Imagining Women's Property in Victorian Fiction

Imagining Women's Property in Victorian Fiction

JILL RAPPOPORT

OXFORD
UNIVERSITY PRESS

Great Clarendon Street, Oxford, OX2 6DP,
United Kingdom

Oxford University Press is a department of the University of Oxford.
It furthers the University's objective of excellence in research, scholarship,
and education by publishing worldwide. Oxford is a registered trade mark of
Oxford University Press in the UK and in certain other countries

© Jill Rappoport 2023

The moral rights of the author have been asserted

All rights reserved. No part of this publication may be reproduced, stored in
a retrieval system, or transmitted, in any form or by any means, without the
prior permission in writing of Oxford University Press, or as expressly permitted
by law, by licence or under terms agreed with the appropriate reprographics
rights organization. Enquiries concerning reproduction outside the scope of the
above should be sent to the Rights Department, Oxford University Press, at the
address above

You must not circulate this work in any other form
and you must impose this same condition on any acquirer

Published in the United States of America by Oxford University Press
198 Madison Avenue, New York, NY 10016, United States of America

British Library Cataloguing in Publication Data
Data available

Library of Congress Control Number: 2022947949

ISBN 978–0–19–286726–1

DOI: 10.1093/oso/9780192867261.001.0001

Printed and bound in the UK by
Clays Ltd, Elcograf S.p.A.

Links to third party websites are provided by Oxford in good faith and
for information only. Oxford disclaims any responsibility for the materials
contained in any third party website referenced in this work.

Contents

Acknowledgments	vii
Introduction: Women's Property Matters	1
I. Unsettling Women's Property	1
II. Wives and Sons: Problems with Women's Property	5
III. Law and Disorder: Legal Doctrine, Family Duty,	
and Other Narrative Claims	18
IV. Properties	26
V. Chapters	31
1. "How Can Money Be a Corpse's?" Wealth, Women, and Wills	
in *Our Mutual Friend*	36
I. Willed Away	38
II. Wills That Won't	41
III. "That Mysterious Paper Currency"	46
IV. "In My Name, Which Is the Same as Mrs. Boffin's, and Means	
Both of Us"	51
V. "A Kiss for the Boofer Lady"	55
VI. "Is That Your Wish? Yes, Certainly."	59
VII. Not "Born a Lady"	62
2. "A Purse in Common": Money, Mutuality, and Darwinian	
Survival in *Wives and Daughters*	66
I. Self-Interest and Struggle	70
II. "Going Together Will Make the Enjoyment": Accounting for	
Common Interest	81
3. Greed, Generosity, and Other Problems with Unmarried	
Women's Property	98
I. "Greedy, Blood-Sucking Harpies": The Problem with	
Possession in *The Eustace Diamonds* (1873)	101
II. Generous to a Fault: The Problem with Giving in *Can You*	
Forgive Her? (1865) and the Phineas Novels (1869, 1874)	108
III. Can You Forgive Her? The Problem of Punishment	117
4. "That Blent Transmission": Women's Property Law and	
Jewish Cultural Inheritance in *Daniel Deronda*	123
I. "Some Struggle about the Diamonds"	125
II. "A Sacred Inheritance"	136

vi CONTENTS

5. "Giv[ing] All She Had": *Hester's* Pearls and the Obligations of
Women's Property   153
    I. "Awful Clever" Women   153
    II. A Wife's Rights   154
    III. Family Obligations   161
    IV. "She Never Looked One Ten-Thousandth Part So Well
All Her Life"   171
    V. "What Can a Young Woman Desire More Than to Have Such
a Possibility of Choice?"   176

Afterword: Women's Property Matters Now   183
    I. Marginal Accounts   183
    II. Invisible Labor   185
    III. "The Reasons Women Should Get the Same Things as Men"   187

Works Cited   193
Index   213

Acknowledgments

When I shared the news of this book's contract, my 6-year-old was unimpressed. "That's a *horrible* title! Call it, 'The Reasons Women Should Get the Same Things as Men.'" Despite the somewhat deflating feedback—I'd been so glad to avoid the scholarly subtitle!—his immediate grasp of how a story about the past could be an argument for the present resonated with (and no doubt responded to) feelings I've had about this project during its long gestation. *Imagining Women's Property in Victorian Fiction*, a study rooted in the literature and history of nineteenth-century England, is also indebted to my place in the twenty-first-century world that produced it. In various ways, this book has been impacted by tumultuous circumstances personal, professional, and political: parenting during my household's dissolution and reconstitution; teaching and advising during a time when the social rights and the physical and mental well-being of so many people have been threatened through persistent racial inequities, the systematic reduction of abortion rights, and legislative attacks on the LGBTQ community; and conducting scholarship during the global COVID-19 pandemic.

I completed the full draft of this manuscript during the pandemic's first year. Before beginning each day of my children's initially chaotic attempts to learn from home and my own efforts to keep them safe, educated, and entertained, I sat at my desk and set a timer for an early morning writing session because I was afraid of losing momentum and didn't want my promotion to full professor delayed any further. With heightened consciousness of how much longer it takes women than men to achieve promotion in my field, I was simultaneously mindful of my extreme good fortune in tenured employment at a time when so many people were losing their jobs or forced to continue labor that seemed increasingly unsafe. This complicated awareness of privilege and inequity is important to my understanding of the past I study and my hopes for the future my children will inhabit. It inflects every page of this project as well as the academic labor I practice. I felt daily the incredible advantages of being able to work from home, of having the resources to adjust to a life that at times had four people on Zoom simultaneously, and of having such incredibly rich interpersonal support systems to encourage and sustain me along the way.

I am grateful to many people and communities, including members of various writing groups: Sarah Hagelin, Ellen Malenas Ledoux, and Jolie Sheffer; Diana Bellonby, Shalyn Clagget, Jill Galvan, Nora Gilbert, and Deanna Kreisel; Mary Jean Corbett, Susan Griffin, Nancy Henry, Deborah Lutz, Ellen Rosenman, Marion Rust, Susan Ryan, and Michelle Sizemore; scholars such as Sean Grass

viii ACKNOWLEDGMENTS

and Deborah Denenholz Morse, who responded to early drafts of chapters; editors who helped me to refine my arguments at various stages, including Lee Behlman and Anne Longmuir, Lucy Hartley, Ivan Kreilkamp, and Rae Greiner; anonymous readers at *Victorian Studies* and Oxford University Press; and many helpful conversations at NAVSA, the Dickens Universe, VISAWUS, INCS, and two SEC Faculty Research Colloquia.

At the University of Kentucky, three department chairs—Ellen Rosenman, Jeff Clymer, and Jonathan Allison—supported my efforts to balance parenthood with professional progress in meaningful, tangible ways; I received research insights and assistance from smart, capable graduate students including Deirdre Mikolajcik and Valerie Stevens; and my involvement in various UK College of Arts & Sciences DEI initiatives with Cristina Alcalde, Ben Braun, Christia Brown, DaMaris Hill, Sarah Lyon, and Mel Stein helped to broaden my understanding of how this project fits into that work, and how much work remains to be done.

In the past decade, there have been many people who have supported and nurtured me in other ways, reminding me just how capacious, flexible, generous, rewarding, and sturdy kinship and communities of choice can be. My deep thanks go to Ann and Paul Rappoport, Julie and Ryan Crowell, Janet and Noah Gusdorff, Janice Crane, Larry Crane, Will and Beth Crane, Shani and David Bardach, Laura and Brian Beiting, Jeff Clymer, Janice Fernheimer, Janice Fernheimer, Mandy Genovese, Kerstin Genovese, Jordana Greenwald, Beth McGinnis, Rachel Mundy, Laura Papero, Hannah Pittard, Hallie Richmond, Moshe and Talia Smolkin, Lisa Zunshine, and so many more.

For Isaac, Max, and Ezra Genovese: This book has, in some ways, grown up with you. Thanks for sharing me with it. I'm sorry about its "horrible title"—check out section III of the Afterword for yours!—but I couldn't be prouder that my three sweet mensches are learning to understand its questions of social justice. I love you dearly.

For Eli Crane: What good fortune to have found you. Thank you for your kindnesses, large and small, your humor, patience, perceptiveness, compassion, and love. I'm overjoyed to begin the next chapter with you.

Introduction

Women's Property Matters

I. Unsettling Women's Property

"Unfortunately, the property of Madame Rigaud was settled upon herself. [...] consequently, Madame Rigaud and I were brought into frequent and unfortunate collision. Even when I wanted any little sum of money for my personal expenses, I could not obtain it without collision—and I too, a man whose character it is to govern!"[1]

"Supposing [...] a man wanted to leave his property to a young female, and wanted to tie it up so that nobody else should ever be able to make a grab at it; how would you tie up that property?"

"Settle it strictly on herself," the professional gentleman would complacently answer.

"But look here," quoth the turnkey. "Supposing she had, say a brother, say a father, say a husband, who would be likely to make a grab at that property when she came into it—how about that?"

"It would be settled on herself, and they would have no more legal claim on it than you," would be the professional answer.

"Stop a bit," said the turnkey. "Supposing she was tender-hearted, and they came over her. Where's your law for tying it up then?"

The deepest character whom the turnkey sounded, was unable to produce his law for tying such a knot as that. So, the turnkey thought about it all his life, and died intestate after all.[2]

These passages from Charles Dickens's *Little Dorrit* (1855–7) offer a glimpse of how married women's property rights in mid-nineteenth-century England were seen as far from "settled."[3] In the opening scene, a "sinister and cruel"

---

[1] Charles Dickens, *Little Dorrit* (unbound edition) no. I, London: Bradbury & Evans (Dec. 1855): 8, 9.
[2] Charles Dickens, *Little Dorrit* (unbound edition), no. II, London: Bradbury & Evans (Jan. 1856): 51.
[3] Though the wealth disputed in the Rigaud marriage is, of course, not English, its depiction in *Little Dorrit* is. I am interested here in popular Victorian perceptions of women's property and the English national stories they comprise.

Imagining Women's Property in Victorian Fiction. Jill Rappoport, Oxford University Press. © Jill Rappoport 2023.
DOI: 10.1093/oso/9780192867261.003.0001

2 IMAGINING WOMEN'S PROPERTY IN VICTORIAN FICTION

fortune-hunter recounts his dealings with the wealthy widow he marries and then murders;[4] in another early moment of the novel, a man hoping to benefit his impoverished goddaughter gives up entirely when he realizes that even law cannot preserve her wealth. In each case, special legal settlements have been presented as a mechanism for protecting women's property from those ("say a husband") who might make their own claims on it, financial workarounds that highlight both the marital law that would otherwise strip these women of their economic rights as soon as they cease to be single as well as the existence of someone sufficiently concerned about those women and their rights to consider recourses outside common law. But together, these cases also suggest law's inadequacy for the job. Whether through "frequent and unfortunate collision" or through "tender-heartedness," because a husband takes it as his prerogative "to govern" or because someone else ("say a brother, say a father") tries to "make a grab at it," villainy and compassion alike threaten women's rights. Fictional portrayals of such "collisions" show repeatedly how a wide range of familial demands can undermine women's apparently independent claims to property, even as they acknowledge the necessity of finding some law to settle and secure those claims.

Imagining Women's Property reframes how we think about Victorian women's changing economic rights and their representation in fiction. Although the (ironically insolvent) legal advisors of Dickens's novel might have been unable to conceive of or "produce [...] law for tying" the kind of "knot" required by women's financial claims in 1855, the reform of married women's property law between 1856 and 1882 nonetheless constituted one of the largest economic transformations England had ever seen,[5] as well as one of its most significant challenges to family traditions. At the start of this period, marriage meant the complete loss of a woman's common-law property rights to her husband; by its end, wives could independently claim their own income and inheritance, choose how to spend, invest, or give away their money, and write wills bequeathing their property. Unsurprisingly, marriage and marital law have been useful lenses for viewing these changing financial rights: wives once "covered" by their husbands through the doctrine of coverture reclaimed their own assets, regained economic agency, and forever altered the legal and theoretical nature of wedlock by doing so. Yet in many literary accounts, married women's property reform was neither as decisive nor as limited as this model suggests. Not only did legal mechanisms coexist and frequently "collide" with familial claims,[6] but the reallocation of

---

[4] Charles Dickens, *Little Dorrit* (1855–7), ed. Stephen Wall and Helen Small (London: Penguin Books Ltd., 2003): 20. Subsequent references will be made parenthetically in the body of the text.

[5] Lee Holcombe, *Wives and Property: Reform of the Married Women's Property Law in Nineteenth-Century England* (Toronto and Buffalo: University of Toronto Press, 1983): 217.

[6] As Tim Dolin has noted, propertied women in Victorian fiction are frequently "united as women of property not by their financial independence so much as by the very tenuousness of that independence" (*Mistress of the House: Women of Property in the Victorian Novel* (New York: Routledge, 2016; 1997 by Ashgate Publishing): 3.

WOMEN'S PROPERTY MATTERS   3

wealth affected far more than spouses or the marital state. Indeed, even fictional contemplation of women's greater economic agency, in the years leading up to these legal changes, produced narratives that show the ramifications of women's property rights for other kin ("say a brother, say a father") and communities. Understanding the reform of married women's property as both an ideologically and materially significant redistribution of the nation's wealth as well as one complicated by competing cultural traditions, I explore the widespread ways in which women's financial agency was imagined by prominent literary authors and their readers during this transformative period.

By highlighting the literary stakes of marital property reform, this book joins a wealth of recent scholarship that has sought to account for women's lives, relationships, and property beyond marriage.[7] As we now know, British women during this period were not entirely without economic agency or material means, nor were they generally presented as such in fiction. From those like Lucy Snowe of Charlotte Brontë's *Villette* (1853), who teaches "'for the sake of the money I get [...] for the roof of shelter I am thus enabled to keep over my head; and for the comfort of mind it gives me'" to wealthier types, such as widowed and "impetuous[ly] genero[us]" Dorothea Casaubon of George Eliot's *Middlemarch* (1871), who is "very uneasy" with her twenty-six hundred a year and eager "to have something good to do with my money [...] to make other people's lives better,"[8] Victorian women as an aggregate earned, invested, inherited, and bequeathed considerable amounts of money. The significance of these funds to families, businesses, and public works has been increasingly well documented.[9] Though some, like the "tender-hearted" goddaughter described above, contributed

---

[7] See, as a sampling, Karen Chase, *The Victorians and Old Age* (Oxford and New York: Oxford University Press, 2009): e.g., 14–36, 71–3, 139–40, 144–9; Kay Heath, *Aging by the Book: The Emergence of Midlife in Victorian Britain* (Albany: State University of New York Press, 2009): e.g., 93–8; Rebecca Rainof, *The Victorian Novel of Adulthood: Plot and Purgatory in Fictions of Maturity* (Athens: Ohio University Press, 2015): 12–14, 60, 81–5, 110–15; Leonore Davidoff, *Thicker Than Water: Siblings and Their Relations, 1780–1920* (Oxford: Oxford University Press, 2012): e.g., 78–102, 133–64, 167–9; Valerie Sanders, *The Brother-Sister Culture in Nineteenth-Century Literature: From Austen to Woolf* (Houndmills: Palgrave Macmillan, 2002): 2; Dara Rossman Regaignon, *Writing Maternity: Medicine, Anxiety, Rhetoric, and Genre* (Columbus: Ohio State University Press, 2021): e.g., 12–13; Tamara S. Wagner, *The Victorian Baby in Print: Infancy, Infant Care, and Nineteenth-Century Popular Culture* (Oxford: Oxford University Press, 2020): 14–15, 37–42, 164–5; Elizabeth Langland, *Nobody's Angels: Middle-Class Women and Domestic Ideology in Victorian Culture* (Ithaca: Cornell University Press, 1995): e.g., 71, 151–71; Dorice Williams Elliott, *The Angel Out of the House: Philanthropy and Gender in Nineteenth-Century England* (Charlottesville: University of Virginia Press, 2002); Martha Vicinus, *Independent Women: Work and Community for Single Women, 1850–1920* (Chicago and London: University of Chicago Press, 1985); Talia Schaffer, *Communities of Care: The Social Ethics of Victorian Fiction* (Princeton: Princeton University Press, 2021): e.g., 166–8; Jill Rappoport, *Giving Women: Alliance and Exchange in Victorian Culture* (Oxford: Oxford University Press, 2012).

[8] Charlotte Brontë, *Villette* [1853], ed. Helen M. Cooper (Penguin Random House, 2004): 317; George Eliot, *Middlemarch* [1871], ed. Rosemary Ashton (London: Penguin Books Ltd., 1994): 733, 765.

[9] See, e.g., Leonore Davidoff and Catherine Hall, *Family Fortunes: Men and Women of the English Middle Class, 1780–1850*, rev. ed. (London: Routledge, 1987, 2002); Nancy Henry, *Women, Literature and Finance in Victorian Britain: Cultures of Investment* (Cham: Palgrave Macmillan, 2018); George

4 IMAGINING WOMEN'S PROPERTY IN VICTORIAN FICTION

to family finances in their single state, many of these women as well as their families also went on to benefit directly from married women's property reforms. Literary portrayals of women with money in the years preceding legal change often reflect on the real or imagined consequences of these reforms. Appearing to affect primarily wives and marriage through the reworking of coverture, married women's property reforms are becoming a critical part of our account of women's financial agency.[10] Yet they remain marginal to the larger narratives literary studies tell of nineteenth-century property and economic history, preventing us from taking stock of how women's newfound rights further impacted not only those very categories—women and marriage—but Victorian culture in general. This book instead emphasizes the social significance of married women's property reform to show some of the ways in which women's dramatically changing access to and autonomy with property shaped notable literary texts as well as perceptions of family finances and public institutions.

Fiction by some of the best known and most highly regarded writers of the period depicts women's already existing economic agency as alarming and the prospect of their increased financial authority as a problem to be solved. Changes to the legal allocation of property were imagined as having wide-ranging, plot-shaping impact not just on marriages and the women in or contemplating them, but on the many other economic relationships they create and value during this time of considerable historic change: extended networks of families and friends, as

---

Robb, "Ladies of the Ticker; Women, Investment, and Fraud in England and America, 1850–1930," *Victorian Investments: New Perspectives on Finance and Culture*, ed. Nancy Henry and Cannon Schmitt (Bloomington: Indiana University Press, 2009): 120–40; George Robb, *Ladies of the Ticker: Women and Wall Street from the Gilded Age to the Great Depression* (Urbana: University of Illinois Press, 2017); Anne Laurence, Josephine Maltby, and Janette Rutterford, eds., *Women and Their Money, 1700–1950: Essays on Women and Finance* (New York: Routledge, 2009); Janette Rutterford,"'A Pauper Every Wife Is': Lady Westmeath, Money, Marriage, and Divorce in Early Nineteenth-Century England," in *Economic Women: Essays on Desire and Dispossession in Nineteenth-Century British Culture*, ed. Lana L. Dalley and Jill Rappoport (Columbus: Ohio State University Press, 2013): 127–42; David R. Green and Alastair Owens, "Gentlewomanly Capitalism? Spinsters, Widows, and Wealth Holding in England and Wales, c. 1800–1860," *Economic History Review* 56.3 (2003): 510–36: http://www.jstor.com/stable/3698573; David R. Green, "To Do the Right Thing: Gender, Wealth, Inheritance and the London Middle Class," in *Women and Their Money 1700–1950: Essays on Women and Finance*, ed. Anne Laurence, Josephine Maltby, and Janette Rutterford (London and New York: Routledge, 2009): 133–50; Alastair Owens, "Property, Gender and the Life Course: Inheritance and Family Welfare Provision in Early Nineteenth-Century England," *Social History* 26.3 (2001): 299–317; Janette Rutterford, David R. Green, Josephine Maltby, and Alastair Owens, "Who Comprised the Nation of Shareholders? Gender and Investment in Great Britain, c. 1870–1935," *Economic History Review* 64.1 (2011): 157–87: http://www.jstor.com/stable/27919486.

[10] See Nancy Henry, *Women*; and Cathrine O. Frank, *Law, Literature, and the Transmission of Culture in England, 1837–1925* (London and New York: Routledge, 2016 [2010 by Ashgate Publishing]), particularly 58, 105–16, both of which consider women's rights with regard to particular aspects of property. Deanna K. Kreisel, *Economic Woman: Demand, Gender, and Narrative Closure in Eliot and Hardy* (Toronto: University of Toronto Press, 2012), examines the feminized depiction of economic demand and accumulation (e.g., 9, 75, 79, 91). For discussions focusing on fictional depictions of women's property and roles in the context of reforms, see Dolin 8, 16 and Deborah Wynne, *Women and Personal Property in the Victorian Novel* (New York: Routledge, 2016; 2010 by Ashgate Publishing): e.g., 6–7.

well as a much broader group that included shopkeepers, investors, and community leaders. Children—whether actual or anticipated—are particularly significant to narratives contemplating women's wealth, which, as we will see, frequently posit tensions between women's financial claims and those of an heir or heirs. As this book will show, the imagined costs of married women's legal property reform appear most significantly in the zero-sum equations posited for family wealth.

But the changing legal allocation is only part of the story Victorian fiction tells about property. Though many of the financial claims that appear within its pages are indeed defended by law, others, as our opening examples indicate, find support in cultural traditions and family expectations instead. If, on the one hand, *Little Dorrit's* suggestion that legal devices are inadequate mechanisms for protecting women and their wealth might seem to undercut a burgeoning political movement for the reform of such laws, similar views appear in novels by authors such as Elizabeth Gaskell and George Eliot, who, as we will see, explicitly signed on to the political movement to support women's economic rights. Victorian literature engages with but also diverges from law in accounts of women's economic choices and transactions. Repeatedly, its narratives suggest both that the law is inadequate to account for the way property enables and disrupts relationships, and that the form of the Victorian novel—in its ability to track intimate and intricate exchanges across generations—is better suited to such tasks.

II. Wives and Sons: Problems with Women's Property

Although an unmarried woman, or *feme sole*, had independent economic rights throughout the nineteenth century, limited education and employment options as well as family expectations restricted her access to earned wealth and upward social mobility. For most of the century two common law doctrines further diminished her economic position: *primogeniture* and *coverture*. The first passed over daughters' rights of inheritance in favor of an eldest son's, compelling many to secure their social status and subsistence through marriage, while the second denied wives economic agency within such marriages. A *feme covert* was "covered" by her husband, who controlled any personal property or land she brought into the marriage or received subsequently through income, inheritance, or gift. In this "one-flesh" understanding of marriage, married women had no independent legal identity and were barred from signing contracts or devising property through wills.[11] This doctrine "covered" her debt or legal infractions, yet despite the

---

[11] See Mary Lyndon Shanley, *Feminism, Marriage, and the Law in Victorian England* (Princeton: Princeton University Press, 1989): *passim*, e.g., 8, 26, 66; also Susan Staves, *Married Women's Separate Property in England, 1660–1833* (Cambridge, MA: Harvard University Press, 1990): 27–36, 129–30, 217; and Lee Holcombe, *Wives And Property*. Even widows' rights were "largely determined by their dead husband"; see Owens, "Property, Gender and the Life Course" 312.

6   IMAGINING WOMEN'S PROPERTY IN VICTORIAN FICTION

dubious advantage of this legal "protection," coverture also stripped a wife of her previous rights as a single woman.

During the early decades of the nineteenth century, fiction tended to show how these economic traditions worked together, blaming inheritance practices (particularly, though not always, what Eileen Spring has referred to as "customary primogeniture")[12] as well as marital coverture for women's economic disadvantages. This earlier view of women's doubled marginalization allows us to see the discursive shift that occurs around the Victorian reform of women's property law. Coverture's unique drawbacks came under closer scrutiny after mid-century. The Divorce or Matrimonial Causes Act of 1857 (20 & 21 Vict., c. 85) not only established the conditions and terms for the dissolution of marriage but also led to public and sometimes dramatic revelations of these marital failures, both in courts and in popular journalism.[13] As the movement to reform married women's property rights increasingly gained traction, marital breakdowns also featured prominently in debates about women's needs. During this time, primogeniture was no longer showcased as among women's most significant economic disadvantages. Instead, in works from the 1860s and 1870s, the claims of primogeniture begin to appear as an argument against women's rights to property; women's claims to private wealth appear to clash with and detract from sons' inheritance. This change is critical. At stake in this shifting narrative of two common law doctrines is the relational axis guiding the transmission of property: marriage or parenthood. Coverture as a legal doctrine governs lateral, conjugal ties first and foremost, while primogeniture governs vertical, generational transmission, though of course both have implications for other relationships. Significantly, the ideological and legal erosion of coverture was not necessarily understood as foregrounding a wife's needs. Instead, husbands' former financial authority is displaced onto sons, who emerge as the new focus of narratives' economic concerns. As I'll discuss in the rest of this section, the shift from understanding marital and filial laws as working in concert to seeing them in tension formed an important part of debates about women's property. This divergence meant that kin who formerly treated their economic circumstances as intertwined were subsequently seen as competing for resources.

So that we may understand how the relational narrative changes, I turn to two novels by Jane Austen that illustrate the backstory of coverture and primogeniture working together to women's disadvantage, before moving on to works that begin

---

[12] "[L]egal primogeniture," which transmitted property to an eldest son in cases of intestacy, was of little practical consequence to larger landowners who rarely died without wills, but it was "the symbol for customary primogeniture, for the habit of entailing estates on eldest sons." See Eileen Spring, "Landowners, Lawyers, and Land Law Reform in Nineteenth-Century England," *American Journal of Legal History* 21.1 (1977): 40–59, 43–4: https://www.jstor.org/stable/844924, accessed Sept. 25, 2020.

[13] See, e.g., Deborah Cohen, *Family Secrets: Shame and Privacy in Modern Britain* (Oxford and New York: Oxford University Press, 2013): 47–84.

to treat primogeniture more favorably. In Austen's era, according to Ruth Perry, "the basis of kinship" shifted from an emphasis on blood lineage to that of conjugal ties, with significant economic consequences for women. Daughters of the landowning classes received diminished inheritances and settlements as families sought to secure wealth for eldest sons, while daughters of working families faced reduced access to their means of subsistence as large estates were consolidated.[14] Austen herself experienced financial dependence. She never married, and her combined earnings over twenty years—roughly £1,500—yielded "less than the annual income Austen imagined for [*Pride and Prejudice*'s] Mr. Bennet," forcing her to rely upon her brothers' matching contributions to the household income she shared with her mother and sister.[15] Although others have argued that historical daughters received more in practice than the common law dictated during this time,[16] fictional representations of inheritance often perpetuate the images of unequal distribution, dependence, and precarity discussed by Perry. Many of Austen's heroines, openly dependent upon marriage because their fathers' homes and wealth descend to a brother or male cousin, typify the plight of imbalanced inheritance and suggest that it is to blame for their economic trouble.[17] Elinor, Marianne, and Margaret Dashwood of *Sense and Sensibility* (1811), for instance, do not benefit from their father's inheritance of his single uncle's considerable estate because it has been secured to their elder half-brother, John Dashwood. This inheritance increases John's already considerable income by "four thousand a-year" while a flat sum of 10,000 pounds (yielding, possibly, £400–500 per year) will provide the total income and fortune of three once extremely well-to-do sisters and their mother.[18] In *Pride and Prejudice* (1813), Jane, Elizabeth, Mary, Catherine, and Lydia Bennet similarly lack fortunes because their father's estate "was entailed, in default of heirs male, on a distant relation."[19]

---

[14] Ruth Perry, *Novel Relations: The Transformation of Kinship in English Literature and Culture, 1748–1818* (Cambridge: Cambridge University Press, 2004): 2. See also 2, 24, 34, 40, 47, 64, 212–13.

[15] Donald Gray, "A Note on Money," in Jane Austen, *Pride and Prejudice* [1813]: *An Authoritative Text, Backgrounds and Sources, Criticism*, ed. Donald Gray, 3rd ed. (New York: W. W. Norton & Company, 2001): 403–5, 405, 404.

[16] See Owens, "Property, Gender and the Life Course" 313–14, though Owens cautions against overstating this point (307–10). Also against the narrative of women's economic diminishment, Amanda Vickery finds "no systematic reduction in the range of employments available to laboring women"; see "Golden Age to Separate Spheres? A Review of the Categories and Chronology of English Women's History," *Historical Journal* 36:2 (June 1993): 383–414, 405.

[17] For female displacement and homelessness in Austen's novels, see Claudia J. Martin, "Place and Displacement: The Unsettling Connection of Women, Property, and the Law in British Novels of the Long Nineteenth Century" (Diss. Binghamton University—SUNY (2018), *Graduate Dissertations and Theses* 70: 149, 150: https://orb.binghamton.edu/dissertation_and_theses/70, accessed July 8, 2020.

[18] Jane Austen, *Sense and Sensibility* [1811]: *Authoritative Text, Contexts, Criticism*, ed. Claudia L. Johnson (New York: W. W. Norton & Company, 2002): 7. Subsequent citations will appear parenthetically within the text.

[19] Jane Austen, *Pride and Prejudice* [1813]: *An Authoritative Text, Backgrounds and Sources, Criticism*, 3rd ed., ed. Donald Gray (New York: W. W. Norton & Company, 2001): 19. Subsequent citations will appear parenthetically within the text. With regard to *Pride and Prejudice*'s entailment, Sandra Macpherson argues that, despite its appearance of injuring the Bennet girls, entailment or at

8   IMAGINING WOMEN'S PROPERTY IN VICTORIAN FICTION

The unlikeable nature of the heirs in both cases make this distribution appear particularly unfair. That Mr. Collins acts as the foolish mouthpiece for the one-flesh doctrine of coverture—claiming, against all evidence to the contrary, that his wife and he "have but one mind and one way of thinking" (142)—aligns marital law with the privileging of male inheritance and suggests that both doctrines are financially and socially flawed.[20]

Support for women's right to property thus comes, during the first half of the nineteenth century, in relation to primogeniture at least as much as to coverture. Indeed, even the unlikeable matriarch Lady Catherine de Bourgh is momentarily sympathetic when she declares, in reference to the Bennet sisters' circumstances, "I see no occasion for entailing estates from the female line" (109). In each novel, the daughters' meager inheritance and their father's inability to compensate for it has direct bearing on the necessity of marriage and the difficulty of finding a suitable match. If primogeniture assumes male financial competence, Austen and others show that such competence is far from assured. Mr. Bennet and Mr. Dashwood fail to provide adequately for their daughters and wives, both because the legal situation securing their estates to individual male heirs is apparently out of their hands and because they are poor financial managers of the marital wealth they do control. "Mr. Bennet had very often wished [...] that, instead of spending his whole income, he had laid by an annual sum, for the better provision of his children, and of his wife, if she survived him. He now wished it more than ever" (199–200). Mr. Dashwood, too, despite his best intentions of "living economically" in order to "lay by a considerable sum" for his wife and daughters, dies before ever managing to do so (6). Their failure to legally provide for their families, common enough in fiction, would have been seen as "'culpable,'" according to Alastair Owens, whose study of early nineteenth-century inheritance demonstrates a cultural emphasis on such provisions.[21]

---

least the logic of entailment enables ethical subjectivity and a sense of responsibility in the novel; see "Rent to Own: or, What's Entailed in *Pride and Prejudice*," *Representations* 82:1 (Spring 2003): 1–23, 8, 16. Peter A. Appel finds evidence against Macpherson's claim that the entailment would actually have been a "strict settlement," a different legal mechanism for land's transmission that, he argues, "would likely come with shares for every one of the Bennet children" (624–6, 624). The distinction matters because, as Appel notes, Mr. Bennet's use of a "common recovery" could have barred an entail, and his failure to do so, along with evidence in the novel that "the law did provide a means for protecting the future of daughters like the Bennets," suggest that "societal norms constituted the means of oppression, not the law itself" (635). See "A Funhouse Mirror of Law: The Entailment in Jane Austen's *Pride and Prejudice*," 41 Ga. J. Int'l & Comp. L. (2013): 609–36. For the purpose and operation of the "strict family settlement," see Eileen Spring, "Landowners" 41–2.

[20] As Elsie B. Michie has noted, Austen's novels resist the notion that individuals should accumulate excessive wealth through inheritance or marriage. See *The Vulgar Question of Money: Heiresses, Materialism, and the Novel of Manners from Jane Austen to Henry James* (Baltimore: Johns Hopkins University Press, 2011): 1–2, 28–9.

[21] Owens, "Property, Gender and the Life Course" 303–4. Strict settlements, the form that, as Macpherson notes, most "entails" took during this period (though not necessarily, as Appel argues, the form taken in Austen's novel), specifically "empowered the life tenants" to provide for a surviving wife and other children; see Macpherson 8, Appel 625, and John Habakkuk, *Marriage, Debt, and the*

WOMEN'S PROPERTY MATTERS   9

As historians and literary critics have demonstrated, primogeniture—particularly among the middle classes—was never absolute,[22] and entailments did not absolutely have to—though they usually did—privilege male heirs.[23] Nevertheless, the general preference for consolidating wealth and endowing male lineage meant that marriage was an important source of financial security for women, even as women conscious of this financial motivation were depicted as selling themselves for an establishment.[24] Yet wives, too, were far from financially secure.[25] Coverture stripped them of economic rights during marriage, while the Dower Act of 1833 (3 & 4 Will. 4. c. 104) eliminated the legal protections that once followed it. Dower had previously given widows life interests in a third of their husbands' land, but after 1833 men no longer had to make posthumous provisions for their wives.[26] As Tim Dolin, Mary Jean Corbett, and Talia Schaffer have discussed, marriage—particularly though not only in the form of exogamous alliances with strangers—could present terrifying risks to women's independence, intimate networks, and property.[27]

Estates System: English Landownership 1650–1950 (Oxford: Clarendon Press, 1994): 2. For the perspective that strict settlements were nonetheless "primogenitive in thrust," see Eileen Spring, "The Strict Settlement: Its Role in Family History," *Economic History Review* 41.3 (1988): 454–60, 459: https://www.jstor.org/stable/2597370, accessed Sept. 25, 2020; and Eileen Spring, "Law and the Theory of the Affective Family," *Albion: A Quarterly Journal Concerned with British Studies* 16.1 (1984): 1–20, 3, 10, 12: https://www.jstor.org/stable/4048903, accessed Sept. 25, 2020.

[22] See, e.g., Amy Louise Erickson, *Women and Property in Early Modern England* (London: Routledge, 1993): 26, 78, 224; Owens, "Property" 313–14; Rappoport, *Giving Women*, e.g., 46, 50.

[23] Entailment as a legal mechanism for permitting a donor to control property beyond his lifetime was not, in itself, a function of the common law doctrine of primogeniture, and could in fact be used to disrupt it, by allowing the donor to choose recipients of his wealth well beyond his own lifetime (Macpherson 7). However, Adam Smith, Austen's near contemporary, *presents* entails as directly and naturally related to primogeniture (*An Inquiry into the Nature and Causes of the Wealth of Nations*, ed. R. H. Campbell and R. S. Skinner (1776; reprint, Indianapolis, 1981), 1:384, cited in Macpherson 7). And as others have shown, although it may have had the legal potential to disrupt the claims of first-born sons, entailment was "biased towards primogeniture" (Habakkuk 30, also 6; see also Macpherson 6; Appel 611, 615). Austen's *Sense and Sensibility* and *Pride and Prejudice*, by assigning wealth to a first-born son and suggesting that the lack of a son disinherits the sisters, suggest that circumstances favor the principle of primogeniture, even if the legal mechanisms do not always fit that common law doctrine precisely.

[24] For women's increasing reliance on conjugal families, see Perry 31–4. For the "paradox" of heterosexual exchange, see Kathy Psomiades, "Heterosexual Exchange and Other Victorian Fictions: *The Eustace Diamonds* and Victorian Anthropology," *NOVEL: A Forum on Fiction* 33.1 (1999): 93–118, 94.

[25] For a classic contemporary response to coverture, see Barbara Leigh Smith Bodichon, "A Brief Summary, in Plain Language, of the Most Important Laws Concerning Women: Together with a Few Observations Thereon" (1854), excerpted in Dorothy Mermin and Herbert F. Tucker, eds., *Victorian Literature 1830–1900* (Fort Worth and Philadelphia: Harcourt College Publishers, 2002): 87–90.

[26] Holcombe 21; Staves 49; Perry 53. Dower could be barred even before the Dower Act, and a widow's jointure theoretically replaced dower with more secure and alienable property, but it was often of far less value than dower and in many cases no more guaranteed (Staves 32–7, 96, 114, 130).

[27] Dolin 3, 13, 86; Mary Jean Corbett, *Family Likeness: Sex, Marriage, and Incest from Jane Austen to Virginia Woolf* (Ithaca: Cornell University Press, 2008): e.g., vii, 20–4; Talia Schaffer, *Romance's Rival: Familiar Marriage in Victorian Fiction* (New York and Oxford: Oxford University Press, 2016): e.g., 13, 81, 120, 124; Kelly Hager and Talia Schaffer, "Introduction: Extending Families," *Victorian Review* 39.2 (2013): 7–21, 10: https://doi.org/10.1353/vcr.2013.0055.

10   IMAGINING WOMEN'S PROPERTY IN VICTORIAN FICTION

Despite this bleak picture of legal and social limitations, married and unmarried women were everyday economic actors and sometimes significant financial figures throughout the nineteenth century. Female characters in the novels explored here are actively involved in property transactions with wide-ranging impact. In its focus on them, my work is part of an emergent body of historical and literary scholarship that emphasizes the real and imagined ways in which some Englishwomen exercised economic agency, used legal and extralegal mechanisms to get around legal limitations, and made financial contributions, both small and large, to domestic, national, and even global economies. While acknowledging the serious legal and social disadvantages living women faced during this period, as well as cultural ideologies that worked to separate women from the "sphere" of financial interest or activity, the story I tell is not one of women suffering dispossession or serving as domestic angels to soothe men's anxieties about Victorian materialism and the volatility of wealth.[28] Instead, this book examines the ways in which women's everyday property management disturbs cultural efforts to idealize, stabilize, or account for their position or value, within and beyond their own households.

Although Victorian middle-class separate spheres ideology assigned women to private domesticity and men to public or commercial life, the 1851 census, as Lee Holcombe notes, recorded that one fourth of married women had employment outside the home and that this number was just less than a quarter of the women employed.[29] Charles Dickens's *Our Mutual Friend*, in which nearly all of the women outside of the wealthier Podsnap and Veneering circles labor for pay in a range of occupations including schoolteachers, business owners, factory workers, and dress-makers, reflects the pervasiveness of female employment in the cultural imagination as well. Even when women were not employed themselves, and long before legal reforms were instituted, women found degrees of economic agency by contributing labor and wealth to family enterprises, as occurs in Oliphant's *Hester*.[30] Their inheritances, income, and investments—often government bonds but also riskier stocks[31]—supported families and public works; as Nancy Henry has noted, "[o]ver the course of the nineteenth century, women comprised between 5 and 20% of the investing public."[32] They also participated in

---

[28] See, e.g., Michie 3; Jeff Nunokawa, *The Afterlife of Property: Domestic Security and the Victorian Novel* (Princeton: Princeton University Press, 1994): 50. As many Victorianists have shown, these spheres were far less separate in practice than in theory. See, for instance, Mary Poovey, *Uneven Developments: The Ideological Work of Gender in Mid-Victorian England* (Chicago: University of Chicago Press, 1988); Karen Chase and Michael Levenson, *The Spectacle of Intimacy: A Public Life for the Victorian Family* (Princeton: Princeton University Press, 2000): *passim*, e.g., 85; Elliott.

[29] Holcombe 8.

[30] See Davidoff and Hall 279–89.

[31] Helen Doe, "Waiting For Her Ship To Come In? The Female Investor in Nineteenth-Century Sailing Vessels," *The Economic History Review* 63.1 (2010): 85–106, 85–7: http://www.jstor.com/stable/27771571.

[32] Henry, *Women* 7, 6. See also Green and Owens, "Gentlewomanly" 512, 519, 523–4, 531; Janette Rutterford, David R. Green, Josephine Maltby, and Alastair Owens, "Who Comprised" 158, 169–70; Janette Rutterford, "'A *pauper* every wife is' 137–41; George Robb, *White-Collar Crime in Modern*

WOMEN'S PROPERTY MATTERS   11

an expanding commercial sphere through production, shopkeeping, and purchases.[33] As Margot Finn and others have shown, strategic uses of credit and legal practices such as the law of necessaries (which required men to provide their wives with the items appropriate for their station in life) absolved women of their husband's debts, giving wives both authority and a degree of impunity as consumers.[34] These strategies afforded opportunities for economic activity and also provided one way for women and their supporters to resist the limitations of coverture, which they did on multiple fronts.

Some Victorian women and men avoided coverture by cohabiting without legal marriage, as Ginger S. Frost has discussed. Such arrangements, comprising "a significant minority" of the working classes, were common enough to be "not shockingly exceptional," and although many of the cases Frost highlights show women's economic dependence, others suggest that sharing a home outside of marriage protected women's finances and property from their male partners.[35] Talia Schaffer has suggested that the "quasi-marital arrangement" of partnerships involving a disabled individual also gave women access to relationships "freed from the lopsided constraints of coverture."[36] Within marriage, other women benefited from *separate estates* set up for them through premarital settlements or trusts made in courts of equity. Such legal settlements were seen by legislators as significant methods for protecting women's property.[37] In *Pride and Prejudice*, Mr. Darcy's alarm that his sister's inheritance could have become the property of the fortune hunter Mr. Wickham is surely compounded by the fact that, had they eloped as planned, no marriage settlements could have been made to protect Miss Darcy's wealth (133). Yet as we have seen, settlements were imperfect

---

England: Financial Fraud and Business Morality, 1845–1929 (Cambridge: Cambridge University Press, 1992): 29–30; Lucy A. Newton, Philip L. Cottrell, Josephine Maltby, and Janette Rutterford, "Women and Wealth: The Nineteenth Century in Great Britain," in *Women and Their Money, 1700–1950: Essays on Women and Finance*, ed. Anne Laurence, Josephine Maltby, and Janette Rutterford (London: Routledge, 2009): 86–94, 89–91. For female investors in nineteenth-century America, see George Robb, *Ladies of the Ticker*, e.g., 45–56.

[33] See Erika Diane Rappaport, *Shopping for Pleasure: Women in the Making of London's West End* (Princeton: Princeton University Press, 2000) and Krista Lysack, *Come Buy, Come Buy: Shopping and the Culture of Consumption in Victorian Women's Writing* (Athens: Ohio University Press, 2008).

[34] Margot Finn, "Women, Consumption and Coverture in England, c. 1760–1860," *Historical Journal* 39.3 (1996), 703–22: 706, 707: http://www.jstor.com/stable/2639966; Margot Finn, "Working-Class Women" 129–30, 145; Rappaport, *Shopping* 50–65; Joanne Bailey, "Favoured or Oppressed? Married Women, Property, and 'Coverture' in England, 1660–1800," *Continuity and Change* 17.3 (2002): 351–72, 353; Erickson, *Women and Property* 150, 224; Staves 131.

[35] Ginger S. Frost, *Living in Sin: Cohabiting as Husband and Wife in Nineteenth-Century England* (Manchester and New York: Manchester University Press, 2008): quotes are from 123, 231; for the greater instances of cohabiting among the working classes, see also 3, 5; for women's economic vulnerability see 126; for cohabiting as a means of protecting women's property, see 35, 125, 128. See also Ellen Ross, *Love and Toil: Motherhood in Outcast London, 1870–1918* (New York and Oxford: Oxford University Press, 1993): 63.

[36] Schaffer, *Romance's Rival* 11.

[37] Shanley 15, 25, Holcombe 44. For distinctions between strict settlements and marriage settlements, see Eileen Spring, "The Settlement of Land in Nineteenth-Century England," *American Journal of Legal History* 8.3 (1964): 209–23, 214–15, n. 13: https://www.jstor.org/stable/844170, accessed Sept. 25, 2020.

12 IMAGINING WOMEN'S PROPERTY IN VICTORIAN FICTION

mechanisms: they did not grant wives property rights equal to those of men or unmarried women; securing them required both sufficient wealth and attentive male guardians; and, as the example of *Little Dorrit* suggests, their protections were not foolproof. Furthermore, they did not protect women of all classes. Only 10 percent of marriages involved such settlements, which were expensive to produce.[38] The discrepancy in women's legal conditions was one example of the nation's inconsistent judicial system, with what amounted to different laws for rich and poor. Public opinion about this inconsistency contributed to the reforms of the Judicature Act of 1873 (36 & 37 Vict., c. 66), which aimed to reconcile the different rulings of equity and the common law and give preference to equity in matters of conflicting rules.[39] The Petition for Reform of the Married Women's Property Law, which was presented in 1856 and included twenty-six thousand signatures, noted the injustice of these different systems: "if these laws often bear heavily upon women protected by the forethought of their relatives [...] and [...] the rank to which they belong, how much more unequivocal is the injury sustained by women in the lower classes [...]."[40] This petition began a twenty-six-year effort by lawmakers and public women to grant married women legal control over their own wealth and earnings, finally achieved in part by the Married Women's Property Act, 1870 (33 & 34 Vict. c. 93), which gave married women rights to their wages and bequests of up to £200, and more fully by the Married Women's Property Act, 1882 (45 & 46 Vict. c. 75), which extended their rights to "any real or personal property."[41]

---

[38] Holcombe 46. Staves clarifies that this group includes more than the "very privileged" (59). For the prevalence of settlements among the "comfortable" classes, see also Janette Rutterford and Josephine Maltby, "Frank Must Marry Money: Men, Women, and Property in Trollope's Novels," *Accounting Historians Journal* 33.2 (2006): 169–99, 185: http://www.jstor.com/stable/40698346.

[39] Holcombe 15, 16. Married women's property reform has been seen as much as a function of this larger Judicature reform as of a feminist agenda (Holcombe 17). For the argument that the Act came about primarily to prevent spouses from colluding on debt, see Mary Beth Combs, "'A Measure of Legal Independence': The 1870 Married Women's Property Act and the Portfolio Allocations of British Wives," *Journal of Economic History* 65.4 (2005): 1028–57, 1029: http://www.jstor.com/stable/3874913. For the ways in which other law affecting married couples, notably divorce law, was part of a broader program that stripped the ecclesiastical courts of their jurisdiction, see R. B. Outhwaite, *The Rise and Fall of the English Ecclesiastical Courts, 1500–1860* (Cambridge: Cambridge University Press, 2006): 157–73.

[40] "Petition for Reform of the Married Women's Property Law Presented to Parliament 14 March 1856," quoted in Appendix 1, Holcombe 237.

[41] Shanley 33; for details on the two Acts see chs. 2 (49–78) and 4 (103–30); Holcombe, 237–8 for full reprintings of the petition, 243–6 for the full text of the 1870 Married Women's Property Act, and 247–52 for the full text of the 1882 Act. For the 1870 Act, some key points are as follows: "The wages and earnings of any married woman acquired or gained by her after the passing of this Act in any employment, occupation, or trade [...] and also any money, or property so acquird [*sic*] by her [...] and all investments of such wages, earnings, money or property, shall be deemed and be taken to be property held and settled to her separate use, independent of any husband [...]. Where any woman married after the passing of this Act shall during her marriage become entitled to any personal property [...] or to any sum of money not exceeding two hundred pounds under any deed or will, such property shall [...] belong to such woman for her separate use [...]" ("An Act to Amend the Law Relating to the Property of Married Women (9 August 1870)," quoted in Appendix 4, Holcombe 243–4). The 1882 Act decreed that "A married woman shall, in accordance with the provisions of this Act, be capable of

For the most part, these practical efforts to improve women's economic status after mid-century focused on their lack of money within marriage, not on their lack of paternal inheritance, yet this is a departure from previous understandings of women's fortunes. Earlier fiction such as Austen's emphasized the interconnectedness of the two common law doctrines, one emphasizing the financial ramifications of wedlock, the other emphasizing the financial ramifications of birth. Understanding how Austen combines the two to highlight women's disadvantages sheds light on their subsequent deployment, when, as we'll see, primogeniture becomes not a point of sympathy for women but a sign of their own moderate or excessive desires and a rallying cry against women's increased property rights.

In the early part of the century, inheritance and marital law worked together to consolidate wealth in male hands. *Sense and Sensibility*'s John Dashwood, for example, not only receives his father's estate but also benefits from his own mother's wealth, apparently secured to her as her separate property. He "was amply provided for by the fortune of his mother, which had been large, and half of which devolved on him on his coming of age" (5); the other half of his mother's wealth would also be his because it "was also secured to her child, and [her husband, John's father] had only a life interest in it" (6). On the one hand, John's mother's wealth, her family's response to coverture, is evidence of the safeguards already put into place for protecting (some) married women's property even before the legal reforms of the later century. His father could not access the principal of his mother's money, only its interest during his own lifetime. Despite the claims of coverture, her marriage did not merge her property with his—an example of the kind of trusts established for wealthy women outside of the court of common law, and, in its evasion of the common law, something of an argument against it. Yet this protection of the late Mrs. Dashwood's property ultimately seems less a triumph for the wife than for her son, whose father, we learn, would have been very pleased to ignore the custom of primogeniture and divide the wealth with his three less privileged female children from his second marriage instead. The narrative emphasis on those children—whose fortunes and marriage plots occupy the rest of the novel—also diminishes any sense that this episode reflects a feminist victory or even a real disruption of the common law. As Cheri Larsen Hoeckley has argued, "equity settlements often simply allowed a father to preserve family property [...] for future male heirs."[42] Thus even a wife's "separate estate" here ultimately serves the purpose of primogeniture. The novel's

---

acquiring, holding, and disposing by will or otherwise, of any real or personal property as her separate property, in the same manner as if she were a feme sole, without the intervention of any trustee. [...She] shall be capable of entering into and rendering herself liable in respect of and to the extent of her separate property on any contract, and of suing and being sued [...] in all respects as if she were a feme sole [...]" ("Married Women's Property Act, 1882," quoted in Appendix 5, Holcombe 247).

[42] Cheri Larsen Hoeckley, "Anomalous Ownership: Copyright, Coverture, and *Aurora Leigh*," *Victorian Poetry* 35.2 (1998): 135–61, 149; Staves 4, 84. Widows were typically treated as custodians of their children's future inheritance (Owens, "Property" 310).

14 IMAGINING WOMEN'S PROPERTY IN VICTORIAN FICTION

discussion of inheritance reminds readers that the doctrines of primogeniture and coverture—the economics of birth and marriage—collaborate to limit women's financial options and suggests that addressing one independently of the other will not guarantee women's economic security.

Coverture and primogeniture again join hands as John Dashwood's wife, Fanny, directs his interests in favor of their son. On the one hand, she appears to have a kind of economic agency through him, in keeping with both coverture's theories of joint interest and separate-spheres' theories of wifely influence. She "did not at all approve" of her husband's initial intention to provide for his half-sisters, and her "consent to this plan"—which she refuses to give—seems necessary to it. As she persuades him to reduce the gift from three thousand pounds to "sending presents of fish and game" (12), she effectively manages both her husband and his finances and, as Elsie B. Michie's study of rich women in fiction has shown, becomes the scapegoat for self-interested wealth.[43] Yet in a "more amiable woman" (7), Fanny's narrow maternal anxiety for her child's interests might have aligned her with the mother of her disinherited half-sisters-in-law, whose love of her own children similarly obscures any wider vision she might have of the world. Fanny has no more legal power over the situation than they do, and, unable to make any claims upon her husband's recent inheritance, must resort to "begg[ing]" and "argu[ing]" (9, 12) to prevent an act that she perceives as equivalent to "rob[bing] his child" (9). Although she entered her marriage with a substantial fortune, the larger part of her father's vast wealth will go to her brother's family, not to her son (264). Her apparent greed stems from those same joined common law doctrines of primogeniture and coverture that shaped her half-sisters' fortunes. The implication is that both sympathetic and unsympathetic characters would be better off—and perhaps even more generous—under different legal conditions.

Following Austen, novelists continued to unite criticism of coverture and primogeniture. In Charlotte Brontë's *Jane Eyre* (1847), for example, Bertha Mason's life and thirty thousand pounds alike fall victim to Rochester's father's "resolution to keep the property together" for his older son while letting his younger son "be provided for by a wealthy marriage."[44] In a similar vein, Anne Brontë's *Tenant of Wildfell Hall* (1848) deplores both the dissolute lifestyle that Arthur Huntingdon's family estates have enabled and the financial control he exerts over the wife he abuses.[45] Not only does he take her money and jewels but

---

[43] Michie 28. For Fanny's "will" with respect to the novel's treatment of inheritance, see Gene Ruoff, "Wills," in *Sense and Sensibility [1811]: Authoritative Text, Contexts, Criticism*, ed. Claudia L. Johnson (New York: W. W. Norton & Company, 2002): 348–59, 350–3.

[44] Charlotte Brontë, *Jane Eyre* [1847], ed. Richard J. Dunn, 3rd ed. (New York and London: W. W. Norton & Company, 2001): 260.

[45] Anne Brontë, *The Tenant of Wildfell Hall* [1848], ed. Herbert Rosengarten (Oxford: Oxford University Press, 1992, 2008). Helen wishes he had "something to do, some useful trade, or profession, or employment" (191); he neglects his tenants (208). His debts arise from his excesses but are enabled by his reputation as a landed gentleman (208–9).

WOMEN'S PROPERTY MATTERS   15

he demands a further "confiscation of property" (310), destroying the art supplies she has planned to use to support herself and her son after running away to safety.[46] In each case, a son's inheritance of paternal wealth and a wife's loss of both freedom and property in marriage appear to coincide to her detriment.

In subsequent decades, however, debates about women's property began deploying primogeniture in new ways. The 1856 Petition for property reform and the Divorce Act of 1857 both drew attention to the imbalanced economics of marriage. In their willingness to address divorce prior to property, legislators emphasized their duty to protect women within marital relationships (thus ensuring the smooth functioning of coverture), rather than advocate for their equal rights (which would rupture the fiction of coverture altogether).[47] But as marital ties come under close inspection, one proof of a wife's merit (and hence her blamelessness for a failing marriage) appears in her parental relationship. Being a "good mother" begins to mean, in part, a willingness to cede economic needs or claims to a child.[48] The 1856 Petition treats the (working-class) wife's property needs explicitly in terms of her maternal role, accusing "the law [... of] depriving the mother of all pecuniary resources [...]."[49] With growing attention given to bad marriages and the failures of the "one-flesh" doctrine, novels from the 1860s balance criticism of mercenary or otherwise incompatible marriages with the celebration of motherhood and primogeniture. In Anthony Trollope's *Orley Farm* (1862), for instance, a second marriage poses problems primarily because it (sensationally) threatens the claims of a first-born son. Betrayal, forgery of her dying husband's will, and perjury in order to claim an estate for her own younger son mark Lady Mason as "a castaway among the world's worst wretches";[50] despite her legal acquittal, the novel exposes her deed to those she cares most about and ultimately secures the estate to her stepson, reinforcing both primogeniture and the inadequacy of the law to effect the customary practices that fiction more frequently safeguards. Yet Lady Mason receives sympathy and love despite her criminal activity because she seemingly commits the crimes not for personal "aggrandisement" or economic self-interest but as a mother, on behalf of her son. Claiming to have married "'not caring for [her husband's] riches'" for

---

[46] Tenant 310–11.

[47] Shanley 71–4, 77–8.

[48] Motherhood's presumed incompatibility with self-interested economic claims aligns with the anti-material (and perhaps anti-materialist) ideal that Carolyn Dever discusses in *Death and the Mother from Dickens to Freud: Victorian Fiction and the Anxiety of Origins* (Cambridge: Cambridge University Press, 1998): 19, 27. For maternal sacrifice and its destructive results, see Ellen Ross, *Love and Toil* 54–5; "Introduction," *Other Mothers: Beyond the Maternal Ideal*, ed. Ellen Bayuk Rosenman and Claudia C. Klaver (Columbus: Ohio State University Press, 2008): 1–22, 14; and Heather Milton, "'Bland, Adoring, and Gently Tearful Women': Debunking the Maternal Ideal in George Eliot's *Felix Holt*," in *Other Mothers: Beyond the Maternal Ideal*, ed. Ellen Bayuk Rosenman and Claudia C. Klaver (Columbus: Ohio State University Press, 2008): 55–74, 55, 56, 63, 65.

[49] "Petition for Reform," Holcombe 238.

[50] See Anthony Trollope, *Orley Farm* [1862] (Oxford and New York: Oxford University Press, 2008): II:128.

16 IMAGINING WOMEN'S PROPERTY IN VICTORIAN FICTION

herself, she adds, "'But then came my baby, and the world was all altered for me. [...]
Why should not this other child also be his father's heir?'" (II: 203). If Victorian
wives are deemed mercenary by demanding property, mothers seeking money
for their children are justified by biblical analogy ("Did she love [...] her babe,
less than Rebekah had loved Jacob?"), even as Victorian fiction works hard to
restore the birthright of Esau and other first-born sons.[51] Subsequent novels such
as Dickens's *Our Mutual Friend* and Gaskell's *Wives and Daughters* further
acknowledge the inadequacy of legal frameworks for marital property but take
extralegal, collaborative pains to ensure the patrilineal transmission of property to
the eldest male or his heir. Attention to the reform of marriage and marital
property, in other words, initially appears to aid not only wives but children,
from the numerous poor offspring of struggling working mothers to wealthier,
first-born children whose inheritance seemingly everyone works to protect.

The rights afforded by marriage and birth—coverture and primogeniture—
diverge further in additional works from this period that explore the two doctrines
through women's sequential relationships. Wilkie Collins's *The Woman in White*
(1860), for instance, demonstrates sensational trouble in Laura Fairlie's first
marriage, while celebrating birthright in her second. This novel illustrates her
extreme suffering when her first husband goes to drastic measures to steal her
separate property; both his "cruel hand" and her false imprisonment in an asylum
testify to the need for protecting a wife's economic and bodily rights.[52] Yet her
property is never presented as intended for her use. Marital reform here serves the
ends of primogeniture. The last spoken words of the novel joyfully align the first-
born son of her (second, happier) marriage with his economic prerogative by
naming him "'the Heir of Limmeridge.'"[53] Similarly assigning unequal merit to
coverture and primogeniture and also affording them different places in its
narrative arc, *Middlemarch* protests against Casaubon's demands on his living
wife, as well as his posthumous control over Dorothea's financial agency. Yet even
after she has remarried against everyone else's wishes and despite repeated threats
of disinheritance, the novel supports her son's customary position as "the heir of
the Brookes." Repeated plans to disinherit her son ("I can cut off the entail, you
know") last only until Dorothea has given birth, when her uncle and the brother-
in-law whose family would benefit from this disinheritance determine instead to
"let things remain as they are." Not only does *Middlemarch*'s conclusion applaud
this decision as a sign of the family's "reconciliation" but it underscores the

---

[51] Ibid., II: 355.

[52] Wilkie Collins, *The Woman in White* [1860], ed. John Sutherland (Oxford: Oxford University
Press, 1998): 304.

[53] Ibid., 643, original emphasis. For a wife's separate property in this novel, see Esther Godfrey,
"'Absolutely Miss Fairlie's Own': Emasculating Economics in *The Woman in White*," in *Economic
Women: Essays on Desire and Dispossession in Nineteenth-Century British Culture*, ed. Lana L. Dalley
and Jill Rappoport (Columbus: Ohio State University Press, 2013): 162–75.

importance of masculine birthright to its narrative resolution by explicitly confirming that her uncle's "estate was inherited by Dorothea's son."[54]

In novels such as these, coverture appears restrictive, while patrilineal inheritance—that scourge of Austen's Dashwood and Bennet families—begins to seem just. But the two doctrines take an even more divergent, competitive turn in other works from the late 1860s to mid-1870s, as property reforms were codified into law. The Married Women's Property Act of 1870, as I have mentioned, gave wives limited control over specific forms of property, notably their earnings and small legacies. It came about not to secure independent property rights for wives of the wealthier classes portrayed by Austen or Collins but to eliminate legal distinctions between poor and wealthy families, and, like the Divorce Act, to protect women of the working or lower-middle classes from husbands sensationally viewed as disreputable, abusive, and often absentee. (Such arguments worked in part by ignoring the possibility that wealthier women might need similar protection.[55]) As if in exchange for these protections, however, women's larger fortunes at this point are described as posing problems for children. No longer a means of helping their offspring, women's economic actions in several novels by Anthony Trollope as well as in George Eliot's *Daniel Deronda* appear to threaten lines of inheritance.

The new legal precedent of recognizing a wife's claim to *any* property within marriage appears, for some writers, tantamount to a wife's claiming *all* property within marriage. Although common law doctrine had previously ensured that a woman's property would become her husband's upon marriage, it never mandated the opposite, that a man's property would become his wife's during his lifetime. Indeed, even provisions for widows were not secure. After 1833, dower became "largely defeasible at the will of the husband," and wives didn't always receive the jointures which were intended to replace dower and depended upon settlements.[56] Much depended upon a husband's conscious legal effort: the bewilderment that meets *Our Mutual Friend*'s Mr. Boffin when he attempts to secure his property to Mrs. Boffin suggests the rarity of such action. Certainly, the 1870 Married Women's Property Act did nothing to transfer a man's wealth to either

---

[54] George Eliot, *Middlemarch* [1871], ed. Rosemary Ashton (London: Penguin Books Ltd., 1994): 836, 817, 837.

[55] See, e.g., Frances Power Cobbe, "Wife-Torture in England" [*Contemporary Review*, April 1878], reprinted, *Prose by Victorian Women: An Anthology*, ed. Andrea Broomfield and Sally Mitchell (New York and London: Garland Publishing, Inc., 1996): 291–333, 295, 324. For domestic abuse in Victorian fiction in general as well as specifically middle- or upper-class violence, see Lisa Surridge, *Bleak Houses: Marital Violence in Victorian Fiction* (Athens: Ohio University Press, 2005): e.g., 45–7, 53–5, 58–61; Marlene Tromp, *The Private Rod: Marital Violence, Sensation, and the Law in Victorian Britain* (Charlottesville: University Press of Virginia, 2000): e.g., 76–8, 156–9, 207–9. For discussion of women who fought back rather than "cower under the hands of violent or abusive husbands," see Marlene Tromp, "'Til Death Do Us Part: Marriage, Murder, and Confession," in *Replotting Marriage in Nineteenth-Century British Literature*, ed. Jill Galvan and Elsie Michie (Columbus: Ohio State University Press, 2018): 127–44, 143.

[56] See Staves 27, 96, 114, 130.

18 IMAGINING WOMEN'S PROPERTY IN VICTORIAN FICTION

his wife or widow, although it does appear to have had an effect on women's investments and other economic decisions.[57] Despite its limited reach, however, the cultural anxieties attending this Act were as great as if it had done much more. In fiction written after the 1870 Act, we find women whose marriages secure them great wealth but whose claims to that wealth appear to conflict with the claims of their husbands' first-born sons. Wives' independent possession of property even begins to be represented as theft. In contrast with Fanny Dashwood's seemingly selfish but also maternally solicitous plea that her husband not "rob" her son of his birthright, novels by Trollope and Eliot suggest that wives themselves are the robbers whose selfishness threatens the next generation. Along these lines, even unmarried women are found to be at fault for generous acts that others equate with robbery because they remove their own wealth from its potential generational transmission. Coverture and primogeniture again appear together, but to different effect: once wives can claim property as their own, primogeniture becomes as much a reason to withhold that property as a reason to grant it. Or, to look at it another way, once women are recognized as productive economic agents having a right to money earned by their labor, they are punished (narratively) for their reproductive function. At this point, mercenary marriage becomes problematic not simply for what it suggests about the wife or the institution of marriage but because it enables a wife or widow to claim as her "own" property that the novel assigns to a son.

The Married Women's Property Act of 1882 would finally grant women independent rights to property within marriage, and though it came about as much to streamline and reform the messy English court system as to address women's economic grievances,[58] its even greater recognition of women's economic agency gave rise to additional configurations of the new rivalries between generational and lateral transmission. In Oliphant's *Hester*, for example, a wife's wealth no longer detracts from her offspring's; instead, her dedication to preserving her property for her daughter is seen as injurious to her husband and his financial responsibilities. Her choice of consanguineal transmission over concern for conjugal ties contrasts painfully with an older model of obligation that at first challenges and finally accedes to the new order of property and family ties.

III. Law and Disorder: Legal Doctrine, Family Duty, and Other Narrative Claims

Competition between spouses and children—wives and sons, husbands and daughters—is just one of the many ways in which fiction from this period sets

---

[57] Combs, "'A Measure of Legal Independence'" 1031, 1033, 1039–40, 1042.
[58] Holcombe 15, 16; Outhwaite 157–73. I discuss these reforms in "'Clutch[ing] Gold': Wives, Mothers, and Property Law in *The Ring and the Book*," *Victorian Poetry* 60:1 (Spring 2022): 1–26; see 18–22.

WOMEN'S PROPERTY MATTERS   19

its exploration of the perceived benefits and threats of legal property reform on a larger stage than marriage and coverture. Repeatedly, narratives show that women's increased economic autonomy affects more than the woman, wife, or marriage touched most directly by legal change and also exceeds legal jurisdiction. By insisting that we write and teach about married women's property reform not only or even primarily through the lens of coverture, *Imagining Women's Property* joins with other literary criticism about women and economics that emphasizes women's broader lives.[59] Foundational feminist scholarship explored women's economic affairs productively through sexual economies, particularly heterosexual transactions including but not limited to marriage,[60] but marriage itself—its forms, history, motivations, mechanisms, exclusions, and effects—has undergone substantial and important revision in Victorian studies. Building on earlier work that took marriage as the narrative mechanism for understanding ideological changes, overt or hidden desires, and even seemingly unrelated points such as sympathetic reading practices,[61] more recent kinship studies have reconsidered how different allegiances (among them consanguineal and conjugal, exogamous and endogamous, heterosexual and homosexual, romantic and familiar) motivated marital choices and determined structures of inheritance.[62] They ask what "taking marriage as a literary and cultural given [has] concealed from our view" and insist on seeing the marriage plot "as more than marriage and more than single plot."[63] Still others have looked beyond marriage to show that women's economic actions, in fiction as in life, cannot be reduced to their choice of husbands. Nancy Henry, for instance, argues that "the history of women's financial lives is as important as the romance or marriage plots through which their stories are usually told," while Eileen Cleere has shown "that attention to the avunculate makes alternative models of kinship visible, family relationships that are economically rather than affectively maintained."[64] Kelly Hager and Talia Schaffer, describing the uncles, siblings, and friends that critics including Cleere, Leonore Davidoff, Sharon Marcus, and others have shown to be central to

---

[59] For a terrific discussion of Victorian families that asks us to "relinquish our assumption that the small nuclear family was normative" see Hager and Schaffer 7.

[60] For a key treatment of marriage-plot economics, see, e.g., Nancy Armstrong, *Desire and Domestic Fiction: A Political History of the Novel* (New York and Oxford: Oxford University Press, 1987): 50–1. For Victorian ideas of "fallen women" or the economics of prostitution, see Judith R. Walkowitz, *Prostitution and Victorian Society: Women, Class, and the State* (Cambridge: Cambridge University Press, 1980).

[61] See, for instance, Armstrong 4–5; Rachel Ablow, *The Marriage of Minds: Reading Sympathy in the Victorian Marriage Plot* (Stanford: Stanford University Press, 2007): 5–7.

[62] For these revisionist approaches to understanding Victorian marriage and its representations, see Corbett; Sharon Marcus, *Between Women: Friendship, Desire, and Marriage in Victorian England* (Princeton: Princeton University Press, 2007); Michie, *Vulgar*; Psomiades, "Heterosexual"; Perry, *Novel Relations*; and Schaffer, *Romance's Rival*.

[63] Jill Galvan and Elsie Michie, "Introduction," in *Replotting Marriage in Nineteenth-Century British Literature*, ed. Jill Galvan and Elsie Michie (Columbus: Ohio State University Press, 2018): 1–11, 2, 5.

[64] Henry, *Women* 15; Eileen Cleere, *Avuncularism: Capitalism, Patriarchy, and Nineteenth-Century English Culture* (Stanford: Stanford University Press, 2004): 21.

20 IMAGINING WOMEN'S PROPERTY IN VICTORIAN FICTION

Victorian experiences of family, contend that "Victorian endogamous life was profoundly shaped by figures we minimize when we focus on the conjugal or nuclear family."[65] Extending these powerful lines of scholarship to prioritize both women's wide-ranging relationships and their financial actions, *Imagining Women's Property* follows the money and other objects of women's economic deliberations. By putting property first, we get a view of economic actions that did not necessarily result from or operate in the service of matrimony, however broadly conceived. Yet doing so also shows how these transactions—gifts, thefts, transfers, refusals—constitute their own kinds of familial and extrafamilial webs and urge us to think more expansively about the ways in which the Victorians imagined kinship, community, and the limits of law.

Returning briefly to Austen, *Pride and Prejudice*, which has prompted important readings of marriage-plot economics,[66] also showcases the significance of sibling relationships, their role in facilitating marriage, and their subsequent interests in marital property. Having early noted and been attracted by Elizabeth's "affectionate behaviour" to her own sister (249), Darcy, in pursuing Elizabeth, also procures a good sibling for Georgiana: "the attachment of the sisters was exactly what Darcy had hoped to see" (253). Elizabeth similarly learns to love Darcy as she sees him through the vantage point of this relationship: "'He is certainly a good brother'" (162). Siblinghood here, in facilitating marriage, appears to serve the function that female friendships do in Sharon Marcus's study. Marriage returns the favor, facilitating sibling closeness. Jane and Elizabeth, "in addition to [the vague advantage of] every other source of happiness, were within thirty miles of each other" (252). The importance of sibling ties here accords with what Talia Schaffer has shown to be the impetus behind "familiar" marriage; Jane and Elizabeth secure their consanguineal kinship circles (as well as conjugal romance) in their choice of life partners.[67] But these marriages have additional value for their younger sisters. "Kitty, to her very material advantage, spent the chief of her time with her two elder sisters" (252), and even the disreputable Lydia profits from Jane and Elizabeth's strategic use of their marital allowances. Economic benefit to siblings, not just pleasurable community, drives or at least follows from these marriages, Kitty in the form of a "very material," marketable improvement that will aid her own marriage prospects, and Lydia and her husband in the form of her sisters' recurring financial aid. Of particular interest here, the novel's only commentary on the marital spending of the new wives concerns this less fortunate sister. "Such relief [...] as it was in her power to afford, by the practice of what might be called economy in her own private expences, [Elizabeth] frequently sent them" (253); or again, " ... whenever they changed their quarters, either Jane or herself were sure of being applied to, for

---

[65] Hager and Schaffer 14.
[66] E.g., Michie, *Vulgar* 21, 30.
[67] Schaffer, *Romance's Rival*, e.g., 101–2.

some little assistance towards discharging their bills" (253). Despite Darcy's dislike for and Elizabeth's own ambivalence about this couple, she uses her new wealth not, as her mother anticipates, to be a "great" lady—"'What pin-money, what jewels, what carriages you will have!'" (247)—nor even to enrich her own line or family estates, but rather to help her youngest sister. The fact that she does so out of her "own private expences" is important. It reiterates that under coverture she cannot access the larger store of household wealth; Darcy's great fortune is not, legally or even practically, hers. It reminds us that she has significant advantages that would not have been available to most women through the common law, in the form of special marital settlements and an unusually rich and generous husband. And it highlights the forms of economic agency women were understood to exercise long before legal changes gave wives independent financial rights.[68] Significantly, the drive to assist a sister who is sometimes mentioned with compassion but also with "disgust [...]" (204) also suggests the strength of economic ties and family feelings or obligations beyond marriage.

The strength of these ties further demonstrates the inadequacy of existing legal or financial mechanisms (coverture, settlements, pin money) to account for women's economic lives. Nineteenth-century fiction, in its depictions of families and communities, frequently questions whether property law can address the economic actions women might take when they control resources. Just as *Little Dorrit*'s turnkey ponders how to keep women's property secure from anyone trying to make a "grab" at it, other novels present family demands as posing obligations at least as compelling for women's financial choices as those demarcated by such traditional legal instruments as entailments or coverture. At a time when women's economic agency fell increasingly under scrutiny, narrative depictions of their wider families and relational dynamics suggest that law is only one of the many factors shaping financial claims and duties. Alongside the straightforward trajectory set out by legal reforms—women lacked financial rights and then gained them—novelists from Austen through Oliphant remind us that women's economic actions emerge out of and produce social situations unimagined by the law. Thus in addition to emphasizing how the movement to reform women's property affected relationships beyond marriage, *Imagining Women's Property* also takes up those relationships to show how novels make a case for their own value in debates about changing economics. As they repeatedly show through heightened attention to women's property during this period, economic relationships come with social complications that the law—unlike fiction—is not flexible or powerful enough to cover.

Tracking the movement of women's resources throughout narratives with the care that we afford to characters themselves changes how we understand some of

---

[68] For "pin money," see Staves 133, 132.

our most familiar literary texts and also forces us to reconsider both economic history and family in the nineteenth century. When we read for money, for example, an intimate exchange between working-class women in *Our Mutual Friend* matters as much as the novel's well-known depiction of mercenary marital speculation, while a testimonial team ultimately has greater financial consequences for women than the novel's infamously objectifying will. In the decade following the 1856 Petition for Married Women's Property rights, notions of economic success as an individual pursuit frequently give way to models of communal benefit in Victorian works grappling with the possibility of women's private property and the vulnerability of those in greatest need. Whereas the period's legal reforms focus on each person's separate property rights, its fiction offers different, collaborative scenarios that explore and manage larger networks of relationships.[69] Whether this literary emphasis reflects real women's historical privileging of shared profits and interpersonal priorities, a tactic to make women's economic agency appear more palatable, or a strategy for suggesting that women, unlike men, do not, cannot, or should not pursue individual advantage, collaboration is both a central method for handling money in these novels and also—for better and worse—a lingering cultural mandate for women and their wealth even today.

The 1870 Married Women's Property Act protected the income and small holdings of working-class wives. Following this first Act, political efforts turned from safeguarding these poorer women to advocating for the rights of wives from wealthier classes. Protecting vulnerable women was an easier concession for legislators and literary authors alike than conceding women's right to make their own economic decisions in times of relative comfort, which is one reason that, despite the need for further scholarship on working women, this book spends more time on depictions of the latter, turning, in the years leading up to the 1882 Act, to those women more likely to benefit from substantial family money and to challenge their families' economic traditions most significantly. As Amy Louise Erickson has noted of an earlier period, "historically, the most important component of wealth was not wages, but inheritance."[70] Working women contributed food and farthings to materially assist others in their local communities,[71] but these forms of financial aid, though highly significant to recipients, appear to have been less problematic for lawmakers than the sums potentially wielded by wealthier women, whose economic actions had more visible opportunities to impact larger communities. Reading for money allows us to better see and understand

---

[69] For communal relationships in terms of theories and actions of care, see Talia Schaffer, *Communities of Care: The Social Ethics of Victorian Fiction* (Princeton: Princeton University Press, 2021): e.g., 6–7, 22.

[70] Erickson, *Women and Property* 3. For inheritance's significance in the racial distribution of American wealth, see Jeff Clymer, *Family Money: Property, Race, and Literature in the Nineteenth Century* (Oxford: Oxford University Press, 2013): 10.

[71] For forms of community childcare in particular, see Ross 156, 135.

these women's choices, which are imagined as far more capacious than their marital options. The wealth of siblings and children becomes as important to trace as that of suitors, and even cousins and friends become significant sources and recipients of women's financial acts. In the decade preceding the more comprehensive 1882 Married Women's Property Act, political debates began opening up the prospect of more women with greater financial agency making independent choices. Fiction from this period explores the consequences of these choices, while often restricting them through forms of illness, popular censure, or, in the case of Eliot's *Daniel Deronda*, a fantasy of spiritual property that reinstates the paths of transmission seemingly threatened by married women's claims.

One of the striking aspects of women's economic choices in many of these novels is that, even when most subject to rebuke, they remain centered on those they consider to be family. Though this pattern aligns with the historical contributions of women to their families recorded by Amy M. Froide as well as by Leonore Davidoff and Catherine Hall, a gap persists between those practices and the representational strategies of scholarly and fictional works alike.[72] Susan Staves notes that historiography tends to portray women as "individuals competing against the 'family' interest rather than integral and necessary parts of the 'family.'"[73] Nineteenth-century literature, too, often frames women's interests as being at odds with those of their families. Yet for the most part, women's property rights in these novels don't lead them into flights of self-indulgent consumerism, dangerous business ventures, or a desire to spurn matrimony and reproduction altogether. Fictional women with money are often presented as possessing attractions beyond those of wealth, and they don't appear any less likely than their penniless counterparts to love or desire the partners who seek them.[74] They simply do not treat a husband, an heir, or their potential future instantiations as the only or even the most important recipient of their fortunes. Instead, they direct their love, loyalty, and financial assistance to a much broader range of familial recipients. Brothers, cousins, or, in the case of Oliphant's *Hester*, a daughter and a whole town of extended kin and community members benefit from women's financial choices, reminding us that marriage and reproduction were not the only possible repositories for their wealth and that marital property reform was understood as having wide impact.

In the decades after the 1851 census revealed a disproportionately high number of women to men, literary authors and social reformers struggled with how to best

---

[72] Amy M. Froide, *Never Married: Singlewomen in Early Modern England* (Oxford: Oxford University Press, 2005): 44, 75, 135; Davidoff and Hall, *Family Fortunes* 279.

[73] Staves 203.

[74] For the ways in which economic autonomy gave single women in an earlier period the "ability [. . .] to choose their state" see Judith M. Bennett and Amy M. Froide, "Introduction," in *Singlewomen in the European Past, 1250–1800*, ed. Judith M. Bennett and Amy M. Froide (Philadelphia: University of Pennsylvania Press, 1999): 1–37, 22–3.

24 IMAGINING WOMEN'S PROPERTY IN VICTORIAN FICTION

serve or be served by this "surplus" population, offering educational and professional opportunities, Anglican Sisterhoods, and emigration schemes for the historical "problem" of what Amy M. Froide has called "never-married women."[75] As
I have suggested elsewhere and as Sharon Marcus, Martha Vicinus, Talia Schaffer,
and others have shown, Victorian women found not only work, community, and
financial support, but also family, intimacy, and romantic love in their connections with other women.[76] The emphasis on single women and widows as well as
wives in many of the works I am discussing gives the novels space to explore the
choices outside of the marriages that conclude some of their threads but that leave
many other characters unwed, with largely unrestricted rights to their own lives
and property as well as active roles with respect to both.[77] In the contested
discourse concerning whether wives' separate property would ruin marriage or
improve it by equalizing partners, Victorian fiction offers representations of social
situations which marital law cannot create or forestall.

Property rights for the *feme sole* and for married women following the 1882 Act
did not mean, of course, that all women had property to protect. The fiction
I discuss here focuses primarily on women of means, whether meager or vast, but
certainly many other women found the daily struggle to sustain life more significant than potential rights to wealth they would never enjoy. It continues to be a
challenge in our field, I think, to acknowledge both the extreme privilege of
wealthier white women in Victorian England and the significant inequalities
they also faced.[78] Nor did property rights necessarily preclude questionable
sources or uses of that property. The wealth of women, when they had it, was
just as likely as that of men to derive from or be used for imperialist exploitation

[75] Froide 12. For "surplus women" see Rappoport, *Giving* 93; also William Rathbone Greg, "Why
Are Women Redundant?" [*National Review*, 1862], reprinted in *The Broadview Anthology of British
Literature: The Victorian Era*, 2nd ed. (Ontario: Broadview Press, 2012): 106–7 and Frances Power
Cobbe, "What Shall We Do with Our Old Maids?" (*Fraser's Magazine*, Nov. 1862), reprinted in *Prose
by Victorian Women: An Anthology*, ed. Andrea Broomfield and Sally Mitchell (New York: Garland,
1996): 236–61.

[76] For intimacy, eroticism, and romantic love between women, see, for instance, Rappoport, *Giving*
104, 114; Marcus, *Between*; Martha Vicinus, *Intimate Friends: Women Who Loved Women, 1778–1928*
(Chicago: University of Chicago Press, 2004); Martha Vicinus, *Independent Women: Work and
Community for Single Women, 1850–1920* (Chicago: University of Chicago Press, 1985): 158–62,
187–210; Margaret R. Hunt, "The Sapphic Strain: English Lesbians in the Long Eighteenth Century,"
in *Singlewomen in the European Past, 1250–1800*, ed. Judith M. Bennett and Amy M. Froide
(Philadelphia: University of Pennsylvania Press, 1999): 270–96, 271, 272, 275. As Margaret R. Hunt
points out, lesbian relationships had economic benefits compared with heterosexuality, since female
partnerships were not subject to coverture (289). For the possibility of "care performativity"—"repeating acts of caregiving [that] can produce the feeling of caring" and examples of the affection and even
love between women that arises from nursing, see Schaffer, *Communities of Care* 50–1.

[77] For single middle-class women's "active role in promoting their own economic welfare," see
Green and Owens, "Gentlewomanly" 512. For the importance of an "underinvestigated middle" rather
than "narrative culmination," see Galvan and Michie 5.

[78] "[T]he possibility of movement between, across, and among genders" is an important consider-
ation when we discuss such concepts as "women's rights." See, for instance, Lisa Hager, "A Case for a
Trans Studies Turn in Victorian Studies: 'Female Husbands' of the Nineteenth Century," *Victorian
Review* 44.1 (2018): 37–54, 37. Although my analysis treats "women" and "men" as fiction and

WOMEN'S PROPERTY MATTERS 25

and the shoring up of class privilege. Women in England and the British colonies, for example, benefited from slavery; when £20,000,000 was distributed as compensation to British colonial slave-owners after emancipation, from 1835–45, most "small-scale" awards (less than £500) went to women.[79] Wealth that the Married Women's Property Acts were called on to protect stemmed in part from slavery and its compensation. Moreover, nineteenth-century women's "capital was crucial to underwriting national and imperial projects" through investment in government debt.[80] Women were 47.2 percent of investors in the national debt by 1840 and were also a "crucial presence as investors throughout the nineteenth century" on the London Stock Exchange, in the East India Company, and in "banks, domestic and colonial railroads, shipping, docks, foreign bonds, and other global securities."[81] Nancy Henry has discussed how some of these projects had highly controversial histories; the St. Katharine Docks, for example, in which both Elizabeth Gaskell and George Eliot invested, "required the defiling of a graveyard [...] and the displacement of 11,300 residents."[82] In the novels that I discuss here, some characters consider the sources of their wealth. *Our Mutual Friend*'s Mrs. Boffin wishes to benefit another child in remembrance of the one whose presumed death has occasioned her fortune; *Daniel Deronda*'s Gwendolen hopes to do right by the illegitimate child she feels her marriage has wronged. Yet other sources of wealth also go unchallenged in these and other narratives. Characters seem unconcerned by the West Indian derivation of Gwendolen's mother's fortune or the national origins of the titular Eustace diamonds. The novels themselves are quick to denounce the economic decisions of various female characters, but without fail their criticism is about these women's divergence from gendered norms as much as or more than about economics or social justice. The point here is not that women's wealth, in fiction or life, is free of fault or put to good use, but that we can acknowledge the shortcomings of certain financial choices without using them as justification to withhold economic rights. Since others have,

legislation label them, I wish to acknowledge the limitations of those labels and of the binary that the novels and laws relied on even while they were suggesting a range of gender expression that often belied some of Victorian England's strictest assumptions about those binaries.

[79] Stephanie E. Jones-Rogers shows how slave-owning women in antebellum America made economic choices that "created freedom for themselves" in the process of denying that freedom to the enslaved. See *They Were Her Property: White Women as Slave Owners in the American South* (New Haven: Yale University Press, 2019): xvii. For British compensation to female slave-owners, see Nicholas Draper, *The Price of Emancipation: Slave-Ownership, Compensation and British Society at the End of Slavery* (Cambridge: Cambridge University Press, 2010): 105–6, 110, 127, 133, 134–7, 183, 184, 204, 207–9. See also Henry, *Women* 7 and Gordon Bigelow, "Forgetting Cairnes: *The Slave Power* (1862) and the Political Economy of Racism," in *From Political Economy to Economics through Nineteenth-Century Literature: Reclaiming the Social*, ed. Elaine Hadley, Audrey Jaffe, and Sarah Winter (Cham: Palgrave Macmillan, 2019): 85–105, 85, 86.

[80] Henry, *Women, Literature and Finance* 6.

[81] Henry 33, Green and Owens, "Gentlewomanly" 524–5, Henry 43, Henry 33–45.

[82] Henry 140. See Henry 139–41, 85–7.

26 IMAGINING WOMEN'S PROPERTY IN VICTORIAN FICTION

historically, denied women rights in precisely that manner, we should be aware of and critical regarding the terms by which their financial choices are framed, celebrated, or condemned.

The financial choices we see in these novels resonate with debates about married women's property rights during this period, but one of the key points that *Imagining Women's Property* makes is that those choices have implications— of keen interest to the literary authors under discussion here—far beyond the married or marriageable woman. We have not yet taken adequate notice of how intensely the aftershocks of even women's imagined possession reverberated through major works of the period, suggesting the degree to which women's management of private property was seen as threatening men's power to transmit money and to determine family ties. Women with money present unresolved problems within Victorian narratives not simply because they are acquisitive or represent the era's materialism, but because—in the decades between the onset of legal debates about married women's property law reform and the legislation that finally granted women separate economic identities—they suggest some of the familial anxieties and hopes attending women's financial management. As we will see, women's claims to ownership provide insight into the rich relationships forged through property transactions and also offer us a lens to examine a wide range of other social matters, including testamentary practices, wills, and copyright law (Chapter 1); economic and evolutionary models of mutuality (Chapter 2); the twin dangers of greed and generosity (Chapter 3); inheritance and custody rights (Chapter 4); and the economic ramifications of loyalty and family obligation (Chapter 5). Exploring the significance of women's economic actions across these and other domains, I show that married women's property legislation was about far more than either marital relationships or legal rights.

IV. Properties

As my allusions to settlements, inheritance, income, jewels, carriages, and "presents of fish and game" have already suggested, Victorian novels mean many different things when they talk about property. Just as a fuller understanding of property reform necessarily complicates our conceptions of "married women" and "rights," it reminds us that "property," too, is a capacious category. If nineteenth-century novels demonstrate that "married women's property rights" engage relationships and customs beyond marriage or law, they also grapple with the fact that such relationships and customs were in a state of constant flux during this period because property was neither static nor unitary. We see this dynamic sense of property in broader legislative attempts to pin down what property could do, for whom. The 1832 and 1867 Reform Acts, for example, changed class thresholds for property-based male suffrage, while other mid-century laws targeted the property

WOMEN'S PROPERTY MATTERS   27

claims and obligations of business corporations.[83] In addition to reflecting on such legal regulations, nineteenth-century novels also signal multiple and changing conceptions of what constituted property itself.[84]

Even before the nineteenth century, "real" estate—property as income-producing land—was subject to different laws and conventions from other forms of "personal" property, a divide we see in the way that male characters such as *Pride and Prejudice*'s Darcy inherit paternal land, while his privileged sister's fortune comes in the monetary form of "thirty thousand pounds" (133). Austen's novel also reminds us of the more contemporary shift from status based on inherited land and longstanding family wealth to individual salary, contract, and changing fortunes. For instance, the Bingleys' relatively new money "had been acquired by trade" (11). Additional avenues for wealth open up later in the century. In *Middlemarch*, Will Ladislaw's political journalism and subsequent public career offer a sharp contrast to the landed family wealth of the Brookes and Chettams and to the older, respectable professions of clergymen and medical practitioners. Here and elsewhere, changing conceptions of the professions lend legitimacy to diverse forms of wealth creation and changing status. They also—as we will see through Dickens's mid-century engagement with authorial copyright and through Gaskell's depiction of new fields of scientific discoveries as well as stolen medical knowledge—showcase newly recognized or contested forms of individual property based in skills, community knowledge, and intellectual labor.[85] Women's

---

[83] I.e., the Representation of the People Act 1832 or 1832 Reform Act (2 & 3 Will. IV c. 45) and the Representation of the People Act 1867 or Reform Act 1867 (30 & 31 Vict. c. 102). Legislation governing corporations, such as the Limited Liability Act 1855 (18 & 19 Vict c. 133), was also part of this broader effort to define and regulate property rights.

[84] Though the following works do not specifically focus on women's changing rights and relationships, important treatments of Victorian property that inform my broader understanding of the period include (but are not limited to): Nunokawa; Andrew H. Miller, *Novels behind Glass: Commodity Culture and Victorian Narrative* (Cambridge: Cambridge University Press, 1995); Regenia Gagnier, *The Insatiability of Human Wants: Economics and Aesthetics in Market Society* (Chicago: University of Chicago Press, 2000); Elaine Freedgood, *The Ideas in Things: Fugitive Meaning in the Victorian Novel* (Chicago: University of Chicago Press, 2006); Catherine Gallagher, *The Body Economic: Life, Death, and Sensation in Political Economy and the Victorian Novel* (Princeton: Princeton University Press, 2006); John Plotz, *Portable Property: Victorian Culture on the Move* (Princeton: Princeton University Press, 2008).

[85] For professions and professionalism in the nineteenth century, see, e.g., Harold Perkin, *The Rise of Professional Society: England Since 1880* (London and New York: Routledge, 1989, 2002): e.g., 9, 79–80, 117, 120–3; Monica F. Cohen, *Professional Domesticity in the Victorian Novel: Women, Work and Home* (Cambridge: Cambridge University Press, 1998): 7–9, 28, 35–6, 101, 108; Nicholas Daly, *Modernism, Romance, and the Fin De Siècle: Popular Fiction and British Culture, 1880–1914* (Cambridge: Cambridge University Press, 1999): 32, 39, 40, 44–6; Bruce Robbins, "The Village of the Liberal Managerial Class," in *Cosmopolitan Geographies: New Locations in Literature and Culture*, ed. Vinay Dharwadker (New York: Routledge, 2001): 15–32, 16–17, 23; Bruce Robbins, "How to Be a Benefactor without Any Money: The Chill of Welfare in *Great Expectations*," in *Knowing the Past: Victorian Literature and Culture*, ed. Suzy Anger (Ithaca: Cornell University Press, 2001): 172–91, 186–7, 189: https://www.jstor.org/stable/10.7591/j.ctv3s8qqv.12; David Babcock, "Professional Subjectivity and the Attenuation of Character in J. M. Coetzee's 'Life & Times of Michael K,'" *PMLA* 127.4 (2012): 890–904, 890–1: https://www.jstor.org/stable/23489094.

28   IMAGINING WOMEN'S PROPERTY IN VICTORIAN FICTION

increasing access to and profit from professional work appears in the many working- but also middle-class and even genteel female laborers who populate the novels discussed throughout this book, from the more conventional seams-tresses, teachers, and governesses to shopkeepers, professional musicians, and bankers. Both their salaries, which would be protected by the 1870 Married Women's Property Act, and their intellectual and artistic talents, presented in these novels, were forms of property, though only after the 1882 Married Women's Property Act could wives formally enter into contracts regarding their labor.

Forms of personal property associated with and afforded to women before the 1870 and 1882 reforms were, more frequently, concrete, tangible goods. Women often took charge of the care and circulation of items ranging from shawls to silver tea services, items which became sources of personal value, pride, and self-possession even when that property legally belonged to a household and could thus be treated by creditors as part of a husband's estate. In Eliot's *The Mill on the Floss* (1860),[86] Bessy Tulliver is so entirely enmeshed with her personal property that her core identity is shaken by the fact that her husband's debts necessitate the sale of "treasures" she began amassing before her marriage:

> Poor Mrs Tulliver, it seemed, would never recover her old self [...]: how could she? The objects among which her mind had moved complacently were all gone: all the little hopes, and schemes, and speculations, all the pleasant little cares about her treasures which had made this world quite comprehensible to her for a quarter of a century, since she had made her first purchase of the sugar-tongs, had been suddenly snatched away from her, and she remained bewildered in this empty life. (288)

The emptiness that she experiences stems both from her loss of property and from her loss of its right of bequeathal. Like many women unable to legally create wills but nonetheless taking care to transmit their property, she has already designated certain special linens as her children's legacy:[87] "'I meant 'em for you. I wanted you to have all o' this pattern'" (214). Bessy Tulliver's distress at this loss contrasts with the more confident sense of ownership we will see in fiction by Trollope and Oliphant, in which female characters are able to keep their personal belongings separate from their husbands' estates. In cases such as theirs, certain tangible items of jewelry or clothing became the sole property of wives during their marriages without requiring special settlements. However, as we will see, legal designations of such property as "paraphernalia" stood in tension with social understanding of rightful ownership and obligation.

---

[86] George Eliot, *The Mill on the Floss* [1860], ed. A. S. Byatt (London: Penguin Books, Ltd., 1979, 2003).

[87] For women and wills, see Chapter 1 of this study.

The novels explored in the last three chapters of the book use such tangible, traditionally feminine personal property to stand in, metonymically, for women's ownership in general, a move which facilitates consideration of women's economic claims but also limits their reach and sidesteps larger issues of economic rights. Diamonds in *The Eustace Diamonds* and *Daniel Deronda* and pearls in *Hester* illuminate a wide range of interpersonal connections as well as the ways in which those connections are constituted by or engaged in a variety of economic traditions and obligations. The value of this jewelry, as John Plotz has discussed, is both sentimental and commercial, "ineffable and fungible simultaneously," opening up important questions about customary transmission and affective claims as well as property rights.[88] The gems' familial settings and their portable, personal nature authorize the circulation of such property among women, who are more likely to be shown in possession of gemstones than of other, similarly valuable property. Women had greater legal claims to their jewelry than to other property, as *The Eustace Diamonds* reluctantly acknowledges, and jewelry was popularly seen as belonging in (or on) a woman's arms.[89] However, its association with feminine adornment also made it somewhat easier to dismiss the serious financial agency of women whose wealth took that form. The novels I consider in these chapters showcase three tremendously valuable necklaces, any of which could apparently provide the means for an independent living; but debate about them, even when it invokes their great cost or speculates on their sale, remains centered on physical possession rather than exploring the use or management of any proceeds from such precious property. In staging the circulation of gemstones among women both as gifts and thefts, that is, Trollope, Eliot, and Oliphant focus on whether women's hold on the gems is illicit, not on what they can do with them. This emphasis on acquisition and possession reflects larger cultural interest in gemstones' imperial origins but also averts attention from the consequences that might follow women's rightful claims. One of these was the potential for political enfranchisement: ownership had long been seen as a prerequisite for male suffrage, and some advocates of women's rights argued that property ownership should secure women the vote.[90] But another consequence of women's rights to broader forms of property was, simply, choice. During this period, women had far

---

[88] Plotz 15.

[89] *The Eustace Diamonds* emphasizes women's legal possession of some property under the category of paraphernalia. For shifts in property holding following the 1870 Act, see Combs, "'A Measure of Legal Independence'" 1032–3. Rutterford, Green, Maltby, and Owens show the effects of the 1882 Act on women's shareholding ("Who Comprised" 171–2). For jewel-adorned female bodies "stand[ing in] for consumer culture and for the striving men who supply the gems," see Adrienne Munich, *Empire of Diamonds: Victorian Gems in Imperial Settings* (Charlottesville: University of Virginia Press, 2020): 14.

[90] See, e.g., Dolin 34. The 1867 Reform Act expanded the level of ownership that counted, still excluding women but roughly doubling the electorate. For the "self-possessed individual, literally a subject who possesses its self, where the self is implicitly figured as a type of property" who was "the male subject considered most deserving of the vote," see Elaine Hadley, "The Past Is a Foreign Country: The Neo-Conservative Romance with Victorian Liberalism," *Yale Journal of Criticism* 10.1 (1997):

30   IMAGINING WOMEN'S PROPERTY IN VICTORIAN FICTION

more choices about their money—which they could save or spend, invest or transmit, opening up new lines of social relation—than those implied by authors' focus on women's expensive accessories.

Through women's investments, we see the expansion and financialization of the nineteenth-century economy, a shift away from property in concrete objects (land, jewels, even money in its bullion form)[91] circulated within tightly knit communities to those forms of wealth represented by increasingly abstract symbols such as bank notes, shares, or futures and circulated globally among strangers. Tangible forms of wealth—the pennies sewn into Betty Higdon's dress in *Our Mutual Friend*, or, at the other end of the social spectrum, the "heap of napoleons" that Gwendolen Harleth wagers at the roulette-table in *Daniel Deronda*'s opening scene (11) and the "heavy boxes" brought in by the "Bank of England porters" to reassure a panicked community when Catherine Vernon saves her family bank in Margaret Oliphant's *Hester* (22)—give way to the more nebulous sense of ownership offered by investments and speculations. Shares in a company might produce future wealth, but that wealth is deferred, inaccessible, and uncertain. *Hester*'s villain Edward Vernon calls speculation "a capital horse when it carries you over the ford—and everything that is bad when you lose'" (*Hester* 377). Novelists from Dickens to Trollope to Oliphant associate this conjectural property, which promises everything but may ultimately yield nothing, with the spectacular rise and sensational fall of men and fortunes alike. The narrator of *Our Mutual Friend* satirically highlights the abstraction of both property and its possessors:

> traffic in Shares is the one thing to have to do with in this world. Have no antecedents, no established character, no cultivation, no ideas, no manners; have Shares. [...] Where does he come from? Shares. Where is he going to? Shares. What are his tastes? Shares. Has he any principles? Shares.
>
> (*Our Mutual Friend* 114)

7–38, 12 doi:10.1353/yale.1997.0003. For a rich discussion of possession and personhood in the different context of American slavery, see Stephen M. Best, *The Fugitive's Properties: Law and the Poetics of Possession* (Chicago and London: University of Chicago Press, 2004): e.g., 18–19, 62–5.

[91] For the argument that "'money, properly speaking, consists only of a certain quantity of precious metal,'" see Robert William Dickinson, *Two Addresses on the Depreciation of the Currency* (London: J. Clarke, 1843): 9–10, quoted in Timothy Alborn, *All That Glittered: Britain's Most Precious Metal from Adam Smith to the Gold Rush* (Oxford: Oxford University Press, 2019): 34, 205 n. 31. For nineteenth-century currency debates, see also Alborn, *All that Glittered* 28–46. For discussions of financialization itself, see C. D. Blanton, Colleen Lye and Kent Puckett, *Representations* 126:1 (Spring 2014, Special Issue: Financialization and the Culture Industry): 1–8, 3: https://www.jstor.org/stable/10.1525/rep. 2014.126.1.1; Garrett Ziegler, "The City of London, Real and Unreal," *Victorian Studies* 49.3 (2007): 431–55, 433–5: https://www.jstor.org/stable/4626329; Nancy Henry and Cannon Schmitt, "Introduction: Finance, Capital, Culture," in *Victorian Investments: New Perspectives on Finance and Culture*, ed. Nancy Henry and Cannon Schmitt (Bloomington: Indiana University Press, 2009): 1–12, e.g., 4, 7.

WOMEN'S PROPERTY MATTERS 31

Emptier than Bessy Tulliver's life without her treasures, a world of speculation here threatens the dissolution of character itself in its sacrifice of history and community to the chance of future wealth. Nonetheless, as Nancy Henry and others have shown, women benefited as well as lost from low- and high-risk investments.[92] Still other forms of further abstracted property remained for women to perhaps lose but not gain: virginity, reputation, custody, and cultural inheritance, for instance, all might signal value of some kind but, as we will see in Chapters 2 and 4, they offered women little of the agency or control we associate with property rights and could not easily be legislated.

Victorian property appears in various forms, with different affordances,[93] and as I discuss in each chapter of this book, these specific differences matter. But the novels I treat never deal with only one, showing both the widespread awareness of property's multiplicity and changing nature and also the greater capacity of fiction than law to present their many and at times competing forms. Ultimately my interest here, as in my previous study of gift exchange, is less on a single type of property than on the dynamic transactions that isolate or draw people together; property as a force more than an object; and the way that literature imagines people's interests and actions with regard to such forces.

V. Chapters

Following this introduction, I turn to two novels written in the mid-1860s, after the Petition to reform married women's property law was presented but before the first Act legislated reform. These works, by Charles Dickens and Elizabeth Gaskell, showcase unsuccessful marriages and strained relations between fathers and sons consistent with contemporary concerns about coverture and the dangers of primogeniture, but they also suggest alternative models for loving relationships. They foreground collaborative ways to safeguard property and protect working-class women, and they offer extralegal solutions to celebrate primogeniture itself as a means of mutual benefit.

When John Harmon's inheritance is made contingent on his marriage to Bella Wilfer, a woman he has never met, his father's will becomes a fulcrum for Dickens's meditations on value and exchange, the subject of Chapter 1, "'How Can Money be a Corpse's?' Wealth, Women, and Wills in Dickens's *Our Mutual Friend* (1865)." By objectifying Bella and laying bare the financial interests of the

---

[92] For the suggestion that "The fact that investing was open to women, as other avenues to wealth and power were not, meant that female authors' treatment of investing and capitalism [...] was not characterized by the same types of critique that appear in" works by Dickens, Trollope, and other male authors see Henry, *Women* 3.

[93] For the "affordances" of different forms, see Caroline Levine, *Forms: Whole, Rhythm, Hierarchy, Network* (Princeton: Princeton University Press, 2015): e.g., 6–7.

32 IMAGINING WOMEN'S PROPERTY IN VICTORIAN FICTION

marriage plot, Harmon's attempted transaction most obviously showcases the economic dispossession of middle-class women that was central to debates about property rights in the 1860s, but it is also central to a different economic problem—the failure of written documents to distribute property. Through Harmon's will, Dickens makes authorship important to his speculations on property ownership, compelling us to connect three points of longstanding critical interest: the novel's ambivalent depiction of women with wealth, its preoccupation with literacy and writing, and its fascination with death and inheritance. Willed property proves to be little more than a fiction in a novel that questions the posthumous power any author can have over his or her writing (whether as property or regarding property). Yet the novel also imagines extralegal ways to push beyond the limits of legal ownership, using female characters both to restore John Harmon's estate and to protect a woman's burial wishes. Ultimately, this chapter will demonstrate, *Our Mutual Friend* attempts to resolve a crisis in gendered and authorial property rights through collaborative exchanges. It grants working-class women greater economic roles and testamentary rights in the service of securing at least the fantasy of stable authorship, patrilineal property, and more reliably directed legacies.

Similarly emphasizing collaborative strategies for property management, Chapter 2, "'A Purse in Common': Money, Mutuality, and Darwinian Survival in *Wives and Daughters* (1866)," highlights Gaskell's interest in the importance and diversity of cost-sharing practices within families and communities. Gaskell's final, unfinished novel has interested critics primarily for the way that its two sibling pairs struggle for scarce economic and marital resources. Molly Gibson and Cynthia Kirkpatrick, like Roger and Osborne Hamley, are primed to resent and compete with one another. Yet they find ways to coexist with affection. The novel attempts to replace competition with common interest, privileging mutual over individual benefit in a model of sibling relations that pools resources, giving emotional connection both an economic counterpart and a grounding in alternative evolutionary strains. By making working-class women, in part, the motivation for and beneficiaries of these new models, Gaskell—like Dickens and other writers in the 1860s—prioritizes the safeguarding of poorer women's household needs over more unconditional property reforms, but her models are expansive in other ways. By juxtaposing sibling relations with visions of marital unity and discord, Gaskell shows how extralegal economic practices can promote wellbeing and intimacy within both family ties. Productive parallels between sibling relations and marriage in Gaskell's novel further suggest the critical value of assessing individual relationships (siblings, friends, spouses) alongside and through one another, rather than in social or political isolation. The marriage plot of Gaskell's novel is as much a story of how to be a good brother, sister, or friend as the story of a developing heterosexual romance, and of the way that changing economic relationships can advance the needs of both.

WOMEN'S PROPERTY MATTERS 33

Economic changes were not always viewed in such a positive light, of course. Novels written after the 1870 Act highlight the trouble with women's economic choices. In Chapter 3, "Greed, Generosity, and Other Problems with Unmarried Women's Property," I focus on the property problems of four unmarried female characters whose financial decisions are divorced from marital or sexual desire and instead directed toward or against platonic blood relations. Alongside Anthony Trollope's generally sympathetic depiction of women's legal position, his acknowledgment of their capacity for financial management, and his tendency to consolidate unusually great sums in the hands of female characters, these novels' unusually punitive plotlines suggest the threat that single women's independent economic actions might pose to established family structures and financial traditions. Whether these women are condemned as "blood-sucking harpies," as Lady Lizzie Eustace is described in *The Eustace Diamonds* (1873) (1:245), or praised like Lady Laura Standish in *Phineas Finn* for being "generous as the sun" (409), their greed and generosity present equal dangers to these novels' social worlds because they obstruct customary forms of property transmission. By challenging principles of inheritance and heterosexual exchange, injuring the very families they claim to help, and creating unacceptable burdens for their male kin, these characters underscore contemporary fears and fantasies about the intrafamilial stakes of women's financial choices and also showcase the contested roles of female custodians and creditors that became salient during a time of increased agitation for married women's property rights.

Women's economic choices continue to pose problems in George Eliot's 1876 *Daniel Deronda*, as I discuss in Chapter 4, "'That Blent Transmission': Women's Property Law and Jewish Cultural Inheritance." Discussions of gender and property in Eliot's novel tend to highlight the economic necessity of marriage for women, the mercenary nature of the marriage market, and the economic power of husbands over their wives. In contrast, I'm interested in Eliot's more comprehensive response to women's changing property rights, both through the novel's treatment of non-marital exchanges within Gwendolen's story and also through its emphasis on property transactions within its other story, the "Jewish plot" of cultural inheritance. Together, the narratives map contemporary tensions between social and legal definitions of ownership. If, as I suggest, the novel's so-called "English marriage plot," like that of Trollope's *The Eustace Diamonds*, uses diamond theft to stage the competing economic claims of wives and sons, its "Jewish plot" uses stolen diamonds to resolve this familial conflict by consolidating more fluid kinship ties. This "blent transmission" of spiritual inheritance counters the fraught transfer of Gwendolen's diamonds through a form of inalienable property that, despite "theft," adheres to its path of descent. Although both plots align in keeping property out of women's reach, Eliot's expansive conception of family ties beyond marriage, her understanding of non-monetary property value, and her defense of socially sanctioned transmission over property law

34 IMAGINING WOMEN'S PROPERTY IN VICTORIAN FICTION

also point to the shortcomings of that law and suggest some of the ways in which legal rights and individuals' priorities attending personal property diverge.

Margaret Oliphant's *Hester* (1883), published after the 1882 Act granted wives economic rights, uses the intense feelings provoked by a pearl necklace to explore two different models for thinking about women's relationship to property. The first is that of the changing legal rights this study explores, from coverture to independent property ownership, as principles of equity were incorporated into the common law. The second, which attention to these legal patterns sometimes obscures but which is evident in the economic choices previous chapters also highlight, is that of family feeling and tradition. In Chapter 5, "'Giv[ing] All She Had': *Hester's* Pearls and the Obligations of Women's Property," awareness of these two models allows us to see how the novel takes what initially appears to be a contest between a naïve, helpless wife and a successful, single businesswoman— once rivals for the same man—and transforms it into opposing visions of daughters, one who manages to protect a maternal legacy for herself and the next generation against another who cannot. This shift in perspective forces us to see how these roles coexist, in tension, and changes how we understand characters' choices and relationships. Suggesting that their newfound rights to private property will not make women abandon other family traditions, *Hester* remains ambivalent about the costs and benefits of these rights and reminds us of the other extralegal forces and relational obligations that continued—and, perhaps, continue—to shape women's financial lives.

My afterword, "Women's Property Matters Now," turns to contemporary workplaces to consider the legacies left to us by Victorian stories of women's property. In this brief conclusion, I note that the Victorian discipline of economics emerged precisely as women's financial rights were changing. Pointing to a neglected but highly suggestive conjunction of legal and theoretical developments, I speculate on what this neglect has meant for women's economic lives today. Finally, I argue that a keener sense of the continuities between Victorian fictions and twenty-first-century labor markets might allow us to better understand the economic challenges women still face and eventually even help to improve these financial circumstances.

Women, the relationships they prioritize, and the property they hold take multiple forms in the Victorian popular imagination during the period of reform from the mid-1850s through the early 1880s. Widows, wives, and unmarried women; grandmothers, mothers, and daughters, aunts and nieces, sisters, cousins, and friends all play roles in fictional renderings of what women's economic action might look like, and those women run the gamut from nursery-maids and shop-keepers to middle-class investors and wealthy heiresses. Their diverse holdings come from wages, business, rents, debts, financial markets, and inheritance, and they include not only money and material personal items but also homes, larger estates, and less tangible property including talent and cultural traditions. This book grapples with the wide range of women's property through exploration of individual works of fiction deemed significant by readers both then and now. All of the authors I discuss at length in this study—Dickens, Gaskell, Trollope, Eliot, and Oliphant—"experienced a drain on [their] finances due to the behavior of family members" including fathers, husbands, brothers, and children, and they all supported their families financially.[94] Three of them—Gaskell, Eliot, and Oliphant—did so under the additional liabilities of gender. It is not surprising that these authors would be particularly interested in the far-reaching ramifications of their characters' economic choices. The novels I focus on here, while only a small sample of the period's fictional output, constitute significant and representative windows into how the Victorians presented those choices, as well as the forms of action and connection they occasioned. By engaging deeply with these works, I show how women's changing property rights mattered to family and communities that extended well beyond individual wives and marital structures. Whether they welcomed such rights, mocked them, viewed them with ambivalence, or bluntly condemned them, these novels' attentiveness to them signals the impact of these pervasive, changing economic systems. They offer insight into how the Victorians imagined women's property and how we still imagine women's property today.[95] As the actions and effects of women's economic choices increasingly enter and influence our narratives, they also help us tell more inclusive stories of the lives, real and imagined, that women's property shapes.

[94] Henry, *Women* 230.
[95] For literary realism as a mode of creative thinking about economics rather than a straightforward reflection of the status quo, see Anna Kornbluh, *Realizing Capital: Financial and Psychic Economies in Victorian Form* (New York: Fordham University Press, 2014): 11–15.

1

"How Can Money Be a Corpse's?"

Wealth, Women, and Wills in *Our Mutual Friend* (1865)

Although inheritance was often figured as a sign of nineteenth-century women's legal vulnerability, literature nevertheless offers important alternatives to the financial dispossession that, as we have seen, characters such as Austen's Bennet and Dashwood sisters face. In *Mill on the Floss*, for example, Eliot's Mrs. Glegg has no legal claim to separate property but nonetheless appears to exercise full authority over "my money as was my own father's gift" (225).[1] She anticipates the glory of "leav[ing] an unimpeachable will" (285) that "divided her money with perfect fairness among her own kin" (138) right down to "the smallest rightful share in the family shoe-buckles [...]" (286). Like Mrs. Glegg, women in wide swaths of fiction were imagined as having significant roles in the transmission of property. From Jane Eyre, who nudges her uncle into making her his heir, to *Little Dorrit*'s Mrs. Clennam, who as "sole executrix [...has] the direction and management of [her late husband's] estate" (60), female characters in Victorian literature take active roles in the disposal of their own or other people's property.

This testamentary agency appears in equivocal forms, however, as women are increasingly associated with the misdirection of men's posthumous wishes. In the decades preceding the first Act to reform married women's property rights, Victorian fiction offers multiple accounts of women's economic agency appearing to interfere with men's last financial directions. Jane Eyre ignores her uncle's wishes by dividing his fortune with her cousins;[2] Lady Mason forges a codicil to her husband's will to benefit his second son in *Orley Farm* (1862); Madame Max rejects the Duke of Omnium's attempt to leave her a sizeable bequest in Anthony Trollope's *Phineas Redux* (1873); Mrs. Clennam conceals a codicil granting two thousand guineas;[3] and Little Dorrit, coming into possession of this codicil and its

---

[1] Mr. Glegg has apparently "allowed [her] to keep her own money the same as if it was settled on her" (134), and when angered she makes reference to the money he has "pretended to leave at my own disposal" (225), comments that serve as reminders both of the inability of law alone to account for women's property movement and also of the precariousness or even pretense, for women, of property not legally guaranteed.

[2] For a larger discussion of Jane's inheritance, see Rappoport, *Giving Women*, ch. 2, esp. 48–54.

[3] The will that Mrs. Clennam conceals is that of her husband's late uncle, who belatedly and somewhat bizarrely wishes to benefit not only his son's former lover but also her music teacher's child or youngest niece (811–13).

Imagining Women's Property in Victorian Fiction. Jill Rappoport, Oxford University Press. © Jill Rappoport 2023.
DOI: 10.1093/oso/9780192867261.003.0002

WEALTH, WOMEN, AND WILLS IN *OUR MUTUAL FRIEND* 37

explanation, continues to suppress both by having Arthur Clennam blindly burn the document and all knowledge of his origins (857).[4] Regardless of whether they act out of self-interest or conscientiousness, malice or love, women in these novels repeatedly and dramatically undercut men's wills or final requests. *Middlemarch's* Peter Featherstone cannot make Mary Garth assist him in burning one of his own wills, and despite the unreasonableness of a three a.m. demand which "might lay [her] open to suspicion" (316), her refusal to comply results in Fred Vincy's disinheritance and leaves her feeling "as if she had knocked down somebody's property and broken it" (406–7). Together, these examples remind us that fiction written in an era of legal property reform often presents women as already controlling wealth and women's financial control as conflicting with men's wishes. They also and crucially show how fiction was emphasizing the inadequacy of property law in these matters.

The failure of law to distribute property either in accordance with a testator's wishes or fairly is a concern that Charles Dickens takes up repeatedly throughout his career. We see it in *Oliver Twist* (1837–8), where another will is vindictively "burnt" but then "joyfully" ignored even once its contents are known.[5] Additional examples appear in *A Christmas Carol's* forecast of Scrooge's robbed corpse (1843),[6] *Bleak House's* longstanding Chancery case of Jarndyce and Jarndyce (1853),[7] and the *Little Dorrit* scenes mentioned above. In his final completed novel, *Our Mutual Friend* (1865), Dickens again registers skepticism about the power of wills, this time coupling his sense of their limitations with larger concern about written words in general and the lack of guaranteed property rights with respect to both. At this key moment in the movement to reform women's property rights, however, his narrative resolution of these concerns differs. In place of the redistribution of property by a Scrooge or Mr. Brownlow, women become the chief financial agents; in place of middle- or upper-class women exercising financial control, as we see in the examples by Brontë, Trollope, and Eliot, working women find protection; in place of individual fears, desires, and actions, Dickens's novel presents collaborative efforts emerging from and oriented toward a wider community. The worst intentions are thwarted not by burning a will but, as we will see, through communal investment in primogeniture, while that same community restores power to select written documents by lovingly safeguarding better final wishes and words than those of the notorious Harmon will.

---

[4] See also *Little Dorrit* 817–18, 822–4.

[5] Charles Dickens, *Oliver Twist* [1838], ed. Kathleen Tillotson and Stephen Gill (Oxford: Oxford University Press, 1999): 419, 437.

[6] Charles Dickens, *A Christmas Carol* [1843] *and Other Christmas Writings*, ed. Michael Slater (London: Penguin Books Ltd., 2003): 100–2.

[7] For a religious reading of testamentary failure in *Bleak House*, see Paula Keatley, "'It's about a Will': Liberal Protestant Theology in Dickens' *Bleak House*," *Nineteenth-Century Contexts* 39.2 (2017): 77–86, e.g., 80, 84.

38   IMAGINING WOMEN'S PROPERTY IN VICTORIAN FICTION

I. Willed Away

When wealthy, eccentric dust collector John Harmon makes his son's inheritance contingent on that son's marriage to Bella Wilfer, a woman he has never met, his will becomes a fulcrum for *Our Mutual Friend*'s meditations on value and exchange. By objectifying Bella and laying bare the financial interests of the marriage plot, Harmon's attempted transaction most obviously showcases the economic dispossession of middle-class women that has concerned Victorianists, in various ways, for decades. But it is also central to a different economic problem, one that the novel links to authorship: the failure of written documents to properly will property away. Nobody cares that Harmon is ultimately unable to do as he wishes, of course. Dickens presents Harmon's effort to direct people's fortunes as spiteful and overreaching; he selected his estranged son's wife to-be after witnessing her childhood tantrum ("I was stamping my foot and screaming, when he first took notice of me").[8] Yet, as we will see, *Our Mutual Friend*'s repeated rewriting and eventual recuperation of testamentary action nonetheless suggest anxiety about the forms of failed circulation and reception that may appear most clearly with regard to Harmon's will but remain relevant to many other texts within and including the novel itself. Alongside this anxiety about where words go and how they are interpreted after they are made public, then, Dickens highlights a desire to find more acceptable forms of authorial control—and, perhaps, to distinguish his own plotting from that of Harmon. Through Harmon's will, Dickens thus makes authorship important to his speculations on property ownership, compelling us to connect three points of longstanding critical interest in this novel: its ambivalent depiction of women with wealth, its preoccupation with literacy and writing, and its fascination with death and inheritance. Willed property proves to be largely a fiction in a novel that questions the posthumous power any author can have over his writing (as property, regarding property). Significantly, though, the novel also imagines ways to push beyond the limits of legal ownership. *Our Mutual Friend* attempts to resolve a crisis in gendered and authorial property rights by crafting collaborative exchanges, granting working-class women greater economic roles in order to secure fantasies of stable authorship, patrilineal property, and more reliably directed legacies.

Among Victorianists, Bella's story has become a familiar indictment of women's economic position in the nineteenth century. Born to a clerk who can barely make ends meet, she will not inherit wealth and has few options for earning money respectably: "'I feel that I can't beg it, borrow it, or steal it; and so I have resolved that I must marry it'" (320). Though she initially takes an active role in business, witnessing her father's transaction with a "free dash of the signature,

---

[8] Charles Dickens, *Our Mutual Friend* [1864–5] (Oxford: Oxford University Press, 2008): 42. Subsequent references will be made parenthetically in the body of the text.

WEALTH, WOMEN, AND WILLS IN *OUR MUTUAL FRIEND*   39

which was a bold one for a woman's" (39), the novel quickly recasts her as an object for others to toy with and traffic in.[9] "'[W]illed away, like a horse'" (377) or "a dozen of spoons" (37) to the younger John Harmon and disappointed in her financial prospects after his presumed murder, Bella has become a "mercenary little wretch" (319) by the time she meets the apparently poor John Rokesmith (Harmon incognito). Finally trading avarice for affection, however, Bella aces the infamously cringeworthy character test orchestrated by her future husband and friends. She "yield[s]" herself gratefully to John—"'Yes, I AM yours if you think me worth taking!'" (606)—and "shrink[s] to next to nothing in the clasp of his arms" (606). Her physical diminution foreshadows her diminished economic and legal status as a married woman;[10] as a wife, Bella's rights, along with her once bold signature, are subsumed under those of her husband's in accordance with the common law's "one flesh" doctrine of coverture. The uncomfortable alchemy that makes her "'the true golden gold'" (773) measures her own worth only in accordance with her husband's "triumph" (759).[11]

Such gendered dispossession was of ideological importance to a culture alarmed by its own acquisitiveness, market instabilities, and the prospect of women having more than a metaphorical relationship to wealth.[12] Unlike other forms of material property, such as the elder Harmon's dust mounds, which can be scavenged, sold, or dispersed, Bella-as-property—her husband's "true [...] gold"—is, at least in theory, longer lasting wealth, offering men what Jeff Nunokawa has understood as

---

[9] Classic accounts of men's traffic in women include Gayle Rubin, "The Traffic in Women: Notes on the 'Political Economy' of Sex," in *Toward an Anthropology of Women*, ed. Rayna R. Reiter (New York: Monthly Review Press, 1975): 157–210; Luce Irigaray, "Women on the Market," in *The Logic of the Gift: Toward an Ethic of Generosity*, ed. Alan D. Schrift (New York: Routledge, 1997): 174–89; and Eve Sedgwick, *Between Men: English Literature and Male Homosocial Desire* (New York: Columbia University Press, 1985). For more recent discussions, see Psomiades 93–118; Rappoport, *Giving* 4–5; Godfrey 162–75. For the way that Bella's circumstances merge inheritance with speculation, see Noa Reich, *Relational Speculation: Rereading Inheritance in Victorian Fiction*, Diss. (University of Toronto, 2018, digital file shared by author in Sept. 2020): 1, 40–1.

[10] Under the common law doctrine of coverture, married women could not earn, inherit, possess, or will away money in their own names, but were instead "covered" by their husbands; as Mr. Boffin understands it, "my name, which is the same as Mrs. Boffin's, [...] means both of us" (92). See Shanley 8–9. As the Introduction of the present study discusses in further detail, many women maneuvered around these legal limitations. See, e.g., Margot Finn, "Women, Consumption and Coverture in England" 707; Bailey 353; Rutterford, "'A *pauper* every wife is'" 133–41; and R. J. Morris, *Men, Women and Property in England, 1780–1870* (Cambridge: Cambridge University Press, 2005): 261–3.

[11] For Bella's (and other female characters') narrow escape from commodification, see Catherine Gallagher, *The Body* 115–16. For Bella's transformation, see Hilary M. Schor, *Dickens and the Daughter of the House* (Cambridge: Cambridge University Press, 1999): 184–5; George Levine, *Dying to Know: Scientific Epistemology and Narrative in Victorian England* (Chicago: University of Chicago Press, 2002): 168; Cathy Shuman, "Invigilating *Our Mutual Friend*: Gender and the Legitimation of Professional Authority," *Novel* 28.2 (1995): 154–72, 159. For the significance of Bella's "gold" in terms of terms of genre as well as gender, see Mary Poovey, *Genres of the Credit Economy: Mediating Value in Eighteenth- and Nineteenth-Century Britain* (Chicago: University of Chicago Press, 2008): 382, 383.

[12] Elsie B. Michie, *Vulgar* 7–9; Mary Poovey, *Making a Social Body: British Cultural Formation, 1830–1864* (Chicago: University of Chicago Press, 1995): 160–1.

40   IMAGINING WOMEN'S PROPERTY IN VICTORIAN FICTION

the fiction of "safe estate" secured against the "vicissitudes of capital circulation."[13] Along these lines, Rokesmith can confidently categorize Bella as "'mine'" (606). "[A]s a most precious and sweet commodity that was always looking up" (683), she is in many ways the *only* "property" that actually behaves as it is desired to—at least if we understand Bella's marriage to Rokesmith/Harmon as his inheritance, the fulfillment of his father's arbitrary bequest.[14] (I'll say more about this shortly.) Bella's fleeting comparison to spoons is important in this sense because, unlike Harmon's other material bequests, she ends up where the will directed her. Resisting but then succumbing to the bestowal, she directs attention away from the fact that actual property is much less tractable. The novel offers us the image of a woman given, a woman whose own will (eventually) synchronizes with that of the testator, partly because it cannot confidently make the same claims about the tangible objects that fill its pages.

Property is far from secure in the novel. Dickens rails against the speculation and ungrounded social power that lead to financial fluctuations—"Have no antecedents, no established character, no cultivation, no ideas, no manners; have Shares" (114)—but the uncertainty of commercial instruments is only the most explicit threat to men's possession. *Our Mutual Friend* also catalogues, with some fascination, its awareness that women's relation to "gold" was not always symbolic. Most of its female characters find remunerative occupations (at mills, dust mounds, needlework, pawn shops, outfitters, public houses, schools) and prove better financial managers than men.[15] The novel, which was published in parts from 1864–5, appeared less than a decade after the first attempted Parliamentary petition for married women's property rights in 1856.[16] Though the legislation that finally began to grant these rights would take several more years to arrive, discussions about them were ongoing. The first legal strides had already been made to secure the earnings of abandoned, separated, or divorced women, and Dickens himself would take working women's part during the 1868 debates for the 1870 Act.[17] During this time, women's demands for property rights were often seen as encroaching upon men's claims to ownership, making gender a key

[13] Jeff Nunokawa, *Afterlife* 10, 13. Shuman notes the "illusory" influence of women in *Our Mutual Friend* (157–8).

[14] See Anny Sadrin, *Parentage and Inheritance in the Novels of Charles Dickens* (Cambridge: Cambridge University Press, 1994): 129–30, 141–2.

[15] For men's traffic in women as a "fiction," see Psomiades. For women's economic practices, see E. Michie; Rappoport; Dalley and Rappoport; Rappaport; Lysack; Dorice Williams Elliott, *The Angel Out of the House: Philanthropy and Gender in Nineteenth-Century England* (Charlottesville: University of Virginia Press, 2002); Anne Laurence, Josephine Maltby, and Janette Rutterford, eds., *Women and Their Money, 1700–1950: Essays on Women and Finance* (New York: Routledge, 2009).

[16] Although the Married Women's Property Acts of 1870 and 1882 postdate *Our Mutual Friend*, political agitation for wives to hold money in their own names began earlier. In 1856, the Married Women's Property Committee's petition to Parliament contained twenty-six thousand signatures. See Shanley 32–4.

[17] On the Divorce Act of 1857, see Shanley ch. 1, esp. 43–8; for Dickens's contributions to the reform of married women's property rights, see Wynne 59.

WEALTH, WOMEN, AND WILLS IN *OUR MUTUAL FRIEND*   41

category for stoking fantasies about forms of more stable or enduring possession. The fiction that a woman can be willed away to become a man's most reliable treasure compensates both for the precariousness of other property rights and for the cultural reality that women were increasingly exerting their own economic wills. As I'll argue, it also depends upon a fiction of stable authorship—the fantasy that writing can wield perpetual control over people and property alike.

II. Wills That Won't

Dickens repeatedly questions whether a deceased man has any right to direct his estate. In the words of the waterman Gaffer Hexam, whose self-serving defense of his own corpse-robbing practices opens the novel, "'Has a dead man any use for money? Is it possible for a dead man to have money? [...] How can money be a corpse's? Can a corpse own it, want it, spend it, claim it, miss it?'" (4). This passage, which Catherine Gallagher uses as a point of departure for understanding nineteenth-century definitions of value,[18] is also a useful place for beginning to consider the conditions under which the novel thwarts certain forms of testation but eventually does allow (different) "corpses" to own, want, and spend. I will discuss the terms of the novel's two more successful wills later; first, I want to draw attention to the ways that *Our Mutual Friend* repeatedly undermines the legal process of testamentary action in order to ultimately re-imagine both the production and reception of authorial will.

Harmon's will doesn't work. The testament that directs most of the novel—the one that requires his son to marry Bella in order to receive his inheritance[19]—is circumvented when Harmon Jr. disguises himself to study his future bride and, following a twist of events that supposedly leaves him dead, his wealth goes to his father's faithful servant, the "Golden Dustman" Mr. Boffin instead. Although Bella eventually marries Harmon Jr., who eventually attains his father's wealth, the novel takes pains to show that this end is not identical to the one dictated by the will. She takes Rokesmith, not (to her knowledge) Harmon, as her husband, and they are both transformed before Bella belatedly joins the reader in realizing that Rokesmith and Harmon are one. The "'stamping'" and "'screaming'" child his father vindictively selected for him has been extinguished on her husband's chest ("laid [...] as if that were her head's chosen and lasting resting-place!" [606]) or within the volume of the Complete British Family Housewife she tries to study (682),[20] while the not-really-dead Harmon has himself been resurrected by his double life as Mr. Wilfer's lodger and Mr. Boffin's secretary. Even if the terms of

[18] Gallagher 87.
[19] For Dickens's "uneasiness [...] about the power of fathers (or father figures)," see Wynne 56.
[20] See also Wynne 85.

42   IMAGING WOMEN'S PROPERTY IN VICTORIAN FICTION

the will objectify Bella, even if she willingly gives herself to John ("'I AM yours'" [606]), she was never old Harmon's possession, a fact confirmed by his inability to alienate her when and as he wishes.[21] More significantly, for my purposes, the will that guides so much of this plot does not actually express "Old" Harmon's final desires (54); it is only one of the miser's three wills.[22] His second leaves everything but one dust mound to the Crown (493), while his third and last leaves everything to Mr. Boffin (787), who generously but also rather rebelliously conceals and then defies these final wishes, even when they are publicly known.

In the multiple failures of Harmon's will, the novel presents a testamentary vision relevant to the scholarly question of whether nineteenth-century fiction distinguished itself from financial instruments or proved analogous to them, a debate that features prominently in discussions of literature and economics.[23] Harmon's failed will accords, at least in one way, with Mary Poovey's sense of how finance and literature diverge and compete in Victorian fiction; narrative (such as Dickens's) supplants financial documents (such as the will). Along these lines, the will appears less capable than fiction to direct property. Unlike the literary texts that (for Gallagher) appear to function as repositories of vital power for authors such as Dickens, or (for Nunokawa) to provide a safer arena for ownership, this will, as a text, gets away from its author. Yet the testator's will is a document that remains largely absent *as* a document from this cluster of critical ideas about writing and value. Refocusing attention on the will is important for understanding not only how *Our Mutual Friend* devalues legal financial documents but also how material property (of texts and of the other wealth they direct) persists as one of its primary concerns, despite the critical tendency to focus instead on how wealth is either abstracted by financial instruments or displaced by metaphors in the novel. Old Harmon's material legacy depends upon his written will,[24] and when his words repeatedly fail him there are tangible consequences.

Here and in other popular Victorian novels, written documentation promises but fails to allow the dead man to continue directing in what ways his money will be used, spent, or claimed. Harmon is not alone among Victorian characters in creating a will that won't follow its author's wishes. As the examples that

---

[21] For an owner's right to dispose of property, see Vincent P. Pecora, "Inheritances, Gifts, and Expectations," *Law and Literature* 20.2 (2008): 177–96, 192; Allan Hepburn, ed., "Introduction: Inheritance and Disinheritance in the Novel," in *Troubled Legacies: Narrative and Inheritance* (Toronto: University of Toronto Press, 2007): 3–25, 6.

[22] For Old Harmon's many wills as calculated to create mistrust, see Phoebe Poon, "Trust and Conscience in *Bleak House* and *Our Mutual Friend*," *Dickens Quarterly* 28.1 (2011): 3–21.

[23] Poovey (*Genres*), for example, details the ways in which literary texts work to differentiate themselves from and displace financial texts, while both Gallagher (97) and Nunokawa (34, 87) align property with narrative itself. For the ways in which literature allegorizes its own monetary value, see Matthew Rowlinson, *Real Money and Romanticism* (Cambridge: Cambridge University Press, 2010): e.g., 192–3.

[24] I am focusing on where his money goes, not simply what the recipients think of him. See Gallagher 94 for the idea that Harmon's legacy in that other sense is revalued.

WEALTH, WOMEN, AND WILLS IN *OUR MUTUAL FRIEND*   43

introduced this chapter indicate, anxiety about unenforceable documents that become more wishful thinking than "will" proliferates in mid-nineteenth-century literature. Inheritance abounds[25] but frequently also abandons its intended pathway in fiction from the period. Indeed, the conflict between one's last testament and its execution produces significant social and financial development in many Victorian plots.[26] Together, they suggest a cultural fixation on how even the most carefully devised things get away from their authors' intentions.

Yet the fictional treatment of these wills and the rights that would have undergirded actual legal testaments don't match up. It is striking that these depictions of testamentary failure appear during a period which—at least according to legal discourses—overwhelmingly supported an individual's right to will away property as he (and, less frequently, she) liked. Between the Dower Act of 1833 (3&4 Will., IV, c. 105), which eliminated the protection of a wife's life interest in her husband's land, and the Inheritance (Family Provision) Act of 1938 (1&2 Geo. 6, c. 45), which allowed a testator's relatives to apply for support when a will did not include them, England placed few, if any, legal restraints on the content of a will. In the words of one legal scholar, this was "a century during which testators had been at liberty to dispose of their property as they wished," a period when "a system of complete freedom of testation prevailed in England."[27] "Old" Harmon's spiteful will is well within the purview of his testamentary freedom, which protected even the most eccentric documents.[28] This freedom was a peculiarly British phenomenon, "almost unprecedented in history," now considered "an accepted, even cherished, aspect of English law"[29] though viewed at times by contemporary writers with more ambivalence, as "a liberty verging upon license."[30] Victorian novels thus take a heightened interest in "corpses" who can't control their money during a period when—legally speaking—there were fewer restrictions than ever on the ways in which dying men and unmarried women devised their property.

---

[25] See Frank 14, 22–6, 80.

[26] For Reich, Victorian "will stories" suggest anxieties about posthumous power (61).

[27] Richard Schaul-Yoder, "British Inheritance Legislation: Discretionary Distribution at Death," *Boston College International and Comparative Law Review* 205 (1985), vol. 8.1, article 8.204–36, 205, 207: http://lawdigitalcommons.bc.edu/iclr/vol8/iss1/8; see also Pecora 180–1 and Janet Finch, Lynn Hayes, Jennifer Mason, Judith Masson, and Lorraine Wallis, *Wills, Inheritance, and Families* (Oxford: Clarendon Press, 1996): 21–2. Some historians consider the Dower Act of 1833 of less significance to this testamentary freedom, since in practice people had been "getting around" dower for some time (R. J. Morris 103).

[28] Finch et al., 21. See also Dickens's "Postscript, in lieu of a Preface" to *Our Mutual Friend*, in which he insists "that there are hundreds of Will Cases (as they are called) far more remarkable than that fancied in this book; and that the stores of the Prerogative Office teem with instances of testators who have made, changed, contradicted, hidden, forgotten, left cancelled, and left uncancelled, each many more wills than were ever made by the elder Mr. Harmon" (821).

[29] Schaul-Yoder 207, 208.

[30] "The Thwaytes Will Case," *The Saturday Review of Politics, Literature, Science and Art* 24:615 (10 August 1867): 181–2, 181; see "Curious Wills," *The Saturday Review of Politics, Literature, Science and Art* 36: 942 (15 November 1873): 630–1, 631.

44   IMAGINING WOMEN'S PROPERTY IN VICTORIAN FICTION

The freedom to determine how to leave one's property did not guarantee that these plans would be properly received or executed, of course. To some extent, as *Bleak House*'s notorious depiction of Chancery suggests, this is a function of courts and legal bureaucracy. In *Our Mutual Friend*, however, the problem is at least partly a matter of writing—of paper and ink. For many Victorians, one's last will and testament was a newly textual affair. Following the Wills Act of 1837 (1 Vict. c 26), which aimed for uniformity in the written, signed, and witnessed bestowal of property, wills seemingly offered more consistent written evidence of a person's possessions and firmer legal instructions for their disposal, stronger testaments of acknowledged relationships and clearer guidelines for dispersing one's belongings among them.[31] If, as David R. Green has suggested, up to 13.4 percent of adults in England who died in 1841 left wills, then a small but significant number of individuals were now and perhaps newly signing paper documents in order to distribute their wealth.[32] Yet alongside this increase in written wills, a number of real and fictional cases contested the power of the written word to legitimate authorship or allocate property.

In *Our Mutual Friend*, the material form of this newly standardized, written will presents many obstacles distinct from those we see in more abstract financial instruments. It is impermanent. "'[P]apers'" (484)—of great interest to Boffin and the "literary" man, Wegg, who reads to and then blackmails him (59)—can be "'buried'" (787), "'destroyed'" (485), "'cut in half,'" "'mutilate[d]'" (497), "'put [...] in the fire'" (580), or "'dispose[d] of [...] to the parties most interested'" (303).[33] Even should the written text survive all of these physical assaults, it can still be revised. Old Harmon made "'many wills'" (787), and their significant textual variants make it impossible to guarantee the author's final wishes by reading a single copy. Finally, reception itself presents risks: Harmon must hope from beyond the grave that he can trust his executors and that the right will is uncovered and implemented, against equal threats of blackmail and generosity. Wegg's "rapacious" attempts to "'come to terms'" with Mr. Boffin after discovering the second will (779, 655) test the limits of testamentary law less successfully but no more audaciously than Boffin's seemingly benign though also rebellious gifts. John Harmon finally possesses his father's property not "'through any act of my father's or by any right I have [... but ... t]hrough the munificence of Mr. Boffin'" (788). In such a case, the testator can depend on neither the delivery nor the reception of

---

[31] Finch et al., 39. The Wills Act of 1837 also consolidated transmission of land (formerly through devise) and personal property (formerly through testament) in a single document. See Frank 3.

[32] David R. Green, "To Do the Right Thing: Gender, Wealth, Inheritance and the London Middle Class," in *Women and Their Money 1700-1950: Essays on Women and Finance*, ed. Anne Laurence, Josephine Maltby, and Janette Rutterford (London and New York: Routledge, 2009): 133–50, 135.

[33] See also *OMF* 301, 484, and 302. For paper's materiality, see Talia Schaffer, *Novel Craft: Victorian Domestic Handicraft and Nineteenth-Century Fiction* (Oxford: Oxford University Press, 2011): 129 and Michelle Allen, *Cleansing the City: Sanitary Geographies in Victorian London* (Athens: Ohio University Press, 2008): 110–11.

WEALTH, WOMEN, AND WILLS IN *OUR MUTUAL FRIEND* 45

his will, which the law has no power to enforce. And although the novel not only disregards Harmon's will but in fact celebrates the undoing of his wishes, it also uses the uncertainties afforded by his writing and the juxtaposition of that writing with other texts to suggest an authorial problem of concern for more (and, ultimately, better) writers than the spiteful miser.

The unpredictability of how Harmon's will may be received owes something to the secrecy of wills, witnessed away from their beneficiaries and, in *Our Mutual Friend*, repeatedly hidden from view.[34] To claim authenticity, they must be made public, "'dug up and [...] legally produced and established'" (788). Recurrent emphasis on confirming whether or not a will is "'genuine [...]'" or "'correct'" (579, 655) hints at the possibility that it might have been forged.[35] In a novel riddled with blackmail, murder, and other forms of physical and financial law-breaking, however, the crime of forgery is oddly displaced from its legal sense of falsified papers onto narratives of erotic desire. Posing no real threat to testamentary documents that are repeatedly verified as authentic,[36] forgery in *Our Mutual Friend* becomes instead the explanation of a lover's doubtful actions, the self-accusation of a guilt-ridden Eugene Wrayburn who thinks he is assisting in the arrest of Lizzie Hexam's father (166, 168). No wills fail in this novel because of forged legal texts, though such documents—the forged will of *Orley Farm*, for example—were subject to prolonged investigation in other literary works from the period. More than a function of secrecy or forging, the unpredictability of where wills will go and how they will be received in *Our Mutual Friend* is symptomatic of paper in general. Described as a form of litter in a frequently cited line—"That mysterious paper currency which circulates in London when the wind blows, gyrated here and there and everywhere" (144)—it usually catches critics' attention on account of its symbolic financial overtones: paper is "currency" that, like cash or the speculative paper of stock investments, has no firm backing and moves about unsystematically.[37] But we might also think of paper in more material

---

[34] E.g., 497, 787, 788. For the changing relationship of secrecy and privacy, see Deborah Cohen, *Family Secrets: Shame and Privacy in Modern Britain* (Oxford: Oxford University Press, 2013): 3–4 and *passim*.

[35] In the eighteenth century, forgery was a capital offense; even though most forgeries were no longer punishable by death after 1832, forging wills remained a capital offense until the 1837 Forgery Act. See Keith Hollingsworth, *The Newgate Novel 1830–1847: Bulwer, Ainsworth, Dickens, and Thackeray* (Detroit: Wayne State University Press, 1963): 20, 24, 26; Sara Malton, *Forgery in Nineteenth-Century Literature and Culture: Fictions of Finance from Dickens to Wilde* (New York: Palgrave Macmillan, 2009): 2–3, 9; Aviva Briefel, *The Deceivers: Art Forgery and Identity in the Nineteenth Century* (Ithaca: Cornell University Press, 2006): 21, 185 n. 6. For nineteenth-century preoccupations with forgery see Malton 5, 9; for Dickens and forgery, Malton 15, 21–31, 47–8, 66–76. For "opportunities for fraud" occasioned by developments in business and finance, see Robb, *White-Collar* 11, *passim*.

[36] See also Malton 12.

[37] Although earlier bank failures resulted in worthless notes, "[t]he 1844 Bank Act was an attempt to standardize paper money, thus allowing the value signified by the paper to stand in for the 'real' value of

46 IMAGINING WOMEN'S PROPERTY IN VICTORIAN FICTION

terms, as the common medium for executing wills and writing books.[38] If decades of testamentary freedom and the recent standardization of signed wills made it an unusual time for novelists to question the documents' capacity to transmit property, contemporary debates about copyright legislation and property rights made it less surprising for authors to fixate on the unpredictable, unsystematic circulation of paper and the consequences of this circulation after death.

III. "That Mysterious Paper Currency"

Unlike forgery, which carried strict penalties even after it was no longer a capital offense, literary piracy frequently went unpunished.[39] Dickens's desire for control over his own work is legendary, and, like many novelists, he struggled with the cost of his own books circulating "here and there and everywhere" without his permission or profit.[40] His *Sketches by Boz* (1836) had been stolen, reprinted and then sold as "Sketchbook by Bos"; *The Pickwick Papers* (1836–7) competed with the "Posthumous Papers of the Cadger's Club"; *Oliver Twist* (1837–9) was promptly followed by "Oliver Twiss by Poz"; and *Nicholas Nickleby* (1838–9) found imitators in such publications as "Nickelas Nickleberry."[41] As others have shown, Dickens engaged passionately in efforts to combat literary piracy and extend authorial copyright, campaigning for agreements with the United States, repurchasing his own copyrights, and fighting legal battles to protect them.[42] In 1837 he dedicated *The Pickwick Papers* to Sir Thomas Talfourd, the MP who initiated the domestic copyright legislation that would become law in 1842,

---

gold or silver" and making paper money seem more secure than stocks. See David W. Toise, "'As Good as Nowhere': Dickens's *Dombey and Son*, the Contingency of Value, and Theories of Domesticity," *Criticism* 41.3 (1999): 323–48, 334. See also Poovey, *Making* 171–2 and Schaffer, *Novel* 135.

[38] See also Schaffer, *Novel* 142.

[39] Malton also contrasts Victorian treatments of forgery and plagiarism (44, 127–8).

[40] For Dickens's attempt to "control [...] his own narrative" as well as its interpretation, see John R. Reed, "The Riches of Redundancy: *Our Mutual Friend*," *Studies in the Novel* 38.1 (2006): 15–35, 22, 28. See also Andrew H. Miller, *Novels* 138–9. For Dickens's attempt to control his family, see Lillian Nayder, "'The Omission of His Only Sister's Name': Letitia Austin and the Legacies of Charles Dickens," *Dickens Quarterly* 28.4 (2011): 251–60, 254. Other authors in this study such as Trollope were also involved in copyright debates (A. Miller, *Novels* 184–8). Under coverture, married women did not hold their own copyrights.

[41] See Cumberland Clark, *Dickens and Talfourd. With an Address & Three Unpublished Letters to Talfourd, the Father of the First Copyright Act Which Put an End to the Piracy of Dickens' Writings* (London: Chiswick Press, 1919): 17–18.

[42] Larisa T. Castillo, "Natural Authority in Charles Dickens's *Martin Chuzzlewit* and the Copyright Act of 1842," *Nineteenth-Century Literature* 62.4 (2008): 435–64; Clare Pettitt, *Patent Inventions: Intellectual Property and the Victorian Novel* (Oxford: Oxford University Press, 2004); Alexander Welsh, *From Copyright to Copperfield. The Identity of Dickens* (Cambridge, MA: Harvard University Press, 1987): 31–3; Michael Hancher, "Grafting *A Christmas Carol*," *SEL* 48.4 (2008): 813–27; Robert Patten, "Copyright," in *Oxford Reader's Companion to Dickens*, ed. Paul Schlicke (Oxford: Oxford University Press, 1999): 119–22; Chris R. Vanden Bossche, "The Value of Literature: Representations of Print Culture in the Copyright Debate of 1837–1842," *Victorian Studies* 38.1 (1994): 41–68, 61–3; Monica F. Cohen, *Pirating Fictions: Ownership and Creativity in Nineteenth-Century Popular Culture*

WEALTH, WOMEN, AND WILLS IN *OUR MUTUAL FRIEND*   47

protecting an author's work for seven years after death or forty-two years after the work's first publication, whichever came first.[43] Thanking Talfourd, Dickens emphasizes the social good that the law would ensure posthumously: "'many a widowed mother and orphan child [...] would otherwise reap nothing from the fame of departed genius but its too frequent legacy of poverty and suffering."[44] Here, Dickens ties authorial copyright directly to the potential property rights of women and children, suggesting that the protection of legatees, rather than the profit of individual authors (or the publishers who frequently held these authors' copyrights), is at stake in more expansive copyright laws. This emphasis on protection over profit draws on strategies for expanding property rights similar to those that campaigners for women's property reform would subsequently use. But it also genders the "author" as male, a husband seeking to benefit his wife and children, eliding both the possibility of single, married, or widowed women desiring to manage their own literary or other property and potential legatees and also the possibility that property rights more equitable to women could be resolved during marriage rather than after widowhood. I'll return to these points. Although critics tend to focus on earlier works in discussions of Dickens and copyright, the problem of copyright—particularly that of international protections—continued to attract Dickens's attention at and beyond mid-century.[45] It most likely influenced his decision to publish *Our Mutual Friend* simultaneously in England and the United States[46] and is, I am suggesting, one of the factors underlying the testamentary trouble of this novel.

Copyright and wills both attempt to manage inheritance. Indeed, as Larisa T. Castillo has noted, "the idea of inheritance is necessary to ensure a sustainable definition of copyright."[47] In this sense, both direct property. Copyright as an economic function directs the flow of financial profits; a will similarly directs the transmission of the testator's estate. There are other points of congruence between the two, however, which are equally or perhaps more meaningful for considera-tion of Dickens's novel. Significant not merely for what they say about other forms

---

(Charlottesville: University of Virginia Press, 2017), *passim*, esp. ch. 5. For Dickens's personal suit in Chancery against piracy, see David Sugarman, "Chancery," in *Oxford Reader's Companion to Dickens*, ed. Paul Schlicke (Oxford: Oxford University Press, 1999): 70.

[43] Talfourd's original goal was "protection for an author's life and then sixty years after death." See Pettitt 80.

[44] Charles Dickens, *The Pickwick Papers* [1836–7], ed. James Kinsley (Oxford: Oxford University Press, 1988): xxii.

[45] See Pettitt 87, 139; Daniel Hack, "Literary Paupers and Professional Authors: The Guild of Literature and Art," *Studies in English Literature, 1500–1900* 39.4 (1999): 691–713, 693, 705. Despite other agreements in the 1840s, 1850s, and 1860s (see Pettitt 278–9 n. 29), full international protections were not granted until 1891.

[46] See Robert L. Patten, *Charles Dickens and His Publishers* (University of California, Santa Cruz: The Dickens Project, 1978): 308; Sean Grass, *Charles Dickens's* Our Mutual Friend: *A Publishing History* (Burlington: Ashgate Publishing Company, 2014): 80–1.

[47] Castillo 437.

48   IMAGINING WOMEN'S PROPERTY IN VICTORIAN FICTION

of property, wills in *Our Mutual Friend*, like copyrighted texts, are also property themselves. We see this in the materiality of wills that characters possess, trade, or hide away. Like copyrighted texts, then, wills in this novel must be understood in relation to specific and tangible documents. When they fail, they fail not simply as transfers of wealth, but as authored texts, papers with signatures, secreted in bottles or stolen away. Similarly, a novel without the benefit of copyright risks being stolen, an author's work and name removed from legitimate distribution. Dickens can no more control the destination of his texts than Harmon can control who hides or digs up his. Wills and literary writing both risk being mis-circulated.

Just as significantly, wills and literary writing both risk being misconstrued. Authors of fiction and wills alike lose control over their writing. In a sense, of course, any published book is out of its author's hands. Required, like Mary Shelley's "hideous progeny," to "go forth and prosper" (or fail) on their own,[48] Dickens's publications may encounter resistant readers and unintended interpretations. *Our Mutual Friend*, as we will see, highlights this generalized anxiety about writing. But other anxieties about writing correspond more specifically to the novel's depiction of wills. If copyright and wills are both property, as well as items that direct property, they are also property with the potential to direct lives, whether fictional or real. We see this most obviously in Harmon's attempt to plot his son's marriage through his will. Since novels direct the plots of many characters, however, copyright too has a hand in that action, by governing the production of a text and maintaining some control over the literary features and quality of the copyrighted novel. A pirated edition might tamper with anything from character description to plot—might consequently redirect the lives and actions of those fictional figures that Dickens describes, in terms that blur lines of reality, as keeping company with him (822). In this sense, then, old Harmon's will is like any of Dickens's pirated novels, directing lives in his name, but not as he intended. And whereas Harmon's mean-spirited will is hardly the kind of print Dickens wishes to praise or protect, we can see in the multiple editions and maltreatment of this will additional instances of the authorship that suffuses the novel, rendered meaningless in the face of both insufficient legal protections and unreceptive audiences.

Along these lines, the congruence between wills and other forms of writing in *Our Mutual Friend* demonstrates more than the economic value of copyright protection or the mistrust of existing legal strategies for managing either financial or literary legacies. It also suggests one possible source for the ambivalence that Dickens famously shows toward literacy itself in this novel.[49] *Our Mutual Friend*

---

[48] Mary Shelley, "Introduction to *Frankenstein*, Third Edition (1831)," in *Frankenstein* [1818], ed. J. Paul Hunter (New York: W. W. Norton & Company, Inc., 1996): 169–73, 173.

[49] See also Pettitt's discussion of ineffective documents in *Bleak House* (177).

WEALTH, WOMEN, AND WILLS IN *OUR MUTUAL FRIEND*   49

refuses to sanctify the written word. Many of its most virtuous characters—Lizzie Hexam, Jenny Wren, Mr. and Mrs. Boffin—are or at least begin the novel illiterate, better able to read people and circumstances than written texts. Its villains—Charley Hexam, Bradley Headstone, even Silas Wegg—are conversely defined by acquisitive reading abilities, Charley planning to "'seek his fortune out of learning'" (75), Headstone storing his "stock" of education in a "mental warehouse" (217), Wegg shifting from books to blackmail with alarming fluidity. Despite a certain reverence for print—"No one who can read, ever looks at a book, even unopened on a shelf, like one who cannot" (18)—"documents" themselves in the novel frequently prove to be nothing more than hypocrisy or solicitation (211). As others have shown, Dickens's novel reflects changes in education and the increasing democratization of print,[50] but it also exhibits a remarkable degree of anxiety about these changes and the ways that the written word might evade its author's meaning. The persistent problem of misreading in the novel is one that bears directly on the failure of wills as well as on failures of copyright and audience reception. "'I will not have my words misconstrued,'" says one villain to another (427), but everywhere in *Our Mutual Friend* words get away from their authors' intent. Wegg, who believes himself "'equal to collaring and throwing'" any "'piece of English print'" (50), "attached as few ideas as possible to the text" (59) and modifies published works liberally as he reads aloud to Mr. Boffin. He is just one of many figures for the novel's contention that writing, in the wrong hands, will not only miss but betray even the most exemplary author's aim. Although Lizzie Hexam attempts to elude her would-be lovers, the return address on letters she sends a friend inadvertently reveals her whereabouts (540, 628), resulting in one attempted murder and (albeit less directly) two other deaths. Just as pirated copies distort an author's words or send them into circulation for others' profit, writing in this novel frequently lacks allegiance to its authors.[51]

If *Our Mutual Friend* suggests anxiety about authorship—about men's lasting control over their legal and literary texts, in particular—its female authors fare poorly as well, as the tragic results of Lizzie's letter writing reveal. Women writers

---

[50] For Dickens's ambivalence toward literacy see Ruth Tross, "Dickens and the Crime of Literacy," *Dickens Quarterly* 21.4 (2004): 235–45; Patrick Brantlinger, *The Reading Lesson: The Threat of Mass Literacy in Nineteenth-Century British Fiction* (Bloomington: Indiana University Press, 1988): 3, 5, 73; and Richard D. Altick, "Education, Print, and Paper in *Our Mutual Friend*," in *Nineteenth-Century Literary Perspectives: Essays in Honor of Lionel Stevenson*, ed. Clyde de L. Ryals (Durham: Duke University Press, 1974): 237–54, 239, 251. For the "personification and commodification of literature," see Goldie Morgentaler, "Dickens and the Scattered Identity of Silas Wegg," *Dickens Quarterly* 22.2 (2005): 92–100, 99. For writing and social aspiration, see Laura Rotunno, "The Long History of 'In Short': Mr. Micawber, Letter-Writers, and Literary Men," *Victorian Literature and Culture* 33 (2005): 415–33, 424. Even illiterate characters are known by their reading or rewriting the world; see Lothar Černý, "'Life in Death': Art in Dickens's Our Mutual Friend," *Dickens Quarterly* 17.1 (2000): 22–36, 23.

[51] For writing that betrays or fails to protect its authors, see also Tross 240–1 and A. Miller, *Novels* 149.

50   IMAGINING WOMEN'S PROPERTY IN VICTORIAN FICTION

are plentiful in this novel: in addition to Bella's once-bold signature, we have Pleasant Riderhood's rejection of marriage "'in her own handwriting'" (84), letters exchanged between Lizzie and Jenny and later Lizzie and Bella, Miss Peecher's ability to "write a little essay on any subject, exactly a slate long [...] strictly according to rule" (219), and Georgiana Podsnap's feverish desire to "'sign [...] something somewhere'" that will allow her to "'make some of [her money] over somehow'" (648).[52] This abundance reminds us that more and more women in Dickens's time were writing. Many were even earning their living by the pen, though this is, notably, not a group the novel explores in its categories of female writers or working women. In *Our Mutual Friend*, women's ability to write seems to afford them key prerogatives (to witness, reject, communicate, exchange)[53] but, just as other forms of authorship hold little authority in this novel, writing is ultimately one more sign of their powerlessness. Miss Peecher "would probably have replied in a complete little essay on the theme" to Headstone's "written proposal of marriage to her"—but he never writes one (219); Lizzie's letters, as we have seen, betray her; Georgiana, as "soft-headed" as she is "soft-hearted," is unable to transfer her fortune as she desires (647); and male "'influence [... is] brought to bear upon'" Pleasant in the end (786).

Thus women's writing, too, appears inconsequential. Diminishing their authorship, even as that authorship is made extremely visible throughout the novel, serves as oblique recognition that at this time women's relation to their writing was even more precarious than men's. Married female authors lost control over their writing in multiple ways; the one-flesh doctrine of coverture gave their earnings, as well as the right to negotiate their contracts, to their husbands, even before copyright law failed to protect them sufficiently from unauthorized editions, and copyrights themselves were one more form of property the common law took from wives.[54] In *Our Mutual Friend,* the depiction of these gendered authorial failures seems more triumphant than sympathetic: Mr. Boffin presides benevolently over three of them, paternalistically guiding Bella, Pleasant, and Georgiana to their narrative ends.[55] At a time when agitation for married women's property rights seemed poised to threaten men's wealth, the novel invests a good deal of energy into invalidating women's writing, further demonstrating the precariousness of all textual legacies while also eliminating the threat that women's writing might compete with men's. As John Harmon's wife, Bella no longer signs her name boldly. She doesn't know what her legal surname is ("'At least, his name is John, I suppose?'" [769]). Yet even as women's writing loses its force, women themselves become central to resolving the various forms of testamentary and authorial trouble that the novel presents.

[52] See also Schor 189.
[53] Schor 15, 189.
[54] See also Wynne 11–12, 25.
[55] See also Wynne 85.

IV. "In My Name, Which Is the Same as Mrs. Boffin's, and Means Both of Us"

The Boffin marriage offers the first and perhaps most immediately striking glimpse of women's centrality to testamentary resolution by presenting the possibility of a partnership that is both economic and domestic. Though Bella's ability to treat her husband with trust and love despite her confusion about his identity is one version of what the novel presents as successful marriage, coverture in their case—as her wishes, legal identity, and economic prospects are subsumed into his—depends upon blind faith in her husband's affairs, leaving her "certain of nothing in the immediate present, but that she confided in John" (762). In contrast, the Boffin marriage showcases mutual participation, respect, and interest in their common life venture. Coverture's assumptions of masculine protection, shared benefit, and separate spheres presented the rationale for married women's loss of personal property, but the novel showcases the unhappy fate of couples whose lives are bound only through property in order to emphasize how coverture in its ideal form must be more than an economic arrangement. Mr. and Mrs. Wilfer are miserably matched, and even as Mrs. Wilfer dramatically echoes coverture's economic structure ("'It is your house, and you are master'") she rebuts its fuller merger of identities, highlighting their distinct personalities as her daughter "'insist[s] on including me'" in an anniversary toast to commemorate "'the day that made you and Pa one and the same" (455). Mrs. Lammle similarly emphasizes the disparity between the marital economy that yokes her to her husband and any larger unification: "'Always beside him and attached in all his fortunes? Not much to boast of in that [...]. My husband and I [...] must [...] bear one another, and bear the burden of scheming together for to-day's dinner and to-morrow's breakfast—till death divorces us'" (624). Even the economic unity that the Wilfers and Lammles profess in lieu of other shared interests is absent from some of the novel's unhappy marriages; Pleasant Riderhood's dying mother's directs her to her "secret capital of fifteen shillings," which she has hidden from her husband (350).

The Boffins, however, exemplify what the novel presents as idealized marital relations under coverture, from the minor matter of Mrs. Boffin's name, which testifies to her own parents' merged identities—"'Henerietty Boffin—which her father's name was Henry, and her mother's name was Hetty, and so you get it—'" (50)—to the much larger economic decisions they make together. Mrs. Boffin's economic role in the novel is unique. Although women from wealthy families did sometimes have independent property settled upon them outside the court of common law, such settlements were generally made prior to marriage. Georgiana Podsnap, for instance, recalls that "'My grandmamma's property, that'll come to me when I am of age [...], will be all my own, and neither Pa nor Ma nor anybody else will have any control over it'" (648), the "anybody else" in this case standing

52 IMAGINING WOMEN'S PROPERTY IN VICTORIAN FICTION

for a future husband or other economic guardian. But this is not the case for the Boffins, who come into their fortune later in life and without familial protections. Legally speaking, coverture makes their inheritance *Mr.* Boffin's, but practically speaking Mrs. Boffin has equal consideration and access to their newly acquired funds. Mr. Boffin, "who had a deep respect for his wife's intuitive wisdom" (99), describes their possession as joint: "'Boffin's Bower is the name Mrs. Boffin christened it when *we* come into it as a property'" (53, emphasis added). Their unusual domestic arrangement, half "'Comfort'" and half "'Fashion'" reflecting their separate tastes and desires, "'is made by mutual consent between Mrs. Boffin and me'" (56). Mr. Boffin ignores the dictates of coverture in his repeated insistence on Mrs. Boffin's financial role, following her lead in many of their household projects. In informing Mr. Lightwood of the reward offered "'in our names'" for the apprehension of John Harmon's presumed murderer, he notes that "'me and Mrs. Boffin have fixed the sum together, and we stand to it'" (92), only acceding to the lawyer's correction ("'In your name, Mr. Boffin; in your name'") because of his faith that the one-flesh directive of the common law doctrine will represent his wife's interests as fully as he intends to. "'[M]y name [...] is the same as Mrs. Boffin's, and means both of us'" (92).

Through the Boffins, *Our Mutual Friend* presents a vision of marriage seemingly in line with—but also and significantly not requiring—the proposed changes to married women's property rights that advocates argued would not discourage or diminish marriage. In their case, coverture is more a matter of feeling than of legal doctrine. Mr. Boffin's confidence in their shared prosperity falters only at the thought of how to ensure her continued autonomy after his death, and he attempts to draw on legal expertise for this purpose.

> 'Make me as compact a little will as can be reconciled with tightness, leaving the whole of the property to "my beloved wife, Henerietty Boffin, sole executrix." Make it as short as you can, using those words; but make it tight.'
>
> ' ... [I]s the tightness to bind Mrs. Boffin to any and what conditions?'
>
> 'Bind Mrs. Boffin?' interposed her husband. 'No! What are you thinking of? What I want is, to make it all hers so tight as that her hold of it can't be loosed.'
>
> 'Hers freely, to do what she likes with? Hers absolutely?'
>
> 'Absolutely?' repeated Mr. Boffin, with a short sturdy laugh. 'Ha! I should think so!' (92–3)

The lawyer's confusion at the thought of granting a widow absolute economic independence, along with the testamentary trouble the novel has shown elsewhere, justify the urgency of Mr. Boffin's desire to create a "tight" will for his wife. Dickens offers no assurance for the execution of legal wills—and, in fact, the Boffins are the principal agents in undermining that of Harmon. But the Boffins'

WEALTH, WOMEN, AND WILLS IN *OUR MUTUAL FRIEND*   53

extralegal efforts, whether in undermining the miser or in granting Mrs. Boffin unfettered economic sway, seem stronger and more binding than those made by lawyers, endorsed as part of the overwhelming "religious sense of duty and desire to do right" manifested by this "honest and true" couple (101).

Many of these extralegal efforts function to secure posthumous legacies for the people that they love. Just as, during Harmon's life, the Boffins joined together to oppose the mistreatment of his children (89–90), they join together after his death to memorialize them. Notably in a novel that so frequently renders writing meaningless, they do so through attention to those children's signatures.

'[. . .] here's the sunny place on the white wall where they one day measured one another. Their own little hands wrote up their names here, only with a pencil; but the names are here still, and the poor dears gone for ever.'

'We must take care of the names, old lady,' said Mr. Boffin. 'We must take care of the names. They shan't be rubbed out in our time, nor yet, if we can help it, in the time after us. Poor little children!'   (184)

Here, *Our Mutual Friend* offers a pure ("sunny," "white") and rare vision of enduring authorship, valued and preserved beyond its writers' (presumed) demise.[56] We never learn the name of the Harmon daughter who married against her father's wishes and, disowned, died early (14). The novel suggests, in her handwritten name, that she is yet another powerless female writer. But the Boffins nevertheless memorialize her along with her brother, the living, breathing John Harmon, who assumes the names of Handford and Rokesmith following his presumed murder, whose name matters for reasons of legal identification and inheritance, and in whose early scrawl the novel substitutes a child's now-treasured autograph for his father's unheeded wills, preserving one while ignoring the other.

The Boffins' posthumous power over the Harmon children's textual legacy grants them a kind of *de facto* role as executors, not just legatees, of the Harmon estate, graced with a moral authority that supersedes the law. Along with preserving the names and writing of the Harmon children, the Boffins preserve the father's wealth for the remaining child, both in their ongoing understanding of their fortune as belonging to him ("'isn't it pleasant to know

---

[56] The memorializing impulse that prompts the Boffins to preserve the names written by "little hands" also causes them to retire, after his death, the adoptive name of the poor orphan Johnny who was to be yet another John Harmon (101). They fear that it has proven "unlucky" (333) but have other reasons for taking it out of circulation: "'I think I should feel as if the name had become endeared to me, and I had no right to use it so,'" says Bella, agreeing with Mrs. Boffin's decision to "'let it rest in the grave'" (334). In both cases, there is an ethical mandate to preserve a name. Johnny's is not at risk of being painted over or ignored; his benefactors simply wish not to "'revive'" it by "g[iving] it to another dear child" (333). Refusing to make further copies of the original, they acknowledge (as Dickens does in his fight for copyright law) the risks of unauthorized replication.

54 IMAGINING WOMEN'S PROPERTY IN VICTORIAN FICTION

that the good will be done with the poor sad child's own money?'") (101) and later, when they learn that the child has survived, in passing it along to him. As noted previously, the younger John Harmon finally receives his father's wealth not through the mechanism of legal inheritance—the will that trades his fortune for a mercenary marriage is not, after all, his father's final word on the subject—but through "'the munificence of Mr. Boffin'" (788) which the novel and Harmon junior take pains to clarify is very much also the munificence of Mrs. Boffin, who has directed most of the couple's spending in fashion and philanthropic efforts alike, though Mr. Boffin wholeheartedly agrees with every project. If Mr. Boffin is responsible for the actual transfer of wealth, John Harmon acknowledges its source in their joint generosity: "'I owe everything I possess solely to the disinterestedness, uprightness, tenderness, goodness (there are no words to satisfy me) of Mr. and Mrs. Boffin'" (788).

Mrs. Boffin is, then, unusually situated as a loving and beloved wife without independent money who nevertheless occupies both the moral heart of her marriage—Mr. Boffin fondly recalls how "'Mrs. Boffin has given [Harmon] her mind respecting the claims of the nat'ral affections'" (90)—and its economic center. By using her "wisdom" for good ends (in agreement with her husband and with his hearty endorsement) she is at once evidence in support of a wife's rights to possess property, and also evidence of the opposing view: that such a loving, like-minded wife has marital and moral "influence" and, consequently, no need of independent property during her doting husband's life. The Boffins' treatment of Harmon's will, which has failed as a last testament, successfully reconciles these competing stances. Mr. and Mrs. Boffin together rebel against unjust uses of paternal, testamentary, editorial, and spousal power, standing up for Harmon's children, refusing to abide by his will, protecting the authorship of an "orphan child" over that of an enriched miser, and insisting on joint economic decisions within their marriage. Yet in practice, their flouting of these injustices amounts to the most conventional of property pathways: the return of wealth to the man whose birth would have made him heir had his father died intestate, the passing of fortune along patrilineal lines, according to the guidance of another common law doctrine, that of primogeniture, which served as a rationale for denying more equitable rights both to daughters (as we saw in the introduction's discussion of Austen) and to wives (as we will see in later chapters of this study). It resolves the problem of Harmon's will by making it superfluous, just as it resolves a wife's independent direction of property by matching it to her husband's desires and to the most conservative principles of inheritance. The Boffins' benevolence may not make the father's will work and in fact runs counter to doing so, but as a partial solution to the novel's multiple property predicaments it endorses a wife's economic agency while simultaneously neutralizing the social disruption of that agency by putting it in the service of preserving a son's name, his writing, and his wealth. It also, like many other literary meditations we will see on property at this time, emphasizes personal choice over bloodlines or legal mandate.

V. "A Kiss for the Boofer Lady"

The Boffins offer an extralegal but socially sanctioned mechanism for inheritance that thrives on collaborative execution, gives primacy to women and children, and finds a way to preserve certain words, even while ignoring a legally authorized text. In addition, it emphasizes the moral authority of the (deserving) working class over that of the wealthy. Despite their current wealth, the Boffins are repeatedly identified with their former condition: they "had worked too, and had brought their simple faith and honour clean out of dustheaps" (384). The two other testamentary acts of the novel that are more faithfully executed than Harmon's share these characteristics. They also share, in contrast with his will but in keeping with the Boffins' working-class roots and moral compass, a limited command of property and an emphasis on community rather than power. The fulfillment of working-class characters' more modest posthumous wishes reminds us that public sentiment about property rights in the years before the first Married Women's Property Act in 1870 leaned toward securing smaller earnings and legacies for working-class women and children, not toward reallocating the massive inheritances of the wealthy. Extending protection, not power, drove reform. Yet distinctions between the execution of Harmon's will and those of his more successful counterparts exceed differences of scale and allow us to see how Dickens manages both property distribution and anxieties about authorship through collaborative efforts. The general mistrust of writing and the related failure of written wills to allocate property that we have seen so far give oral property transmission particular significance in the two cases I'll discuss here. In the first, speech replaces writing altogether; in the second, it supplements and clarifies it. Both indicate the importance of having (or cultivating) receptive audiences, replacing insufficient legal transactions with fantasies of intimate, interactive community.

One of the two "wills" in *Our Mutual Friend* that appear to have greater success than Harmon's[57] is voiced by little Johnny, the poor orphan who dies in a children's hospital before the Boffins can adopt him (330). In his final moments, witnessed by Rokesmith and a doctor, Johnny makes over his small estate—a toy horse on wheels (204), "a Noah's ark, and also a yellow bird with an artificial voice in him, and also a military doll" (326)—to another small patient. "'Him!' said the little fellow. 'Those!'" One more directive follows:

> [...] the child heaved his body on the sustaining arm, and seeking Rokesmith's face with his lips, [he] said: 'A kiss for the boofer lady.'
>
> Having now bequeathed all he had to dispose of, and arranged his affairs in the world, Johnny, thus speaking, left it.   (330)

---

[57] For the most part. Betty Higden, as I will discuss, acquires one of the toys he gives to the child.

56   IMAGINING WOMEN'S PROPERTY IN VICTORIAN FICTION

Johnny's labored yet insistently vocal bequest ("thus speaking") does not meet the formal requirements mandated by the 1837 Wills Act; legally, his "will" is meaningless.[58] From a material or financial standpoint, it is also far less consequential than Harmon's will; instead of immense wealth, he leaves four small toys and a kiss. But Johnny's "will" is treated as far more sacrosanct than Harmon's, and in practical terms, it seems to work, throwing into relief the far more tormented and less effective production, reception, and execution of Harmon's many wills. Literacy itself appears inversely proportional to characters' success at choosing their legacy. (This child, unlike the young Harmons, has no handwriting to preserve, though his adoptive name will be similarly "'[l]aid [...] up as a remembrance'" [334] by the Boffins after his death.) A sentence suffices to dispose of Johnny's objects as he has willed: "The doctor was quick to understand children, and, taking the horse, the ark, the yellow bird, and the man in the Guards, from Johnny's bed, softly placed them on that of his next neighbour, the mite with the broken leg" (330). The "kiss for the boofer lady"—Bella Wilfer (327)—takes longer and requires additional help but arrives finally at its destination as well.

Over two hundred pages elapse between the child's formulation of this bequest and Rokesmith's delivery of that kiss (606), but the narrator explicitly recalls little Johnny's wishes shortly before Bella's engagement: "O boofer lady, fascinating boofer lady! If I were but legally executor of Johnny's will! If I had but the right to pay your legacy and to take your receipt!" (531). This narrative interruption—suggesting the paired erotic desires of a narrator who is not "legally executor of Johnny's will" and of a character who, having received that kiss in trust for Bella, might be poised to act that part—significantly reminds us that Bella features in Johnny's will as well as Harmon's and affords us the opportunity to consider the two testamentary attempts in relation to one another. Shifting the focus from Harmon's will to Johnny's draws attention, albeit briefly, to Bella's relationships outside of the novel's marriage plot and improves Bella's economic position. Left like spoons in Harmon's will, Bella could only be its object, the reward for his son's conformity with his demands, the condition for her husband's wealth. In little Johnny's bequest, however, the object is a kiss and Bella the legatee, who stands to inherit something of her own—though the inheritance is sentimental rather than financial in this case. Johnny's will gives Bella some power of acceptance or rejection, which she feels she lacked as "'the willed-away girl'" subject to young Harmon's "'approv[al],'" "'dragged into the subject without my consent'" (523). She is not entirely bound to receive items left to her, as we see through Madame Max's unusual but nonetheless firm rejection of the Duke's bequest in Trollope's

---

[58] In addition to requiring written documents, the 1837 Act limited children's power to create wills. See Hepburn 11.

Phineas Redux.[59] This is an important caveat, should the bequeathed kiss be unwelcome or unwanted, though the novel appears to sidestep the problem of consent and bodily autonomy in Bella's case by displacing the risk of unwanted physical touch onto Lizzie's working-class plot and making Bella happy to receive Johnny's kisses, whether from him or from his executors.

The priority accorded to Johnny's will valorizes youth over age, generosity over selfishness, poverty over wealth, affect over law, and sentiment over financial gain, but beyond these Dickensian truisms, it also suggests that Victorian fiction valued a wider range of family ties than the conjugal, that women were the recipients, not just objects, of exchange, and that oral transmission could have priority over written documents. Johnny's will and Harmon's take different forms. Dickens, by the time *Our Mutual Friend* was serialized, had given over two hundred profitable public readings of his works.[60] Something, surely, of the celebrated intimacy of these performances—Dickens's "passionate engagement" with his own listening audience, the "'personal affection'" he sought to engage—shapes little Johnny's deathbed bequests and their prompt execution.[61] After death, authors and testators alike lack control over their property, but if Harmon's case shows us a "corpse" who cannot "own," "spend," or "claim" property, Johnny's suggests that mechanisms beyond the law's purview, though well within the novelist's imagination, might allow it. But Johnny's will, though far more effective than Harmon's, is only partly successful. Although Johnny leaves all of his toys to his young hospital neighbor, and the doctor does present them to him, we later see his great-grandmother Betty Higden tuck into her dress the toy guard "who had been on duty over Johnny's bed," and "then put her old withered arms round Bella's young and blooming neck, and sa[y], repeating Johnny's words: 'A kiss for the boofer lady'" (391). Betty's appropriation of the toy soldier and kiss[62] qualifies, somewhat, the privileged status the narrator gives to the child's oral transmission. (As we will see, a more collaborative approach to testation allows the novel to finally reconcile orality with the written word, as Dickens could do in his own career, and to shape a "tight[er]" will.) If the sentimentalized soldier is removed from its intended destination, however, the kiss does still reach it; Betty delivers Johnny's kiss to Bella long before Rokesmith/Harmon, who received that kiss in trust for her, can. In this way, Betty disrupts the pathway, not the legacy, challenging both the authority of the executor (as much or more than that of

---

[59] Anthony Trollope, *Phineas Redux* [1874], ed. John Bowen (Oxford: Oxford University Press, 2011): 186–7.

[60] See Malcolm Andrews, *Charles Dickens and His Performing Selves: Dickens and the Public Readings* (Oxford: Oxford University Press, 2006): appendix, esp. 268–78.

[61] Andrews 258, 171. On the profit from Dickens's oral performances, see Andrews 45 and Sean Grass, "Commodity and Identity in *Great Expectations*," *Victorian Literature and Culture* 40.2 (2012): 617–41, 626. Grass briefly links Dickens's public readings to the question of property rights (626).

[62] For property's erotic qualities, see Nunokawa 17.

58 IMAGINING WOMEN'S PROPERTY IN VICTORIAN FICTION

the testator) and the primacy of heterosexual romance in the novel's determination of property distribution.[63]

Rokesmith, who received Johnny's kiss in trust for Bella, is the presumptive executor of his will. As a secretary, he is well suited to carry out the precise details of others' wishes, but his personal desires dovetail with the execution of this particular legacy. Betty's usurpation of that role thus undermines Rokesmith, rendering his erotic desires superfluous (as they should be) to the child's transaction by becoming another executor herself.[64] Though he can contrive against his father's will through subterfuge and surveillance, Rokesmith/Harmon has limited power to act upon Johnny's, and so the kiss he gives Bella is his own romantic offering, distinct from the legacy that the narrator recalls. In this way, Betty Higden's execution of Johnny's will offers yet another example of men's inability to control the terms of property transmission in this novel, varied as that property may be. While women did serve as executors for their husbands' or others' wills, such arrangements were rare, as Dickens suggests earlier, when Mr. Boffin bewilders his lawyer by attempting to "leav[e] the whole of the property to 'my beloved wife, Henerietty Boffin, sole executrix'" (92).[65] Shifting focus from Harmon's will to Johnny's not only offers women greater economic roles (as legatees and executors of estates) but also curbs the authority of men and heterosexual romance in plotting the transmission of property.

As I have argued, the novel demonstrates the difficulty of any corpse claiming property by showcasing how the law cannot protect an author's rights to his words, whether through the failure of wills or the haphazard circulation of paper in general, and it emphasizes women's still more precarious relationship to property. Johnny's nearly successful will, in contrast, emphasizes the spoken word over written documents, benefits two women, and engages multiple people (the doctor, Rokesmith, Betty) ready to fulfill his wishes, though they appear, regardless of their intentions, to operate more at cross-purposes with one another than collaboratively. Significantly, Betty's small challenge to Johnny's property transmission, like the Boffins' challenge of Harmon's will, commands respect within the novel: one of its pet characters, this "strong" but "tender" working-class

---

[63] For the significance of women's same-sex relationships and homoerotic desire to *Our Mutual Friend*, see Michael D. Lewis, "The Challenge of Female Homoeroticism in *Our Mutual Friend*," *Dickens Studies Annual: Essays on Victorian Fiction* 48 (2017): 207–29.

[64] For Betty's importance to this novel, see Schaffer, *Novel* 119–43.

[65] In R. J. Morris's study of wills in Leeds from 1830–4, only "18 percent of the men who left widows did not bother with the protection of any trust mechanism and made an absolute grant of all or part of their property to their widow" (104). For discussion of such grants and of female executors, see also Green, "To Do the Right Thing" 140–6. Contemporary writers considered this role significant. See "Duties of Executors and Administrators," *The Leisure Hour: A Family Journal of Instruction and Recreation* 998 (11 Feb 1871): 91–4. In George Eliot's *Middlemarch*, Dorothea Brooke "'is an executrix'" of her late husband's will, and worries family members because the role enables economic activity, however vaguely stated: "'she likes to go into these things—property, land, that kind of thing. She has her notions, you know [...] and she would like to act'" (483).

WEALTH, WOMEN, AND WILLS IN *OUR MUTUAL FRIEND* 59

woman who lives in fear of losing her independence (197, 198) is the mouthpiece for Dickens's decades-old bitterness against the New Poor Law and the workhouse: "'Kill me sooner than take me there'" (199). Johnny's brief deathbed scene and the posthumous resolution of his property, then, not only address the novel's testamentary troubles—highlighting the differences between two wills and their relationship to gendered and authorial concerns—but also draw attention to Betty as a key figure in resolving the property crisis that *Our Mutual Friend* has established. As we will now see, Betty's death, and the wishes that prevail beyond it, finally grant a "corpse" control over her property, draw on and restore posthumous authority to speech and writing alike, and bring together a community of like-minded people in the mutual service of her will.

VI. "Is That Your Wish? Yes, Certainly."

Dickens introduces Betty Higdon through the texts that she reads and the texts that are read to her. Betty is a moderately literate working-class woman; though she "ain't [...] much of a hand at reading writing-hand [...] I can read my Bible and most print" (198). The text generally associated with her, however, is the newspaper, which she listens to instead. She admits that "I do love a newspaper" and praises her adopted son Sloppy as "a beautiful reader of a newspaper" before joining him in "cheerful," extended laughter (198). Betty's early and positive association with the written word is important. Although nearly two hundred pages of the novel elapse before another text takes a prominent place in her life, the letter that Dickens ties to her last days and to her own successful final testament gains force from its connection to the joyful, loving, and communal way in which she earlier receives the written word. This letter is crafted when Betty, determined to avoid pauperism and the dreaded workhouse to the last, decides to earn her living on the road after little Johnny's death.[66] As she prepares to depart, Rokesmith creates a document for her, the written directive that will finally prove successful after death. "'I think,' said Rokesmith [...] 'that at least you might keep a letter in your pocket, Mrs. Higden, which I would write for you [...] stating, in the names of Mr. and Mrs. Boffin, that they are your friends [...]'" (389). The "friend[ly]" group is surprisingly adamant about this offer. "'As to the letter, Rokesmith,' said Mr. Boffin, 'you're as right as a trivet.

---

[66] For "what 'Betty' saw" about workhouses in contemporary newspapers as well as "another context in which to place [her] as she made her way up the Thames, with her basket of goods, an aged figure pursuing her trade vigorously and alone," see Chase, *The Victorians and Old Age* 20–4, 29–30. For the social annihilation of workhouse paupers, see Sambudha Sen, "From Dispossession to Dissection: The Bare Life of the English Pauper in the Age of the Anatomy Act and the New Poor Law," *Victorian Studies* 59.2 (2017): 235–9, 242, 245.

60   IMAGINING WOMEN'S PROPERTY IN VICTORIAN FICTION

Give her the letter, make her take the letter, put it in her pocket by violence'"
(390). No such physical force proves necessary; Betty again "laugh[s]" gratefully as
she agrees to their proposal.

> The letter was written, and read to her, and given to her.
>
> 'Now, how do you feel?' said Mr. Boffin. 'Do you like it?'
>
> 'The letter, sir?' said Betty. 'Aye, it's a beautiful letter!'   (390)

In a novel that has previously questioned the power of authorship, this letter—a
"beautiful," aesthetically appealing object, intended to protect its carrier and
conveyed in both material and spoken form—draws on elements of wills, copyright, and fiction and accordingly carries greater weight than its brief contents
might otherwise suggest. Despite the good-natured exchange, the laughter, and
the desire to protect Betty, the "violence" of thrusting the letter upon her ("'make
her take the letter, put it in her pocket'") suggests its unusual significance to its
authors. The care she then takes of the letter and the novel's near sanctification of
it at her death make it equally remarkable for the novel at large.

Rokesmith, not Betty, writes this document, and to a certain extent he and
Mr. Boffin, by crafting the letter that stands in lieu of her own last testament and
"covering" her with their protection, underplay the "indomitable purpose" (197)
and voice of this forceful woman in order to preserve her will. Betty could not have
written or read this letter, but other Victorian women did produce their own wills.[67]
Unmarried women and widows could do so legally, and although the common law
did not recognize married women's wills, many wrote them anyway and some wives
managed to circumvent official or legal procedures in bequeathing money, as
we saw in the case of Pleasant Riderhood's mother. If Betty must sacrifice some
of her independence to "friends," however, the transaction also alters the status of
Rokesmith's writing, making it just one part of a larger, collaborative system, shaped
by Betty's needs, the Boffins' urging, and the people she will encounter.

After Betty has walked herself nearly to death, she prepares for the end with two
actions, one religious, the other textual. She "commit[s] herself to Him who died
upon [the Cross]" (512) and in the very next sentence takes care of Rokesmith's

---

[67] Although some critics have suggested that the Wills Act of 1837 removed married women's rights
to make wills (see Wynne 97), it seems to have left women in the same legal position they held
previously. See J. B. Matthews, ed., *Hayes & Jarman's Concise Forms of Wills, With Practical Notes*, 12th
ed. (London: Sweet and Maxwell, Limited, 1905): 9m. For women's wills, see Morris 237–40 and Green,
"To Do the Right Thing" 135, 137. Mary Beth Combs shows that married women's wills "increased from 17.7
percent in 1860 to 34.3 percent at the turn of the century" (1039), a shift that corresponds to the
increase of married women's economic rights. See also Green and Owens, "Gentlewomanly" 517 and
Frank 47 n. 33. Even after married women's property law reform, a wife's will included only property
she had at the time of writing, rather than at the time of death, until 1893 (Frank 113).

WEALTH, WOMEN, AND WILLS IN *OUR MUTUAL FRIEND* 61

paper: "Her strength held out to enable her to arrange the letter in her breast, so as that it could be seen that she had a paper there" (512). She has a few final words— "'Paper. Letter'" are among them (513)—and they guide Lizzie Hexam to discover her will: "'This paper in your breast? [...] Am I to open it? To read it?'" This scene allows Betty to die confident that Lizzie will honor her will: "'Will I send it to the writers? Is that your wish? Yes, certainly. [...] Most solemnly. [...] Faithfully'" (513). Betty's acknowledged wishes are few and relatively straightforward: to contact the Boffins, to escape the workhouse, and to avoid a pauper's grave (203–4) by paying for her burial with the money "[s]ewn in the breast of her gown" (511).[68] The next chapter confirms what Lizzie has pledged, opening upon the memorial service where Betty's friends congregate at her "lowly grave. Not a penny had been added to the money sewn in her dress: what her honest spirit had so long projected was fulfilled" (515). Unlike Old Harmon's overreaching, alienating directives, her modest, open desires for community and financial agency are not only obeyed but even cherished.

It is no small matter here that a document finally carries weight in this novel, that a piece of writing permits a character's material decisions to matter after death. Whereas wealthy Old Harmon's writing fails him, his son helps a less fortunate woman create an untouchable legacy. Despite its earlier refusal to allow a "corpse" to claim or direct the use of money, the novel here offers a more hopeful vision of property rights than those afforded either by insufficient copyright or intractable audiences: that authorship will gain longer lasting authority, that a reader-recipient will interpret an author's words correctly and follow both the letter and spirit of his directive, that "beautiful" words (390)—whether in Rokesmith's letter or perhaps in a piece of fiction itself—can have their way.

But they can't do so alone. The reinstatement of authorship and its prerogative to claim and direct property and people, during and after life, requires something more than writing, whether legal or literary. Though the novel earlier refuses to let a solitary, secretive "corpse" claim or direct the use of money, here it offers a testamentary team that works more successfully. Rokesmith and the Boffins anticipate the setting which might require written documentation of Betty's desires, while an intimate exchange—Betty's deathbed communication with Lizzie—directs attention to the document she carries and allows Lizzie to confirm "solemnly" and "[f]aithfully" (513) that she will fulfill Betty's wishes. Compelling us to revisit both the individualist, masculinist logic that still characterizes most economic criticism and the heterosexual norms that often overlook exchanges of property between women, this remarkably collaborative effort highlights women's

---

[68] Betty's emphasis on burial derives in part from anxiety about the treatment of paupers' bodies. For a detailed discussion of the circumstances leading to and arising from the 1832 Anatomy Act, which made the bodies of workhouse paupers available for dissection, see Ruth Richardson, *Death, Dissection, and the Destitute*, 2nd ed. (Chicago: University of Chicago Press, 2000): *passim* but, e.g., xv, 108–30, 186–9, 198–202, 215–23, 263, 266–70, 276.

62 IMAGINING WOMEN'S PROPERTY IN VICTORIAN FICTION

extralegal contributions to economic activity and the importance, in Dickens's novel as in his own career, of oral delivery to the written word.[69]

The paper supplies the necessary details, but the brief encounter makes them matter. In that encounter, we see the novelist's fantasy of a single reader-recipient—a unified audience—who is intent on carrying out an author's wishes and who does so both by attending to the written word and by reading its larger spirit. Channeling the Dickens of public readings, whose material books became mere props as he personally presented his works to thousands, the voice supplementing the text here creates a "bond" with an "audibly responsive" and "interactive" audience.[70] Lizzie's execution of Betty's will requires her newly acquired literacy, which allows her to read the document and write to Betty's friends, but it also requires the longstanding, sympathetic vision she has had since her more impoverished days of lovingly reading "'fortune-telling pictures'" in the hearth (29). Both together allow her to engage with and understand Betty, who by that point can barely speak. Although Gallagher has suggested that Dickens's ideal reader will blindly "wait and trust [...] very much like the reformed Bella Wilfer at the novel's end,"[71] Lizzie's interaction with Betty suggests another, more active model for receptive readership (and women's economic engagement) than that of wifely submission. Lizzie as Betty's reader is an "earnest" woman (512), intent on "understand[ing]," and sympathetic to the meaning she will strive to learn. No passive repository of trust, she is an audience who will also *act*, quickly and bravely, to ensure that a "last request [is] religiously observed" (516) and that a will can finally find its way.

VII. Not "Born a Lady"

Betty and Lizzie together, like Mrs. Boffin earlier, further remind us that Victorian novelists such as Dickens were imagining women as more than merely objects of men's will; nineteenth-century women's economic agency is not simply our more recent critical discovery. It is telling, though, that these working-class women, rather than Bella (or Mrs. Wilfer or Georgiana Podsnap or Mrs. Lammle), demonstrate this point. Though we see Mrs. Boffin wealthy and "'go[ing] in for fashion'" (99), she insists on her more humble background: "'Bless ye, I wasn't

---

[69] For consideration of collaboration and intersubjective economic activity rather than individual competition, see, for instance, Gordon Bigelow, "The Cost of Everything in *Middlemarch*," in *Economic Women: Essays on Desire and Dispossession in Nineteenth-Century British Culture*, ed. Lana L. Dalley and Jill Rappoport (Columbus: Ohio State University Press, 2013): 97–109. For community in Dickens's fiction, see also John Bowen, *Other Dickens: Pickwick to Chuzzlewit* (Oxford: Oxford University Press, 2000): 19–20.

[70] Andrews 136, 70.

[71] Gallagher 114, 115. Rachel Ablow suggests another marital model for novel-reading (*The Marriage of Minds* 19).

WEALTH, WOMEN, AND WILLS IN *OUR MUTUAL FRIEND* 63

born a lady any more than you'" (203). Using her fortune to enrich others, particularly John Harmon, Jr., she ultimately reinforces existing structures of familial wealth and class through her nevertheless remarkable economic agency. Betty and Lizzy also, for the most part, support the status quo in this exchange.[72] They are working women who, despite their seemingly innate gentility, possess little money and—as a widow and an orphaned single woman, respectively—earn their own livings without seeking "a penny" of additional support. Posing no private threat to husbands or fathers, their small-scale economic agency seems unlikely to disturb larger economic operations either: Betty's insistence on her own grave will not shut down the workhouse, and Lizzie's execution of Betty's desires doesn't even make her late to her job at the mill (517).

Granting working-class women moderate levels of economic agency even as it depicts middle-class women such as Bella as "shrink[ing] to next to nothing" (606), Dickens's novel, published after nearly a decade of debates about women's property rights and five years before the first major legislative response, accords with prevailing attitudes toward (or at least prevailing strategies for enacting) legal change. The idea that a woman could have or control independent means threatened middle-class ideals of marriage, and advocates initially found it easier to argue for protections rather than rights—the protection of working women's meager means from (reputedly) alcoholic, abusive, or absentee men. Just as Dickens emphasized the protection of women and children (rather than the property rights of authors, whether male or female) as a rationale for expanded copyright law, legislators who disliked the idea of women's separate wealth within their own economic spheres nevertheless acknowledged its value in other socio-economic groups. The first steps toward property reforms were frequently framed in terms of protection from mistreatment or neglect, not in terms of more proactive rights to preserve, spend, invest, or bequeath. When the first Married Women's Property Act was passed in 1870, it focused on working-class women, protecting their earnings and small inheritances from untrustworthy husbands, but doing little to protect or enrich women of higher ranks.[73]

Though discussions of married women's property reform generally center on married women, the most prominent working-class women in Dickens's novel—Lizzie Hexam, Jenny Wren, Pleasant Riderhood, and Betty Higden—are unmarried. The three younger women pass most of the novel under *feme sole* classification and are more visible in their roles as daughters than as (future) wives,[74]

---

[72] Lizzie's marriage to Eugene Wrayburn, which occurs later in the novel, is the exception here.

[73] See n. 37, Shanley 74, and Rachel Ablow, "'One Flesh,' One Person, and the 1870 Married Women's Property Act," *BRANCH: Britain, Representation and Nineteenth-Century History*, ed. Dino Franco Felluga. Extension of *Romanticism and Victorianism on the Net* (Web, Nov. 23, 2015).

[74] For Jenny's relationship to Lizzie, see Lewis, "Challenge" 210–15. See also Holly Furneaux, "Sexuality," in *Charles Dickens in Context*, ed. Sally Ledger and Holly Furneaux (Cambridge: Cambridge University Press, 2011): 358–64, 362–4.

64 IMAGINING WOMEN'S PROPERTY IN VICTORIAN FICTION

while Betty is a widow seen primarily in terms of her grandmotherly relation to her adoptive children, Johnny and Sloppy.[75] Yet their domestic circumstances nevertheless reinforce popular middle-class understandings of working families that reformers would use to advocate for the property rights of working-class women. The novel highlights these working women's hard and honest work and pairs it either with upper-class protection (in Betty's case) or with evidence of why such protection is necessary, in the cases of Lizzie, Jenny, and Pleasant. Their rough and disreputable fathers, who claim their companionship, homemaking, affection, and support (29, 240, 445), are given to some combination of theft, deceit, alcoholism, and physical violence "in the form of a fist or a leathern strap"[76] (351), and they actively thwart their children's efforts to create more stable futures. We never see them as husbands. Lizzie, Jenny, and Pleasant's mothers die early, and all we know about their marital relationships we must glean from Jenny's father, Mr. Dolls, who uses most of his earnings to drink (242), and from efforts such as those of Pleasant's mother, who, as we have seen, found it necessary to hide "a secret capital of fifteen shillings [...] in a pillow" from her husband (350),[77] actions suggestive of precisely those working-class spousal struggles that advocates of married women's property rights described. Lizzie, Jenny, and Pleasant similarly strive to earn a living despite the additional challenges of caregiving for men who impede their efforts. Freed from these burdens not by divorce but by their fathers' untimely deaths, these daughters achieve financial and personal independence through mortality rather than legislative means, but their stories as "deserving," unmarried working women stand alongside those of countless working-class wives whose lives were being imagined or narrated in the popular press and for whom legal measures such as the Married Women's Property Act of 1870 were enacted. Though this Act would not directly protect the earnings of daughters, the novel's accounts of Lizzie, Jenny, and Pleasant not only offer glimpses of what their lives might have been had their mothers been able to freely leave them financial support but also remind us that debates about the protection and management of women's property engaged representations of unwed as well as married women.

When we look exclusively at the middle-class women and wives threatened by commodification or the fiction of being someone's "safe estate" in the novel, we miss the characters whose plot lines offer a different story about gender, class, and economics. In Dickens's novel, of course, these stories intertwine. Lizzie is the daughter of Gaffer Hexam, the corpse-robbing waterman who dragged John

---

[75] Johnny is actually her great-grandson ("the child of my own last left daughter's daughter") while Sloppy, the orphan of unknown parents, was brought up in the workhouse (198, 199).

[76] Lizzie's praise of her father includes the point that, "let him be put out as he may, [he] never once strikes me" though his son seems less fortunate (37).

[77] Lizzie and Jenny unconsciously follow the late Mrs. Riderhood's lead, concealing money from their fathers in order to aid a brother or secure their own well-being.

WEALTH, WOMEN, AND WILLS IN *OUR MUTUAL FRIEND*   65

Harmon's (supposed) body in from the Thames and first raised the question of whether or not a dead man could own, want, or spend money. After Gaffer's death, Lizzie strives to make "'Any compensation—restitution'" for his thefts (227). In her ability to help another poor woman direct her own burial, she offers a model distinct from her father's in every way. The money found on Betty's body goes where Betty intended; Lizzie's aid to her quietly but firmly rebuts Gaffer's assertion that "money [cannot] be a corpse's" (4). Literary critics have long noted that *Our Mutual Friend* (1864–5) is obsessed with money.[78] Its characters squeeze livings out of dust, water, ribbons, and flesh, while human relations are monetized through blackmail, begging, volatile markets that deal as easily in orphans as in stocks (195–6), and marriages that result as much from financial speculation as from love. Lizzie's "earnest," "Angel[ic]," "compassionate" actions (512, 514) work differently, but they are also economic choices which bear significantly on the novel's larger discourses about authorship and property and which allow her, like the Boffins, to construct alternative forms of connection beyond bloodlines or the marriage plot, beyond coverture or the common law. They come more clearly into focus when we expand our understanding of ownership beyond the bounds of competitive individualism and when we take seriously the way that female characters create and execute legacies of their own. Offering the possibility that an author might have a lasting claim upon readers' actions, the novel makes the most successful forms of writing intimate and interactive, shared property for its mutual friends.

---

[78] See, e.g., J. Hillis Miller, "Our Mutual Friend," in *Dickens: A Collection of Critical Essays*, ed. Martin Price (Englewood Cliffs, NJ: Prentice-Hall, Inc., 1967): 169–77, 169.

2

"A Purse in Common"

Money, Mutuality, and Darwinian Survival in *Wives and Daughters* (1866)

Collaboration is an ongoing economic strategy for households in Victorian fiction. Communal living, as a means of cost-sharing as well as companionship, assists working-class characters Lizzie Hexam and Jenny Wren in Dickens's *Our Mutual Friend*, for example. In the decades before the 1870 Act began the legislative work of reforming married women's property rights, other authors similarly envisioned economic cooperation as a means for those with limited resources, especially women, to sustain themselves. Such cooperative efforts derive but also differ from the economic assistance that appears in many Austen moments of support for poorer kin or connections: one sister's ongoing aid to another in *Pride and Prejudice*, as I discussed in the Introduction; the maintenance of an impoverished niece in *Mansfield Park* (1814) who grows up conscious of her cousins' great difference in "'rank, fortune, rights, and expectations'"; and even the various subsidized visits that Bennet, Dashwood, or Elliot sisters make in order to uphold their present-day lifestyles or launch their possible economic futures.[1] Instead, the cooperative domestic units that interest me here strive to erase knowledge of their members' different means. From the unevenly financed sisters of Wilkie Collins's *The Woman in White* (1859), who continue to share a home even after one has married, to the female households of extended Stanbury and Rowley kin and friends in Anthony Trollope's *He Knew He Was Right* (1869); from Aurora Leigh, who supports the impoverished Marian Erle and her child as her "own" in Elizabeth Barrett Browning's eponymous epic poem (1856), to Lizzie of Christina Rossetti's "Goblin Market" (1862), who comes to the aid of her penniless sister and appears to co-parent with her years later; Victorian fiction and poetry published during this period are filled with non-heteronormative domestic

---

[1] Jane Austen, *Mansfield Park* [1814]: *Authoritative Text, Contexts, Criticism*, ed. Claudia L. Johnson (New York and London: W. W. Norton & Company, 1998): 10. For a great economic reading of Fanny Price and of her differences from the Bertram sisters, see the first chapter of Eileen Cleere's *Avuncularism* (33–75). For the Elliot sisters, see Jane Austen, *Persuasion* [1818]: *A Norton Critical Edition*, 2nd ed., ed. Patricia Meyer Spacks (New York: W. W. Norton & Company, 2013): e.g., 25, 34.

Imagining Women's Property in Victorian Fiction. Jill Rappoport, Oxford University Press. © Jill Rappoport 2023.
DOI: 10.1093/oso/9780192867261.003.0003

arrangements that, in various ways, allow women to stretch their means and get by with a little help from their friends.[2]

How these and other economic practices define and shape a wide range of relationships are of particular concern in Elizabeth Gaskell's fiction. Denouncing the self-interest of individuals who operate according to their financial benefit alone,[3] her works explore how economic interactions create and accompany conditions for different forms of interpersonal intimacy. In *North and South* (1854), for instance, factory employment, labor unions, charity baskets, cost-sharing schemes, inheritance, and speculation all shape professional and personal relationships. Group allegiance and exile are tracked in the gift-giving systems of *Cranford* (1851–3) that I have discussed elsewhere[4] and in the £50 sent to the abandoned heroine of *Ruth* (1853) by her seducer's mother to sever ties.[5] Among Gaskell's works, *Wives and Daughters* (1866) is a meaningful case study for the ways in which it situates individual desire within a social context and highlights the importance and diversity of cost-sharing practices within families and communities. Like Dickens's Bella Wilfer, many of the female characters in Gaskell's final, unfinished novel struggle with their inability to earn, "beg [...] borrow [...] or steal" sufficient money (*OMF* 320), while other characters go about their daily business of spending and investing their resources, going into debt, and making or receiving gifts. In *Wives and Daughters*, however, the acquisition and disposal of money seem to matter less than the systems through which people manage (or fail to manage) these financial acts *together*. The varied forms of these systems underscore the significance of economics to a wide range of domestic plots and also the ways in which those many relationships and story lines allowed Gaskell to imagine alternative models for property management beyond those dictated by common law.

In its meditations on extralegal, collaborative property management, Gaskell's novel offers an important perspective on debates about married women's property. Gaskell herself supported the movement to improve women's property rights; she signed her name to the 1856 petition for their legal reform. Yet just

---

[2] *Aurora Leigh* VII: l. 119. The domestic unit of sibling surrogates Jane Eyre forms with her cousins, first at their expense, then at hers, is yet another example. For women's alliance-forming gift-giving strategies in general, and those in "Goblin Market," *Aurora Leigh* and *Jane Eyre* in particular, see Rappoport, *Giving Women*, esp. chs. 2 and 4. For mid-century novelists' emphasis on "the basic social unit as communal, rather than individual," see Ilana M. Blumberg, *Victorian Sacrifice: Ethics and Economics in Mid-Century Novels* (Columbus: Ohio State University Press, 2013): 11. For the homoerotic attachment underlying some of these cohabitations, see, e.g., Lewis, "The Challenge of Female Homoeroticism in *Our Mutual Friend*," 212, 228 and Marcus, *Between Women*, e.g., 91–102, 193–204.

[3] See, e.g., Elizabeth Gaskell, *North and South* [1854], ed. Patricia Ingham (London: Penguin Books Ltd., 1995): 117, 118. For that self-interested economic individual, see Elaine Hadley, "Human Capital: Becker the Obscure: Human-Capital Theory, Liberalisms, and the Future of Higher Education," in *From Political Economy to Economics through Nineteenth-Century Literature: Reclaiming the Social*, ed. Elaine Hadley, Audrey Jaffe, and Sarah Winter (Cham: Palgrave Macmillan, 2019): 29–57, 34.

[4] See Rappoport, *Giving Women*, ch. 3.

[5] Elizabeth Gaskell, *Ruth* [1853], ed. Angus Easson (London: Penguin Books Ltd., 1997): 78, 90.

68　IMAGINING WOMEN'S PROPERTY IN VICTORIAN FICTION

as significantly, her life testified to the irrelevance of the law, at least in certain privileged contexts. Despite coverture's contrary mandate, for example, she entered into her own publishing negotiations and purchased a house without her husband's knowledge.[6] As Gaskell observed, however, the irrelevance of the law could be far more injurious in other cases. Like *Little Dorrit's* disappointed benefactor in the example that opened this book, she doubted whether any legal reform could help: "'[A] husband can coax, wheedle, beat or tyrannize his wife out of something and no law whatever will help this.'"[7] Along similar lines, *Wives and Daughters* showcases both the limitations of coverture and the need for reforms that step outside of legal frameworks. Arguing against the common law doctrine of coverture by demonstrating both the destructive nature of its lopsided economic structure and the repeated absence of the shared interest that this doctrine presumes, Gaskell suggests a different form of economic partnership that grows out of, rather than mandates, mutual concerns. More interested in mutuality of affect and mutual access to shared resources than in women's independent financial ownership or agency, her version of property reform is not the one that Parliament would go on to enact or that sits comfortably with most feminist scholarship today. Yet that is one more reason why it remains critical for our understanding of how changing attitudes toward property fit into the nineteenth-century women's movement. Gaskell's complicated, hopeful, and at times problematic stance on economics and intimacy evinces deep skepticism about the ability of law to protect or provide for these ties. Her novel insists on the power of the written word (as well as the affections of those it associates most strongly with reading and writing) to supplement or supplant the law. It also tells the story of how, in the years leading up to legislative change, popular ideas about married women's property rights intertwined with broader understandings of siblinghood, friendship, primogeniture, and, as we will see, even evolutionary science.

When discussions of *Wives and Daughters* delve into its economics, they generally do so in terms of the novel's Darwinian framework. Along these lines, the novel has interested Victorianists for the way that its two sibling pairs struggle for scarce resources, participating in a world of evolutionary inheritance and rivalry. Gaskell had a keen interest in contemporary scientific discoveries,[8] and Mary Debrabant and others have argued that this novel "deserves to be recognized as a notable instance of the interaction of Darwin's ideas and Victorian

---

[6] Gaskell famously butted heads with Charles Dickens over control of her writing in *Household Words* and negotiated with her publisher Edward Chapman. For the home purchase, see Mary Elizabeth Leighton and Lisa Surridge, "Evolutionary Discourse and the Credit Economy in Elizabeth Gaskell's *Wives and Daughters*," *Victorian Literature and Culture* 41.3 (2013): 487–501, 489–90.

[7] Elizabeth Gaskell, *The Letters of Mrs. Gaskell*, ed. J. A. V. and A. Pollard (Cambridge, MA: Harvard University Press, 1967): 379, quoted in Dolin 12.

[8] See, for instance, Rappoport, *Giving Women*, ch. 3.

MONEY, MUTUALITY, AND DARWINIAN SURVIVAL 69

literature."[9] Citing Gaskell's relationship to Charles Darwin and her efforts to model naturalist Roger Hamley after him, scholarship has explored the novel's engagement with natural selection and sexual competition.[10] Roger, the hearty, scientifically-minded second son of a squire, appears more fit for mid-Victorian life and professionalism than his languid, feminized older brother Osborne, whose position as heir renders him helpless to forge his own way, despite his parents' favor, early academic promise, and what initially seems a financially secure future. Molly Gibson is similarly poised to struggle with her new stepsister Cynthia Kirkpatrick. Framing them as unconscious rivals for Roger's love, ranked against each other by onlookers, the novel tests Cynthia's "power of fascination" and bold beauty against Molly's "courageous innocence" and "perfect grace."[11] Critics explain these characters through Darwinian "self-interested survival strateg[ies]" and adaptive abilities, which, for Mary Elizabeth Leighton and Lisa Surridge, include the ability to enter and succeed within a credit economy.[12] The novel's characters and economic actions, that is, are typically read in accordance with popular ideas of Darwinian competition. When other relational modes such as altruism and sympathy emerge, Darwinian readings of the novel tend to explain them as competitive edges—the one-sided survival skills of mature, moral, or prosperous individuals and scientists. Molly and Cynthia, like Roger and Osborne, are thus primed to resent and compete with one another.

But they don't. Molly and Cynthia, like Roger and Osborne, manage to coexist and support one another with real affection. A different part of Darwin's legacy and a different economic mode—less individualist, less competitive—better

---

[9] Mary Debrabant, "Birds, Bees and Darwinian Survival Strategies in *Wives and Daughters*," *Gaskell Society Journal* 16 (2002): 14–29, 28. See also Phoebe Poon, "Popular Evolutionism: Scientific, Legal and Literary Discourse in Gaskell's *Wives and Daughters*," in *Elizabeth Gaskell: Victorian Culture and the Art of Fiction: Original Essays for the Bicentenary*, ed. Sandro Jung (Lebanon, NH: Academia, 2010): 195–213, 210; Leighton and Surridge 487; Anne DeWitt, "Moral Uses, Narrative Effects: Natural History in Victorian Periodicals and Elizabeth Gaskell's *Wives and Daughters*," *Victorian Periodicals Review* 43.1 (2010): 1–18, passim.

[10] Linda K. Hughes, "*Cousin Phillis, Wives and Daughters*, and Modernity," in *The Cambridge Companion to Elizabeth Gaskell*, ed. Jill L. Matus (Cambridge: Cambridge University Press, 2007): 90–107, 98. See also Pam Morris, "Introduction," in Elizabeth Gaskell, *Wives and Daughters* [1864–6, 1866], ed. Pam Morris (London: Penguin Books Ltd., 1996): xi–xxxv, xxv. Though Gaskell had direct ties to Darwin and Darwinism, "most Victorian readers got their Darwinism not from Darwin and Huxley but from non-professionals." See Jonathan Smith, "Introduction: Darwin and the Evolution of Victorian Studies," *Victorian Studies* 51.2 (2009): 215–21, 218. Smith's general source is Bernard Lightman, *Victorian Popularizers of Science: Designing Nature for New Audiences* (Chicago and London: University of Chicago Press, 2007), who cites one science writer's letter to Gaskell (115). Lightman's detailed account shows that "at least half a dozen books by popularizers surpassed the *Origin* [in sales]" (34, see also 491); for some of these writers, see 219–23, 247, 270, 354.

[11] Elizabeth Gaskell, *Wives and Daughters* [1864–6, 1866], ed. Pam Morris. (London: Penguin Books Ltd., 1996): 217, 479, 320. Subsequent citations appear within the text. The novel's competitive assessments of them include 320, 392. For their distinct types of femininity, see Jennifer Panek, "Constructions of Masculinity in *Adam Bede* and *Wives and Daughters*," *Victorian Review: The Journal of the Victorian Studies Association of Western Canada and the Victorian Studies Association of Ontario* 22.2 (1996): 127–51, 128, and Hughes 106.

[12] Debrabant 26; Poon, "Popular" 202; Leighton and Surridge 487, 492.

70 IMAGING WOMEN'S PROPERTY IN VICTORIAN FICTION

explain how these relationships work and offer us important ways to think about money, evolution, marriage, and other forms of kinship during this period. Darwin himself, despite his alignment with practices "red in tooth and claw,"[13] has long been associated with sympathy and selflessness as well.[14] What's important, though, is that selflessness, like self-interest, necessitates a "self" and an "other."[15] They are equally out of place in Gaskell's fictional world and in the aspect of Darwinian thought that I am stressing here. Darwin, as we will see, emphasizes mutuality, not just individuals, and common purpose as well as struggle.[16] Through the sibling relationships of Molly, Cynthia, Roger, and Osborne, Gaskell depicts this more collaborative side of survival *along with* the more combative and even parasitic forms of individualism that also appear in the novel. In ways that resemble models of Darwinian interdependence, *Wives and Daughters* attempts to overcome the difficulties of competition and other inequitable relations by offering visions of common interest in their place. Gaskell's proposed relational model privileges mutual over individual benefit, showing how material cooperation can strengthen intimate ties. Furthermore, by juxtaposing the siblings' close friendships with visions of marital relations, and by emphasizing the economic aspects of both, Gaskell acknowledges the changing notions of marriage prevalent in the 1860s, challenges the sufficiency of the common law for friendship and marriage alike, and suggests the importance of extralegal measures to ensure both intimacy and economic well-being. Parallels between sibling relations and marriage in her novel further suggest the critical value of assessing different relationships (spouses, siblings, friends) alongside and also through one another. The marriage plot of Gaskell's novel is, surprisingly, as much a story of learning how to be a good brother or sister as it is a story of a developing heterosexual romance. Cost-sharing in accordance with mutual need and affection proves important to both.

I. Self-Interest and Struggle

Wives and Daughters repeatedly highlights problems inherent in unequal relationships in ways that have bearing on mid-century debates about marriage and

[13] Alfred, Lord Tennyson, *In Memoriam A. H. H.* 56:15, *Tennyson's Poetry: A Norton Critical Edition*, ed. Robert W. Hill, Jr. (New York: W. W. Norton & Company): 238.

[14] For a "kinder, gentler" Darwin, see not only *Origin* itself but also George Levine, *Darwin Loves You: Natural Selection and the Re-enchantment of the World* (Princeton: Princeton University Press, 2006): ch. 7, 202 and *passim*, 214; George Levine, *Darwin and the Novelists: Patterns of Science in Victorian Fiction* (Cambridge, MA: Harvard University Press, 1988); 10–11, also DeWitt 7, Poon, "Popular" 199, Jim Endersby, "Sympathetic Science: Charles Darwin, Joseph Hooker, and the Passions of Victorian Naturalists," *Victorian Studies: An Interdisciplinary Journal of Social, Political, and Cultural Studies* 51.2 (2009): 299–320, 300; Leighton and Surridge 498.

[15] Levine, *Darwin Loves* 212.

[16] Levine, *Darwin and the Novelists* 11, 47; Levine *Darwin Loves* 47, 78; Gillian Beer, *Darwin's Plots: Evolutionary Narrative in Darwin, George Eliot, and Nineteenth-Century Fiction*, 2nd ed. (Cambridge: Cambridge University Press, 1983, 2000): 7, 19, 93, 159.

property, though daughters (and siblings) are as important to Gaskell's intervention as wives. In one poignant scene, Molly Gibson, the earnest daughter of a middle-aged doctor, attempts to approach her father's hasty remarriage with the selflessness advocated by her new mentor Roger Hamley: "'I will think of others. I won't think of myself,' she kept repeating."[17] Despite striving to think "more of others' happiness than of her own," she struggles against the sacrifice entailed: "did it not mean giving up her very individuality, quenching all the warm love, the true desires, that made herself?" (134) Molly's dilemma at this early point in Gaskell's novel pits the self and its individual desires against others' happiness in an extreme, zero-sum equation: there is seemingly no way to meet the needs or desires of both sides, as her response to Roger's platitude ("'by-and-by you will be so much happier for it'") insists:

> "No, I shan't!" said Molly, shaking her head. "It will be very dull when I shall have killed myself, as it were, and live only in trying to do, and to be, as other people like. I don't see any end to it. I might as well never have lived. And as for the happiness you speak of, I shall never be happy again."
>
> There was an unconscious depth in what she said, that Roger did not know how to answer at the moment [...]. (135)

Gaskell renders this heart-broken daughter's declaration of enduring unhappiness with something more than just the sympathy of an experienced mother toward adolescent drama. Though Molly's intense grief largely subsides in the everyday negotiations of her new household life, the real and pressing emotions which find voice here and to which the older and wiser Roger tellingly has no answer are a powerful indictment of the sacrificial femininity advocated by such conduct book writers as Sarah Stickney Ellis and novelists such as Dickens.[18] In this scene, Gaskell showcases the dangerously stultifying risks of "quenching" or "kill[ing]" oneself in order to secure other people's happiness; acknowledges that the problem of balancing individuals' different and at times competing needs—a problem of scarce resources: economic, emotional, and evolutionary—requires more than a "moment" to address;[19] and signals her interest in using the longer duration of narrative time to explore other models, beyond the competitive poles of selflessness or selfishness, for managing the social world of this novel.

---

[17] Elizabeth Gaskell, *Wives and Daughters* [1864–6, 1866], ed. Pam Morris (London: Penguin Books Ltd., 1996): 125. Subsequent references will appear parenthetically within the text.

[18] E.g., Sarah Stickney Ellis, *The Women of England, Their Social Duties, and Domestic Habits* (New York: Appleton, 1843). See also Holcombe 79 and Blumberg, *Victorian Sacrifice* 7–20.

[19] The American Economic Association defines economics as "the study of scarcity, the study of how people use resources and respond to initiatives, or the study of decision-making. It often involves topics like wealth and finance, but it's not all about money": https://www.aeaweb.org/resources/students/what-is-economics, accessed Jan. 7, 2020.

72 IMAGINING WOMEN'S PROPERTY IN VICTORIAN FICTION

Molly's awareness that she has been asked to "quench" herself in order to benefit her father and "other people" depends on the logic of competition, hierarchy, and unequal resource distribution that seems to structure most of the primary relationships of the novel, including but not limited to marital arrangements. Coverture, the common-law doctrine that erased a woman's independent legal and financial identity within marriage, is one obvious Victorian analogue for Molly's profound sense that thinking of others' happiness at her own expense will "kill" her. As Dolin and others have noted, coverture is the married woman's substitute "for individuality" (11). We have already seen how Dickens's Bella "shrink[s] to next to nothing" in her lover's arms, "vanishing" in their marriage (*Our Mutual Friend* 606, 607). As Gaskell's novel insists, however, coverture cannot actually erase the fact of one's "very individuality" or "true desires," and thus fails to provide the shared interest that the legal doctrine presumes.

In the 1820 setting of Gaskell's novel, and until the reform of married women's property law in 1870 and 1882, a woman's property became her husband's upon marriage, and his financial actions as the head of the household were expected to "cover" her; wives without the legal protection of a separate estate (an expensive privilege, typically reserved for women whose male kin cared about preserving wealth for the next generation) depended upon their husbands to provide for them. Such financial dependence takes a few different forms within *Wives and Daughters*. Hyacinth Kirkpatrick, a woman who has disliked working as a private governess and schoolteacher, explicitly views marriage as a better way to procure an income and looks forward to the economic aspect of her marital disenfranchisement. Her daydreams feature an "imaginary breadwinner" (104), one "who would be bound to support her without any exertion of her own" (159). Although "she liked" the widowed physician attending her former employer, she "accepted Mr Gibson principally because she was tired of the struggle of earning her own livelihood" (125). What she doesn't accept is the dissolution of her own self-interest within this new relationship. Whereas Mr. Gibson naively attempts to understand marriage in its idealized legal sense, as an act that will make them "one" (383), the new Mrs. Gibson expects financial support, not the merger of being or interest implied in the "one-flesh" doctrine of marriage. Economic dependence may unite them legally but it cannot produce intimacy.

The marriage of Squire and Mrs. Hamley is represented in more loving terms than Mr. Gibson's breadwinning—the squire "jealously guarding" his job of carrying breakfast up to his invalid wife (81) and "gathering [...] a sweet fresh nosegay every day" for her (44)—but it too is based less on mutual interest than on dependence and lopsided support, and this is also apparently one source of Mrs. Hamley's decline. "[P]ossibly Mrs Hamley would not have sunk into the condition of a chronic invalid, if her husband had cared a little more for her various tastes [...]"; "he showed so little sympathy with her [...] that she ceased caring" about her previous enjoyments (42). In place of "sympathy" or mutual interest, Squire

MONEY, MUTUALITY, AND DARWINIAN SURVIVAL   73

Hamley "quench[es]" his wife with paternalistic kindness, "giving his consent" to her activities and "furnishing her amply with money. 'There, there, my little woman, take that! Dress yourself up as fine as any on 'em, and buy what you like, for the credit of Hamley of Hamley; and go to the park and the play, and show off with the best on 'em'" (42). His putative generosity underlines the inequality in their marriage, as he infantilizes his wife ("my little woman"), turns her "various tastes" into the superficial acts of dressing up, and displays his own status ("for the credit of Hamley of Hamley"). Their financial arrangement, which adheres to the economic strictures of coverture without its implied merger of interests, undermines not only their marital intimacy but even the physical well-being of Mrs. Hamley, whose status as a "chronic invalid" progresses inexorably throughout the first third of the novel. Even Mr. Gibson cannot cure this form of invalidism. In fact, the physician seems ignorant of the danger he unwittingly works to perpetuate; he helps to orchestrate his own beloved daughter's marriage by keeping her in a similar state of dependence, ignorant not only of her lover's regard but also of her own financial circumstances. "'Molly has some money independently of me,—that she by the way knows nothing of,—not much—and I can allow her something,'" he informs a suitor (643). Implied is that she will make what was considered to be the most important economic decision of a Victorian woman's life, that of marriage,[20] without full knowledge of or control over her own economic circumstances; any possible financial "independen[ce]" will only come to her—as in the case of Mrs. Hamley—under cover of her husband, with no guarantee of shared sympathy or interest.

Wives and Daughters criticizes the marital dependency and dissonance we see in the Squire's control over his wife's finances and Mr. Gibson's breadwinning, but unequal financial arrangements are not unique to marital relations or legal doctrines, as Gaskell's novel, like Austen's before her, pointedly demonstrates.[21] When middle-aged Phoebe Browning briefly (albeit erroneously) anticipates a marriage proposal, the "question of questions" that occupies her—"Could she leave her sister?" (144)—reminds us to think about the ways that, for some women, the significance of a sibling or other relationship could rival that of marriage.[22] The two relationships could also resemble each other. The Browning sisters' financial dynamic, like those of the Gibsons and Hamleys, is one of control and dependence. Despite the fact that each sister legally possesses her own small property, the elder Miss Browning restricts her younger sister's access to it, as Phoebe explains in a description of "a large miniature set round with pearls" that she wears to a charity ball:

---

[20] See, for instance, Schaffer, *Romance's Rival* 13, 23.

[21] Austen's novels emphasize both the dependence of poor single women such as *Mansfield Park*'s Fanny Price and, in Cleere's terms, their "constant" and ongoing "obligations" to those who provide for them (51).

[22] See Marcus; Rappoport, *Giving Women*.

74 IMAGINING WOMEN'S PROPERTY IN VICTORIAN FICTION

It is a likeness of my dear mother; Sally has got my father on. The miniatures
were both taken at the same time; and just about then my uncle died and left us
each a legacy of fifty pounds, which we agreed to spend on the setting of our
miniatures. But because they are so valuable Sally always keeps them locked up
with the best silver, and hides the box somewhere; she never will tell me where,
because she says I've such weak nerves, and that if a burglar, with a loaded pistol
at my head, were to ask me where we kept our plate and jewels, I should be sure
to tell him; and she says, for her part, she would never think of revealing under
any circumstances. (I'm sure I hope she won't be tried.)   (284)

The scenario envisioned here, in which jewelry and silver are valued more highly
than their owners' lives, may seem hard to take seriously. But perhaps in moments
such as this one we might think more generously about these characters' circumstances, as Molly insists upon doing when she rebukes Lady Harriet for mocking
the Browning sisters as "Pecksy and Flapsy" (161, 163). Women's inheritance
often took the form of personal property, and for unmarried middle-class women
without employment, the preservation of that property may well have felt necessary for the preservation of life.[23] If, alternatively, we find humor here, we might
consider how this example, by making the sisters' uneven property management
appear ridiculous, also reveals the absurdity of unequal economic control between
two cohabiting adults more generally, whether or not one is perceived as the
"weak[er]" of the two. Sally Browning's sharp economic dictates to Phoebe may
sound less gentle or generous than Squire Hamley's to his wife—we are accustomed to hearing them in the lower ranges of a masculine voice—but they differ in
pitch, not in tune. In both cases, the novel suggests that financial dependence is
neither a safe nor natural part of relationships, though the sisters and wives in
question may accept or even welcome it as part of the social order. Importantly,
the parallel between sibling relations and marriage here does not privilege the
latter. Indeed, the source of these women's small fortune and the way that they use
it—an avuncular legacy, spent entirely on jeweled settings which function as
memorials to their parents—highlight additional, cross-generational relationships
that they value highly and prioritize, in their expenditure, over the benefit of
having additional money to bring to or attract a future marriage.[24]

If unequal financial relationships appear ridiculous, injurious, or simply irrelevant to sympathy in these cases, they register as frankly manipulative in others;

---

[23] See, for instance, Amanda Vickery, "Women and the World of Goods: A Lancashire Consumer
and Her Possessions, 1751–81," in *Consumption and the World of Goods*, ed. John Brewer and Roy
Porter (London: Routledge, 1993): 274–301, 294; Erickson 224; Wynne 89.

[24] Eileen Cleere 21, though in Gaskell's novel the Browning sisters' use of their uncle's wealth to
memorialize their parents differs from Cleere's understanding of distinct paternal and avuncular
models. See *Avuncularism: Capitalism, Patriarchy, and Nineteenth-Century English Culture*
(Stanford: Stanford University Press, 2004): 24–5, 74–5.

MONEY, MUTUALITY, AND DARWINIAN SURVIVAL   75

the "'unlucky debt'" that Cynthia naïvely enters into, for instance, entangles her with Mr. Preston, who transmutes their financial relationship into an engagement by turning the loan into an "'advance'" of her future dependence and who views economic power as the means to affection even after her repeated attempts to repay him and sever their ties (470, 463). If the novel has a villain, it is this steward of the local aristocracy, whose management of relationships and money alike are apparently at odds with the property management that the novel elsewhere endorses and who alone experiences multiple characters' "instinctive distaste," "'poor opinion,'" and "'hate'" (273, 442, 461).[25] Yet his treatment of Cynthia is in many respects only a more conscious and malicious wielding of the power that financial disparity grants him than that we see in the Gibson, Hamley, and Browning examples, an extreme case of the lack of sympathy or common interest that often goes along with lopsided economic relationships. Through all of these fraught relationships, the novel teaches us to be wary of relationships based in or settled around unequal finances. It also reminds us that arrangements such as economic dependence need not be particular to any one familial tie (marital, sibling) and that the lessons we learn from one relationship might, for better or for worse, carry over to another, regardless of the different forms intimacy takes in each.[26]

Whereas Preston's overt attempts to purchase love and then blackmail Cynthia are denounced and Mrs. Gibson seems mercenary for seeking a breadwinner over a romantic partner, another unequal financial model comes across as less obviously dangerous because it is so common to British economic traditions and to the Victorian novel: primogeniture. Primogeniture, the common-law form of patrilineal property transmission to an eldest son, appears to connect father with son but also pits one against the other.[27] While on the one hand, Osborne Hamley's position as heir gives him a coveted status—wealth, land, and status on the horizon—the novel makes clear the high costs of this economic custom, not, in this case, to the younger son, who neither needs nor wants the money, but to Squire Hamley, whose hands are tied during his life and whose son's inheritance can come only at the expense of his father's life. The logic of this filial substitution, wherein a father's death ultimately provides a son's wealth, is competitive: even should they wish it, strict entailments on the Hamley estate (248) prevent any sharing of resources, which must go to the two men sequentially, not

---

[25] Despite this depiction of Preston, Gaskell is not opposed to economic exchanges in general, particularly those that support useful relationships. As Nancy Henry has argued, although much of Victorian fiction appears anticapitalist, resisting the monetization of people and services, female authors such as Gaskell often had more nuanced depictions of the economic benefits of capitalism. Along these lines, the novel appears neutral about the way Mr. Gibson builds his practice by attending Lord and Lady Cumnor for a discounted payment (321).

[26] For the logic of relational substitution, whereby the economic value held by *Mansfield Park*'s niece Fanny Price allows her to stand in as daughter, sister, and eventually wife, see Cleere, e.g., 60.

[27] See Rutterford and Maltby, "Frank Must Marry" 177.

76   IMAGINING WOMEN'S PROPERTY IN VICTORIAN FICTION

simultaneously. Unsurprisingly, their relationship suffers. Its competitive nature appears most explicitly when the squire erroneously believes that Osborne has been borrowing money based on his expectations of future wealth; "the squire believed that Osborne and his advisers had been making calculations, based on his own death. [...] he imagined that [...] his first-born grudged him his natural term of life" (248–9).[28] Even when the two are on good terms, however, the transmission of wealth from father to son appears as a form of *quid pro quo* in expectations that prove as crushing to Osborne as generosity without sympathy was to his mother. The squire spends money improving the estate for Osborne ("'we never thought anything of economies which would benefit Osborne in the long run,'" explains his mother ˙191]) but does so under the understanding that Osborne will "'hoist the old family up again'" (433), both by marrying wealth and also through his own achievements: "'he was the heir, you know; and he was so clever, every one said he was sure of honours and a fellowship'" (191–2). Mr. Gibson wonders, after Mrs. Hamley's death, that the estranged father and son "'are not drawn together by their common loss'" (222), but whether the father sacrifices himself for his son or the son counts on his father's death, the relationship is one that eschews commonality, even in loss, in favor of unequal distribution, obligation, and resentment. Underscoring the mortal competition at work here, Osborne's death, like that of Mrs. Hamley, is represented as more than a result of bodily ailments. The squire, mourning this loss, grieves that the high expectations he had so often voiced for his son lead Osborne to keep his own marriage a secret: "'He was afraid of me [...]. And it made him keep all to himself, and care killed him. They may call it heart-disease—[...] I know better now'" (566–7). In the structure of primogeniture, as well as in other financial arrangements including marital coverture, *Wives and Daughters* thus showcases the detrimental nature of unequal financial control within relationships, particularly when such inequality seems to overlay the insistently separate interests of individuals whose needs, desires, or tastes remain independent of their economic arrangements.

For many relationships in the novel, including but not limited to marriage and heirship, the clash of interests within these financial arrangements appears to entail a dangerous struggle for limited emotional and material resources. We might understand this conflict, as other scholars have described Gaskell's sibling pairs, in Darwinian terms, as the "struggle for existence" that comprises one part of "natural selection," though the novel takes some liberties with evolutionary theory in its translation of scientific discovery to narrative plotting.[29] Competition

---

[28] For inheritance's structural relation to speculation, see Reich, e.g., 41, 81.

[29] For instance, natural selection for Darwin is largely about minor, "infinitesimally small" modifications to the species that occur over "the long course of time" to favor a group's position in the "struggle for life," rather than the forms of individual struggle better traced within the scope of

for scarce resources offers one way of viewing many of the economic and affective problems the novel traces. Such scarcity seems ready to undermine Molly's relationship with her new stepmother and stepsister and with even her father. There is not enough of Mr. Gibson to go around. When Mrs. Gibson and Cynthia visit London, Molly scolds him for agreeing to go to tea instead of enjoying their "perfect freedom [...] of old times come back again": "'how could you go and waste one of our evenings. We have but six in all, and now but five'" (437, 439). Time, like other resources in *Wives and Daughters*, is in short supply, and in this brief scene, Molly wants to hoard it. Mrs. Gibson, in contrast, opts for equalizing expenditure without taking account of need. Refurnishing the house shortly after her marriage, and assuming a competition that doesn't yet exist, she remarks to Molly that she is planning to update Cynthia's bedroom "'and yours, too, darling; so don't be jealous'" (182). Despite Molly's repeated protests that her room be left as it is, Mrs. Gibson worries "'what would be said of me by everybody'" if she were to treat the girls differently: "'Every penny I spend on Cynthia I shall spend on you too; so it's no use talking any more about it'" (183). Though from a financial standpoint this treatment may seem an improvement on primogeniture's uneven distribution of resources, it, too, sacrifices filial feeling and individual desire for a parent's unilateral will; equal expenditure, which Mrs. Gibson claims to "'owe [her]self,'" pits her desires against Molly's, silencing Molly's voice, disregarding her wishes as "'a selfish fancy,'" and erasing her history by removing "cherished relics of her mother's" (183).

The struggle over resources, a struggle that the novel depicts in both economic and sexual terms, threatens even the newfound affection that Molly feels for her new stepsister—"a companion, a girl, a sister her own age!"—the one part of her father's re-marriage that brings her joy at the outset (213). Cynthia "captivate[s] Molly" and everyone else she meets, and the two immediately become close (216). Although Cynthia's "intimacy" is "superficial" (414), and she is at least initially "not capable of returning [...] true love" (331),[30] their asymmetry of feeling is only part of the problem with Molly and Cynthia's relationship, which is threatened more profoundly by sexual competition. This too has Darwinian echoes: while "sexual selection," for Darwin, entails more than competition, such competition is certainly part of the process whereby individuals vie for mates through courtship, at times even at the cost of their own survival.[31] Though she is seemingly unaware of her own romantic feelings toward him, Molly triangulates

narrative time (60, 95, 109, 61; see also 320). As this essay will go on to discuss, Darwin's natural selection also operates, at least with "social animals [...] for the benefit of the community" (87), rather than purely individual success.

[30] The novel reiterates that Cynthia cannot match Molly's depth of feeling with respect to affection (219) or even (as Molly informs Mr. Preston), hate (481).

[31] For Darwin in the first edition of *Origin*, sexual selection is typically "a struggle between the males for possession of the females" in which failure results in "few or no offspring" (88). Sexual selection does not always guarantee and in some cases actually compromises survival, however. Darwin's later

78 IMAGINING WOMEN'S PROPERTY IN VICTORIAN FICTION

her affection for her new stepsister around Roger when he becomes engaged to Cynthia before departing for Africa as a naturalist: "'I think if she were really wicked, and I did not love her at all, I should feel bound to watch over her, he loves her so dearly'" (520). Here and elsewhere, Molly's regard for Cynthia takes Roger as a reference point. When she tells her stepsister, "'I love you doubly because he has honoured you with his love'" (377), she highlights her inability to separate out her feelings for each.[32] Such unconscious competition seems to compromise the directness of the women's regard for each other even as it may appear to amplify their emotion.

But Molly's love for Roger does not actually "doubl[e]" her love for Cynthia; on the contrary, Gaskell's novel emphasizes the ways in which competition threatens these women's relationship and eventually Molly's own marital future, despite its insistence that neither Molly nor Cynthia initially understands Molly's feelings for Roger (e.g., 354, 377, 549). As soon as her new stepsister has met Roger, Molly feels "uneasy" (242) around Cynthia, uncomfortable with the difference in Roger's manner to them, aware "of Roger's attraction" to Cynthia (310), "angry" in her knowledge "that Cynthia did not love him" (354), and "uneas[y]" about "Cynthia's ways and manners about Roger" after their engagement (411). Roger alone strains both the bond between the girls and even the relational language that associates them: "Molly's love for Cynthia was fast and unwavering, but if anything tried it, it was the habit Roger had fallen into of always calling Cynthia Molly's sister in speaking to the latter. From anyone else it would have been a matter of indifference to her [...], it vexed both ear and heart when Roger used the expression" (312). Love and sisterhood alike falter in the struggle presented by Gaskell's rendition of sexual selection. The narrative, picking up on Molly's feelings, reflects on her "keen insight into her 'sister's' heart" (354), Gaskell's quotation marks reflecting the relational tension brought about by Roger's presence as well as the distinction Molly makes in her feelings for each as she observes Cynthia's actions: "'I am his sister,'" she would say to herself. [...] I must wait and watch, and see if I can do anything for my brother'" (354).[33] Though she

---

writing details other examples of self-destructive courtship rivalry in which a bird "will sometimes sing till he drops down dead" or birds engaged in a dancing competition may "become so absorbed that a skillful archer may shoot nearly the whole party." See Charles Darwin, *The Descent of Man* [1871], ed. James Moore and Adrian Desmond (London: Penguin Books Ltd., 2004): 418, 446. Darwin also notes in a later edition of *Origin* that certain favored traits in sexual selection, such as the peacock's long and ornamental tail feathers, would be injurious for the group's survival if passed to female descendants. See *Descent* 498 n. 1 and Charles Darwin, *On the Origin of Species by Means of Natural Selection, or the Preservation of Favoured Races in the Struggle for Life,* 4th ed., with additions and corrections (London: John Murray, 1866): 241: https://catalog.hathitrust.org/Record/011619025/Home.

[32] See Corbett, *Family Likeness* 165.

[33] On tensions between sisters, see Helena Michie, *Sororophobia: Differences among Women in Literature and Culture* (New York: Oxford University Press, 1992); for female friendship facilitating heterosexual union, see Marcus 79, 84; for the relationship of marriage to adoptive kinships see Corbett, e.g., 154–5, 170–3.

MONEY, MUTUALITY, AND DARWINIAN SURVIVAL 79

repeatedly avows love for her stepsister (485), at times, as she "chafe[s]" against Roger's "entrap[ment]," she seems to love more by compulsion than consent: "she could not help loving Cynthia, come what would" (346). When she sacrifices her own reputation in order to help Cynthia break her prior engagement to Mr. Preston—a sacrifice that risks Molly's conjugal prospects—she keeps silent less for Cynthia's promise of eternal love and gratitude (477) than "in thoughts of Roger – how he would feel, what he would say" (475). Pondering (with some unconscious malice) whether she should "conceal it from him" even though "she felt how it would disturb his love for Cynthia" (475), she embarks on the task "almost more pitiful to her friend's great distress and possible disgrace, *than able to give her that love which involves perfect sympathy*" (478, emphasis mine). The tension between Molly and Cynthia sharpens immediately after the engagement and again right before its dissolution, when both long for a privacy—"'Leave me alone'" (545, see also 376)—that their lives and relationship do not usually permit.

For much of the narrative, then, this romantic triangle—sexual competition, a struggle over affective resources—threatens Cynthia and Molly's "unwavering" love. Divided in their interests and feelings, they are no more "able to give [each other] that love which involves perfect sympathy" (478) than Squire and Mrs. Hamley. Dependence, obligation, generosity, competition: each of these unequal models entails an understanding of relationships as involving two discrete beings with separate resources, separate needs, and separate interests. Gaskell's novel suggests that none of them allows for "that love which involves perfect sympathy" and which permits communal loss or communal gain. Yet such sympathy of interest and feeling, *Wives and Daughters* insists, is a necessary component of successful interpersonal intimacy, both in friendship and in marriage. It is no coincidence that the strains in Molly and Cynthia's relationship come into view just as it becomes evident to Molly that "her father was not satisfied with [his new] wife" (410). If the prospect of marriage troubles female friendship, it also provides a provocative parallel. Molly and Cynthia, like Mr. and Mrs. Gibson, reveal that ideal forms of intimacy cannot exist when one person thinks of her welfare as separate from another's. Mr. Gibson assumes, in keeping with coverture's ideology, that marriage will merge two people's disparate interests, that his wife "'and I [should be] one in all [...] respects,'" and that she "'cannot do a dishonourable act without my being inculpated in the disgrace'" (383). His assumption, naïve as it appears within the novel, is irrevocably overturned when Mrs. Gibson eavesdrops on her husband's medical consultation and attempts to benefit from the information she gathers, "'betray[ing] a professional secret'" and "'trad[ing] on that knowledge'" (383) as she speculates on her daughter's marital options. Both Mr. Gibson's claims to private property in professional knowledge and Mrs. Gibson's desire to benefit her daughter at the expense of her husband's integrity reveal their conflicting economic and affective interests, though this seems to surprise only him. In their naivete about marriage, the professional men of the

80   IMAGINING WOMEN'S PROPERTY IN VICTORIAN FICTION

novel—medical doctor Gibson as well as scientist Roger—are revealed to have less practical intelligence than the self-interested Mrs. Gibson, who assesses Roger as "'A great awkward fellow [...], who looks as if he did not know two and two made four, for all he is such a mathematical genius'" (235). Though she underestimates Roger in many ways, her comment obliquely points to the folly of marital math under coverture, which assumes that one plus one can somehow equal one.

Mr. Gibson's disillusionment as he realizes that he and his new wife make two, not one, responds in part to the wave of marital reforms that were perceived as threatening the "one-flesh" doctrine of coverture and that would have been within the scope of Gaskell's knowledge, though not Mr. Gibson's in the 1820s. The Matrimonial Causes Act of 1857 made divorce available to the middle classes, and the 1856 petition for the reform of married women's property rights, as we have seen, sparked a wave of debate about wives' economic and legal autonomy which culminated in the 1870 and 1882 Married Women's Property Acts.[34] Opponents of these property reforms decried separate spousal interests, suggesting that giving women the right to hold independent wealth within marriage would threaten marital harmony. The fact that *Wives and Daughters*, in 1866, makes Mr. Gibson's unifying ideal the more "honorable" position here suggests, to a certain extent, the novel's discomfort with his wife's autonomous actions, a discomfort seemingly incompatible with the property reform Gaskell supported when she added her name to more than twenty-six thousand others petitioning for married women's independent financial rights.[35] Yet the Gibson scenario nonetheless forms an important part of Gaskell's criticism of contemporary marital arrangements and her call for a different kind of reform. It shows, first, that coverture was already a failed doctrine. Since, as she suggests, the spousal dissonance feared by opponents of property reform was already present, it could not be blamed solely on legislative change. It further emphasizes the difficulty of translating legal directive into marital practice. As Victorian fiction reiterates time and time again, the unity mandated by the "one-flesh" common law doctrine of coverture could not guarantee—and often hindered—the "perfect sympathy" that in theory bound spouses together as one.[36] By showcasing the failure of legal models, then, the Gibson union points to problems with existing marriage law along with the need for extralegal resolution. Finally, Gaskell demonstrates these marital ideals and disappointments in a way that makes them analogous to the failed expectations of other relationships, including sibling friendship: Molly's reluctant dealings with Mr. Preston on Cynthia's behalf entail a similar division of economic interest, as

---

[34] Shanley, e.g., 14; Rappoport, "Wives and Sons: Coverture, Primogeniture, and Married Women's Property," in *BRANCH: Britain, Representation and Nineteenth-Century History*, ed. Dino Franco Felluga. Extension of *Romanticism and Victorianism on the Net* (Web, Nov. 30, 2015).

[35] See Holcombe 72–3, Leighton and Surridge 487–501, 489–90.

[36] See Rachel Ablow, "'One Flesh'"; Shanley, *Feminism* 8–9, 12.

she agrees, despite misgivings, to secret meetings and financial exchanges in order to release her stepsister from financial liability. In both instances, those of marriage and of friendship, separate interests threaten the "perfect sympathy" that the novel idealizes but also presents as generally out of reach. Through these parallel cases, Gaskell underscores her own vision of relational unity, one not limited to marital relationships or dependent upon Parliamentary acts. Though *Wives and Daughters* does not seek the legislative rights that became central to feminist claims or demand the improvement of women's independent lives in the terms we best recognize today, the novel offers us another mode of seeing how Victorian literature was recognizing deficiencies within marriage and other relationships and calling for change. It challenges us to see as reformist, albeit in different ways, the alternative, interpersonal solutions it offers in the face of real skepticism about the power of legal change. *Wives and Daughters* suggests that intimacy itself required adjustment. In Gaskell's novel, as the rest of this chapter will argue, a better model of sibling friendship showcases the economic and affective practices of the "perfect sympathy" that so many relationships appear to lack. Through it, she insists that successful intimacy, whether marital or non-marital, requires the common interest that fiction can imagine, as much or more than any mandates by the common law.

II. "Going Together Will Make the Enjoyment": Accounting for Common Interest

Attaining "perfect sympathy" seems a tall order, however, since common interest is often at odds with the struggle for survival (financial, sexual, affective) that so much of the novel's social world charts and provokes. Marriage secures a livelihood, not a soulmate, for Hyacinth Kirkpatrick, and friendship—no matter how meaningful it becomes—is as much a function of proximity as of any real compatibility. Molly and Cynthia are thrown together as companions following their parents' marriage, and none of the other young women who make brief appearances at card games or balls are ever treated as even potential friends for either. The Hamley brothers similarly "knew but few young men of [their] own standing in the county" (250); as Anna Unsworth has noted, the squire's "refusal to entertain their social equals [...] means that they do not feel able to accept invitations,"[37] thereby limiting the relationships they are able to form until, in the course of the narrative, they develop other romantic and professional attachments. Though the brothers are not friends by default alone, their friendship makes a virtue of necessity in a setting that makes friends as rare as romantic partners and

---

[37] Anna Unsworth, "Some Social Themes in *Wives and Daughters*, I: Education, Science, and Heredity," *Gaskell Society Journal* 4 (1990): 40–51, 45.

82 IMAGINING WOMEN'S PROPERTY IN VICTORIAN FICTION

other desirable objects. The insularity of friendship (between siblings and step-siblings, with few outside reinforcements) reflects the conditions of scarcity and competition that fascinate Gaskell in this novel.

As we will see, the close relationship between Osborne and Roger Hamley provides *Wives and Daughters* with its most successful model of interpersonal intimacy, one that has important ramifications for the novel's treatment of both sibling friendship and marriage. While the brothers' longstanding love has many factors, their intimacy within the plot is intertwined with their economic relationship. The way in which Osborne and Roger treat the common interest of their material circumstances both reflects and helps to produce the unusual degree of "perfect sympathy" that they have with one another.

Before we meet Osborne and Roger, they are framed as rivals, competing for their parents' affections and resources. The "heir of the Hamleys" and his brother sustain themselves on vastly unequal monetary allowances (192, 258) as well as vastly unequal expectations: Osborne is reputed to be both "'beautiful'" (65) and "'a bit of a genius'" (73), while Roger "'was never to be compared with him'" on either point (65). In fact, the brothers, like Molly and Cynthia, are incessantly compared. Miss Phoebe Browning moves almost instantly from admiring Roger ("'Such a fine-looking young man'") to privileging his unseen brother: "'And yet they all say Mr. Osborne is the handsomest'" (166). Mrs. Gibson sets them against each other more severely: "'I do like that Osborne Hamley! [...] The other is but a loutish young fellow, to my mind'" (182). Before meeting either, Molly prepares to hate the younger brother who comes bearing the elder's sad report: "Her unconscious fealty to Osborne was not in the least shaken by his having come to grief at Cambridge. Only she was indignant—with or without reason—against Roger, who seemed to have brought the reality of bad news as an offering of first-fruits on his return home" (85). Despite the narrator's hint that appreciating one brother may not afford "reason" for resenting another, characters and critics frequently pit them against each other.[38]

Even when a turn of events reverses the brothers' status—Osborne's university failure, financial debt, and illness subordinating him to Roger, who successfully navigates his mathematical examinations and new scientific opportunities—they remain subject to comparison, though the preference shifts. Squire Hamley, frustrated with Osborne, goes to Roger for comfort, measuring them against each other with the reflection that Roger is "'twice as much a son to me as Osborne'" (367). Mrs. Gibson similarly turns to Roger as the target of her marital plotting when she determines that Osborne's poor health might actually make his brother heir instead (380). The legal framework of primogeniture means that one brother's hold on specific property entails the other's inability to hold that same

---

[38] E.g., Panek 128, 142, 147; Leighton and Surridge 488.

MONEY, MUTUALITY, AND DARWINIAN SURVIVAL 83

property. In this financial sense, with brothers, as with fathers and sons, one's gain is the other's loss. Yet Gaskell's novel refuses to privilege this struggle as the most important relation between the Hamley brothers. Not only does *Wives and Daughters* create the material conditions that could conceivably allow both sons and their offspring to flourish financially—Osborne as heir, Roger as self-made man of science—but it also rejects competition as the primary way to view these men. Instead, it implicitly argues in the words of Mr. Gibson's more direct protest to the disappointed squire, that "'we may praise one without hitting at the other'" (367). By doing so, *Wives and Daughters* grants the brothers sufficient freedom from competition to enable what it understands or promotes as the "perfect sympathy" of true love. The brothers' relationship thus offers a model of good rapport that both allows us to understand the subsequent shift in female friendship, when relations improve between Molly and Cynthia, and forms a prototype for considering successful marital union.

For, despite the comparisons to which the Hamley brothers are subjected by everyone else and which, incidentally, parenting experts describe as precisely the way to create lifelong rancor between siblings,[39] they maintain a remarkably noncompetitive friendship by ignoring outside influences in favor of their own bond. Molly's initial impulse to pit them against each other ceases as soon as she sees them together, when she "intercepted a glance between the two brothers—a look of true confidence and love, *which suddenly made her like them both under the aspect of relationship*—new to her observation" (168, emphasis mine). This relationship shapes Roger and Osborne alike, reinforcing their ties apart from any external influences, and Molly learns that any judgement of them has to take these ties into account. Mr. Gibson, too, recognizes that "'whatever those lads may be to others, there's as strong a brotherly love as ever I saw, between the two'" (196). Instead of resenting Osborne's favored position, "Roger in his boyhood had loved Osborne too well to be jealous" (369). When Osborne falls into debt to provide a home for Aimée, the "'thoroughly good'" but also French, working-class, and Catholic woman he has secretly married in defiance of his father's approval, prejudice, and longstanding plans for him (494), Roger becomes his brother's most ardent supporter. Defending his character (202–3), he takes it upon himself to provide both Osborne and his wife with material means. Without a thought toward the unequal allowance they had previously received from their parents, Roger enthusiastically refers to his forthcoming fellowship income as belonging to them both: "'we'll have a purse in common'" (303). Osborne understands that "as long as Roger had a penny his brother was sure to have half of it" (332). Some see Roger's contributions to the household as primarily self-beneficial, but even if, as Leighton and Surridge suggest, Roger is "a man of productive credit who invests

---

[39] E.g., Adele Faber and Elaine Mazlish, *Siblings without Rivalry: How to Help Your Children Live Together So You Can Live Too* (New York: W. W. Norton & Company, Inc., 2012).

84   IMAGINING WOMEN'S PROPERTY IN VICTORIAN FICTION

his intellectual capital [...] in order to support Osborne's family and to re-finance the work of improving the estate," self-serving economic questions of future "interest" and "return [on] the capital" appear far less important to Roger than those of family care (353).[40]

Significantly, those motives, which might be relevant with regard to the estate improvements he funds for his father, do not arise at all in the context of maintaining Osborne and his wife.

Eschewing financial formulations of credit, debt, and economic competition as well as expectations that gifts will keep one person dependent or produce obligation and reciprocity, Roger's generosity appears less as an exchange, even one formulated in terms of reciprocal gifts, and more as a merger, the "purse in common" standing in for an intimacy that appears to leave little room for a division of interest despite facilitating individuality: "He reserved enough of money for his own personal needs, which were small, and for the ready furtherance of any project he might see fit to undertake; the rest of his income was Osborne's; *given and accepted in the spirit which made the bond between these two brothers so rarely perfect*" (347, emphasis mine). Not only does Roger give to his brother, but he then understands that money as equally Osborne's, not as the means of establishing his brother's financial or other dependence on him but as an extension of their bond. Roger tells Osborne of the upcoming travel required by his professional pursuits, "reddening as if he had been accused of spending another's money instead of his own" (353). Having a "purse in common" here means not that he shares his wealth with his brother but, importantly, that he views that money as no more his own than it is Osborne's.

He also works hard to ensure that he does not inadvertently take anything from his brother. Overriding Osborne's confidence in him, a confidence—"'I can trust you as I can myself'"—which speaks to their "perfect sympathy" of feeling and interest, Roger goes to what Osborne calls "'a great deal of trouble, unnecessary trouble, and unnecessary expense'" to ensure that Osborne and Aimée's marriage was entirely legal so that their (unborn) child will legitimately inherit the Hamley estate, in the event of Osborne's death (351, 352). He sees Osborne's advantage as his own and makes it a point to secure it. Although some of their shared desire is about keeping property away from the "'Irish Hamleys'" (352), Roger is equally adamant that the estate follow in his brother's line rather than come to him. When Osborne does die, Roger's first work, utterly incomprehensible to Mrs. Gibson and others who see the siblings in terms of competition and struggle (638), "was to put his brother's child at once into his rightful and legal place" (590). This "rightful and legal place" as heir in a system of primogeniture emerges from the brothers' affective, economic collaboration and suggests a way to celebrate the inheritance of a first-born son.

---

[40]   Leighton and Surridge 498.

As I have discussed, early debates about marital property reform worked to decouple primogeniture from coverture in assessments of women's financial circumstances. Gaskell, like Dickens, keeps the common law doctrine of primogeniture in place even as she alters the spirit around it. In addition to revising intergenerational conflict, offering Osborne's son an inheritance free from the competition or struggle that we saw with Osborne and Squire Hamley (or, in the case of *Our Mutual Friend*, between the Harmons senior and junior), she also makes this depiction of a son's gains newly compatible with a wife's interests. I'll return to the important ways in which Roger and Osborne's collaborative model actually speaks to coverture's distribution of property and the financial interests of middle- or upper-class women. Here, however, we see how Gaskell (again like Dickens) positions a working-class woman's financial needs in terms of protection, not rights. In the decade before the first Married Women's Property Act, which gave working women ownership of their own earnings, arguments for their rights to property emphasized their need for security. Gaskell's discussion of Osborne's wife Aimée similarly incorporates this working woman into discourses on property not through concern over any separate rights she might desire but by emphasizing her need for financial protection, first by Osborne, whose poetry fails to provide an income, then by Roger, who provides for them both, and subsequently by the Squire, who hopes to "'make [her] comfortable for life in her own country'" (568) before finally accepting her as a daughter of the house. Aimée will not assert herself or lay claim to property rights on the basis of having married or produced an heir. Making no demands at all for herself, Osborne's grief-stricken widow is roused into action only to care for her son (574, 577, 628), or, later, to express her sense of Roger's "'goodness'" and "brotherly friendliness" (629, 628). In Aimée's case, Gaskell not only aligns primogeniture's care for the heir with a wife's interest but also distinguishes the rights of working-class women, who were seen as requiring protection, from the rights of wealthier women; as we'll see shortly, the novel implies that this latter group might benefit more directly from the forms of economic collaboration modeled by Roger and Osborne.

Critics who recognize Roger's remarkable generosity and kindness to his brother and to his brother's surviving wife and child attribute these traits to the same science that, they claim, also provides the basis for the brothers' evolutionary struggle for fitness. Anne DeWitt, for instance, argues that Roger exemplifies popular Victorian ideas of scientific morality, resembling Darwin, Isaac Newton, and Étienne Geoffroy Saint-Hilaire as much in character (or at least in widespread representations of their character) as he does in scientific theory.[41] Roger's ability to be a "faithful friend" has been attributed to contemporary representations of

---

[41] DeWitt 1–18, 2–3; see also Leighton and Surridge 498.

86 IMAGINING WOMEN'S PROPERTY IN VICTORIAN FICTION

specific scientific men, to new developments in professional "fraternities,"[42] and to Darwinian interpretations of his personality; his altruism is thus a "survival strateg[y]," while "[s]ympathy was a scientific skill," both offering him a competitive edge in evolutionary struggle.[43] Showing how Roger's rational and emotional strengths work together, these arguments explain the Hamley brothers' friendship from the side of the "successful" brother and his relation to the same scientific frameworks that presumably elevate him above Osborne professionally as well as physically and morally; Roger, according to these ideas, is a kind and loyal friend *in spite of* "the opposition established between Roger and his brother."[44]

Yet Osborne, despite his inability or lack of desire to compete and long before he stands to benefit materially from his younger brother's success, is also a kind and loyal friend to Roger. The bond that both Molly and Mr. Gibson recognize, is, importantly, "*between* the two" (168, 196, my emphasis), not unidirectional. If Osborne, by the time we meet him, has less to offer Roger from a material or intellectual standpoint, this seems to be beside the point; even in the Gibson and Hamley marriages, disparities of wealth before marriage are far less significant than the kinds of common interest or the "spirit" of "giv[ing] and accept[ing]" that fail to appear in those unions but strengthen the bonds of the brothers. If Osborne makes no financial contribution to their common purse, he certainly meets Roger with regard to affection, speaking about his brother "in a warm, longing kind of way" (206) with the forms of generosity that are still available to him: "[E]very word, every inflexion of the voice breathed out affection and respect—nay, even admiration!" (235) Cynthia, whose talent for observing people matches Rogers's for observing the rest of the natural world, notes that Roger "'is the one subject on which Osborne Hamley becomes enthusiastic'" (235). The readiness with which he confides in his brother is a sign that he, like Roger, considers their interests undivided (261). Osborne takes pride in Roger's growing fame as "'a first-rate fellow'" (301). Osborne may struggle somewhat more with the comparison—he "strove against any feeling of envy or jealousy with all his might; but his efforts were conscious" (369)—but "the brotherly affection [was] so true between Osborne and Roger" (369) that it prompts such valiant efforts, despite Osborne's characterization as generally "too indolent to keep up an unassisted conscience" (352). Even then, Osborne reserves his resentment for his own failures, not for his brother's burgeoning success, "a sting of self-reproach mingling with his generous pride in his brother" (301). Osborne struggles with himself, not his brother, despite the prevailing opinion of critics and characters

---

[42] Karen Boiko, "Reading and (Re)Writing Class: Elizabeth Gaskell's *Wives and Daughters,*" *Victorian Literature and Culture* 33.1 (2005): 85–106, 94; also DeWitt 11; Lisieux Huelman, "The (Feminist) Epistemology of the Nineteenth-Century Periodical Press: Professional Men in Elizabeth Gaskell's *Wives and Daughters,*" *Nineteenth-Century Gender Studies* 5.2 (2009): para. 17.

[43] Debrabant 17; Endersby 300; see also Endersby 305, 312 and Poon, "Popular" 196, 199, 202.

[44] DeWitt 7.

that he and Roger are competing. He "wins" when he is able to be generous to both, managing, as Mr. Gibson recommends, to "'praise one without hitting at the other'" (367) when Roger secures employment in order to address the Hamleys' financial needs. "'Roger, you're the providence of the family,' exclaimed Osborne, suddenly struck by admiration at his brother's conduct, and forgetting to contrast it with his own" (353). Their "true[st]" intimacy apparently lies in this forgetfulness of self: recognizing their interest as the *family*'s interest, rather something individual, brings them closer to "perfect sympathy" with one another.

And this is where, in assessing the different economic model Gaskell presents, scholarship on this novel also needs to emphasize a different aspect of Darwinian thought. Darwin was famously interested in interdependence, not just individuals, mutuality, not just competition.[45] He marvels, toward the end of *Origin of Species* (1859), at "an entangled bank, clothed with many plants of many kinds, with birds singing on the bushes, with various insects flitting about, and with worms crawling through the damp earth, and [...reflects] that these elaborately constructed forms, so different from each other, and dependent on each other in so complex a manner, have all been produced by laws acting around us."[46] Of more particular use for our understanding of *Wives and Daughters*, Darwin describes this complex entangling or interdependence with "enthusiastic admiration" in his observations of the "Cell-making instinct of the Hive-Bee," noting "that a multitude of bees all work together; [...] a score of individuals work even at the commencement of the first cell. [...] The work of construction seems to be a sort of balance struck between many bees, all instinctively standing at the same relative distance from each other, all trying to sweep equal spheres, and then building up, or leaving ungnawed, the planes of intersection between these spheres."[47] Like understanding the construction process of Darwin's bees, accounting for the relationship "between the two" requires attention to the Hamley brothers' shared investment in a "common" interest, not just one-sided assessments of scientific character, survival strategies, admiration, or generosity, though all of those points contribute to Gaskell's picture of "true" friendship and affection. "[S]o different from each other, and dependent on each other in so complex a manner," the Hamley brothers "give [...] and accept [...]" according to their "perfect bond," rather than according to the evolutionary doctrine of struggle or the common law doctrine of primogeniture, whereby one brother gains at the other's expense. Their relationship rejects competition, whether economic, legal, or evolutionary.

---

[45] Claudia C. Klaver notes that John Stuart Mill's *Principles of Political Economy* [1848] also discusses "profit-sharing and cooperatives" and remarks on this book's popularity by the 1860s (152–3, 161).

[46] Charles Darwin, *On the Origin of Species by Means of Natural Selection, or the Preservation of Favoured Races in the Struggle for Life* (London: John Murray, 1850), *A Facsimile of the First Edition with an Introduction by Ernst Mayr* (Cambridge, MA: Harvard University Press, 1964): 489.

[47] Darwin, *Origin* 224, 231–2.

88   IMAGINING WOMEN'S PROPERTY IN VICTORIAN FICTION

Importantly, bees in *Wives and Daughters*, as in *Origin*, help to showcase this healthier mutuality and also suggest a more tranquil way of moving beyond individualism, one associated with the Hamleys in general and most strongly with Roger and Molly. During Molly Gibson's first, homesick hours at Hamley Hall, she attends to a "summer silence broken by the song of the birds, and the nearer hum of bees. Listening to these sounds, which enhanced the exquisite sense of stillness [...] Molly forgot herself" (63). In place of "killing" herself for others, she experiences self-forgetfulness here as "exquisite," something that brings her closer to the inhabitants, including Mrs. Hamley, with whom she quickly develops a deep friendship. This version of forgetting oneself, which comes in part with the near "hum of bees," is similar to Osborne's, when he forgets himself in admiration of his brother; the differentiated self with its personal needs and interests remains, but it is not the primary concern. Again, when Roger returns home bearing news of Osborne's difficulties, Molly "sit[s] at the pleasant open window, and los[es] herself in dreamy out-looks into the gardens and woods [...] And there was scarcely a sound out-of-doors but the humming of bees, in the flower-beds below the window" (83). Molly's pleasant, dreamy, movement outside of herself bears little resemblance to the forms of quenching self-loss against which she rebels, and reminds us that individuals need not always be the central figures in narrative.

Roger teaches Molly about these bees and their activities, urging her to "'notice how many bees I saw [....] There are more than two hundred kinds of bees in England, and he wanted me to notice the difference between them and flies'" (149). He lends her books about the shapes of bee hives (267) and, when he brings her the gift of a wasp's nest, helps her to learn about "'the wasps [who] have turned the bees out of [their] hives, taken possession and eaten up the honey'" (165). That Roger cares about the bees, their hives, and their honey suggests this naturalist's interest in (and perhaps affinity for) apian lifestyle. In Darwin's reflections on bees, unknown to Roger in the earlier timeframe of the novel but most likely familiar to Gaskell, "A large store of honey is indispensable to support a large stock of bees during the winter; and the security of the hive is known mainly to depend on a large number of bees being supported."[48] The well-being of all, that is, depends upon the well-being of each member of the community, and shared resources are what make all of this possible. *Our Mutual Friend*'s languid Eugene Wrayburn, inveighing against Mr. Boffin's advice to imitate the bees, misses this key collectivity by focusing on their reputation for labor: "'they work; but don't you think they overdo it?'" (*Our Mutual Friend* 94). In contrast, for Gaskell as for Darwin, the bees' mutuality is the point. Having a store of honey—or, in the case we have seen of Roger and Osborne, a purse—in common is good for the hive (or other kinship networks). The 1820s setting of *Wives and Daughters*, before

---

[48] Darwin, *Origin* 234. For Gaskell's knowledge of Darwin, see Debrabant 14–16.

MONEY, MUTUALITY, AND DARWINIAN SURVIVAL 89

Darwin's voyages on the HMS Beagle in the early 1830s and the 1859 publication of his theories, allows Roger's interests and priorities as a naturalist to stand in for but differently emphasize the evolutionary discoveries Gaskell's generation would witness.

The Hamley brothers' model—the non-competitive, hive-building version of Darwin, the anti-individualist alternative to "economic man"—has ramifications for other sibling friendship in the novel. Cynthia, that keen observer of Osborne and Roger, understands the place she and her mother may hold in Molly's perception. "'I often think what interlopers we must seem, and are in fact—'" (437). Cynthia's comment aligns the stepsister and stepmother with those wasps who intrude upon the bees, "'t[ook] possession, and [ate] up the honey'" (165), interfering with the previously peaceful Gibson hive. Understanding the Hamley brothers' relationship allows us to note a shift in Molly and Cynthia's rapport, as I will address before long. Moreover, it reflects on the changing marital norms of the 1860s, offering a reformist view of how a husband and wife might also "give [...] and accept [...]" in common interest, whether or not they enter their marriage with equivalent wealth or are compensated equivalently for their labor within it. Whereas the lack of "perfect sympathy" in Molly and Cynthia's friendship at least briefly mirrors the rift in the Gibson marriage, the "perfect bond" between Roger and Osborne conversely suggests a better model for friendship and other forms of intimacy, including but not limited to marriage. By suggesting that this model emerges out of 1820s scientific discovery rather than 1850s petitions, the novel to a certain extent attempts to depoliticize marital reforms, proposing them as a natural outgrowth of generational developments rather than partisanship. It also significantly, establishes them as functions of affection rather than law, and makes them the work of readers and writers (such as Gaskell) rather than of legislators: Osborne the poet and Roger the published man of science are initially better poised to model them than Molly and Cynthia, but the stepsisters read Roger's books on "'the different cells of bees'" and both find this suggestive material "'very interesting'" (267).[49]

The "purse in common" which the brothers' affectionate mutuality grants them stands as an extralegal alternative not only to primogeniture but also to the economic unity that coverture decreed for married couples who did not have special financial settlements. Spouses, too, theoretically enjoyed a "purse in common," but only because a woman's property became her husband's upon marriage; she lacked legal access to or determination over that purse. (How often, in Victorian novels, do we see husbands blush over spending wealth they view as belonging equally to their wives?) Just as coverture promised but failed to "cover"

---

[49] For the ability of literature, particularly the novel, "to encourage sympathy" in ways that "resembl[e] the sympathetic influence of the wife" in Victorian domestic ideology, see Rachel Ablow, *The Marriage of Minds*, e.g., 4–7, 14.

90 IMAGINING WOMEN'S PROPERTY IN VICTORIAN FICTION

wives' economic interests, the novel suggests that it promised but failed to unite spousal interests, financial or affective as well. Rather than mandate such unity through law, or approximate it with reciprocal obligations based on credit and debt, dependence and duty, *Wives and Daughters* suggests the need for emotional and financial intimacy grounded on love, trust, and a voluntary pooling of resources. Describing the difference between pooling and reciprocity, anthropologist Marshall Sahlins reminds us that even mutually beneficial reciprocity necessarily "stipulates two sides, two distinct social-economic interests."[50] In sibling relations and friendship, as in marriage, Gaskell asks us to consider what relationships might look like when those interests merge instead, when "persons [...] are cooperatively related."[51] Such a relationship, with a cooperative economic component that need not be limited to matrimony, is distinct from the "companionate" marriages that literary critics and historians have long used in describing the shift to "marital choice" from the seventeenth century on and that, in Talia Schaffer's analysis, have meant everything from amicable partnership to romantic love, usually but not always including affection and never specifying this form of pooled resources.[52] For middle-class women, who had fewer opportunities for the collectivity that the workers of Gaskell's earlier, industrial novels experience, or for the entrepreneurial endeavors that allow younger sons such as Roger to succeed, the stakes of such economic mergers in friendship or marriage were high— particularly in this moment, when Gaskell is imagining their economic agency before, and independent of, legal reform. If Osborne's working-class wife receives protection rather than a shared purse, Roger's own future wife is from the professional class that this novel takes greater pains to explore, and it suggests that she, like his brother, might be able to count on relations of greater mutuality.

As the Gibson and Hamley marriages suggest, *Wives and Daughters* calls into question the "one-flesh" doctrine, highlighting changing expectations for marriage and the need to underwrite any legal tie with the same bond of "perfect sympathy" that it advocates for friendship and sibling relations. Even while Lady Cumnor preaches wifely subordination of reverence and conformity, the novel quickly overturns such marital platitudes: "It was as well that Lord Cumnor was not amongst the audience; or he might have compared precept with practice" (606). Again, Gaskell shows that conventional, legal models of marital subordination, like those of marital interest, can prove fictitious.

---

[50] For pooling, the material side of "collectivity," see Marshall Sahlins, *Stone Age Economics* (Chicago: Aldine & Atherton, Inc., 1972): 189; for mutually beneficial reciprocity, such as the "reciprocal altruism" that George Levine describes, see *Darwin Loves* 212.

[51] Ibid. Here we might also think of the cooperative kitchen that Gaskell's John Thornton and Nicholas Higgins experiment with toward the end of her earlier novel, *North and South*.

[52] Schaffer, *Romance's Rival* 26–7. Schaffer cites Lawrence Stone's definition of companionate marriage as "settled and well-tried mutual affection" on 47. Schaffer distinguishes between rival forces of familial affection and romantic love in her analysis, though her focus remains on marriage. See, e.g., 8.

MONEY, MUTUALITY, AND DARWINIAN SURVIVAL 91

Challenging common-law visions of marriage in which a wife's interests can be entirely covered by or merged in her husband's, but also seeking to eliminate "sides," Gaskell nonetheless preserves one traditional principle of Victorian marriage within her most exemplary relationship: gender complementarity, as an alternative to competition. In this vein, Osborne's feminization, often discussed in terms of his similarities to his mother and his hereditary failure in the struggle against the sturdier and in some ways more conventionally masculine Roger,[53] might be seen in terms of his heteronormatized compatibility with Roger instead. Gaskell, after all, attributes his openness with Roger to "the feminine part of his character [which] made him always desirous of a confidant" (261). Within a marital context such complementarity is in some respects highly conservative: their gendering suggests their potential enactment of Victorian domestic ideology, whereby assumptions of separate spheres policed gender differences, gender expression, and gender inequalities.[54] Yet through Osborne, Gaskell also offers a more fluid conception of gendered identity,[55] and within the context of the brothers' friendship, Osborne's feminization allows Gaskell to articulate a form of intimacy based on mutuality rather than competition or independence. This model is not about granting women (or feminized men) their own, private property. Again, Gaskell's vision for improved conditions of intimacy and mutual financial agency differs significantly from the reforms that the Married Women's Property Acts would go on to enact. But it argues against coverture and similarly unequal relationships in other ways. For example, Gaskell uses the bond between Osborne and Roger to reject a fundamental aspect of separate spheres ideology, that of influence. Proponents of separate spheres such as Ellis had long justified domestic ideology based on the idea that, in the absence of legal rights, a wife's power (economic, political, moral) derived from her ability to positively influence her husband; other writers, such as Anne Brontë in *Tenant of Wildfell Hall*, had shown the devastating results of wives counting on such influence.[56] In *Wives and Daughters*, Gaskell invokes the idea of "influence" within the Hamley brothers'

---

[53] For the novel's feminization of Osborne, see 74, 167, and 392. Critical discussions include James Najarian, "'Mr. Osbourne's Secret': Elizabeth Gaskell, *Wives and Daughters*, and the Gender of Romanticism," in *Romantic Echoes in the Victorian Era*, ed. Andrew Radford and Mark Sandy (Aldershot: Ashgate, 2008): 85–101, 93. For Osborne's resemblance to his mother and his socialization to replace a deceased daughter, see Panek 46; for Roger as paternal, see Poon, "Popular" 202. Endersby notes that sympathy, though "increasingly [...] regarded as a feminine virtue," was also important "to *male* naturalists requir[ing] us to rethink the way gender roles were negotiated in Victorian natural history"; according to him, Roger's "unusual sensitivity" and his "manly qualities" go hand in hand (300, emphasis original).

[54] For the relationship of Darwin's thought to similarly conservative ideas of gender and gender roles, see Smith, "Introduction" 217.

[55] Despite his feminization, Osborne produces a hearty son (573, 575); see Panek 148.

[56] Anne Brontë, *Tenant* 126, 129, 222. See also Doreen Thierauf, "Guns and Blood: Reading *The Tenant of Wildfell Hall* in the Age of #MeToo," Special Issue: Victorian Literature in the Age of #MeToo, ed. Lana L. Dalley and Kellie Holzer, *Nineteenth-Century Gender Studies* 16.2 (2020): paras. 23, 6, and 11.

92   IMAGINING WOMEN'S PROPERTY IN VICTORIAN FICTION

relationship more than once not to praise or denounce it but simply to deny its place in intimacy or economic equality. "'[M]uch as he loves me,'" Roger explains, "'I've but little influence over him, or else he would tell my father all'" (203). Or, again, though Osborne "never did conceal anything long from Roger," we also learn that "Roger's opinion had no effect on Osborne's actions; and Roger knew this full well" (261). But this is not a problem for their relationship. Roger may occasionally sigh over the negative consequences of his brother's decisions (203), but they don't appear to affect the brothers' bond or easy communication. Even their mutual acknowledgment of independent thought—Roger telling his brother frankly "'you know, old boy, you don't follow out my advice when you've got it'" and Osborne responding with equal frankness, "'Not always, I know. Not when it does not agree with my own opinion'" (261)—does nothing to shake their shared interests, intimacy, or wealth-sharing. In this way, Gaskell's novel challenges the premise that "influence" is a necessary or effective strategy within relationships. The brothers' relationship indicates that the pooling of resources within relationships should be a function of love, not power, and along similar lines suggests that marrying with the hope of influencing a partner relies on a false idea of control that should be exchanged for something closer to joint decision making or collaboration.

The ideal of common interest that helps to explain the Hamley brothers' own friendship also helps us to understand developments in the novel's primary female friendship. We see hints of it during Roger's second meeting with Cynthia, when he asks if she will attend an upcoming charity ball with Molly.

> For the first time during this little conversation she glanced up at him—real honest pleasure shining out of her eyes.
>
> "Yes; going together will make the enjoyment of the thing. It would be dull without her."
>
> "You are great friends, then?" he asked.
>
> "I never thought I should like anyone so much,—any girl I mean."
>
> She put in the final reservation in all simplicity of heart; and in all simplicity did he understand it.   (268–9)

Here, friendship with Molly affords Cynthia "real honest pleasure"—not common in her daily pursuit of admiration—and gives Roger something more substantial than Cynthia's captivating beauty to justify his growing regard for her. The connection to Molly that Cynthia expresses here is not expressed in the terms of erotic attraction, but its strength ("'I never thought I should like anyone so much'") is made parallel to the courtship plots that the novel charts ("'any girl I mean'"). It serves as another reminder that, as Talia Schaffer has suggested in her study of the "familiar" marriages that rivaled romance, siblinghood, friendship, or

MONEY, MUTUALITY, AND DARWINIAN SURVIVAL 93

other relationships might have felt as important as heterosexual love for some Victorians.[57] The rivalry works both ways: as we have seen, heterosexual love also threatens the stepsisters' friendship. Later in the novel, after Cynthia is no longer engaged to Roger, we are better able to see the two girls (as Molly earlier learned to see Roger and Osborne) "under the aspect of relationship" (168), one deeper and more direct than their previously "uneasy" rapport. After wearing herself out tending to the grief-stricken Hamleys, Molly becomes seriously ill, and when Cynthia learns this she immediately leaves a pleasurable London vacation and a new suitor to nurse her. The "inarticulate sounds of love" Molly utters at her arrival "sank deep into Cynthia's heart" (586). If Cynthia's emotion now takes deeper root than her earlier, "superficial depth of affection and intimacy," Molly, in her turn, experiences her stepsister's return with "delight" and "pleasure" that appear to have no immediate reference to Roger (586).

Even more important than the new depth or delight of their feelings for one another, however, is the way that Molly and Cynthia begin to develop common interest in place of their earlier competition. Just as Roger and Osborne demonstrate their "perfect bond" in part through shared income, the "purse in common" that both reflects and also ensures their continued mutuality, the stepsisters' developing relationship appears most tellingly in terms of shared benefit, in this case through gifts. Leighton and Surridge, observing that "success or failure in this most Darwinian of Gaskell's novels extends beyond bloodlines to money," measure Gaskell's characters in terms of the credit-debt relations that characterize the period's market economy.[58] Along these lines, they draw attention to the "handsome" (albeit "dull") wedding present that Lady Cumnor gives Cynthia (608): in addition to a luxuriously bound bible and prayer-book, Cynthia receives "a collection of household account-books, at the beginning of which Lady Cumnor wrote down with her own hand the proper weekly allowance of bread, butter, eggs, meat, and groceries per head, with the London prices of the articles, so that the most inexperienced housekeeper might ascertain if her expenditure exceeded her means" (608). Lady Cumnor's intrusion into Cynthia's future household—reminiscent of Lady Catherine de Bourgh's "familiar [...] and minute [...]" inquiries and advice regarding Charlotte's domestic concerns in Austen's *Pride and Prejudice*—similarly suggests "that nothing was beneath this great Lady's attention, which could furnish her with an occasion of dictating to others" (*Pride and Prejudice* 109). Leighton and Surridge, noting the conflation of Cynthia's sexual and financial credit in her matrimonial dealings, comment on her need for "the very proper present" (611). More remarkable to me about this scene, however, is the way that it highlights a traditional form of accounting—allowance per person, expenditure versus means—mainly to undermine it. Not only does the

[57] Schaffer, *Romance's Rival*, e.g., 13, 36–8, 156, 166.
[58] Leighton and Surridge 488, 498.

94   IMAGINING WOMEN'S PROPERTY IN VICTORIAN FICTION

novel align this accounting with a Lady simultaneously nosy and out of touch with the people she wishes to manage, it also strongly suggests that such management tips will be ignored: Cynthia receives the gift "without testifying any very great delight or gratitude" (611). Gaskell offers this impersonal and undesired present to showcase Cynthia's contrasting response to another, less material gift, the offer of hospitality for Molly, who is still too ill to travel to London for Cynthia's wedding. The bride gives no indication that she will ever open, much less learn from the account books and prayer aids of this pedantic present.

> But when she heard her mother quickly recapitulating all the details of the plan for Molly, Cynthia's eyes did sparkle with gladness; and almost to Lady Harriet's surprise, she thanked her as if she had conferred a personal favour upon her, Cynthia. Lady Harriet saw, too, that in a very quiet way, she had taken Molly's hand, and was holding it all the time, as if loth to think of their approaching separation—somehow, she and Lady Harriet were brought nearer together by this little action than they had ever been before.   (611)

The form of accounting that measures "expenditure" against one's "means" may be crucial to the credit economy in which they live, but it appears that Gaskell endorses a different form of economy within the intimate relations of friends, siblings, and spouses in this novel. Just as Roger and Osborne's friendship is marked partly by their "purse in common" (303), here, Cynthia evinces more "gladness" and gratitude for the gift offered to Molly than she does for the "handsome, dull present" she herself receives, experiencing Molly's treatment as "a personal favour" that assumes their joint interest and shared gifts. Even before Cynthia expresses her thanks socially, her immediate, presumably unconscious reaction suggests a deep connection to Molly. Cynthia's "sparkl[ing]" eyes (like her "shining" eyes in the early conversation with Roger) physically respond to the thought of her stepsister's comfort in a way that reads as genuine ("real" and "honest") because of longstanding literary associations of eyes with the soul; the "quiet" action of joining hands appears to be another unconscious but significant physical response. In place of "two sides, two distinct social-economic interests," the scene emphasizes a form of "collectivity"[59] that makes one woman's gain equally another's. Personal profit gives way to mutual benefit. Witnessing Cynthia and Molly's interaction makes Lady Harriet (in the words of Molly's earlier response to watching Roger and Osborne together) "like them both under the aspect of relationship—new to her observation" (168). Within Gaskell's novel, close relationships alter individuals in ways that not only help each appear to best advantage but also transform what "advantage" can mean. Identifying "the proper

---

[59] Sahlins 189.

weekly allowance of bread, butter, eggs, meat, and groceries per head" (608) is a form of household management that treats each person's needs on an individual basis and budgets by allocating some part of the whole to each accordingly. In this moment, however, Cynthia doesn't have to think in terms of scarcity or separate desires. A favor to Molly will not lessen the gifts that Cynthia can receive, nor will Cynthia's presents detract from Molly's. On the contrary, Cynthia takes greater pleasure, here, in learning of an arrangement that will give Molly greater peace of mind: she gets more out of common interest and mutual benefit.

Unlike the "one flesh" doctrine that preached the covering or submerging of one person by another in marriage and that increasingly, in the 1860s and 1870s, seemed to threaten female autonomy in the process, idealized intimacy in *Wives and Daughters* occurs in feelings and actions "between the two" (168, 196), in common, not through competition or coverture. The projected marriage of Roger and Molly suggests how friendship and heterosexual coupling might effectively build on the same basis of common interest and mutual benefit that seemed so effective in the Hamley brothers' relationship and that ultimately appears between Molly and Cynthia.[60] Molly's effort to help Cynthia disentangle herself from Preston while thinking of Roger—"how he would feel, what he would say" (475)—may not have enhanced her intimacy with her stepsister, but it does resemble Roger's quiet forms of acting on her behalf during the visit when he has realized that he loves her but worries that she does not reciprocate: "unknown to her, Roger was exerting himself to make her visit pleasant. [...I]t was Roger who arranged all these simple pleasures—such as he knew Molly would enjoy. But to her he only appeared as the ready forwarder of Aimée's devices" (630). Neither Molly nor Roger attempts to take credit for actions that will benefit the other, but in both cases the loved one's feelings are uppermost in the lovers' mind, and they respond with greater "gladness" and "gratitude" to things that will benefit the other than to those that will benefit only themselves. Although Gaskell's death left their marriage unwritten, it appears—despite the financial secrets that Mr. Gibson, troublingly, shares with Roger but keeps from Molly—as if it could offer a substantial improvement over that of the Hamleys and Gibsons, replacing generosity and self-interest not only with "true confidence and love" but a purse or at least interest in common as well. In this way, the novel reminds us that we may understand more about the marriage plot and the ways in which nineteenth-century writers were thinking about marriage when we look to other relationships—in this case, those of siblings and friends.

But the idealized intimacy of the Hamley brothers or of Molly and Cynthia does not matter only or even primarily because of what it suggests about marriage. This vision of common interest and the unique strength of the ties it allows importantly

---

[60] For homosocial friendship as an important basis for heterosexual marriage, see Marcus, e.g., 85–96.

96 IMAGINING WOMEN'S PROPERTY IN VICTORIAN FICTION

offers a model of relation that is centered in, not merely based upon, bonds of siblinghood and friendship that the novel depicts as richly complicated and meaningful in and of themselves. If Cynthia's gratitude for Molly's advantages and the "purse in common" that gives Roger and Osborne financial unity as well as a shared sense of benefit provide us with models for improved marital economics, they also remind us that marriage in 1866 was in general a less equitable relationship than siblinghood or friendship could be. Phoebe Browning's momentary question of whether she could leave her sister in order to marry may not be required by narrative circumstances—she gets no proposal—but it underscores the significance of relationships outside of marriage, as, in a different way, does Molly's determination to help her stepsister regardless of whether or not she damages her own reputation and marital prospects while doing so (518). Similarly, Molly's utter lack of interest in learning of the "desperate love-letter" once written to her is juxtaposed with the thoughts of Osborne's death that consume her instead; grief and preoccupation with the ramifications of this loss for his father, brother, wife, and son are far more pressing to her than any personal romantic prospect (561). Yes, these relationships tell us about alternate visions for marriage, and about marital reforms, but they also tell us about how Victorian authors imagined other forms of connection and belonging that may at times have been equally or more valuable to them.

These models open up on a potentially broader social world. Within the sibling friendships and marriage of *Wives and Daughters*, mutual benefit and intimacy do typically take the restricted form of the dyad, but such intimacy seems capable of drawing in other people too. As Lady Harriet's response to Cynthia's physical demonstration of affection suggests, we do not have to limit our conception of intimate, shared interest to only two. "[S]omehow, she and Lady Harriet were brought nearer together by this little action than they had ever been before" (611). In this case, shared interest unconsciously brings people "nearer together"; in another, it inadvertently involves them in shared business: Molly learns Osborne's secret and later takes close care of his grieving widow. Observers in these instances not only understand two people differently when they see them together, but to a certain extent also join in their intimacy, giving it the potential to expand outward. Although the novel only gestures toward this broadening, it is an important reminder that pairing, whether in friendship or in the legal and fictional coupling of characters in marriage, is only one form of human intimacy, that "heterosexual marriage," as Mary Jean Corbett puts it, may be "understood as one tool among others for forging a nondyadic relationality that implicitly critiques liberal autonomy and rationality."[61] This unfinished novel thus leaves us with a possible

---

[61] Mary Jean Corbett, "Afterword: Real Figures," in *Replotting Marriage in Nineteenth-Century British Literature*, ed. Jill Galvan and Elsie Michie (Columbus: Ohio State University Press, 2018): 229–37, 233.

model—the beginning cells of a hive, perhaps?—for friendship, marriage, and other, less exclusive forms of intimacy and community. At the same time, and perhaps paradoxically, it raises questions about the longevity and scalability of such relationships. The early death of Osborne Hamley and the fact that his wife and son do not appear directly within the narrative until after his death prevent us from seeing how his friendship with Roger holds up against competing ties. Cynthia's marriage to a London barrister and her subsequent removal from the neighborhood similarly prevent her new depth of feeling for Molly, and Lady Harriet's interest in them both, from being tested against other relationships, whether friendly, marital, or maternal. In the context of such extremely insular relationships, external forces can be threatening. Whether by design or simply because of Gaskell's death, the novel ends without addressing these changes and possible threats. But these challenges to intimacy—death and procreation, marriage and moving—if not purposeful are nevertheless meaningfully destabilizing. They show that marriage is only one element, not the grand telos, of the novel's plotting. And they highlight the ways in which not only these but all relationships change over time as a result of circumstances biological and circumstantial, legal and geographical, affective and financial. For a novel that has a great deal to say about marriage, siblinghood, and friendship at a time when authors such as Gaskell were advocating the reform of property law within relationships, those changes are as potentially hopeful as they are threatening. They remind us that literature has the power to imagine, not just record; that relationships are historically and culturally contingent; and that economic law, personal feeling, and choices, both individual and mutual, have the power to shape and reshape what relationships look like as people strive in various ways to attain both a "livelihood" and also "true confidence and love."

3
Greed, Generosity, and Other Problems with Unmarried Women's Property

Women's economic choices took on heightened meaning at the cusp of married women's legal reform. As their common-law rights to property grew, the decisions they made about it fell under increasing scrutiny. A critical attitude toward women's economic activity was not, itself, anything new; depictions of women as poor financial managers or superficial spendthrifts have a long literary history, including, in the nineteenth-century, everything from Lydia's thoughtless purchase of an ugly bonnet she doesn't need in Austen's *Pride and Prejudice* to the Jenkyns sisters' misplaced trust in a failing bank in Gaskell's *Cranford* and Cynthia's disastrous personal debt in *Wives and Daughters*. As Elsie B. Michie has shown, women's wealth signaled cultural anxieties about materialism, while the suggestion that women couldn't manage their money justified precepts such as coverture. What is different and more surprising about criticism of women's financial choices during this transitional period, however, is the extent to which it targets even women who are not portrayed as attempting extravagant purchases, pursuing dangerous business ventures, or proving themselves to be gullible victims of economic crimes.[1] The characters I explore in this chapter simply keep hold of their property or give it to others within their own families. The extreme hostility they awaken by doing so thus offers us a lens for understanding some of the newer problems associated with the extension of women's economic rights and also highlights the different forms of kinship those rights potentially affect.

Seismic shifts in married women's property law—real and anticipated—shook far more than the conjugal dyad. Victorian fiction also registers increasing discomfort with how women's control of their property impacts other family dynamics, portraying vexed transactions between mothers and sons, sisters, brothers, and cousins. The generosity and collaboration we have seen so far in works by Austen, Dickens, and Gaskell give way to suspicion and blame in the social worlds of novels by Trollope, Eliot, and Oliphant, as this and the next two chapters will show. Relationships, no longer governed as uniformly by common law, begin to compete for primacy in women's personal economic decisions. A sharpened focus on these other relational dynamics enables us to better assess

---

[1] See, e.g., Robb, *White-Collar* 29–30, 184–5 and Robb, *Ladies* 22.

Imagining Women's Property in Victorian Fiction. Jill Rappoport, Oxford University Press. © Jill Rappoport 2023.
DOI: 10.1093/oso/9780192867261.003.0004

GREED, GENEROSITY, AND OTHER PROBLEMS   99

the cultural aftershocks of mid- to late century property debates. It also provides us with models for interpreting female economic agency that do not focus primarily upon marriage and other sexual economies. Even as critics have complicated traditional accounts of heterosexual exchange and mapped women's financial action onto diverse marital choices and erotic desires,[2] scholarship continues to explain female economic agency largely through sexuality and the desiring or desirable body. In contrast, the following pages emphasize the importance of blood ties in wide-ranging depictions of women's financial activity. By attending to images of intrafamilial greed and generosity in several novels by Anthony Trollope, I emphasize the generational dynamics of marital property law and show how two seemingly opposite arguments against women's financial rights rely on a shared understanding of their financial responsibilities: that even unmarried women possess property primarily for the benefit of their (future, potential) children or heirs.

Trollope is a key figure for assessing Victorian anxieties about married women's property rights not only because his novels endow numerous women with startling degrees of financial control[3] but because many of their transactions occur outside of sexual economies. We might think of Jemima Stanbury supporting her niece in *He Knew He Was Right* (1869),[4] or Aspasia Fitzgibbon paying her brother's debt in *Phineas Finn* (1869). Some of Trollope's female characters seem eager to "give up the heavy burden of [their] independence" and embrace the financial conditions of coverture (*Barchester Towers* II: 240); the once wealthy Marie Goesler, for instance, seems content with the economic conditions of her marriage: "'I haven't a shilling. [...] You forget that I've got a husband'" (*The Prime Minister* 80). Yet others evade the common law and maintain control of their wealth. Contemplating a second marriage, one widow declares, "'I shan't let any of the money go into his hands [...]. I know a trick worth two of that'" (*Can You Forgive Her?* II: 242).[5] Trollope challenges the "one flesh" doctrine most explicitly in depictions of extreme marital discord. Scenes between Robert and Laura Kennedy in *Phineas Finn*, for example, or Louis and Emily Trevelyan in *He Knew He Was Right* famously expose how the "even

---

[2] See, for instance, Corbett, *Family* 13–24, Michie, *Vulgar* 10–13, and Marcus 193–204. Psomiades (112) shows how correlations between financial and sexual exchanges undermined women's increasing rights. For the continued focus on sex in economics, see Audrey Jaffe, "Trollope in the Stock Market: Irrational Exuberance and *The Prime Minister*," *Victorian Studies* 45.1 (2002): 43–64, 49.

[3] Janette Rutterford and Josephine Maltby explore women's financial management in Trollope's novels, but see it primarily as a function of courtship and marriage. See "Frank Must Marry" 170, 190–2, 194. For Trollope's anxieties about unmarried women's economic position, see Margaret F. King, "'Certain Learned Ladies': Trollope's *Can You Forgive Her?* and the Langham Place Circle," *Victorian Literature and Culture* 21 (1993): 307–26, 311.

[4] See also Chase, *The Victorians and Old Age* 71–2.

[5] On widowhood, see Christopher S. Noble, "Otherwise Occupied: Masculine Widows in Trollope's Novels," in *The Politics of Gender in Anthony Trollope's Novels: New Readings for the Twenty-First Century*, ed. Margaret Markwick, Deborah Denenholz Morse, and Regenia Gagnier (Burlington: Ashgate, 2009): 177–90, 184. Subsequent references to *The Prime Minister* and *Can You Forgive Her?* within the body of the text will be abbreviated *PM* and *CY*.

100 IMAGINING WOMEN'S PROPERTY IN VICTORIAN FICTION

partnership" (*Phineas Redux* 565) or "terms of equality" (*The Duke's Children* 343) endorsed by his better marriages are ethical ideals, not economic or emotional realities.[6] But Trollope undermines coverture just as steadily through the everyday economic conditions of his female characters, who frequently possess separate estates and appear to be at least as savvy as men in the stewardship of their incomes. While characters such as Glencora Palliser, the Duchess of Omnium, showcase what marriage might look like when a wife's wealth remains "her own" (*PM* 46), the rich widows and single women of means who interest me here suggest how the period's shifting property rights might have shaped the financial lives of women and their families outside of marital ties.

This chapter explores the property problems of four unmarried female characters whose economic choices are divorced from marital or sexual desire and instead directed toward or against (platonic) blood relations. Alongside Trollope's generally sympathetic depiction of women's legal position and his acknowledgment of their capacity for financial management, these characters' unusually punitive plotlines suggest the threat that single women's independent economic actions might pose to established family structures. Whether these women are condemned as "blood-sucking harpies," as Lady Lizzie Eustace is in *The Eustace Diamonds* (1873) (*ED* I: 254), or praised like Lady Laura Standish in *Phineas Finn* for being "generous as the sun" (*PF* 409), their greed and generosity apparently present equal dangers to these novels' social worlds because they obstruct traditional forms of property transmission such as primogeniture and marriage. Trollope thus imagines their distinct financial choices as operating similarly: they challenge principles of inheritance and heterosexual exchange, and, by doing so, injure the very families they claim to help and create unacceptable burdens for their male kin. In these novels, similarly disastrous consequences attend women whose property rights serve purposes other than the enrichment of their direct lines. Illustrating the fear that women's property will undermine

---

[6] On equal marriages, see Deborah Denenholz Morse, *Women in Trollope's Palliser Novels* (Ann Arbor: University of Michigan Press, 1987): 39, 77–9. For Trollope's opposition to abuses of marital power, see Deborah Denenholz Morse, *Reforming Trollope: Race, Gender, and Englishness in the Novels of Anthony Trollope* (Burlington: Ashgate, 2013): 91, 107 and Regenia Gagnier, "Conclusion: Gender, Liberalism, and Resentment," in *The Politics of Gender in Anthony Trollope's Novels: New Readings for the Twenty-First Century*, ed. Margaret Markwick, Deborah Denenholz Morse, and Regenia Gagnier (Burlington: Ashgate, 2009): 235–48, 247. For readings of *He Knew He Was Right* and women's property, see Wendy S. Jones, *Consensual Fictions: Women, Liberalism, and the English Novel* (Toronto: University of Toronto Press, 2005): 129, 144–5 and Ablow, *Marriage* 119. For *HKHWR* and divorce law, see John Sutherland, "Introduction," Anthony Trollope, *He Knew He Was Right*, ed. John Sutherland (Oxford: Oxford University Press, 2008): vii–xxiii, xviii, and Suzanne Raitt, "Marital Law in *He Knew He Was Right*," in *The Ashgate Research Companion to Anthony Trollope*, ed. Margaret Markwick, Deborah Denenholz Morse, and Mark W. Turner (Farnham: Ashgate, 2016); see also Kathy Alexis Psomiades, "*He Knew He Was Right*: The Sensational Tyranny of the Sexual Contract and the Problem of Liberal Progress," in *The Politics of Gender in Anthony Trollope's Novels: New Readings for the Twenty-First Century*, ed. Margaret Markwick, Deborah Denenholz Morse, and Regenia Gagnier (Burlington, VT: Ashgate, 2009): 31–44, 33, 36, 39, 42, 44. Subsequent references to *Phineas Redux* and *The Duke's Children* within the body of the text will be abbreviated *PR* and *TDC*. Similarly, subsequent references to *The Eustace Diamonds* and *Phineas Finn* will appear as *ED* and *PF*.

established social conventions, these characters also suggest the intrafamilial stakes of women's financial choices and the contested roles of female custodians and creditors that became salient during a time of increased agitation for married women's property rights.

I. "Greedy, Blood-Sucking Harpies": The Problem with Possession in *The Eustace Diamonds* (1873)

Since most work on married women's property reform focuses on wives or brides within the framework of marriage, we have missed how other relationships reflected or shaped women's economic standing during this period. In *The Eustace Diamonds* (1873), for example, Lizzie Eustace's status as a widow and the diamonds' presence in a marital exchange have obscured the fact that her story also reveals anxiety about competing generational claims to property, compelling us to assess the relative claims of mothers and children. The novel questions whether wealth should travel along conjugal or consanguineal lines, to wives through heterosexual union or to sons through lineal descent. The eponymous diamonds embody the directional tension of these competing kinship priorities. By signaling marriage but also passing from one generation to another, they become the means of asking whether marriage or reproduction provides the right repository for wealth.[7] Though the narrative conflict between legal and social opinions refuses an easy answer, many characters and the narrator himself respond by equating a wife's wealth with theft.[8]

From the start, Lizzie's story engages anxieties regarding married women's property law, reminding us that legal tenets represented only one side of ownership. Unmarried, she borrows money on the prospect of a rich husband, despite her creditor's awareness that Sir Florian Eustace is not legally liable for her pre-nuptial debt (3). Both her underage status and the 1870 Married Women's Property Act absolve him,[9] but the social world of the novel—in this instance and in the larger case that follows—trusts to honor as much as to the law (4). After her husband's death and despite his family's demands, Lizzie refuses to relinquish the diamonds he placed in her hands; the narrator accuses Lizzie of "endeavouring to steal" these jewels (I: 55), which are valued at £10,000. Even though she commits no act legally punishable as a crime, her possession is repeatedly characterized as

---

[7] For the diamonds' relational status, see Stefanie Markovits, "Form Things: Looking at Genre through Victorian Diamonds," *Victorian Studies* 52.4 (2010): 591–619, 597; Marcia Pointon, "Intriguing Jewellery: Royal Bodies and Luxurious Consumption," *Textual Practice* 11.3 (1997): 493–516, 509, 511; and Munich 88.

[8] On Trollope's narrator, see Frank O'Connor, *The Mirror in the Roadway: A Study of the Modern Novel* (London: Hamish Hamilton, 1957): 167–8.

[9] The 1874 Amendment or Creditors Bill restored husbands' liability. For wives' pre- and post-marital debts and fears of wives colluding with tradespeople, see Shanley 104–9 and Rappaport 55–63.

102 IMAGINING WOMEN'S PROPERTY IN VICTORIAN FICTION

theft. In part this is because she lies about the conditions under which she acquires the diamonds (I: 55). Sir Florian presented her with the diamonds to wear and offered to have them reset for her, but—according to the narrator—his description of them as "family jewels" and his jokes about a "future daughter-in-law who should wear them" (I: 42) make it unlikely that he intended to legally gift them to her as her "'own,'" "'for always'" (I: 57), as she claims. Thus, for the novel's many indignant speakers, her repeated and fabricated assertion that they were a gift amounts to nothing more than an attempt to rob her husband's estate.

A lengthy discussion of gifts, heirlooms, and paraphernalia—the discourses through which male lawyers, suitors, and relations attempt to verify the proper legal relationship of people to property—determines that the Eustace diamonds are *not* the family heirlooms that would make Lizzie's possession of them theft (I: 272).[10] The novel even suggests, as property law confirms and literary critics have recognized, that, lying or not, Lizzie can legally claim the stones as her own under the title of "'paraphernalia'" (I: 229):[11] "jewels, which belong to the husband but which the wife is permitted to wear" and which belong to her after his death, permitting her to alienate them by sale, by will, or by gift.[12] But, as Kathy Psomiades notes, the specific property laws cited matter very little.[13] Trollope ignores the ramifications of his extensive legal debate by maintaining that "this selfish, hard-fisted" woman's claims are illegitimate (I: 43).

The novel's emphasis on how fiction is better equipped than legal structures to navigate competing claims to property parallels the sense we have seen, in works by Gaskell and Dickens, of social and narrative power exceeding that of economic law. In the case of Trollope's *The Eustace Diamonds*, the law's "irrelevance" to property arbitration shifts focus instead to the diamonds' cultural and historical weight, which critics have viewed productively in terms of Victorian sexuality, imperialist exploitation, contract-based ownership, Lizzie's "overattachment" to objects, narrative and the literary trade, and the way that "possession not only defines social relations [...but] authorize[s] representations of truth."[14] Such

---

[10] On the legal world of *The Eustace Diamonds*, see Ayelet Ben-Yishai, *Common Precedents: The Presentness of the Past in Victorian Law and Fiction* (Oxford: Oxford University Press, 2013): 119, 123 and R. D. McMaster, *Trollope and the Law* (Houndmills: Macmillan, 1986): 78–84.

[11] For her rights through paraphernalia, see Alan Roth, "He Thought He Was Right (But Wasn't): Property Law in Anthony Trollope's *The Eustace Diamonds*," *Stanford Law Review* 44.4 (1992): 879–97, 890–1, 894 and D. A. Miller, *The Novel and the Police* (Berkeley: University of California Press, 1988): 11. William Blackstone compared a wife's rights to paraphernalia with a husband's common-law rights: "as the husband may thus, generally, acquire a property in all the personal substance of the wife, so in one particular instance the wife may acquire a property in some of her husband's goods [...]. These are called her *paraphernalia* [...]." *Commentaries on the Laws of England*, 4 vols (Oxford: 1745–9) vol. II, 435–6, quoted in McMaster 80–1.

[12] Roth 887 [quoted from 22 Halsbury's Laws, *n.* 29, ¶ 1082].

[13] Psomiades, "Heterosexual" 102.

[14] For "representations of truth," see Andrew H. Miller, *Novels behind Glass: Commodity Culture and Victorian Narrative* (Cambridge: Cambridge University Press, 1995): 179–80. For sexuality, see William A. Cohen, *Sex Scandal: The Private Parts of Victorian Fiction* (Durham: Duke University Press,

GREED, GENEROSITY, AND OTHER PROBLEMS   103

arguments frequently echo the way that Trollope refutes but then insists upon Lizzie's so-called crime. Psomiades, for instance, suggests that the diamonds "to which Lizzie has no right [. . .] distract our attention from the property to which she does."[15] Yet pitting legitimate property against stolen goods confuses a key issue in *The Eustace Diamonds*: since Lizzie does have a legal "right" to the diamonds, the question becomes why her desire to keep them should be treated so punitively. This is why I remain unsatisfied by D. A. Miller's influential Foucauldian argument about the novel. Although Miller, too, acknowledges that "[t]he very status of [Lizzie's] 'theft' is open to question," his argument depends upon her wrongdoing. Recast for his purposes as social "impropriety" rather than crime, Lizzie's misdemeanor nevertheless counts sufficiently as "one theft" to enable it to "lead [. . .] to another," in order to finally separate the novel's more legally legible thefts from the social world which has suffered from this "impropriety."[16] This reading, in which legal and disciplinary regimes correspond, accepts as a given that Lizzie is blameworthy for keeping hold of the diamonds.[17] In contrast, I think the general critical willingness to find her guilty suggests just how powerful Victorian bias against women's property still is. By associating Lizzie's possession with greed and lies, the novel shows the gap between law and social feeling and puts pressure on the very property laws that certain highly biased characters attempt to police. As Andrew H. Miller observes, *The Eustace Diamonds* constructs "dishonesty and theft" as "structurally analogous." Whereas he understands the slippage between these terms as Trollope's response to the publishing industry, I focus on the ways in which this slippage specifically undermines gendered claims to property.[18]

Trollope calls attention to the fact that many of his characters and even his narrator are unreliable sources of information about these diamonds. Mr. Camperdown, the indignant Eustace family lawyer, reflects that "he had never as yet heard of a claim made by a widow for paraphernalia. But then the widows with whom he had been called upon to deal, had been ladies quite content to accept the good things settled upon them by the liberal prudence of their friends and husbands,—not greedy, blood-sucking harpies such as this Lady Eustace"

1996): 161; for contract-based ownership, see Psomiades, "Heterosexual" 102; for object attachment, see Plotz 35; for narrative see Walter M. Kendrick, "The Eustace Diamonds: The Truth of Trollope's Fiction," *ELH* 46.1 (1979): 136–57, 154; and for diamonds' tainted connection to imperial plunder, see Danielle C. Kinsey, "Koh-i-Noor: Empire, Diamonds, and the Performance of British Material Culture," *Journal of British Studies* 48.2 (2009): 391–419; Markovits 595; Plotz 41; Munich 128; Deirdre David, *Rule Britannia: Women, Empire, and Victorian Writing* (Ithaca: Cornell University Press, 1995): 146–7; Suzanne Daly, "Indiscreet Jewels: The Eustace Diamonds," *Nineteenth-Century Studies* 19 (2005): 69–81, 70–2; and Jean Arnold, *Victorian Jewelry, Identity, and the Novel: Prisms of Culture* (Burlington: Ashgate, 2011): 77–80.

[15] Psomiades, "Heterosexual" 104.

[16] D. A. Miller 12.

[17] See also Ben-Yishai for the ways in which "the empirical truth *of* the novel is aligned not with [. . .] legal truth [. . .] but rather with its gossip and propriety" (126).

[18] A. Miller, *Novels* 179, 184–5.

104 IMAGINING WOMEN'S PROPERTY IN VICTORIAN FICTION

(I: 254). The lawyer's ignorance regarding "paraphernalia" reveals his general bias against women's property rights. Having dealt only with wives who were contented with "liberal" settlements, he could disregard the legal details governing women's independent claims. The distinction he draws between contented gift-recipients and "greedy, blood-sucking harpies" is a distinction between women satisfied to take what their husbands or fathers have given them and those ready to assert their own, individual rights—between those whose acceptance of coverture and whatever provisions have been made for their jointure makes them grateful to receive anything at all, and those who, like Lizzie, lack those caretaking "friends" and have to look more carefully to their own interests. The crass insult signals, among other things, its speaker's impassioned prejudice. The lawyer, no friend to women's property, cares more about the case than his client does; Sir Florian's brother would "sooner replace the necklace out of his own property, than be subject to the nuisance of such a continued quarrel" (I: 249).

Like the legal debates, moral judgments about Lizzie's falsity or "greed" distract from the fact that authority figures in the novel work hard to represent Lizzie's legal possession of the diamonds as illegitimate. This vitriol is not a blanket condemnation of women's wealth on Trollope's part. On the contrary, cameo appearances by Marie Goesler and Glencora Palliser (e.g., II: 68–70), whose independent wealth features more prominently in other Palliser novels,[19] remind us that the social world Trollope imagines includes and in many respects approves of other capable rich women. Depicting Lizzie's hold on the jewels as intrafamilial greed or theft protests a very specific form of women's property ownership, one in which a wife's wealth appears to come at the expense of a child's.

After all, we cannot accuse Lizzie of "endeavouring to steal" her diamonds without reflecting on the identity of her (presumed) victim. The language of theft and the seeming "sacrifice" of Lizzie's forgiving brother-in-law[20] deflect attention from the fact that his benevolence is beside the point. Even discounting her claims of paraphernalia, the prospective owner whose rights Mr. Camperdown defends so fiercely is her "'own child'" (I: 213), still a minor. No one contests her rights to that child. In this respect, Lizzie is fortunate, because fathers were legally entitled to choose testamentary guardians. Custody law was still determining widows' claims to their children until the Infant Custody Act of 1886, and Sir Florian, before his death, ominously "knew what his wife was" (I: 9).[21] Lizzie appears to be her son's legal guardian, and the Eustace family lawyers seem uninterested in

---

[19] Trollope leaves *The Eustace Diamonds* out of his reflection on the Palliser novels' consecutive ordering, suggesting for Morse and others that it was not originally included in that series, despite contemporary recognition of their shared characters and the novel's current marketing as "the third in the Palliser series." See Trollope, *An Autobiography*, vol. 1 (London: Blackwood, 1883): ch. 10, 245–6; Morse, *Women* 2; John N. Hall, *Trollope: A Biography* (Oxford: Clarendon, 1991): 379; back cover matter, *ED*.

[20] Ben-Yishai 124.

[21] See Shanley 131, 148–50.

GREED, GENEROSITY, AND OTHER PROBLEMS   105

fighting that point. Even if she does have the "property of the heir[...] in her custody" (I: 39; also I: 155, 213–14)—a point that is never proven—she is also the rightful guardian of that property until he comes of age. She indicates as much when she declares, truthfully or not, "'I mean to—keep them—for—my child'" (I: 52; also I: 94), and reiterates that "'It will be my pleasure, when my boy marries, to hang them round his bride's neck'" (I: 183). But Lizzie's present possession of the diamonds outrages Mr. Camperdown less than her claim that they are her own, "'always'" (II: 30), with the right to give or sell them. Her fantasy of a wedding gift to a future daughter-in-law posits a female succession that skips over the possibility of her son's birthright and affords his mother the freedom to alienate property according to her own wishes, freedom that, as others have noted, "is a proof of ownership."[22] In this case, a wife or widow's possession appears as theft, regardless of the legal status of that possession, because it challenges patrilineal descent.[23] When Lizzie insists, "'My husband's diamonds were my diamonds'" (I: 52), she inserts herself in the line of inheritance, suggesting coverture's inverse: that a wife could be entitled to claim her husband's property. The Married Women's Property Act of 1870 granted women no such right; indeed, while widows could (attempt to) claim both paraphernalia and any jointure settled upon them, wives in ongoing marriages had neither of those limited rights to their household's property. Nevertheless, the 1870 Act, by beginning the process of allowing wives to withhold property from their husbands, was associated with larger challenges to the common-law doctrine that privileged men's possession. Lizzie's hold on the diamonds is painted as "bloodsucking" because it is perceived as a drain on her nearest blood tie and forces lawyers and lovers to confront the possibility of wealth's lateral rather than vertical transmission.

Lizzie is seen as a thief, that is, at least partly because the novel's frustrated narrator, lawyer, and implied readers want property to pass by descent, not sexual exchange. Lizzie rejects that claim. Her status as a thief also depends upon her ignorance of property law, figured by the novel as a kind of gendered dispossession: "[w]ere she once to get hold of that word, paraphernalia, it would be as a tower of strength to her" (I: 231). Hardly a reinforcement of legal power or its diffuse disciplinary power, this statement underscores the instability at the heart of married women's rights and the inability of either law or social feeling to protect women from public opinion. Finally, Lizzie's status as a thief hinges on her refusal to agree with the lawyer's "courteous" suggestion that "it would be for the advantage of all parties that the family jewels should be kept together" (I: 38).

---

[22] Ilana M. Blumberg, "'Unnatural Self-Sacrifice': Trollope's Ethic of Mutual Benefit," *Nineteenth-Century Literature* 58.4 (2004): 506–46, 532.

[23] See also Dagni Bresden, "'What's a Woman to Do?': Managing Money and Manipulating Fictions in Trollope's *Can You Forgive Her?* and *The Eustace Diamonds*," *Victorian Review* 31.2 (2005): 99–122, 117 and Psomiades, "Heterosexual" 102.

106 IMAGINING WOMEN'S PROPERTY IN VICTORIAN FICTION

Lizzie, in keeping with women's increasing claims to separate property, recognizes "her own interests" apart from those of the collective Eustace family and questions how the lawyer's "arrangement" would further them (I: 38). Notably, Lizzie's "interests" are primarily financial, not particularly maternal, but also not romantic or marital. Her economic decisions cost her more than one potential suitor; Lord Fawn, for instance, ends their engagement when she refuses to give up the diamonds (I: 183), but this does not deter her.

The tension between individual advantage and a larger family's interests in Lizzie's case resembles concerns we have seen elsewhere. In *Wives and Daughters*, for instance, Molly Gibson wonders if thinking of the rest of her household means "giving up [...] the true desires, that made herself" (*WD* 134), while Osborne prioritizes his own "true desires" rather than serving his family's financial interests by marrying wealth. Similar family frictions appear elsewhere in Trollope's novels, which are just as likely to protest against fathers who squander their sons' patrimony as to indict "greedy" mothers or sisters-in-law. The squire of Greshamsbury in *Doctor Thorne* (1858), to take one example, regrets "'injur[ing]'" (47) his son by not leaving him "'the property entire'" (*DT* 47). Such plotlines, along with many others that question the justice of putatively legal inheritance—in *Castle Richmond* (1860), *Orley Farm* (1861–2), *The Belton Estate* (1865), and *Ralph the Heir* (1871), to name a few—suggest how pervasive the struggle for resources within families is in Trollope's works during this period. Still, the characters at fault in these other Trollope novels are tolerated with far greater equanimity than *The Eustace's Diamonds*' "blood-sucking harpy." Whereas Lizzie's friends and lovers turn against her, the squire's friends assure him (and *Doctor Thorne*'s marriage plot guarantees) that his son "'will do very well yet'" (*DT* 47). Along similar lines, many men who handle money poorly in Trollope's novels are forgiven their selfishness or ineptitude and even turned into objects of narrative solicitude and "'tender feeling'" (*FP* 402; see also 300, 337–8). As we have seen, Lizzie's role as a "greedy" woman and mother is more problematic.

Part of the problem, I think, is that her characterization conflicts with the version of motherhood publicly circulating and driving popular interest in married women's property reform. Outside of fiction, mothers with money feature prominently in contemporary Victorian debates about property and shed light on how wives' financial interests come to matter primarily when couched in terms of protection, not rights, and when aligned with—if not entirely supplanted by—those of their children. Unlike wealthy Lizzie Eustace, the mothers appearing in these debates are poor and self-sacrificing. Journalistic images of such mothers, who were reputedly living lives of "quiet self-denial" in order to feed their children, served as rallying points for increasing the property rights of working women.[24] The

---

[24] "English Laws of Divorce with Regard to Women," *Englishwoman's Domestic Magazine*, n.d., 82–6, 85.

GREED, GENEROSITY, AND OTHER PROBLEMS 107

1856 petition for married women's property rights inveighs against a legal state of affairs in which husbands might seize upon their wives' hard-earned provisions: "for a robbery by a man of his wife's hard earning there is no redress—against the selfishness of a drunken father, who wrings from a mother her children's daily bread, there is no appeal."[25] In the wake of this petition, newspapers ranging from the *Englishwoman's Domestic Magazine* to *The Times* presented real and hypothetical case studies of "idle, heartless, and unprincipled" fathers—negligent or downright abusive, drunken or debauched—who return to their abandoned households only long enough to take bread out of their families' mouths before again leaving their wives "to the mercy of the wide world" with no means to support their children and no legal recourse to prevent the scenario from replaying "at any moment."[26] We have already seen such fathers in *Our Mutual Friend*. Additional examples of hardworking mothers, starving children, and paternal robbery proliferate in journalism from the period: "the children had had no food that day nor had she herself, but now she had money to buy food, [...] unluckily however she met her husband in the door-way. He forced her hand open and took away the money, as he had a legal right to do."[27] Coverture joined with brute strength to force a mother's hand during her lifetime and even beyond, since wives were legally unable to create wills without their husbands' consent. "Should death come and release her," one paper protested, "she may not even bequeath to her own children the scanty portions of her often painful sacrifices."[28] Such conditions called for desperate measures, according to an article that described a wife's murder of her husband as the understandable and even natural "instinct of a mother to protect her young" when "[t]he law refused to protect her or her children."[29]

Popular opinion overwhelmingly sympathized with working mothers attempting to support their children, and the impulse to protect these children contributed powerfully to the fight for married women's property rights. The 1870 Act, which permitted married women to possess their own earnings and up to £200 in their own names, targeted these working wives and mothers. However, this impulse to protect starving children also appears to have provided a rationale for denying increased property rights to wealthier women, whose financial claims

[25] M. S. R. "The Property of Married Women," *Englishwoman's Domestic Magazine*, n.d., 234–8. For wives' struggle to have their husbands provide their income for family needs, see Ross 72–6.
[26] "Married Women's Property," *Women's Union Journal: The Organ of the Women's Protective and Provident League* (Sept. 1, 1882): 72; "Central Criminal Court, Jan. 14," *The Times* (Jan. 15, 1869): 9, *The Times Digital Archive* (Web, Sept. 21, 2015); M. S. R. "Property" 273; also "Divorce," *John Bull and Britannia* (Feb. 21, 1857): 121.
[27] "I.—The Property Earnings and Maintenance of Married Women," *Englishwoman's Review* (Oct. 1, 1867): 263–75, 273. See also "Imperial Parliament: The Property of Married Women," *Bell's Life in London and Sporting Chronicle* (Mar. 16, 1856): 8; "The Property of Married Women," *Lady's Newspaper and Pictorial Times* (Jun. 7, 1856): 355. For images of working men as brutes, see Michael D. Lewis, "Pictures of Revolutionary Reform in Carlyle, Arnold, and *Punch*," *Nineteenth-Century Contexts: An Interdisciplinary Journal* 34.5 (2012): 533–52, 537, 541.
[28] "English Laws" 85.
[29] "Property Earnings" 273.

108 IMAGINING WOMEN'S PROPERTY IN VICTORIAN FICTION

were portrayed as competing with, rather than reinforcing, those of their offspring, and whose common-law rights moved to the forefront of property debates between 1870 and the subsequent Married Women's Property Act of 1882. Accordingly, rich mothers who rob their children join poor thieving fathers as characters in popular fiction's deliberations over women's property. Novels such as Trollope's, which were written during the height of the debates on married women's property, use children's financial needs or rights as evidence for why wealthier women should not be granted independent property rights, reversing the more sympathetic, working-class cases presented by journalism and by earlier novels such as *Our Mutual Friend*. *The Eustace Diamonds* reveals the tension between the law and social order by asking onlookers to choose between the primacy of a wife's or a child's property rights, a choice that comes into view when we consider Lizzie's financial choices in terms of her role as a mother rather than solely in terms of her roles as wife and widow.

II. Generous to a Fault: The Problem with Giving in *Can You Forgive Her?* (1865) and the Phineas Novels (1869, 1874)

At least initially to protect the rights of children, then, advocates fighting to secure married women's property rights in the decades between the 1856 petition and the 1870 and 1882 Acts sought for wives the same economic rights that unmarried women had: unlike a wife, the *feme sole* could earn, inherit, possess, and transmit considerable property. Alongside mothers such as Lizzie, the portrayal of single females who possess and choose to alienate significant wealth thus stages another side of the property reform debate, one in which women's independent economic rights are undermined as much by generosity as they are by greed, and unmarried women are as significant as wives and mothers. Even to an author like Trollope, who is known for granting strong female characters economic protection and power, the overly generous *feme sole* poses an economic danger as great as that of the selfish mother or self-interested speculator when her unregulated generosity thwarts the expected movement of wealth.

If Lizzie Eustace's self-interested approach to marriage and motherhood makes her a relatively easy target for opponents of women's property rights, the three characters I now turn to are more surprising because they err on the opposite side. More anxious to give than to take, they seek—largely against their own material welfare or marital interests—to share their wealth instead. In *Can You Forgive Her?* (1865), Alice Vavasor resolves to put "'any portion'" of her £400 a year or its principal at her cousin George's service (*CY* I: 332); George's sister Kate also pledges first her own annual "'mite'" of £90 and then a larger income of £500 per year to him (*CY* I: 38); and Lady Laura Standish of *Phineas Finn* and *Phineas Redux* (1873) uses her £40,000 fortune to discharge the debts of her brother

GREED, GENEROSITY, AND OTHER PROBLEMS   109

Oswald, Lord Chiltern. Their open-handedness threatens to overturn both their own and their families' fortunes, and they are crushed in remarkable outlays of narrative energy, punished for what we still think of as the most socially sanctioned form of female economic agency in Victorian England: being "generous as the sun" (PF 409).

Such blame-finding is startling. Women in nineteenth-century fiction generally appear to best advantage when they treat money as nothing next to the male kin they love—even when their children, suitors, brothers, or fathers prove consistently unworthy of these economic sacrifices.[30] In Charles Dickens's Our Mutual Friend, as we have seen, Bella Wilfer is a heroine in part because she learns to prize people over wealth, while in George Eliot's Middlemarch that innate ability is part of what makes Dorothea Causabon a modern-day Saint Theresa. Whether these characters attempt to redistribute wealth along equitable lines, like Trollope's Miss Mackenzie (1865) and Lady Anna (1874), or simply assume, with Trollope's Hetta Carbury, "[t]hat all [their] interests in life should be made subservient to [a brother]" (The Way We Live Now 15–16), the noblest female protagonists in Victorian fiction eschew avarice. They are most likely to achieve happy narrative ends when they conform to gendered ideals of selflessness, placing—as Dickens phrases it—"'a woman's heart'" above any "'gain'" (Our Mutual Friend 527).[31] Trollope's Alice Vavasor, Kate Vavasor, and Lady Laura Standish are stunning exceptions to this rule. As Deborah Denenholz Morse suggests, their plotlines reveal "the inadequacy of the feminine ideal of self-sacrifice."[32] Yet the extreme financial generosity that these single female characters show to their male kin is as much an economic choice as a feminized virtue. The extensive chastisement they receive for this generosity thus demands attention as a monetary matter as well as a moral one.

Attending to the feme sole in her single state instead of always seeing her as a potential bride means considering financial decisions—such as gifts to brothers and cousins—that do not easily fit into frameworks of marriage or other sexual economies. Unlike Lizzie Eustace's more traditional, albeit passing desire to enrich her own cousin Frank through marriage and his own temptation to accept the help—"He was a rising young man [...] but still he was poor" (I: 47); "Had Lizzie become his wife, her fortune would have helped him to the very highest steps beneath the throne" (I: 220)[33]—the gifts that Alice, Kate, and Laura contemplate have nothing to do with romantic interest or deliberate marital choice. These novels explicitly detach these female characters' financial choices from

---

[30] Our Mutual Friend and The Way We Live Now suggest that the sisters of Charley Hexam and Felix Carbury deserve more, but Lizzie and Hetta are heroines partly because they don't demand it.

[31] Women with money remain scrutinized throughout the nineteenth century, though heiresses begin to represent more positive cultural values than materialism by the 1860s and '70s (E. Michie, Vulgar 102). Many of these characters are portrayed in terms of strength; the Victorians did not necessarily equate selflessness with weakness (e.g., Rappoport, Giving 6 and passim).

[32] Women 20.

[33] See also, e.g., I: 35; I: 111–12; I: 220; I: 241; I: 270; I: 314–15; II: 127–8.

110 IMAGINING WOMEN'S PROPERTY IN VICTORIAN FICTION

matrimonial desires, but then punish their economic autonomy by accusing them of sexual transgression. Since these characters decide to give away their money under conditions that are clearly not erotic, the slippage between money and sex reads more as a cover-up than a correlation. Unable to overtly indict Laura, Alice, or Kate for generosity—that gendered ideal of economic selflessness—Trollope prosecutes them for what he presents as a more familiar, gendered crime, that of sinning against romantic love. The novels thus shift their characterization of female agency from the economic to the sexual, and I will return to the problematic consequences of such a shift. But I also want to attend more fully to the specific economic practices that precede and even oppose this shift, and that Trollope undermines in economic as well as sexual terms.

Redirecting the focus away from sexual economies does not deny their significance. We have long recognized domestic fiction's ability to consolidate class interests through marital choice, and more recent scholarly work has turned to finance and anthropology to explore the various sexual-financial arrangements available in Victorian novels, tracing money as it is funneled into either endogamous or exogamous unions, absorbed under the hierarchical, patriarchal bonds of coverture, or channeled into more equitable marital contracts.[34] Trollope's novels note the relative value of these alliances, underscoring the economic significance of sex as well as the eroticized nature of financial transactions.[35] Even George's devoted sister is shocked that Alice offers up her assets before marriage (*CY* I: 398). "'There seems to me to be something sacred about property that belongs to the girl you are going to marry'" (*CY* I: 398), Kate tells her brother. When George contemplates "getting his hand into his cousin's purse" (*CY* I: 389), Trollope's crude humor rests on the longstanding equation of women's sexual virtue and economic value. His novels suggest additional reasons to safeguard women's wealth, however. The men who vie for access are often scoundrels or at least scapegraces, and ends rarely justify the means. Thousands of pounds spent to secure George's Parliamentary seat can't keep it for long, and Laura's life is beyond repair by the time her brother repays her. Alice, Kate, and Laura are punished for being too free with their money, but we risk eliding those financial actions if we conflate them too narrowly with sexualized indiscretions.

Like the many other moneyed women who inundate Trollope's Palliser novels, these women pass significant parts of their plots unmarried, and in the 1860s and '70s their legal standing as single women makes their economic choices at least as meaningful as their erotic ones. By considering their financial decisions in terms of the *feme sole* status they had when they made them, we can better understand

---

[34] For class consolidation, see Armstrong 48 and 138–9; for endogamy and exogamy, see Corbett, *Family* 24 and 37 and Michie, *Vulgar* 13 and 119; for contracts, see Psomiades, "Heterosexual" 101–4 and Marcus 212–17, 232–9.

[35] See Michie, *Vulgar* 134 and Psomiades, "Heterosexual" 93–4.

GREED, GENEROSITY, AND OTHER PROBLEMS   111

the economic actions they have in common as well as the ways in which contemporary debates about married women's property rights were being staged through depictions of single women. Blood ties, not marriages, are central to the gifts that Alice, Kate, and Laura make. Whereas Ruth Perry has argued that "consanguinity came to be replaced by conjugality as the primary principle of kinship" by the Victorian period, these fictional characters feel greater financial responsibility toward existing consanguineal kin than toward future conjugal ties.[36] That they are punished for this first-family preference accentuates the perceived challenge of their economic practices to traditional kinship arrangements and suggests a contemporary anxiety that women's increased economic rights might entail another revision of kinship patterns and principles.

Choosing consanguineal over conjugal ties, Laura pays her brother's debts and champions his marriage with far more care than she gives to her own. Though she describes her marriage to Robert Kennedy as the result of this transaction—her loss of fortune entailing a loss of romantic choice—never, in her deepest marital sorrows, does she express regret for giving Chiltern her money. Similarly choosing blood kin over matrimony, Alice jilts John Grey, the man she claims to love, and engages herself to her cousin solely in order to give him £8,000. Acknowledging that she "could not love her cousin and marry him," she wishes "to stick close to him like another sister, to spend her money in aiding his career in Parliament" (*CY* I: 112). When George proposes, she readily accepts the financial part of the union: "'He is welcome to it all [...] whether he has it as my friend or as my husband'" (*CY* I: 326). She is not prepared to be his wife, however: "'My money may be absolutely necessary to you within this year, during which, as I tell you most truly, I cannot bring myself to become a married woman. [...] You will take it'" (*CY* I: 339). Though the cousin relationship was not necessarily platonic during the nineteenth century, and indeed, Mary Jean Corbett has shown how cousin marriage could even offer an empowering form of "resistance to 'exogamous' exchange" in Austen's *Mansfield Park*,[37] Trollope's novel resists that form of marriage for Alice. She welcomes her father's advice that she "'give him [her] money without [herself]'" (*CY* I: 354) and shudders at George's embrace. "'[I]t was not in my bargain'" (*CY* I: 383). Critics make much of this revulsion, suggesting usefully that the proposed marriage offers Alice a wife's vicarious political engagement, a vocational marriage, a sacrificial marriage, the allure of a contract-based marriage in place of a hierarchical one, a union with George's sister, a choice between marrying within or beyond the family, or a way to defer marriage itself.[38] Yet foregrounding the proposed marriage in this way misses the

---

[36] Perry 4, 158, 186.

[37] Corbett, *Family* 50; see also 13, 35–7.

[38] Regarding a wife's vicarious political action, see Sara L. Maurer, *The Dispossessed State: Narratives of Ownership in 19th-Century Britain and Ireland* (Baltimore: Johns Hopkins University Press, 2012): 150–6; for vocation, Talia Schaffer, "Why You Can't Forgive Her: Vocational Women and the

112   IMAGINING WOMEN'S PROPERTY IN VICTORIAN FICTION

pecuniary point: sexual exchange does not determine every economic transaction. Here, Alice attempts a consanguineal financial arrangement, one at odds with and independent of her romantic or marital interests.

Kate pledges her smaller fortune of £2,000 to George (*CY* I: 146, 367). Like Laura, she puts a brother's interests first. "'[H]e shall have every farthing [...] though I should have to go out as a housemaid the next day'" (*CY* I: 38). She courts a rich aunt and tends to her grandfather largely on George's behalf. "'I do not want money, but he may. [...I]f I had my way I would spend every shilling of Vavasor money in putting him [in Parliament]'" (*CY* I: 57), she declares, and triumphantly passes along her grandfather's gift of a ten-pound note to George (*CY* I: 57–8), just as she vows to turn over any future inheritance to him (*CY* II: 130). As with Alice and Laura, critics remark on her gendered selflessness; her claim to be "'nothing'" without George (*CY* I: 63) echoes a long line of women, both fictional and historical, who were trained to "sacrifice everything to [a brother's] welfare" (*CY* II: 173). As Leonore Davidoff and Catherine Hall have shown, sisters throughout much of the nineteenth century were "expected [...] to generally underwrite [their brothers'] economic ventures,"[39] a tradition of practical, first-family economic support that would have been familiar to much of Trollope's audience. But Trollope's fiction notably reverses these historical expectations. For these characters, extreme lateral, intrafamilial support defies social convention and is punished accordingly. Rather than conforming to domestic ideals, Laura, Alice, and Kate are presented as challenging them in their attempts to "underwrite" men's "economic ventures."

Kate's financial decision to fund George has drawn less critical attention than the other non-traditional desires (political, homoerotic, incestuous) that appear to fuel that decision. However, the possibility of her brother's political success has little bearing on Kate's desire to support him. Whereas Alice, learning of George's lost election, thinks momentarily "of her money, and the vain struggle in which it had been wasted," Kate continues to offer "'all my share'" (*CY* II: 299). Similarly, basing Kate's economic decisions in passionate, erotic attachments to Alice or to George does not explain why she remains ready to give George "'my right in the property'" (*CY* II: 161) after his violent threats drive both women to conclude that

---

Suppressive Hypothesis," *Victorians: A Journal of Culture and Literature* 128 (2015): 15–35, 15 and 27 and *Romance's Rival*; for sacrifice, Anca Vlasopolos, "The Weight of Religion and History: Women Dying of Virtue in Trollope's Later Short Fiction," in *The Politics of Gender in Anthony Trollope's Novels: New Readings for the Twenty-First Century*, ed. Margaret Markwick, Deborah Denenholz Morse, and Regenia Gagnier (Burlington: Ashgate, 2009): 221–33, 221, 223 and Robert Tracy, "Trollope Redux: The Later Novels," in *The Cambridge Companion to Anthony Trollope*, ed. Carolyn Dever and Lisa Niles (Cambridge: Cambridge University Press, 2011): 58–70, 64; for contract, Marcus 234–5; for a union with Kate, Marcus 236–9; for exogamy and endogamy, Michie, *Vulgar* 119–22; and for the deferral of marriage, Marcus 234.

[39] Davidoff and Hall, *Family* 311. For this underwriting in the two *Phineas* novels as a sign of the "blur[red...] boundaries between financial and domestic spheres," see also Henry, *Women, Literature and Finance* 67.

"[they] never wished to see him more" (*CY* II:174).[40] Ambition, selflessness, or passion for Alice or George cannot explain this unshaken resolve to fund the man who, in Kate's words, "'should have starved'" before accepting Alice's wealth (*CY* II:244) and with whom they both break: "'If he wanted money I would send it to him, but I would not write to him'" (*CY* II:244). What a critical focus on self-abnegation, ambition, or erotic exchange misses is that Kate's financial decisions repeatedly reject the possibility of marriage as a cover (*CY* II: 159; *CY* II: 299–300). Her insistence on funding George aligns with the extreme, intrafamilial giving that occupies Alice and Laura and that refuses even the most endogamous of marriages.

Despite "abundant evidence" that Victorian sisters and cousins contributed capital to first-family enterprises,[41] Trollope's fiction presents a different vision of intrafamilial giving, suggesting instead that it injures the families it is intended to help. Though we should be skeptical when Alice's (negligent) father claims to "'suffer[...]'" financially on her account (*CY* II: 384, also *CY* I: 357),[42] the complaint itself underscores Victorian understandings of women's expenditures as family affairs. The familial costs of women's financial activity come more clearly into view in Laura's case, as her effort to support her brother threatens to detract from her family's wealth. Chiltern repays her through the sale of family property (*PF* 296, 357), but since he does so after her marriage she cannot preserve it from her husband as her own, independent property: "'if it had been paid in the usual way at my marriage, settlements would have been required that it should come back to the family after Mr Kennedy's death in the event of my having no child. But, as it is now, the money would go to his estate after my death'" (*PR* 140). Though Laura wonders "'what use would it be [...] to have a sum of money to leave behind me,'" her father's anger that this arrangement "'has robbed us all'" (*PR* 141) reminds us that a woman's independent fortune was not necessarily considered her own. Whereas Laura's focus on "use" privileges her present ability to spend, invest, or donate her wealth, her father's belief that a woman's money should be "le[ft] behind" privileges the future financial rights and uses of lineal descendants.

Trollope's depiction of these two clashing, thwarted visions of property remains unresolved. Laura regains her property at her husband's death (*PR* 371), at which point she and her father again disagree about its use, her father advising her to invest her money so that it may "go to her brother's child," while Laura contemplates "a different destination" (*PR* 374). Though the novel finally validates neither stance and certainly makes Laura the more sympathetic character of the two, the conflict is important to our understanding of Victorian property debates.

---

[40] For those attachments, see, respectively, Marcus 236–9 and Morse, *Women* 36.

[41] Davidoff and Hall 279.

[42] They share household expenses, so her gifts cause him to briefly consider the future necessity of downsizing (*CY* I: 357).

114   IMAGINING WOMEN'S PROPERTY IN VICTORIAN FICTION

When nineteenth-century women inherited property, they frequently received life interest in but not full ownership of it.[43] These arrangements directed family wealth to the next generation, bypassing husbands in favor of vertical transmission to children—typically their own, in the tradition of primogeniture, but also, as we see in the recommendation of Laura's father, to nephews or other first-family heirs.[44] Under these provisions, women conveyed property to others rather than enjoying it themselves. We see such devices frequently in Trollope's fiction. Kate's grandfather, alarmed by her generosity toward George, leaves her his estate's income but preserves the property itself for a future male heir (*CY* II: 156). A similar spirit drives the "costly pre-nuptial settlements" protecting Trollope's wealthiest female characters.[45] Such settlements provided a rationale against reforming women's property laws in general; they challenge "the very *commonality* of the common law" and demonstrate the much remarked-upon friction between Trollope's liberal politics and his conservative values.[46] Alice's mother's wealth "was settled very closely on herself and on her children, without even a life interest having been given to Mr. Vavasor" (*CY* I: 2). Glencora Palliser has a considerable personal fortune, but chooses the path of dynastic wealth, securing some of it for the next generation; "her own property was separated from [her husband's] and reserved to herself and her children" (*PM* 46). Along these lines, Chiltern's fiancée must choose whether to join her wealth to his—making it part of an eldest son's estate, in accordance with traditions of primogeniture—or keep it for a second son (*PF* 411). As Janette Rutterford and Josephine Maltby have argued, Trollope's female characters "are often portrayed as advocates of primogeniture," yet settlements often made such advocacy redundant.[47] A woman's inheritance was preserved for her children; as one contemporary article describes such arrangements, the wife's funds enter "a state of dead lock. [...N]ot even if the husband go to gaol or the wife be starving can a penny be got at, save the dividends at each quarter-day."[48]

---

[43] See David R. Green, "To Do the Right Thing: Gender, Wealth, Inheritance and the London Middle Class," in *Women and Their Money, 1700–1950: Essays on Women and Finance*, ed. Anne Laurence, Josephine Maltby, and Janette Rutterford (London and New York: Routledge, 2009): 133–50, 140, 142; and Alastair Owens, "Property, Gender and the Life Course: Inheritance and Family Welfare Provision in Early Nineteenth-Century England," *Social History* 26.3 (2001): 299–317, 305–6.

[44] See Davidoff and Hall 209.

[45] "Married Women's Property."

[46] Ben-Yishai, *Common* 6. On Trollope's politics, see Amanda Anderson, "Trollope's Modernity," *ELH* 74.3 (2007): 509–34, 531; Regenia Gagnier, "Conclusion: Gender, Liberalism, and Resentment," in *The Politics of Gender in Anthony Trollope's Novels: New Readings for the Twenty-First Century*, ed. Margaret Markwick, Deborah Denenholz Morse, and Regenia Gagnier (Burlington: Ashgate, 2009): 235–48, 243; Jane Nardin, *He Knew She Was Right: The Independent Woman in the Novels of Anthony Trollope* (Carbondale: Southern Illinois University Press, 1989): 18, 130; Rutterford and Maltby, "Frank Must Marry" 172; and Mark W. Turner, *Trollope and the Magazines: Gendered Issues in Mid-Victorian Britain* (New York: St. Martin's, 2000): 11.

[47] Rutterford and Maltby, "Frank Must Marry" 176.

[48] "The Lady and Her Marriage Settlement," *Englishwoman's Domestic Magazine* (Mar. 1, 1864): 207–11, 208.

GREED, GENEROSITY, AND OTHER PROBLEMS 115

Whereas trusts and settlements typically preserved wealth for future generations, Alice, Kate, and Laura provoke anxiety in part because they control their own funds. The extent of their gifts—every shilling, in Laura's case, and all but "'enough [...] to prevent [her] being absolutely a burden on papa'" (*CY* II:141), in Alice's—highlights the claims that these single women have to their fortunes. Without a case for legal protest, their male kin grow desperate. Kate's grandfather finally threatens her with George's disinheritance "'if he gets your money from you'" (*CY* I: 393), and resorts to name-calling when she offers her brother money anyway, "'[b]ecause it was my own'" (*CY* II: 131). Alice's father realizes in horror that she "might put her name to any other number of bills, and for any amount!" (*CY* II: 211), while Laura is similarly able to make her gift because she "had been left a fortune altogether independent of her father" (*PF* 109). The prospect of such unfettered expenditure similarly worried opponents of the Married Women's Property Acts. Though the 1870 Act would not have directly affected women of Alice's, Kate's, or Laura's high economic status, it seemed to open the floodgates to women's independent control of property by breaking with traditional ideas about marriage.[49] Since the economic status of single women was considered the legal model for what wives might hope to attain with greater property rights, the financial choices made by these three single women speak to contemporary discourses on marital property rights. Not only do their gifts contradict the forms of self-interest so crucial to most understandings of modern finance—indeed, they might exemplify what Lauren Goodlad sees as "Trollope's [...] dissatisfaction with possessive individualism"[50]—but their unsanctioned nature implies that, when left to their own devices, women's property decisions are likely to clash with their own needs as well as social traditions and their families' future welfare.

The problems presented by these characters' independent control of wealth stand out even more when we juxtapose them with another sisterly financier who also appears in *Phineas Finn*. Aspasia Fitzgibbon, a competent manager and "most discreet spinster," secretly pays her younger brother's debt, advising his friends that he is "'bad to lend money to'" (*PF* 165) and cautioning that she will not help again: "'If Laurence began to find that he could get money out of me in that way, there would be no end to it'" (*PF* 237). That Aspasia receives no narrative retribution for her financial transaction allows us to mark some of the differences between her payment and those of the other moneyed women I've described. Unlike Laura, Alice, or Kate, the money she devotes to her brother is strictly bounded, both by frequency (this is a one-time event) and by amount (£220). The sum, though substantial, is hardly the unending aid that Laura, Alice, and Kate pledge, and will not come close to exhausting her much larger "windfall" of

---

[49] See Shanley 74 and Ablow, "One Flesh."

[50] Lauren M. E. Goodlad, "'Trollopian Foreign Policy': Rootedness and Cosmopolitanism in the Mid-Victorian Global Imaginary," *PMLA* 124.2 (2009): 437–54, 446.

116 IMAGINING WOMEN'S PROPERTY IN VICTORIAN FICTION

£25,000 (*PF* 35) or to injuring her own interests. It also approaches the amount that the 1870 Act, a year after *Phineas Finn*'s publication, would permit married women to keep for themselves: "Where any woman married after the passing of this Act shall during her marriage become entitled to any personal property [...] or to any sum of money not exceeding two hundred pounds under any deed or will, such property shall [...] belong to such woman for her separate use [...]."[51] Within Trollope's novel, this sum thus registers the growing sentiment that women's wealth and transactions, when securely bounded, might prove harmless both to them and to their families. Moreover, Aspasia, an "old maid, over forty," ridiculed, disregarded, and "reconciled" to her single status (*PF* 34), poses little threat to patriarchal inheritance, her future family's wealth, or other marriageable women seeking a financial role model (*PF* 34–5, 165–6).

In contrast, the other characters I've discussed are treated in terms of their potential as wives and mothers. Laura's legal right to her own fortune rests uneasily beside her father's claim that his family has been "robbed," and Kate ignores her aunt's hope that inheritance will increase her marital options (*CY* II: 299–300). While "greedy" Lizzie Eustace resists generational transmission by keeping hold of her own wealth, Laura, Alice, and Kate stake their claims to property by showcasing their right to alienate it—a right that, as Jeff Nunokawa notes, is fundamental to the privileges of property.[52] Without that ability, according to Trollope's *Ralph the Heir* (1869), one is "robbed of the true pleasures of ownership" (I: 139). These women actively transmit their money to the people they choose instead of becoming passive vehicles for property transmission. In this sense, their economic plots are echoed by that of Kate's aunt, the widow Arabella Greenow, who similarly enjoys financial independence and resists the conventional generational pull of money in favor of choosing "'liberality'" toward those she "'like[s]'"; but where she "'do[es]n't care much about what you call 'blood,'" the characters I have discussed care deeply about consanguineality, privileging blood over marital or other ties (*CY* I: 141; II: 3). They also emphasize the lateral circulation of wealth (to brothers and cousins) over vertical legacies (to children), but the disastrous results of their efforts to consolidate family wealth in this way emphatically differentiate between a patriarchal inheritance and gifts that pass through a sister's or cousin's hands. Refusing to acknowledge claims to wealth based on either heredity or heterosexual exchange, they are uninterested in their own or their family's reproduction. They are guilty of "robb[ing]" their families, despite their gifts' first-family financial commitments, because they disregard their wealth's value for a future generation.

---

[51] "An Act to Amend the Law Relating to the Property of Married Women (9 August 1870)," quoted in Appendix 4, Holcombe 243–4.

[52] Nunokawa 83.

GREED, GENEROSITY, AND OTHER PROBLEMS 117

First-family blood ties had strong appeal during the nineteenth century, as studies have shown. Adam Kuper demonstrates the financial stakes of endogamous kin marriages,[53] but Trollope's novels suggest the importance of consanguineal transactions outside of sexual or parental economies as well. If, as Mary Jean Corbett argues, the "affective dimension" of "first-family ties [...] intensifies" throughout the period and strong sibling attachments "constituted a significant norm," then the passionate sense of financial duty Trollope's characters feel toward brothers or cousins should be understood as signifying more than the second-place status assigned to sisters.[54] It speaks to a larger vision of women's first-family financial management, one that, as Davidoff and Hall have demonstrated, had historical precedence in nineteenth-century women's economic contributions to their families but that seems magnified in these women's large-scale attempts to support their kin.[55] In Trollope's depictions of extensive consanguineal giving as both "waste[ful]" (*CY* II: 299) and injurious, these novels explore but ultimately reject such contributions.

III. Can You Forgive Her? The Problem of Punishment

Generosity thus generates as much disapproval within these novels as Lizzie Eustace's "greed." Their stories begin with the question of whether or not such a woman can be "forgive[n]," and Trollope leaves at least one of them "'no escape, no hope, no prospect of relief, no place of consolation'" (*PF* 418). Their transactions result in broken lives and limbs. Kate suffers physical injury at George's hands, while Alice blames herself for George's violent rage, determining that she has been "'punished'" for "'behav[ing] badly'" (*CY* II: 211). Laura's punishment is displaced onto her marriage; although she considers her brother's "'affection to me [as] more than a return'" for paying his debts (*PF* 115), the novel stresses the emotional costs of this transaction, yoking her financial decision to what it terms "the fault of her life," marrying for political motives rather than for love (*PR* 461; *PF* 201–2, 233, 409).

Laura's independent financial action becomes the root of her painfully protracted misery. Having begun *Phineas Finn* "worthy of admiration" (*PF* 29), she is, by the end of its sequel, "worn out, withered, an old woman before her time" (*PR* 360), her life "'a burden'" (*PR* 139).[56] The belabored "forgiveness" granted to Alice (and perhaps Kate) in the 1865 novel turns into relentless narrative

---

[53] Adam Kuper, *Incest and Influence: The Private Life of Bourgeois England* (Cambridge, MA: Harvard University Press, 2009): 27, 110, 119.

[54] See Corbett, *Family* viii and 115. For the relative status of sisters and brothers, see Ellis 135–7.

[55] Davidoff and Hall *passim*, e.g., 197.

[56] See also Margaret Markwick, *New Men in Trollope's Novels: Rewriting the Victorian Male* (Burlington: Ashgate Publishing Company, 2007): 135, 132.

118 IMAGINING WOMEN'S PROPERTY IN VICTORIAN FICTION

retribution for Laura in a work published after the first Married Women's Property Act: she concludes *Phineas Redux* (1873) "'as though [...] going down into the grave'" (*PR* 549). Despite the narrative's sympathetic take on her tragedy, the way Trollope draws out her decline seems to support her comment that "'No woman was ever more severely punished'" (*PR* 139). In a literary lineup of loveless marriages, this punishment seems excessive—but only if we misunderstand the crime. Like Alice and Kate, Laura is chastened as much for her specific economic actions and autonomy as for her marital choice.

As we have seen, Alice, Kate, and Laura refuse to steward future family wealth. But their transactions also put pressure on present-day family finances and relations. Intended as gifts,[57] their contributions are quickly reclassified in more quantifiable terms, as loans—temporary affairs that the debtors hope to discharge. Chiltern acknowledges that "'Laura ought to have her own money'" and hastens to repay her "'some day'" or even "'to-morrow'" (*PF* 139, 140). George convinces himself that he is merely "borrowing his cousin Alice's money" (*CY* I: 388), that he will "repay her in full" (*CY* I: 367). The men prefer the finite terms of repayment to the more indeterminate "burden" of reciprocity (*PR* 349). Yet their debts are difficult to repay. Chiltern initially finds that his father, Lord Brentford, "'won't join me in raising money for the sake of paying Laura her fortune'" (*PF* 139). George attempts to verbally "'acknowledge [his] debt'" before asking for "'another loan'" (*CY* II: 56) but finds borrowing hard to "endure" (*CY* II: 113). His inability to discharge his debt makes him conscious that he has "robbed" his cousin (*CY* II: 318).

Here and elsewhere in Trollope's novels, financial obligations are painful and emasculating.[58] Although they lack the economic protections afforded by contract, Alice and Laura hold the place of creditor to their male kin, who demonstrate profound discomfort with this scenario.[59] Chiltern tries to keep his sister from "burden[ing]" another man with her wealth, while George finally flees to America. Whereas other men such as Phineas might feel similarly that "'presents of money are always bad. They stain and load the spirit, and break the heart'" (*PF* 538), he can nevertheless ultimately "enjoy [...] his wife's fortune" (*PR* 559) in accordance with the understanding that "'[w]hen [a woman's hand] and all that it holds are your own, you can help yourself'" (*PF* 538). His own wife, Marie Goesler, is eager to cede her financial claims. In contrast, Chiltern and George face particularly painful situations because they borrow from women but—as a brother and an undesired cousin—cannot subsequently absorb these debts in

---

[57] E.g., *CY* I: 393; *CY* II: 355; *PF* 251.

[58] See also, e.g., *PF* 158; *PF* 237; *PM* 13, 104–5. For Trollope's own obligations at this time, see Walter M. Kendrick, *The Novel-Machine: The Theory and Fiction of Anthony Trollope* (Baltimore: Johns Hopkins University Press, 1980): 110.

[59] For women as creditors see Green and Owens, "Gentlewomanly" 518; Froide, *Never Married* 128–41.

GREED, GENEROSITY, AND OTHER PROBLEMS   119

marriage. Though such a state of affairs was hardly common, it threatened to become more widespread with the extension of married women's property rights. If married women acquired independent financial status, marriage could no longer annul the financial obligations men might have to their brides. With the elimination of coverture, that is, a husband might find himself legally indebted to his wife. Just as idealized brother-sister relations were often seen as prefiguring marriage,[60] portrayals of siblings' financial relationships had stakes for marital economics as well. In Trollope's fiction, consanguineal debt between siblings or cousins stands as a model for the potential tensions of marital debt during this period. Within close kin relations, even when money has been repaid, "the burden of the obligation" (*PR* 349) cannot easily be discharged or, in financial terms, forgiven: canceled, written off.

Can You Forgive Her? resolves this dilemma in part by reversing the status of debtor and creditor and shifting the terms of obligation; it asks us to "forgive" a woman's sexual guilt rather than a man's financial debt, setting the stage for similar slippage between men's economic liabilities and women's romantic indiscretions in the *Phineas* novels. Morse has argued that unworthy men are the real targets of the novels' demands for forgiveness;[61] my point is that the terms of "forgiveness" differ along gender lines. Though Laura and Alice are owed money, Trollope reverses the implications of their loans by requiring their sexual transgressions, not their (unworthy) debtors' obligations, to be forgiven: "can you forgive her, delicate reader?" (*CY* I: 384). Alice confesses to Grey that "'though you may forgive me, I cannot forgive myself'" (*CY* II: 313); Laura, too, feels that she has done Kennedy "'a grievous wrong'" (*PF* 529) and admits, "'it has been my fault'" (*PR* 561). Whatever their feelings, this admission of guilt is a bait and switch, a disavowal of the economic structure in place.

These novels turn female creditors into debtors in need of forgiveness while canceling men's monetary obligations by displacing them onto the social world. According to this logic, Chiltern and George require forgiveness for their ungentlemanly behavior, not for owing vast sums to their female kin. At least in Chiltern's case, Trollope grants that forgiveness.[62] Laura never mentions Chiltern's financial indebtedness; after she spends her entire fortune on him, she refers to him as a debtor only once, to characterize his ineffective marriage proposals: "'he almost flies at [Violet's] throat, as an angry debtor who applies for instant payment'" (*PF* 168). George is similarly taken to task for his manners, not his monetary claims, when he threatens his sister and cousin and insists upon payment (*CY* II: 142, 165). Alice concedes that George's financial demand is "'mainly right'" but disapproves of his "'putting it to me in that hard, cruel

---

[60] Ellis 134 and Davidoff and Hall 348.

[61] Morse, *Women* 9.

[62] William A. Cohen, "The Palliser Novels," in *The Cambridge Companion to Anthony Trollope*, ed. Carolyn Dever and Lisa Niles (Cambridge: Cambridge University Press, 2011): 44–57, 53.

120   IMAGINING WOMEN'S PROPERTY IN VICTORIAN FICTION

manner'" (*CY* II: 142). Kate finds George's "conduct [...] mean and unmanly" (*CY* II: 145) and regrets mainly "'that I should live to be so ashamed of my brother!'" (*CY* II: 165). In accusing the men of bad behavior, the novel absolves them of their real economic obligations, forgiving or writing off their monetary debt by writing them into positions that require a different kind of forgiveness. Freed from the outcomes of their economic actions, these men retain the legal and social force of economic agency, while Alice, Kate, and Laura suffer remorse alongside the economic and social consequences of their financial dealings.

On the other end of the spectrum, Lizzie Eustace retains economic agency— appearing in *The Prime Minister* (1876) with "£4000 a year and a balance at her banker's" (418)—but suffers social chastisement at least in part because, unlike Alice, Kate, and Laura, she never accepts blame for her behavior, remaining "conscious of no special sins" (*PR* 516). Though some characters want her "'locked up'" (*ED* II: 374), Chiltern, who makes a return appearance in *The Eustace Diamonds*, is less severe, perhaps remembering his own social and financial liabilities: "'all that I can hear of her is, that she has told a lot of lies and lost a necklace'" (*ED* II: 375). Walter M. Kendrick has shown that these "lies" trouble Trollope's vision of his "realistic enterprise."[63] Even after time transforms Lizzie's so-called "theft" into "that old story about the jewels" (*PM* 69), the novels shift the terms of her blame to find her still guilty, because "[s]he would still continue to play her game as before, would still scheme, would still lie" (*PR* 516). Although Kendrick argues persuasively that Lizzie's lies are Trollope's commentary on narrative policy, and Andrew H. Miller similarly shows how her dishonesty reflects Trollope's view of the literary market,[64] my point is that by aligning Lizzie's lies with her economic independence, the novels criticize both. Once again, as with Alice, Kate, and Laura, blame and punishment slip easily between economic and social registers in order to find a female economic agent particularly culpable.

Legally speaking, Lizzie needs no financial forgiveness. Her economic liability rests on social expectation, rather than the law. But if we read her "sins" and punishments together with those of the other characters I have discussed, we see a similar translation of independent economic actions into manners. The narrator's exclamation—"Poor Lizzie Eustace! [...] Lizzie the liar! Poor Lizzie!"—reiterates her social blameworthiness even as it expresses pity in ironically economic terms (*PR* 516). (Whatever else she may be, Lizzie is not "poor.") Unable to stop this woman's "continue[d]" financial independence, the novels fuse even her legal economic claims with her "lies" to denounce her particular form of wealth acquisition, continuing to pit her unfavorably against her son and heir, who reappears in *Phineas Redux* seemingly for the sole purpose of being known as a

---

[63] Kendrick, "*Eustace*" 141, 156.
[64] A. Miller, *Novels* 183–8.

GREED, GENEROSITY, AND OTHER PROBLEMS   121

"child [...] who stood [...] high in repute" (*PR* 516). In a doubly punitive measure, then, the novels both refuse to pardon her behavior, and—as with Laura and Alice—punish her economic agency through sexual means. One fiancé dissolves their engagement when she refuses to give up the diamonds (*ED* I: 183), and her second marriage seems a form of narrative retribution. Her husband, firm in the "marital supremacy" that will prevent her intended pre-nuptial "settlements," is guilty of bigamy and suspected of murder (*ED* II: 369: *PR* 512). Although the law annuls their marriage, leaving her wealthy and "free from all marital persecution" (*PM* 69), "decent" society leaves her "alone, weeping in solitude" (*PR* 516; *PM* 69).

D. A. Miller finds that the Palliser novels as a whole "portray a Parliament that, for all its politicking, has no politics,"[65] but—as we have seen—Trollope enacts his visions of contemporary politics as much within the social plots and feelings of these novels as in their citations of the law, which Victorian fiction consistently shows to be inadequate. Although questions of female suffrage (granted for local elections in 1869) appear only long enough to be rejected in favor of vicarious political power (*PF* 75; *CY* I: 111), the novels engage at length in the equally pressing question of reforming women's property rights.[66] Whether by taking or giving, the female characters discussed here lay claim to their property, struggling against even their most ardent well-wishers to control their own financial transactions.[67] Alongside countless Victorian heroines better known for their financial disadvantages, Lizzie, Alice, Kate, and Laura present unresolved problems within these narratives not because they depend upon their male kin, prove overly acquisitive, or make the wrong marriage choices, but because in their most generous and greedy manifestations alike, single women's independent possession and management of property threaten their first-families' economic longevity and—perhaps just as importantly—their male kin's peace of mind.

The novels I have discussed ask readers, pre-emptively, to forgive or punish *her* in the sexual terms most familiar to them, at least in part because they are not ready to cede to women the new financial power to shepherd family wealth, to keep or cancel family debts, to demand repayment, or to refuse forgiveness to kin. Yet even the call for forgiveness, taken in its financial sense, reminds us that by the final decades of the nineteenth century women were increasingly active economic players. Under the common-law doctrine of coverture, a married woman could be neither debtor nor creditor. The property reforms of the 1870s and 1880s

---

[65] D. A. Miller 116; see also Nicholas Dames, "Trollope and the Career: Vocational Trajectories and the Management of Ambition," *Victorian Studies* 45.2 (2003): 247–78, 256–7.

[66] E.g., Maurer 160. Some advocates connected women's suffrage to property rights (Turner 112, Shanley 109–14).

[67] Alice's father and sometimes fiancé pay George out of John's wealth, not hers. Though others read this in terms of her marital options (Schaffer, "Why You Can't Forgive Her" 28; Michie, *Vulgar* 122; Marcus 244), Alice wants to circulate money without committing to marriage.

increased women's financial rights in part by increasing their fiscal responsibilities. As Trollope was writing these novels, even debt in need of forgiveness was becoming a welcome sign of economic responsibility for single and married women alike, a new economic possibility for an increasing number of female creditors and the men and women who owed them money.

4

"That Blent Transmission"

Women's Property Law and Jewish Cultural Inheritance in *Daniel Deronda* (1876)

In George Eliot's *Daniel Deronda* (1876), newlywed Gwendolen Grandcourt expresses delight at "having her own diamonds to try on"; her pleasure vanishes, however, with the belief that she has "robbed" her husband's former mistress of them.[1] Like Molly Gibson in *Wives and Daughters*, Gwendolen experiences conflicting duties to herself and others, but her storyline, rather than supplying the means to mutual benefit, leaves her grappling with the consequences of having chosen to acquire something of "her own." As in the case of Lizzie Eustace from the previous chapter, Gwendolen commits no act legally punishable as crime. Neither woman *steals*. Yet Gwendolen's possession of family jewels, like Lizzie's, is repeatedly characterized as theft.

Stealing typically reinforces the very economic rules it breaks by serving as an index to ownership. When we define theft as the seizure of another's property, we recognize one party as the rightful holder of that property.[2] Yet the theft-which-is-not-theft that Eliot and Trollope describe removes clear-cut ownership as a fixed counterpoint to "illicit" possession. Gwendolen and Lizzie are not criminals, despite accusations or self-consciousness about "theft," in part because nobody else can make a firm case for owning their jewels. In these novels, theft becomes grounds for plot more than imprisonment not simply because it is difficult to identify perpetrators or because social discipline functions as a substitute for police power[3] but because labeling a perpetrator doesn't actually resolve anything. Lizzie is pegged as a thief by chapter five, but this begins rather than ends the novel's action because the language of theft fails to clarify the relationship of a woman to diamonds that once were (and, it turns out, might still be) rightfully

---

[1] George Eliot, *Daniel Deronda* [1876], ed. Terence Cave (London: Penguin Books Ltd., 1995): 358, 427. Subsequent citations to this novel will be made parenthetically.

[2] Similarly, classifying the refusal to repay debt as theft implies that a legitimate creditor exists. See Ilana M. Blumberg, "'Unnatural Self-Sacrifice': Trollope's Ethic of Mutual Benefit," *Nineteenth-Century Literature* 58.4 (2004): 506–46, 537; Ilana M. Blumberg, *Victorian Sacrifice: Ethics and Economics in Mid-Century Novels* (Columbus: Ohio State University Press, 2013): 160. For the shared structure of gifts and thefts, see Ilana M. Blumberg, "Collins's *Moonstone*: The Victorian Novel as Sacrifice, Theft, Gift and Debt," *Studies in the Novel* 37.2 (2005): 162–86, 165; and *Victorian Sacrifice* 174.

[3] E.g., D. A. Miller, *The Novel and the Police* (Berkeley: University of California Press, 1988): 10, 15.

Imagining Women's Property in Victorian Fiction. Jill Rappoport, Oxford University Press. © Jill Rappoport 2023.
DOI: 10.1093/oso/9780192867261.003.0005

124   IMAGINING WOMEN'S PROPERTY IN VICTORIAN FICTION

hers. Similarly, when Gwendolen's bridal diamonds become the "poisoned gems" of robbery (359, 427), the language of theft, rather than identifying owners and criminals, reveals how ill-equipped marital property law is to classify either. In *Daniel Deronda*, such extra-legal theft challenges the concept of rightful owner-ship, particularly for women within the confines of the marriage contract, and undermines the basic premise that legal ownership can mean the rightful posses-sion or transmission of property.

Scholars discussing gender and property in *Daniel Deronda* typically highlight the financial necessity of marriage for women with limited professional options, the mercenary nature of the marriage market, and the power—economic, social, physical—that husbands hold over their wives. In contrast, this chapter looks beyond marriage to explore Eliot's more comprehensive response to women's changing property rights through the novel's treatment of extra-marital property exchanges within Gwendolen's story and also through the emphasis on non-marital property transactions within Daniel's plot of Jewish cultural inheritance. Following the critical tradition that, against F. R. Leavis's desire to remove everything Jewish from the novel, insists on the two plots' meaningful interweaving,[4] I understand them as jointly mapping contemporary tensions between social and legal definitions of ownership. Together, I argue, the storylines expose the inadequacy of property law to account for a wider range of kinship formations and transactional needs outside of marriage.

Focusing primarily though not exclusively on diamond transactions—the "poi-soned gems" (359) transferred from Grandcourt's former mistress to his new bride and the "fine diamond ring" (391) pawned and then stolen in the plot that returns Daniel to his heritage—I show first how the English marriage plot uses the language of theft in order to stage the competing economic claims of wives and sons. As we saw in the previous chapter's discussion of *The Eustace Diamonds*, contemporary debate about property law questioned wealthier mothers' rights

---

[4] A long critical tradition prioritizes one plot (typically Gwendolen's) over the other and debates whether and how they are unified. See, for instance, Terence Cave, "Introduction," in George Eliot, *Daniel Deronda* [1876], ed. Terence Cave (London: Penguin Books, 1995): xv; Deirdre David, *Fictions of Resolution in Three Victorian Novels: North and South, Our Mutual Friend, Daniel Deronda* (New York: Columbia University Press, 1981): 135, 145–6 n. 1; Peter Brooks, *Realist Vision* (New Haven: Yale University Press, 2005): 105; Sarah Gates, "'A Difference of Native Language': Gender, Genre, and Realism in *Daniel Deronda*," *ELH* 68.3 (2001): 699–724, 699, 721–2 n. 2; Nancy Henry, *The Life of George Eliot: A Critical Biography* (Chichester: John Wiley & Sons, Ltd., 2012): 215; Judith Adler, "Hidden Allusion in the Finale of *Middlemarch*: George Eliot and the Jewish Myth of the *Lamed Vov*," *George Eliot—George Henry Lewes Studies* 70.2 (2018): 143–71, 159–60: https://doi.org/10.5325/geo relioghlstud.70.2.0143. For theories of the novel's unity, see Mary Wilson Carpenter, "The Apocalypse of the Old Testament: Daniel Deronda and the Interpretation of Interpretation," *PMLA* 99.1 (1984): 56–71, 56, 57, 67, also 68 n. 1; Joanne Long DeMaria, "The Wondrous Marriages of *Daniel Deronda*: Gender, Work, and Love," *Studies in the Novel* 22.4 (1990): 402–17, 403; Jill L. Matus, *Shock, Memory, and the Unconscious in Victorian Fiction* (Cambridge: Cambridge University Press, 2009): 151. In Hebrew translations, Gwendolen's plot rather than Daniel's was abridged; see Mikhal Dekel, "'Who Taught This Foreign Woman about the Ways and Lives of the Jews?': George Eliot and the Hebrew Renaissance," *ELH* 74.4 (2007): 783–98, 792.

over those of their children; the child's illegitimacy in *Daniel Deronda* removes maternal considerations from the starker pitting of wife against son. Depicting a wife's possession of her husband's wealth as theft is a strike against married women's claims to property rights, but the fact that this fictional theft exists beyond the purview of existing law—that it doesn't reveal a "true" owner and can't be prosecuted as theft—underscores that law's failure as a clear or just arbiter of possession. Eliot seeks resolution in a higher form of law. *Daniel Deronda*'s Jewish plotline echoes but also responds to this familial conflict, using stolen diamonds to consolidate broader, more fluid kinship lines. The "blent transmission" (751) celebrated in this part of the novel counters the fraught transfer of Gwendolen's diamonds through a form of inalienable cultural property, a spiritual inheritance that, despite multiple thefts, adheres to its appointed path of descent. Both plots align in keeping such assets out of women's reach, ensuring that "family property" is never treated as a woman's "own" even when in or passing through her possession. Yet Eliot's expansive conception of family ties beyond marriage, her understanding of non-monetary property value, and her defense of socially sanctioned transmission over that governed by property law also point to the shortcomings of that law and unsettle the way that the rights and priorities attending personal property have been understood.

I. "Some Struggle about the Diamonds"

Legally speaking, when Gwendolen Harleth marries Henleigh Mallinger Grandcourt, she is, or should be, in a much better position than Lydia Glasher, the mistress she has displaced. As his betrothed, it is her right to wear the "splendid diamond ring" he sends her "'as a sign of [their] betrothal'" (312), and she is also entitled to the family diamonds which he "necessarily wished to have [...] for his wife" (343). Morally speaking, of course, the novel questions Gwendolen's right to these diamonds, drawing attention to the mercenary motives behind her marriage. The check Grandcourt encloses with her engagement ring (312) and his wedding-day promise of future financial support for her mother (428) make explicit the simultaneously financial and sexual nature of the bargain and reinforce Gwendolen's sense that "she had sold herself" (669). In both cases, money and marriage go hand in hand, accompanied by diamonds which showcase this fairly conventional pairing of women and wealth in circulation. As Kathy Psomiades has argued, such illustrations of "heterosexual exchange," which draw on theories of "heterosexuality and capitalism as homologous social structures, money and sex as connected because they somehow work in the same way to organize the world in which we live," paradoxically arise in Victorian fiction "at precisely the historical moment in the West in which middle-class women and men to a greater and greater extent are seen as having a claim to equal economic

126 IMAGINING WOMEN'S PROPERTY IN VICTORIAN FICTION

and political agency."[5] Accordingly, Eliot's novel, published during the period between the passage of the first Married Women's Property Act in 1870 and the second in 1882, uses diamonds to highlight Gwendolen's position as a woman "on the market."[6] Though Grandcourt's retention of his own diamond ring reminds us that jewels functioned as significant personal property for men as well as for women (161),[7] and that husbands frequently determined which "family" items a wife might enjoy, Gwendolen actually resembles the gemstones in her "luster" and "brilliancy" (34). She is "cold" and "pale" (10), "delicate" but "immovable" (12); in one of our first encounters with her she "kisse[s] the cold glass" of the mirror that reflects her (18). It is no surprise to learn that the "brilliants suited her perfectly" (428). But the diamonds' even keener association with Lydia—the woman whose "beauty and brilliancy" (340) also "suited diamonds" (343) and to whom Grandcourt had earlier given them—reveals the similar nature of wife and mistress that Catherine Gallagher has observed and that contemporary reformers saw as the result of property laws and customs that encouraged mercenary marriage by giving women inadequate economic opportunities.[8] The diamonds show how even the legally wedded wife is afforded little power in a culture still governed by the "one-flesh" doctrine of coverture. Despite Gwendolen's fleeting thoughts of "having her own" jewels, Grandcourt will control both wealth and its exhibition within their union. Subject to her husband's will in all things, she is compelled to wear these gems. Gwendolen recognizes with a laugh that Grandcourt wants to "'make me put [an engagement ring] on'" (313), but his "imperiousness" about the diamonds she later receives (427) is no laughing matter: these "poisoned gems" entail "struggle" that a number of critics have aligned with marital rape, other forms of domestic abuse, both emotional and physical, and Grandcourt's imperialist tendencies (359, 426).[9] Such moments call into question the nature of a wife's ownership: her "natural" affinity to the stones, her appraisal of them as "her own" (358), and their physical transfer to her fail to give Gwendolen the "freedom

---

[5] Psomiades, "Heterosexual" 93, 94; see also 112.

[6] Ibid. 93.

[7] For the imperial significance of Grandcourt's ring, see Munich 136, 14, 26–7. See also Wynne 117.

[8] Mary Lyndon Shanley, *Feminism, Marriage, and the Law in Victorian England* (Princeton: Princeton University Press, 1989): 61; Catherine Gallagher, "George Eliot and *Daniel Deronda*: The Prostitute and the Jewish Question," in *Sex, Politics, and Science in the Nineteenth-Century Novel: Selected Papers from the English Institute, 1983–84, New Series, No. 10*, ed. Ruth Bernard Yeazell (Baltimore: Johns Hopkins University Press, 1986): 39–62, 51–2. See also Marlene Tromp, "Gwendolen's Madness," *Victorian Literature and Culture* 28.2 (2000): 451–67, 460.

[9] For rape and other forms of domestic abuse and trauma in Gwendolen's plot, see Tromp 454–5; Matus 149, 153; Doreen Thierauf, "*Daniel Deronda*, Marital Rape, and the End of Reproduction," *Victorian Review* 43.2 (2017): 247–69, 257. For Grandcourt's imperialist tendencies, see Kathleen McCormack, "Yachting with Grandcourt: Gwendolen's Mutiny in *Daniel Deronda*," *Victorian Literature and Culture* 43 (2015): 83–95, 83, 89; Katherine Bailey Linehan, "Mixed Politics: The Critique of Imperialism in *Daniel Deronda*," *Texas Studies in Literature and Language* 34.3 (1992): 323–46, 330–1, 334. For Gwendolen's relationship to empire, see Susan Meyer, "'Safely to Their Own Borders': Proto-Zionism, Feminism, and Nationalism in *Daniel Deronda*," *ELH* 60.3 (1993): 733–58, 735; Linehan 328–30; David, *Fictions* 176–7, 193.

WOMEN'S PROPERTY LAW AND JEWISH CULTURAL INHERITANCE   127

to alienate" them associated with property rights[10]—or even the freedom to leave them in her jewelry box, when her husband demands their display.

Gwendolen's discomfort with the diamonds results partly from Lydia's prior claim and partly from Lydia's control over the women's transaction. Despite their avowed function as Grandcourt's marriage gift to Gwendolen, they arrive as a gift from Lydia, not Grandcourt, accompanied by Lydia's "venomous" letter (424).[11] Having previously promised Lydia that she wouldn't marry Grandcourt, Gwendolen is reproached for having "'broken her word'" (358). But the problem with this property appears to exceed its association with the "willing wrong" she commits. The diamonds haunt her, refusing to abide by the de-animating laws of ownership. They become "whispering stones," with "horrible words clinging and crawling about them" (426). No other thing acquired through Gwendolen's broken promise—neither "her own furlong of corridors and [...] her own servants" (357), nor even the emerald jewelry given to her by Grandcourt himself (426)—troubles her to this degree. Far from being "her own diamonds" (358), as Gwendolen anticipated, they are marked and tainted by their history of circulation. The letter enclosed with them reads: "'These diamonds, which were once given with ardent love to Lydia Glasher, she passes on to you. [...] You have chosen to injure me and my children'" (358–9). Gwendolen's marital acquisition of the diamonds and all they entail appears to both women as theft; Lydia resents that Gwendolen will "'possess what was hers'" (358), and Gwendolen regretfully reflects: "'What a privilege this is, to have robbed another woman of!'" (427).

As many have noted and dazzling scholarship attests, diamonds themselves were fraught, multi-faceted things during this period.[12] At the start of Eliot's own *Middlemarch* (1871), Dorothea Brooke, contemplating "a fine emerald with diamonds," is torn between her vision of the "'gems [...] as spiritual emblems,'" "'fragments of heaven,'" and her uncomfortable recognition of their more worldly sources: "'Yet what miserable men find such things, and work at them, and sell them!'" (*Middlemarch* 13, 14). Further developing Dorothea's sense of unease with

---

[10] Blumberg, "Unnatural" 532 and *Victorian Sacrifice* 155.

[11] For the significance of this transmission, see Katherine Dunagan Osborne, "Inherited Emotions: George Eliot and the Politics of Heirlooms," *Nineteenth-Century Literature* 64.4 (2010): 465–93, 483, 487.

[12] For the "social relations [...] in things," see Elaine Freedgood, *The Ideas in Things: Fugitive Meaning in the Victorian Novel* (Chicago: University of Chicago Press, 2006): 54. Recent discussions of diamonds' doubleness have shown how they registered imperial power and plunder, affective and cash value, sexuality and motherhood, and the compressed density of lyric along with the various histories of narrative. For empire, racial conflict, exploitation, and theft, see Danielle C. Kinsey, "Koh-i-Noor: Empire, Diamonds, and the Performance of British Material Culture," *Journal of British Studies* 48.2 (2009): 391–419; John Plotz, *Portable Property: Victorian Property on the Move* (Princeton: Princeton University Press, 2008): 41; Deirdre David, *Rule Britannia: Women, Empire, and Victorian Writing* (Ithaca: Cornell University Press, 1995): 146–7; Arnold, *Victorian Jewelry* 77–80; and Munich 131. For sentiment and economics, Plotz 25, 31. For diamonds as an index to relationships, see Markovits 597 and Pointon, "Intriguing" 493–516, 509, 511; Osborne 484. For diamonds' lyric and narrative play, see Markovits 595, 596–7.

128 IMAGINING WOMEN'S PROPERTY IN VICTORIAN FICTION

diamonds and other jewels, *Daniel Deronda* more explicitly links them to the
commercial practices of "miserable men" by associating the gems with Jewish
diamond markets and the stereotypically disreputable trades of pawnbroking and
money-lending, as I will discuss in greater detail later. For Victorian scholars
today, of course, diamonds also invoke the illicit transactions of Britain's burgeoning empire, and some of Eliot's readers may have been conscious of the exploitation signaled by the gems' movement to England from India, Brazil, and South
Africa as well. As Wilkie Collins's best-selling novel *The Moonstone* (1868) had
previously suggested,[13] for example, diamonds could be emblems of violent dealings, signs of ill-gotten power and wealth. These various connections to questionable forms of trafficking, whether at home or abroad, lend diamonds additional
meaning in Eliot's novel, aligning the engagement token from an imperious
husband and the wretched spoils of a cast-off woman with other patterns of
damaging circulation and exchange. Along these lines, Gwendolen's "struggle
about the diamonds" (*Daniel Deronda* 426) reflects historical problems with the
diamonds themselves. But this struggle also distracts from the fact that, legally
speaking, Gwendolen's claim to possession is as valid as anyone else's within the
novel. Considering diamonds through the lens of theft makes the novel's "struggle
about the diamonds" (436) less a heterosexual power play between Gwendolen
and her cruel husband and more a sign of one woman's profit at another's expense
through marriage, of female power to "injure." At least, this is what Gwendolen
and critics echoing her think when Daniel Deronda describes the ugliness of
" 'see[ing] that our gain is another's loss' " (337).[14] If, in this novel, one person's
gain necessarily entails another's loss, then (as Ilana M. Blumberg has suggested)[15]
profit—from marriage, from diamonds—always entails theft, whether we see the
violence of the transaction as embedded in the stones themselves or in their
manner of acquisition.

But theft of what, and from whom? Lydia's hold on the gems is no less
problematic than Gwendolen's. When Grandcourt "[f]ormerly [...] asked [her]
to put them into his keeping again, simply on the ground that they would be safer
and ought to be deposited at the bank, she had quietly but absolutely refused"
(343), as she again refuses when he demands them a second time, for his wedding
(349). Her insistence on keeping the diamonds in her possession until she can
deliver them to his new bride, a "purpose" compared at one point to a child's grasp
on "a small stolen thing" (351), is no more legitimate than Gwendolen's. One

---

[13] Wilkie Collins, *The Moonstone* [1868], ed. Sandra Kemp (London: Penguin Books Ltd., 1998). For
the novel's popularity, see "Introduction," vii–xii; for some of Collins's sources, see viii–ix.

[14] E.g., Carolyn Dever, *Death and the Mother from Dickens to Freud: Victorian Fiction and the
Anxiety of Origins* (Cambridge: Cambridge University Press, 1998): 164. For relations between Lydia
and Gwendolen, see Munich 137.

[15] Blumberg, " 'Love Yourself as Your Neighbor': The Limits of Altruism and the Ethics of Personal
Benefit in *Adam Bede*," *Victorian Literature and Culture* 37 (2009): 543–60, 544, 546; Blumberg,
Sacrifice 106.

WOMEN'S PROPERTY LAW AND JEWISH CULTURAL INHERITANCE   129

problem with reading Gwendolen as stealing the diamonds from Lydia—a trans-action that Lydia attempts to establish as parallel to profiting from a marriage that has been illegitimately contracted—is that Lydia herself is not the legal owner of the gems she has been keeping.[16] Moreover, the coveted objects in this transaction are not actually metonyms for marriage, marital wealth, or marital love. Grandcourt himself is no jewel, and even the "privilege" of marrying him and of sharing in his wealth is a dubious one, given the control he exerts over his possessions. Gwendolen's "loving him having never been a question with her" (315), her highest romantic aspiration is to have "the least disagreeable of hus-bands" (305), and by this point in the novel Lydia's love has "resolved itself into anxiety" (341), while Grandcourt's "passion" for Lydia is "as dead as the music of a cracked flute" (340). But if marriage ceases to be the primary lens for viewing these women's relationship to property—if we trace the money, instead of the passions and injured feelings of triangulated heterosexuality—we see that the conflict is not actually about marriage or the claims of mistress and wife themselves.[17] Instead, the novel uses diamonds and the clash between two vulnerable women to stage a debate about the relative rights of a wife and a son.

When Lydia first confronts Gwendolen to ask that she not marry Grandcourt, it is because "'[h]e ought to make [her] boy his heir'" (152), and when she yearns for marriage herself it is so that "her son could be made his father's heir" (341). The novel ultimately dismisses her personal complaint "'that [Grandcourt] should be happy and I miserable'"—this marriage will make no one "happy"—but it takes far more seriously her objection to "'my boy [being] thrust out of sight for another'" (152). Along similar lines, Gwendolen treats Lydia's personal status and desires unsympathetically: "'He could have married her if he had liked; but he did *not* like. Perhaps she is to blame for that'" (314). Gwendolen, the eponymous "spoiled child" of the novel's first book, further and somewhat hypocritically condemns Lydia's greed; noting to herself that "'there will be enough for two,'" Gwendolen concludes that "Mrs Glasher appeared quite unreasonable in demand-ing that her boy should be sole heir" (314). Along these self-justifying lines, we might say that Gwendolen considers Lydia guilty of the desire for engrossment that Elsie B. Michie associates with "vulgar" women during this time.[18] Even before Gwendolen receives Lydia's letter, however, the question of the child's inheritance prompts her to feel remorse and generosity. "'Perhaps we shall have no children. I hope we shall not. And he might leave the estate to the pretty little boy'" (314). Despite her disregard for Lydia's own position, Gwendolen

---

[16] See also Wynne 116.

[17] David W. Toise also notes the "failure of heterosexual romance to structure the plot" of *Daniel Deronda*. See "Sexuality's Uncertain History: Or, 'Narrative Disjunction' in 'Daniel Deronda,'" *Victorian Literature and Culture* 38.1 (2010): 127–50, 127.

[18] Michie 1–2, 28–9.

130 IMAGINING WOMEN'S PROPERTY IN VICTORIAN FICTION

recognizes the claims of her child and shares his mother's dread of "injur[ing]" a son by "robbing" him.

In Gwendolen's guilty view of her own "theft" and in the financial arrangements Grandcourt subsequently makes for his families, the novel pits the wife's right to property against that of a son. Significantly, the son in question is not Gwendolen's. Critics have commented extensively on Gwendolen's "sterility" in her brief and unhappy marriage, describing it as a function of Lydia's "curse," a punishment for Gwendolen's "theft of little Henleigh's inheritance," her "exclusion" from reproduction, a narrative means of leaving the future to Jews, or a parallel with Eliot's life.[19] Alternatively, and more in keeping with Gwendolen's own desires—her "repugnance" to and fear of Grandcourt contributing to her wish not to conceive (313, 427)—Gillian Beer views her childless state as a "fairy-tale element" of salvation.[20] What all of this reproductive speculation ignores is the constraint that a child born within the marriage would place on the narrative: in the case of "legitimate" paternity, law and legal precedent had plenty to say about inheritance. Had Gwendolen given birth to a son, the question—should the estates go to this son or to Lydia's—would have been a relatively straightforward legal matter, a contest between two children, one "legitimate," one "illegitimate." Nineteenth-century law passed over children born out of wedlock. Legally speaking, if Grandcourt had died without a will, Lydia's child would have had less claim than Gwendolen to his estate, and even if Grandcourt had married Lydia her son might have no claim; he "*could* be made his father's heir" but would not become so automatically (341, emphasis added). By leaving the Grandcourt marriage childless and assigning his property by will rather than common law, Eliot makes the financial conflict generational (wife or son) and shifts the conversation away from the child's birth status. After Grandcourt's death, that is, inheritance law becomes irrelevant.[21] The heir looks like his father, acquires most of his wealth, and even takes his name. The question of legitimacy (mistress versus wife, bastard versus bride) thus gives way to asking whether wealth should travel along conjugal or consanguineal lines—whether heterosexual union (a wife) or lineal descent (a first-born son) should be the determining factor for obtaining property.[22]

Eliot demonstrated her practical sympathy for wives' economic circumstances by signing the 1856 petition for married women's property rights and by specifying that the substantial annuities she bequeathed to women in her own will were

---

[19] See, respectively, Brooks 101; Thierauf 264; Gallagher 54; Alan T. Levenson, "Writing the Philosemitic Novel: *Daniel Deronda* Revisited," *Prooftexts* 28.2 (2008): 129–56, 143 and David (*Fictions*) 194, 203; Henry, *George Eliot* 105, 230.

[20] Gillian Beer, in *Darwin's Plots: Evolutionary Narrative in Darwin, George Eliot, and Nineteenth-Century Fiction*, 2nd ed. (Cambridge: Cambridge University Press, 1983, 2000): 173, 209.

[21] For Eliot's criticism of primogeniture and entail in multiple novels, see Henry, *George Eliot* 157.

[22] Osborne suggests that that Eliot privileges emotional connection over bloodlines (489, 466–7), but it is worth recalling that Grandcourt passes property consanguineally to a biological son with whom he has little connection and who lacks "any particular liking for this friend of mamma's" (344).

WOMEN'S PROPERTY LAW AND JEWISH CULTURAL INHERITANCE   131

for their separate use, free from their husbands' control.[23] She also showed a great deal of concern for the financial well-being of children, whether "legitimate" or not. In her longstanding "ambiguous position as neither wife nor mistress, or perhaps more accurately, as both"[24] to married partner George Henry Lewes, the financial needs of children at times superseded her own. From the early days of their life together, when her earning was unreliable, through the period when her much larger authorial income made it far easier to have dependents, she helped to support the debts and annual maintenance of his "legal but unfaithful wife"[25] Agnes Jervis Lewes and her seven children, three from her marriage to Lewes and an additional four with Thornton Hunt.[26] As Nancy Henry has discussed, *Daniel Deronda*'s Lydia "represents the ambiguities of Agnes's position and the complexity of Eliot's feelings toward the first wife/former lover of her 'husband.'"[27] Also significant, I think, is the way that the inheritance granted to Grandcourt's "illegitimate" child—at Gwendolen's expense but with her full endorsement—engages Eliot's possible feelings and financial attitudes toward the children she supported so extensively, not only in their youth but also as adults, after Lewes's death and even beyond her own.[28] Her life as well as her fiction suggests an expansive understanding of family obligation.[29] She goes far beyond any legal mandate to affirm that romantic relationships should not detract from children's fortunes and that children conceived out of wedlock, whether by a

[23] For details about Eliot's will, see Frank 58. For her signature, as Marian Evans, on the petition, Holcombe 83. Despite her support for married women's property, many of Eliot's "best" female characters are "avowedly anti-materialist"; see Monica Cohen, "From Home to Homeland: The Bohemian in *Daniel Deronda,*" *Studies in the Novel* 30.3 (1998): 324–54, 336. See also Henry, *George Eliot* 136. Others note Eliot's "ambivalence about political involvement" (Thierauf 247). Despite Eliot's legal status as "Spinster," her financial circumstances were intertwined with those of her partner, G. H. Lewes even after his death. See Rosemary Ashton, *George Eliot: A Life* (London: Hamish Hamilton, 1996): 368.

[24] Henry, *George Eliot* 82.

[25] Holcombe 84.

[26] For Eliot's income in 1853 and 1854, as well as her calculations regarding what Agnes and the children received, see Rosemary Ashton, *G. H. Lewes: A Life* (Oxford: Clarendon Press, 1991): 143 as well as Appendix II from *The George Eliot Letters*, Vol. VII, ed. Gordon S. Haight (New Haven: Yale University Press, 1954): 382–3. Lewes was the legal father of Agnes's children with Hunt (Henry, *George Eliot* 86, 100, 223), and she depended upon Lewes and Eliot for financial support (Ashton, *G. H. Lewes* 178, 179, 239, 212). Special thanks to Nancy Henry, who generously and quickly supplied me with information and pages on this topic during the COVID-19 shutdown of 2020.

[27] Henry, *George Eliot* 212, 213, 85, 88. For Agnes's significance to Eliot's writing, see Henry, *George Eliot* 7, 20, 80, 125–6, 166.

[28] Eliot financially supported the children's professional pursuits (Henry, *George Eliot* 83, 123, 134, 140–1, 158, 223), and after Herbert (Bertie) Lewes's death she supported his widow Eliza and their two children during her life and subsequently in her will (Henry, *George Eliot* 259). Charles Lewes, the oldest son, was "sole executor and residual legatee" of Eliot's estate, and Margaret Harris notes that "In death as in life, George Eliot's earnings supported the extended Lewes family"; see Harris, "Afterlife," in *George Eliot in Context*, ed. Margaret Harris (Cambridge: Cambridge University Press, 2013): 52–62, 53. For more details about Charles's relationship with his "Mutter" Eliot, see Margaret Harris, "Charles Lewes's Career," *George Eliot-George Henry Lewes Studies* 72.1 (2020): 1–19, 3, 5 and Henry, *George Eliot* 127.

[29] See also Henry, *George Eliot* 30.

132   IMAGINING WOMEN'S PROPERTY IN VICTORIAN FICTION

husband such as Grandcourt or a wife such as Agnes Lewes, should not be punished for their parents' actions.[30]

Despite *Daniel Deronda*'s clear privileging of the son over the wife with respect to inheritance, however, there is nothing inevitable about that choice, and diamonds embody the directional tension of these competing kinship priorities. As John Plotz has noted with regard to their sentimental and economic values, diamonds "are at their most distinctive in Victorian novels when they are manifestly *riven*."[31] Though we are now most accustomed to understanding British diamond transactions as unjust because of exploitative trade practices and imperial plunder, their domestic transmission within England was fraught in this period as well. Grandcourt's engagement ring and family jewels represent tensions inherent in family wealth. At this time, a woman's sexuality and offspring alike were seen as her "jewels," and diamonds symbolized marriageable women as well as the children they produced, so their relational affinity is with both Gwendolen and the young Grandcourt.[32] Alongside this symbolic doubleness, their multidirectional physical movement makes family jewels difficult to pin down. Diamonds could either mark marriage (a lateral move) or pass from one generation to another (a vertical trajectory). Whereas *Middlemarch*, despite briefly acknowledging the gems' "miserable" trade practices, simplifies their domestic transfer—a maternal legacy of jewels descends to two generally amicable and still-unmarried sisters without mention of competing familial claims (indeed, without further mention at all)[33]—*Daniel Deronda*'s scenario is more complicated. In this case, they pass to children (Grandcourt possesses his mother's diamonds, or did so before passing them along to Lydia) but they are also associated with the horizontal traffic of marriage: he "necessarily wished to have them for his wife" (343). In some configurations, inherited property, bearing the marks of its intergenerational path even when gifted laterally within marriage, can function to consolidate a family unit through its collective possession of wealth. Not so here, however. Eliot's novel shows clearly that this sense of family property is not a viable option. Not only do Gwendolen and the young heir represent different and competing

---

[30] Lewes himself was illegitimate—see Margaret Harris, "George Eliot's Reputation," in *The Cambridge Companion to George Eliot*, ed. George Levine and Nancy Henry (Cambridge: Cambridge University Press, 2019): 236–58, 245; Rosemary Ashton, *G. H. Lewes* 9—though he may not have known this (Ashton, *G. H. Lewes* 10). For Eliot's privileging of "moral commitment" over "legal bonds," see Henry, *George Eliot* 81, 144.

[31] Plotz 31. See also n. 11 of the present chapter.

[32] Markovits 597. For jewelry as signifying sexuality and as a form of communication, see Brooks 98, 103, and 104.

[33] Despite the fairly quick resolution of Dorothea's inner conflict about gemstones, Eliot's concerns about them seem to linger within *Middlemarch*. Subsequent references to "Diamond" in that novel interestingly displace the exploitative and injurious practices of the trade from gemstones onto the horse that Fred Vincy purchases (239), who not only fails to bring him the wished-for profit but also "ended in laming himself severely" (241) and whose "unsanitary" origins appear responsible for Fred's ensuing and "serious" illness (259, 260).

WOMEN'S PROPERTY LAW AND JEWISH CULTURAL INHERITANCE   133

family groups with no sense of a shared future, but neither Gwendolen nor Grandcourt views property through the lens of collective possession. Gwendolen first covets and then regrets "having *her own* diamonds" (358, emphasis added), while Grandcourt makes clear to her that any determination of "family" wealth excludes consideration of a wife's feelings or claims: "'What you think has nothing to do with it'" (427). Instead of merging interests or consolidating family through wealth, then, Grandcourt's diamonds serve as a sign of the family's internal division as well as its lack of concern for those members not protected by economic law. Their symbolic value and material history come together to suggest that these diamonds do and don't belong with both Gwendolen and the heir, whose tenuous economic positions, in this rendering, oppose one another. These particular circumstances highlight the potentially problematic nature of "family" property in general because, despite the symbolic double valence of the diamonds, they can't actually be owned by or even serve the interests of woman and child at the same time. Analogous, in an extralegal register, to the generational conflict posed by primogeniture in *Wives and Daughters*, the diamonds mark a problem with possession because in practical terms they refute simultaneity and compel a choice.

The novel thus uses diamonds to ask whether marriage or reproduction is the right repository for family wealth. By way of an answer, a wife's wealth appears as theft. Everyone supports the son's claim to inheritance.[34] Even Gwendolen's well-wishers support Grandcourt's choice of his son as heir. Grandcourt's uncle, Sir Hugo, thinks that Gwendolen should have had a more "'handsome provision'" (717) and resents Grandcourt's "'shabby'" legacy to her (757), but he "'say[s] nothing against his leaving the land to the lad'" (716) and eventually remarks that "'since the boy is there, this was really the best alternative for the disposal of the estates'" (757). Daniel, the moral center of the novel, goes so far as to say that "'[Grandcourt] did wrong when he married this wife—not in leaving his estates to the son'" (716). Gwendolen herself is "'quite contented with it'" (717), calling the decision "'all perfectly right'" (759) and expressing relief, after Grandcourt's death, that she is "'saved from robbing others'" (699). Notably, Lydia's other, older three children—daughters—do not figure into these final calculations. We do not know whether Grandcourt ever makes good on his earlier "'th[ought] of by-and-by settling a good sum on [Lydia] and the children'" (347); reports of his will, which indicate at least some distribution of wealth through Gwendolen's annual payments, state simply that "'he has left everything'" to the son (716). His privileging of male lineage and the entitlement of his only son meet with a far

---

[34] Though the son's inheritance might benefit his mother, I disagree that it constitutes "reparation to Mrs. Glasher [...] from Gwendolen" (Dever 169); Gwendolen explicitly differentiates the son's rights from those of his mother. Lydia will not control her son's wealth, and if he is like his father it may provide her with little personal comfort.

134   IMAGINING WOMEN'S PROPERTY IN VICTORIAN FICTION

more favorable reception than we saw earlier in the century, when Austen presented daughters' claims to wealth sympathetically. In Eliot's novel, "'there is no question about leaving [the heir's sisters] in beggary,'" but beyond that they appear not to merit discussion (347). In contrast, the financial circumstances of Gwendolen and the heir appear in direct relation to one another. Nobody argues that a wife should have greater claims than a son. Indeed, by framing a wife's possible gain as a son's loss, Eliot implies the opposite. By representing Gwendolen's acquisition of diamonds as theft, the novel suggests that property accrued through marriage is less legitimate than property acquired through transmission to a son.

These arguments had serious stakes. In 1876, when *Daniel Deronda* was published, the common law still prevented wives from acquiring or controlling much wealth and favored the rights of sons over those of widows. Consequently, providing for widows was a question of personal feeling and a bride's male protectors rather than legal mandate.[35] Grandcourt's decision to overlook his wife may be ungracious, uncaring, even punitive, and it goes against a precedent of giving widows the life interest in their husbands' property,[36] but it is not legally unsound. Recognizing this, Sir Hugo states simply that "'A man ought to have some pride and fondness for his widow. [...] I take it as a test of a man, that he feels the easier about his death when he can think of his wife and daughters being comfortable after it'" (757). Sir Hugo himself has met that test. Unlike the men of so many nineteenth-century novels—Jane Austen's Mr. Bennet, who continues to "spend [...] his whole income" instead of saving "an annual sum for the better provision of his wife and children," for instance, or George Gissing's Dr. Madden, who dies before "insuring [his] life for a thousand pounds" for his six daughters in *The Odd Women* (1893)[37]—Sir Hugo has "husbanded his fortune" in order to provide for his wife and daughters when his life interest in his lands has run its course (159, 158, 585).[38] His desires and foresight are presented as a function of his unusual and "wonderful goodness" to his family, however, not as a matter of justice (442). Along similar lines, Gwendolen's male protectors are annoyed at the individual case, rather than being outraged by laws that have failed to protect her interests. Grandcourt's "'posthumous grudgingness towards a wife'" comes across as a personal character flaw (757), one presented as an outlier among "wonderfully good" men and thus easier both to attack and to remedy than a longstanding legal system.

[35] Significantly, Gwendolen has had no pre-nuptial settlement; given her impoverished state, her male protectors thought it fit to leave financial matters up to her husband.

[36] See, e.g., Alastair Owens, "Property, Gender and the Life Course: Inheritance and Family Welfare Provision in Early Nineteenth-Century England," *Social History* 26.3 (2001): 299–317, 305–6.

[37] Austen, *Pride and Prejudice* 199–200; George Gissing, *The Odd Women* [1893], ed. Elaine Showalter (London: Penguin Books Ltd., 1983): 1, 6.

[38] For the relationship of Sir Hugo's financial plot to Eliot's father's employment, see Henry, *George Eliot* 26.

WOMEN'S PROPERTY LAW AND JEWISH CULTURAL INHERITANCE   135

But the system was in the process of changing. Married women's property rights, as we have seen, were under question during this period. Political agitation for wives' rights to their own property, begun by a petition in 1856, had so far produced the Married Women's Property Act of 1870; a fuller recognition of women's economic rights within marriage would follow shortly, with the Married Women's Property Act of 1882. The 1870 Act, which gave working women the right to money earned by their own labor and to small bequests, postdates the novel's 1860s setting and would not have actually helped a woman of Gwendolen's social standing, for whom marriage had been the financial alternative to other unwelcome or unopen careers and whose marriage would have in turn precluded the forms of income typically protected by the Act.[39] Despite its limited reach, however, the cultural anxieties attending this 1870 law were as great as if it had it had done much more. For many commentators, it "signaled the demise of coverture" by granting some women the possibility of slight economic independence from their husbands.[40] As we have seen in the previous chapter's discussion of Trollope's novels, the new legal precedent of recognizing a wife's claim to *any* property within marriage appears, for some writers, equivalent to letting a wife claim *all* property within marriage. In fact, the Act authorized no such thing: although the common law doctrine of coverture previously ensured that a wife's property would become her husband's upon marriage, neither it nor the new law caused a husband's property to become that of his wife. Even a widow's claims, after the Dower Act of 1833, depended upon the wishes and legal actions of her late husband.[41] Yet it seems striking that after the 1870 Act weakened the doctrine of coverture as absolute, a wife's independent possession of property— diamonds she can call her "own"—should be represented as illicit. During this time of intense debate about property rights, the novel's putative "crime" and its resolution—depicting a wife's wealth as theft and then saving her from "robbing others" by restoring it to a male heir—suggests that when wives claim property as their "own" they do so at the expense of sons. In this zero-sum view of family property, the redistribution of marital resources to include wives injures others— particularly if women with wealth are not recognized as having economic agency, the ability to make reasonable or ethical choices, or a capacious understanding of what family ties might entail. Accordingly, mercenary marriage becomes

---

[39] The novel opens with her gambling losses (11), shows her ill-equipped for a career on stage (255–7), and offers as her only other options the roles of governess or teacher (269).

[40] Rachel Ablow, "'One Flesh,' One Person, and the 1870 Married Women's Property Act," in *BRANCH: Britain, Representation and Nineteenth-Century History*, ed. Dino Franco Felluga, Extension of *Romanticism and Victorianism on the Net* (May 6, 2020). For Victorian understandings and uses of coverture, see Rachel Ablow, *The Marriage of Minds: Reading Sympathy in the Victorian Marriage Plot* (Stanford: Stanford University Press, 2007): 10–13; for 1870 as a clear breaking point in romantic ideals of coverture see Ablow, *Marriage* 15.

[41] See Susan Staves, *Married Women's Separate Property in England, 1660–1833* (Cambridge, MA: Harvard University Press, 1990): esp. 27–8, 32–7, 49, 130.

136 IMAGINING WOMEN'S PROPERTY IN VICTORIAN FICTION

problematic not simply for what it suggests about the financially interested wife or the imbalanced economic conditions of marriage itself but because—at least in this assessment of marital transfers—it enables and even encourages a wife to wrongfully withhold money from the next generation.

At the same time, however, the fact that this son's claim to his wealth depends upon the whim of an entirely unlikeable man and the "unfortunate absence of a legitimate heir" (756–7), rather than the common law doctrine of primogeniture, reminds us of young Grandcourt's own problematic claims to ownership and reflects the inadequacy of both contemporary law and social feeling to allocate rightful possession in such a case. By side-stepping the law in this respect, the novel demonstrates considerably less "grudgingness towards a wife" than Grandcourt does. Its depiction of women's stinted economic autonomy before, within, or without marriage—Gwendolen's step-father having "carried off his wife's jewellery and disposed of it" (274–5), for instance—suggests greater sympathy for women's restricted options. Other unhappy unions (Mirah's "'good'" mother mistreated by a "'scoundrel'" [223], Daniel's mother Leonora Halm-Eberstein "'forced into marrying your father'" [626]) also demonstrate the need for other conceptions of marriage than "coverture," a concept that repeatedly fails to gloss over everything from dissent to dangerous struggle between husbands and wives and that cannot give Grandcourt "the least conception of what was going on in the breast of [his] wife" (670). Unwilling to allow women to profit from marriage, the novel nonetheless portrays marriage as an institution in need of reform, and consequently regards the treatment of husbands with less censure than the treatment of illegitimate sons. When Grandcourt drowns during a boating trip in Genoa, accidentally thrown overboard, Gwendolen's feelings of guilt from having wanted to "'kill him in my thoughts'" (695) and not taking immediate action to save him though "[she] had the rope in [her] hand" (696) fail to incriminate her. Discovered in tears, on her knees, "Such grief seemed natural in a poor lady whose husband had been drowned in her presence" (702); the "cover" of marriage effectively absolves her of any wrongdoing.[42]

II. "A Sacred Inheritance"

Gwendolen's plot—like Lydia's—suggests that neither character, coverture, nor the 1870 Married Women's Property Act is a sufficient measure for justly distributing property, marital and otherwise; both contemporary law and social feeling fail to determine rightful possession. *Daniel Deronda*'s other plot responds to this problem of family property by reframing it, looking for guidance in divine

---

[42] For Gwendolen's trauma, see Matus 142; for her inaction as a form of mutiny, see McCormack 84, 91. For coverture as a means of exonerating wives from debt, see Rappaport 48–50, 57.

WOMEN'S PROPERTY LAW AND JEWISH CULTURAL INHERITANCE   137

commandments and Jewish tradition, rather than the dictates of British property law. As he faces the theft and reclamation of his cultural property and spiritual inheritance, Daniel learns to appraise property in different terms and, crucially, to see family as a more expansive category.[43] The inalienable nature of Daniel's most valuable possession seems to offer a somewhat more reassuring view of inheritance than the one that shapes the lives of Sir Hugo, Gwendolen, Lydia, or her children (or than we saw previously in Dickens's *Our Mutual Friend*). This is no utopian alternative, however. As Amanda Anderson has argued, Daniel's plot is not simply Eliot's "attempt to flee [the] instabilities [of Gwendolen's plot] by constructing Jewish identity as an absolute ideal."[44] Nor, in its "transcendence of an empty materialism," does this version of property ownership merely mean "the spiritual transformation of English society."[45] This plot continues to take seriously the significance of property as something to be desired, transferred, stolen, or treasured. It also continues to favor male ownership and rebuke women who seek to disrupt lines of descent through "theft." Its resolution will not help to secure property rights for the Gwendolens, Lydias, Leonoras, or even Mirahs of the world, nor will it offer a plan for systemic change. Yet by celebrating alternatives to British law, it undermines the Victorian institutions that attempt to regulate family property, removing the power of adjudication from the British courts of common law and equity. This turn to religious precept and the emphasis on inheritance might seem to revive ecclesiastical courts, which, prior to 1857, had jurisdiction over marriage and probate.[46] The novel intimates, though, that tradition, community, and personal choice can organize inheritance more effectively than legal mandate, whether religious or secular. By demonstrating the pull of broader and more fluid forms of connection, *Daniel Deronda* also challenges more restrictive definitions of heteronormative, nuclear, legally authorized "family" for Victorian Jews and non-Jews alike, embracing alternative kinship formations driven by property transactions that ultimately leave material wealth aside.

For Daniel, as for Gwendolen, these deliberations feature diamonds, which signal connections but also disrupt them through theft, showcasing competing claims to property and the conflicting commitments that property represents. His "'fine diamond ring'" (391) receives less attention than Gwendolen's "poisoned gems" (359) or the turquoise necklace (previously her father's) that he redeems for her shortly after their first encounter,[47] but it plays a key role in the second plot of

---

[43] For cultural, literary, monetary, and metaphoric inheritance in *Middlemarch*, see Henry, *George Eliot* 193, 200–1.
[44] Amanda Anderson, *The Powers of Distance: Cosmopolitanism and the Cultivation of Detachment* (Princeton: Princeton University Press, 2001): 121.
[45] Bryan Cheyette, *Constructions of "the Jew" in English Literature and Society: Racial Representation, 1875–1945* (New York: Cambridge University Press, 1995): 54.
[46] Holcombe 11–12, 15. For greater detail about the changing functions of ecclesiastical courts, see also Outhwaite, e.g., 157–73.
[47] E.g., Henry, *George Eliot* 232.

138 IMAGINING WOMEN'S PROPERTY IN VICTORIAN FICTION

Eliot's novel, which returns the English-bred gentleman to his Jewish roots and channels his wide-ranging sympathies into a proto-Zionist nationalist mission.[48] Daniel's ring symbolically stands in for and materially connects him to his larger cultural heritage, having belonged to his biological father whom he later learns was a Jew. By pawning his diamond ring, Daniel becomes acquainted with Mordecai, the man eventually revealed to be Daniel's own spiritual partner as well as the long-lost brother of Mirah, the singer Daniel rescues from the Thames and ultimately marries. Whereas Gwendolen's diamonds represent marriage and procreation as conflicting priorities, Daniel's diamond ring and its multiple connections to a Jewish father, brother, wife, and nation seem aligned with ideas of heritage that supersede direct lineage and thus avoid the conflict posed by Gwendolen's diamonds. By the time that the diamond is detached from both his finger and his cares, its theft valorizes a different kind of property; unlike the gemstones that feature in both plots, Daniel's cultural property can be securely transmitted, despite or perhaps because of its many directional pulls and ability to benefit wide-ranging kin simultaneously.[49]

Although diamonds circulate in both plots, *Daniel Deronda* associates jewelry and commerce most strongly with its Jews. Their eyes "glittered like [. . .] gems" (720), and Mirah's Christian suitor fears that her long-lost brother could turn out to be "'a fellow all smiles and jewellery—a Crystal Palace Assyrian'" (579). Mordecai, whose eyes are "dark gems" (573), wears no jewelry, but he does repair it at Ezra Cohen's pawnshop (400), while Ezra, who specializes in jewelry and watches (382) and alarms Daniel with "his vulgarity of soul" (391), not only "'know[s] stones well'" (399) but also understands how to "bre[e]d more money" out of them (517). He is "'not afraid of taking that ring of yours at [his] own valuation'" (399). The novel's depiction of Jewish pawnshops picks up on and perpetuates Jews' connections with moneylending, one of few occupations historically permitted to them but often invoked to reinforce anti-Semitic accusations of greed and materialism.[50] Early scenes detailing Gwendolen's decision to

---

[48] For the relationship of this "proto-Zionism" to "Zionism proper," see Dekel 784–5; Meyer "'Safely'" 747–50; and Monica O'Brien, "The Politics of Blood and Soil: Hannah Arendt, George Eliot, and the Jewish Question in Modern Europe," *Comparative Literature Studies* 44.1/2 (2007): 97–117, 99–100, 105–6: https://www.jstor.org/stable/25659563.

[49] For the novel's anti-Semitic depiction of "refined" Jews as acorporeal and unencumbered by the riches of "vulgar" Jews, see Susan Meyer, *Imperialism at Home: Race and Victorian Women's Fiction* (Ithaca: Cornell University Press, 1996): 181–2, also "'Safely'" 147; for commerce's embodiment in Jews, see Michie, *Vulgar* 131. Michael Ragussis, in contrast, suggests that *Daniel Deronda*'s project is, in part, "to overturn the anti-Semitism that is specifically based in a kind of racial jealousy"; see Ragussis, *Figures of Conversion: "The Jewish Question" and English National Identity* (Durham: Duke University Press, 1995): 264. See also Munich 137.

[50] See Anderson 127; Meyer, "'Safely'" 745. For usury in *Daniel Deronda*, see Cleere, *Avuncularism* 147; for associations of Jews with ancient histories of wealth, see Heidi Kaufman, "*King Solomon's Mines*?: African Jewry, British Imperialism, and H. Rider Haggard's Diamonds," *Victorian Literature and Culture* 33 (2005): 517–39, 522. According to Mary Wilson Carpenter, pawnshops stand in for the histories which Gwendolen loses and Daniel redeems; see "The Apocalypse of the Old Testament:

WOMEN'S PROPERTY LAW AND JEWISH CULTURAL INHERITANCE   139

part with her father's necklace, for example, insist that such profits are unfair, despite the irony attending these particular losses: "these Jew dealers were so unscrupulous in taking advantage of Christians unfortunate at play!" (19). *Daniel Deronda*'s Mr. and Mrs. Arrowpoint also reflect this stereotypical Victorian view of Jews as financially motivated; they are dismayed by their daughter's engagement to the Jewish musician Herr Klesmer, wrongly suspecting that he wishes only to "'marry [her] fortune'" while they are determined to instead "'place [their] great property in the right hands,'" even if it means disinheriting their daughter (248, 246). While Klesmer emphatically proves them wrong, Ezra Cohen's family seems to confirm such prejudiced views of mercenary behavior through his young son's "aged commercial soul" (390) and his own willingness to conduct business on the Sabbath (392).[51] Finally, Mr. Lapidoth—father of Mirah and Mordecai, whose biblical name conjures the gem-shaping work of lapidaries—carries away Daniel's precious diamond ring, giving in to "a dominance of desire, like the thirst of the drunkard" (790) because he is unable to resist the temptation of acquiring wealth so easily. If the novel's English marriage plot condemns making "'our gain [...] another's loss'" (337), it relies on anti-Semitic stereotypes to associate such "unscrupulous" gain or theft with many of its "vulgar" Jewish characters and their jewelry in its plot of Daniel's heritage.

Eliot's emphasis on diamonds in her "Jewish" novel reflects the history of the European diamond trade and, by the time of *Daniel Deronda*, of English diamond imports, as largely managed by networks of Jewish families.[52] According to Marcia Pointon:

> The first great diamond diaspora was the result of the Inquisition's persecution of Portuguese Jews, which brought wealthy and highly skilled diamond dealers to London, often under assumed names. [...] It has been reliably claimed that London achieved its position in the diamond trade in the eighteenth century as a direct result of the immigration of Jewish diamond merchants from the Netherlands and Portugal, and later also from Leghorn and Germany.[53]

Daniel Deronda and the Interpretation of Interpretation," *PMLA* 99.1 (1984): 56–71, 61. For a discussion of an "ambivalent semitic discourse" in the nineteenth century, see Bryan Cheyette, 53 and 13–54 *passim*.

[51] As others have noted, the novel is particularly critical of Jews who show signs of assimilation; see Anderson 124–6, O'Brien 110. For readings of the Cohen family as "the wrong Jews," see Linehan 338, Cheyette 47, and David, *Fictions* 162. David suggests that Eliot "displaces her ideal of English working-class conduct" onto the novel's Jews (*Fictions* 153, see also 160–1, 162), while Levenson points out that Eliot emphasizes the Cohens's Sabbath rituals (148). For a more sympathetic reading of Cohen, see Levenson 149. For Eliot's reworking of Jewish conversion plots, see Ragussis 268.

[52] For the diamond trade, see Munich 86–7. For an argument regarding *Middlemarch* as also representing Eliot's significant but "*sub rosa*" literary engagement in Judaism, see Adler 157, 143–9, 162, 164. My thanks to Abigail BeDard for bringing Adler's argument to my attention.

[53] See Marcia Pointon, *Rocks, Ice and Dirty Stones: Diamond Histories* (London: Reaktion Books, 2017): 83, also 44, 71, 81.

140   IMAGINING WOMEN'S PROPERTY IN VICTORIAN FICTION

Even the proto-Zionist cause of Jewish return trumpeted by Mordecai and then Daniel in the novel aligned Jews with diamonds by protecting England's overland route to India,[54] one source of British diamonds before the discovery of South African mines in 1867. Furthermore, as Heidi Kaufman discusses, following that discovery, "[e]conomic competition between Jewish and non-Jewish European financiers ensued and instigated a flood of anti-Semitism in the region."[55] As this anti-Semitism suggests, historical ties between Jewish merchants and the diamond trade do not suffice to explain accusations of vulgarity and greed, which have other histories as well. While works such as Collins's *The Moonstone* linked diamonds to chains of imperial plunder and theft from foreign peoples, the gemstones were also problematic among a Victorian readership for their associations with Jews. "'English-born'" but, as *Daniel Deronda*'s Mirah understands, not considered "'English'" (193),[56] Jews could not hold seats in Parliament until 1858. Considered at the time to be racially as well as ethnically other, they were viewed as an internal colony of outsiders, more complicated in their relation to England or Englishness than true foreigners: when Daniel learns that Mirah is a Jew, he reflects that one "might *simply* have guessed her to be Spanish" (193, emphasis added).

Eliot's emphasis on diamonds in this novel thus draws on cultural attitudes toward Jews as much as or more than an understanding of gemstone circulation. Along similar lines, Trollope, whose novels feature in the previous chapter of this study, links his notorious Eustace diamonds to the disreputable Jewish tradesman Mr. Benjamin, who colludes with Lizzie as an accessory to her first marriage and her acquisition of the necklace, provides her with the heavy strong box in which she keeps them for much of that novel's duration (*ED* I: 41), and finally receives fifteen years of penal servitude for his role in stealing the diamonds (*ED* II: 357). Aligning Lizzie throughout the novel with Jewish jewelers who "were not trustworthy" (*ED* I: 42), Trollope assigns similar guilt to her and eventually punishes her through marriage to a criminal (and converted clergyman) later referred to as "'Lizzie Eustace's Jew'" (*PR* 359).[57] As Michie points out, Trollope's depiction of Lizzie resembles Victorian images of Jews, "signifying not racial difference per se but the attitudes toward wealth the Victorians linked to the Jew."[58] In Trollope's novel, this invocation of Jewishness incriminates Lizzie but also differentiates her from (and absolves from greed) those other English "ladies quite content to accept the good things settled upon them" (*ED* I: 254). Eliot's novel also uses Jews in order to resolve the problem of Englishwomen's property

---

[54] Meyer, *Imperialism* 186; Meyer, "'Safely'" 748.
[55] Kaufman 518; see also 519, 525–6.
[56] For Jews as a "dark race," see Meyer, *Imperialism* 160, 168; Anderson 128; Ragussis 275.
[57] See Cheyette 35–6 for discussion of Lizzie's second husband; also Munich 123.
[58] Michie 130, also 129, 131. For Trollope's portrayal of "the Jewish infiltration of English culture," as well as Eliot's "novel as a response" to him, see Ragussis 234, also 234–60. For the "inner rapaciousness" that Trollope associates with Jews see Cheyette 35, 33–4, 40.

WOMEN'S PROPERTY LAW AND JEWISH CULTURAL INHERITANCE   141

acquisition. Eliot, however, connects Jews to diamonds less to limit the liability of women in general or to scapegoat Jews for the materialism that Gwendolen no less than the pawnbroker exhibits than to create a fantasy of a different, cultural property that cannot be stolen, despite various "thefts." As we will see, the inalienability of this property, a function of Daniel's Jewish identity, offers a corrective to yet another incident of a mother "robbing" her son.

Eileen Cleere has argued that the novel "project[s] Daniel's problematic Jewish economic identity onto Gwendolyn Harleth [...] absorb[ing] the ideological contaminations of usury so that Daniel can be cleansed."[59] But as Michie has shown and the plots of Gwendolen, Lizzie Eustace, and others bear out, Victorian women with wealth also appear to need redemption from their "problematic [...] economic identit[ies]," especially since, at that time, it remained an open question whether or not women were entitled to any economic identity at all. If, as Susan Meyer has argued, "proto-Zionism [...] is the central metaphor through which Eliot simultaneously expunges female impulses to transgress social boundaries and expunges those who penetrate England's national boundaries," we need to be more specific about those impulses and the narrative solution.[60] Eliot does not merely "cleanse" Jews—or women—in her conclusion; she cleanses property itself, laundering the narrative money so that wealth by the end of the novel means something entirely different from its meaning at the start. This differs, I think, from simply replacing "empty materialism" with "transcendence," as Bryan Cheyette describes it, or, in Gallagher's words, from substituting a "moral economy" for tainted commercial exchanges.[61] Both of these formulations, in keeping with nineteenth-century suspicions of capitalism, eschew property transactions in favor of other forms of relations. But Eliot's novel suggests a more complicated relationship to wealth, retaining terms such as inheritance, theft, and "possess[ion]" (748), though in Mordecai's words as in Daniel's subsequent mission, "'possession tends to become more universal'" (734). Even Daniel's desire to "'awaken a movement'" comes across as an "'idea that I am possessed with'" (803). Nancy Henry, noting that Eliot "appreciated investment, even of inherited wealth, as a means by which women could find independence," has argued that for the most part "the critique of business and finance [was] a male privilege that even middle-class women could not afford and which women authors [...often] found hypocritical."[62] While Eliot's novel traces the movement of wealth more fully through inheritance and theft than through the lens of investment, Mordecai's vision of possession, like nineteenth-century finance, relies on the expectation of future benefit, of imagining dividends in "'the good

---

[59] Cleere 151. For Cheyette, the plots are linked less by materialism than by powerlessness (53).
[60] Meyer, "'Safely'" 734.
[61] Cheyette 54; Gallagher, "George Eliot" 58.
[62] Nancy Henry, *Women, Literature and Finance* 255.

142 IMAGINING WOMEN'S PROPERTY IN VICTORIAN FICTION

which [...] is to come'" (735). Simply put, property remains a crucial ideal in its present state, its historical legacy, and its anticipation of growth over time.

Religion, spirituality, and culture in *Daniel Deronda* are not just transcendent or moral categories; they are figured as forms of property that can be inherited, shared, invested, robbed, guarded, and held dear, akin to the "'jeweled breast-plate'" with which Mordecai metaphorically endows the impoverished, wandering, and "'trodden on'" Jew (534). Such property even has, at least in part, a material embodiment and physical location, in the form of family papers in a "precious" treasure chest that Daniel must retrieve from a "'banking-house'" with "'an unreasonable sort of nervous eagerness to get it away under my care'" (752, 639, 719). Although Mordecai celebrates making "'possession [...] independent of gross material contact'" (734), Daniel himself does not condemn wealth. Advising Gwendolen to keep her late husband's bequest and "'let [her] remorse tell only on the use that [she] will make of [her] monetary independence'" (768), for instance, he is apparently able to see both tangible and cultural inheritance in less absolute ways than Mordecai, appreciating "material contact" even as he directs himself and others to its spiritual and cultural ends.[63] Along these lines, it is worth noting that those ends require significant funds, which the novel gestures toward in Daniel's father's money (which Daniel does not renounce) as well as the generous wedding gift of "a complete equipment for Eastern travel," which Daniel receives from Sir Hugo (810). While the valuable inheritance from Daniel's plot remains in male hands and privileges transmission between men, its new terms—cultural and spiritual as well as material, universal as well as individualist—give it the potential to challenge traditional understandings of family, property ownership, and the laws determining the relationships between them. Seen in the context of the ongoing movement to reform women's property rights in the 1870s, such a challenge to family and property law is perhaps a more radical contribution to this movement than the novel's depiction of women's property itself might appear, at first glance, to be.

If diamonds signify Jewish greed and familial theft in *Daniel Deronda*, they also have other, less mercenary functions in Daniel's property reclamation, enabling him to secure his most valuable inheritance and reverse two forms of parental robbery. As Mordecai astutely observes to him, "'You did not need money on that diamond ring. You had some other motive for bringing it'" (504). Raised as a gentleman who "did not need money," Daniel's gender and financial circumstances set him apart from Gwendolen and allow his diamond to be more than a symbol of the alienable wealth she finds necessary. Not only or primarily a commercial object, his "'father's ring'" (633) marks Daniel's own paternal heritage. It also signifies non-unidirectional kinship, consolidating broader kinship

---

[63] For philosophical distinctions between Mordecai and Daniel, as well as how the latter "actively resists Mordecai's vision of a complete mind-meld" in favor of dialogue, see Anderson 123–4, 134–8.

WOMEN'S PROPERTY LAW AND JEWISH CULTURAL INHERITANCE   143

ties. He uses it to find Mordecai, and it stands in for their "'hidden connection'": their joint interest in Mirah and, increasingly, in a Jewish nation (570). It unites spiritual partners, a brother and a sister, a husband and a wife. It connotes lateral as well as vertical ties, those within a single blood family (consanguineal) but also those formed through exchange (conjugal). Instead of compelling Daniel toward *either* his paternal legacy *or* his newfound connections, this diamond affords him access to both, providing an alternative to the familial conflict embedded in Gwendolen's gemstones (as well as to *Middlemarch's* more unidirectionally maternal jewels).

Eliot's novel ameliorates the tensions between lateral and vertical ties partly by depicting Jews as endogamous, bound to one another by blood.[64] We see this racialized endogamy in Mirah's refusal to marry a Christian (462) and in the fact that Daniel's mother married her cousin (627, 633). Although cousin marriages were not uncommon among the Victorians and in Victorian fiction, as Mary Jean Corbett and others have discussed,[65] it is significant that early in the novel's other plot Gwendolen rejects the hand offered by her own cousin, whose primary narrative role seems to be to enable that rejection (81). In contrast, Eliot figures marriage and descent alike as functions of close previous ties for Jews. The novel's Jews are so nearly connected that a Jewish stranger in Frankfort recognizes enough of Daniel's features to eventually bring about his reunion with his mother (368). Even when Jewish characters such as Mordecai and the pawnbroker's family have no known familial relationship, they claim "'the kinship of Israel'" (571), and Mirah is tied to Daniel through Mordecai's connection with him as well as this larger kinship long before they marry. In these ways, Eliot aligns Judaism with endogamous transmission over heterosexual exchange. Mordecai's last, dying interest—depicted as the "'sacred inheritance of the Jew'" (500)—belongs to his "yearning for transmission" (472) and inheritance.[66] Daniel echoes this emphasis on transmission in his sense of his own "'inherited yearning'" (750) for his Jewish identity and proto-Zionist mission.

This emphasis on inheritance might at first seem to mirror the other plot's emphasis on vertical ties, privileging generational transmission over marriage just as Grandcourt does when he leaves his estates to his "illegitimate" son rather than to his wife. But inheritance is not straightforwardly generational in Daniel's plot, in part because the novel merges intergenerational, fraternal, and romantic kinship in the bond it describes as existing between Mordecai and Daniel. Their spiritual connection is figured in fluid relational terms, a crucial distinction from

---

[64] For the sustained endogamous marital practices of the Rothschilds, a Jewish banking family, see Kuper 121, also 119–25.

[65] See, e.g., Kuper 18, 27; Corbett 13, 24.

[66] See also 495, 532, 536, 546.

144   IMAGINING WOMEN'S PROPERTY IN VICTORIAN FICTION

the gender fluidity upon which others have remarked.[67] It is both maternal and fraternal: Mordecai's gaze is like "the slowly dying mother's look when her one loved son visits her bedside [. . .] for the sense of spiritual perpetuation in another resembles that maternal transference of self" (495). At the same time, however, Daniel is likened to the "'brother that fed at the breasts of [Mordecai's] mother'" (751). But the relationship is also romantic, "akin to the boy's and girl's picturing of the future beloved" (474), suffused with "as intense a consciousness as if they had been two undeclared lovers" (495). Once declared, they await "'the marriage of [their] souls'" (751). Daniel's relationship to Mirah is similarly ambiguous. Though he seemingly desires her as a lover, he accepts what Mordecai describes as the "'duties of brotherhood'" to her (749) and couches his proposal of marriage to her in language that could as easily make him her brother as her husband: "'Mirah, let me think that he [Lapidoth] is my father as well as yours'" (792). Even Mirah only understands him "gradual[ly]," "by degrees" (792). The "famil- iar" nature of their intimacy suggests that the alternatives to romantic marriage Talia Schaffer has described had appeal for men as well as women. While the erotic undertones of much of the intensity between Daniel and Mordecai suggest that the triangulated relationship of the two men and Mirah is indeterminate partly because of a sexual nature the text cannot name, this indeterminacy also functions to blur lines of both selfhood and kinship, to offer a vision of "'blent transmission'" (751) as an alternative to the choice of specific blood lines or marriage. The question raised by Gwendolen's diamonds, of whether lineal transmission or exogamous exchange should be privileged, is thus answered in Daniel's plot through a series of interconnections that refuse to align themselves with traditional kinship terms.

Eliot's vision of Judaism ensures property transmission through a fantasy of multidirectional movement. Without stripping Daniel of his property, the novel rhetorically offers a maternal inheritance to lovers as well as brothers, and grants its transmission to two men who are both, at times, feminized (e.g., 600). Women themselves are as materially bereft of property rights as we saw them to be in Gwendolen's and Lydia's scenarios; biological mothers lose out to Mordecai's "maternal" presence. Again, their dispossession is figured in terms of theft. Mirah's father "'robbed'" her mother of "'a pearl'" when he took away their daughter, according to Mordecai (542, 776, 223). Mirah and her mother have no

---

[67] For the feminization of Mordecai and Daniel, see Toise 139; Linehan 342; DeMaria 406, 408–11; Gates 706, 708–9, 717; Anderson 139; Meyer "'Safely,'" 738–9; Cohen 342, 245. This relational fluidity includes but also extends beyond Mordecai's vision of the past and future as parent and child (Cheyette 46), or Daniel's "eroticized phantasy of maternal reunion," with Mordecai as the "nurturing," "missing mother" (Dever 157). For their "religious affinity rather than sexual attraction," see David, *Fictions* 137. Similarly for Gates, marital metaphors indicate "prophetic recognition" more than sexuality (715). For "the text's fluid patterns of sexual desire," see Dever 156. In *Communities of Care*, Schaffer understands the relationship between Daniel and Mordecai as belonging to the "euphoric mutuality" of a care community (132, 130–2).

WOMEN'S PROPERTY LAW AND JEWISH CULTURAL INHERITANCE   145

legal recourse for what the novel depicts as a moral crime, however, because nineteenth-century British custody laws privileged fathers. The Infant Custody Acts of 1839 and 1873, which granted mothers the right to petition for custody or access to their children, did not help poor women such as Mirah's mother, who could not have afforded a lawsuit. Even the Infant Custody Act of 1886 would not grant wives joint custody during marriage.[68] Despite calling Mirah's removal theft, a description which sets a "good" mother and daughter against a self-interested father, Lapidoth's unilateral guardianship could not have been prosecuted as such; the language of theft again marks a cultural problem with possession, underscoring the disparity between legal justice and social judgment, and showcasing women's lack of rights as well as their problematic status as objects to be taken. But this novel makes another Jewish woman an agent of theft, in a depiction that similarly makes note of women's limited rights to hold onto or alienate even the products of their own flesh. The decision of Daniel's mother—Leonora Halm-Eberstein, previously the famous singer and actress Alcharisi—to claim that he had died (636) and then have him raised as an "'Englishman'" (634) is repeatedly characterized as robbery: "'robbery of my own child'" (638).[69] Daniel, too, refers to himself as "'stolen offspring'" (750). Such language makes sense in the context of British custody law, which limited even widows' rights to their own children; along those lines, both "robberies" highlight women's legal dispossession of their own blood. Here, though, by endorsing Daniel's assessment of his mother's actions and grouping those actions with Lapidoth's, the novel privileges a son's inheritance over a mother's rights once more. Daniel's case is another example of how even those works generally sympathetic to dispossessed women and their lack of legal options nonetheless retain a vision of idealized primogeniture, often at those women's expense, during this period of married women's property reform.

In their treatment of Mirah and Daniel, Lapidoth and the Alcharisi are both represented as thieves not just because they claim the power to do as they wish with their children or because they take property, though Lapidoth's flight leaves Mirah's mother and brother "'destitute'" (542) and the Alcharisi fantasizes about burning property that she keeps from her son. These material actions matter far less in the novel than the ways in which both characters attempt to thwart the transmission of Jewish identity—figured as a form of valuable cultural property—to these children. Mirah is "'sure that my mother obeyed her religion,'" but her father "'did not follow our religion at New York, and I think he wanted me not to

[68] For discussion of how "children of a marriage 'belonged' to their father," see Shanley 131–55. The earlier Acts did not remove the father's right to establish "a testamentary guardian other than the mother in his will" (Shanley 135). Widows' rights to custody of their own children were not established until the Infant Custody Act of 1886, although this act allowed fathers to establish a co-guardian to serve with their children's mothers. Significantly, though, unmarried mothers such as Lydia had greater custodial rights than wives. See Holcombe 33.

[69] For the relationship of Daniel's mother to debates over "Judaism and modernity," see Anderson 139, 141.

146   IMAGINING WOMEN'S PROPERTY IN VICTORIAN FICTION

know much about it'" (214). Her realization of her father's deceptions and dishonesty emerges concomitantly with her attempt to "'know a little of our religion, and the history of our people'" (214). Only when she reunites with her brother can she learn "'to be a good Jewess—what she [her mother] would have liked me to be'" (582).

Daniel's mother transgresses still more flagrantly. Concealing her son's life from her father's friends while also preventing Daniel from learning about his own identity and even his "'real name'" (637), she withholds from him "'the chest that my father had charged me and my husband to deliver to our eldest son'" (637), a chest filled with papers that will inform Daniel of his Jewish birthright and familial project (662, 663). Like Mordecai, his grandfather "'ardently maintained the fellowship of our race,'" and Daniel recovers and accepts this "'vocation'" (748) as an "'inherited yearning'" (750). Indeed, although his mother has given him "'all your father's fortune. They can never accuse me of robbery there'" (640),[70] her withholding from him this cultural inheritance of his grandfather's is figured as a far greater crime. She observes to him, "'You think I robbed you of something'" (660). Likewise, his grandfather's friend, restoring the chest to him, calls his mother's actions "'A robbery of our people'" (722). Michael Ragussis understands the "robbery of the Jewish child" and Mirah and Daniel's subsequent recoveries and return to Jewish tradition as a "critique of the ideology of assimilation and conversion."[71] Yes; but Daniel's declaration that his mother has been "'saved from robbing my people of my service and me of my duty'" (662) also aligns with Gwendolen's realization that she is "'saved from robbing others'" (699), and suggests within this novel a parallel reading of these women's two "thefts." The repeated insistence on his mother's "robbery" and Daniel's uncharacteristic lack of sympathy for her[72] reinforce the messages of the other plotline: that male children, rather than mothers or wives, ought to inherit ancestral property in keeping with legal and customary ideas of primogeniture and that women function primarily as placeholders for these sons' wealth.

Even women's careers, which allow them to earn their own money instead of depending upon inheritance, become similarly problematic when they exceed the bounds of necessity and entail women's "'great claims'" for themselves (664). Representing theft on the one hand, Daniel's mother is also an economic agent in another way, as an artist with a successful career. She and (to a lesser degree) Mirah earn their own income on the stage. In Mirah's case, this is a material

---

[70] As David notes, this fortune will fund Daniel's journey to Palestine (*Fictions* 169).

[71] Ragussis 287.

[72] O'Brien 109–10; for Daniel's "overdeveloped sympathy" as a "failure to specialize," see Susan Colón, "'One Function in Particular': Professionalism and Specialization in *Daniel Deronda*," *Studies in the Novel* 37.3 (2005): 292–307, 294; Schaffer, in *Communities of Care*, discusses Daniel's sympathy in terms of passivity and his need to learn active care instead (127–8). For the Alcharisi's rejection of motherhood and its cultural ideals, see Dever 145.

WOMEN'S PROPERTY LAW AND JEWISH CULTURAL INHERITANCE   147

requirement, an important response to her gendered disinheritance of both monetary and cultural wealth, but in his mother's case, it also derives from a wish to be "'great,'" "'a queen,'" and "'to live for my art'" (634, 639). Her successful public performances offer a stark contrast with the small-scale, domestic arts of women such as the Meyrick daughters, who illustrate, embroider, and take pupils in industrious support of the home whose modest contents are figured as being "as much a part of their world as the stars [...] seen from the back windows" (196, 210, 481); an artistic career such as the Alcharisi's is also out of reach for Gwendolen, whose brief vision of a life on the stage as an alternative to a financially motivated marriage is disappointed because, as a "'charming young [English] lady'" bred for "'the drawing-room,'" she "'has not yet conceived what excellence is'" (254, 256). Jewish women in this novel seem better equipped to fill in the financial gaps of their dispossession or desire in public, nonconventional, and potentially lucrative ways. Rather than celebrating such professional independence, however, Eliot leaves us instead with Mirah, for whom "'the artist's life has been made repugnant'" (665). If, as Gallagher has argued, *Daniel Deronda* aligns artistic careers with other negative forms of circulation, including usury and prostitution,[73] it also links these public careers, as illicit, morally suspect transactions, to the "theft" of inheritance for both the stolen Mirah and the stealing Alcharisi.

Despite what he understands as his mother's theft, Daniel—like young Grandcourt—gets his inheritance after all, to a certain extent because in Eliot's novel women are written out of Judaism's cultural transmission nearly as much as they are written out of English property law. He, not Mirah, is to be her brother's spiritual inheritor. All she receives of her Jewish heritage is a Hebrew hymn whose words she recalls incompletely from her mother's singing: "'the rest is lisping [...] childish nonsense'" though still "'very full of meaning'" in its "childish [...] tenderness" (373, 374). Despite the novel's indignation at Lapidoth's "theft," it shares Mirah's complacency about her ignorance: "'If I were ever to know the real words, I should still go on in my old way with them'" (374). Even in its most sympathetic moments, the novel privileges men's cultural inheritance over women's possession, substituting women's tender ignorance for the kind of knowledge Daniel intends to acquire, in careful study with Mordecai, of manuscripts written in Spanish, Italian, Hebrew, Arabic, and Latin (748). Daniel's own mother has disliked "'the bondage of [Judaism]'" (627) from an early age, partly as a result of her father's similar desire to pass along his heritage to a male child, not to her: "'He wished I had been a son; he cared for me as a makeshift link'" (631). Or, again, "'he cared more about a grandson to come than he did about me: I counted as nothing'" (634). When his friend restores the sacred chest to Daniel, he too counts

---

[73] Gallagher, "George Eliot" 51–5.

148   IMAGINING WOMEN'S PROPERTY IN VICTORIAN FICTION

Leonora as "nothing" by referring to Daniel as "'the offspring they had robbed him [her father, Daniel's grandfather] of'" (722): his offspring, not hers, despite her direct, immediate blood tie and conviction that "'you were my son, and it was my turn to say what you should be'" (634).

At least in England, legal practice confirmed the novel's declaration that Daniel's upbringing was a crime: "it was a firm rule of law that in the absence of an express statement to the contrary, children should be brought up in the religion of their father."[74] Despite his mother's declaration that because she had given him "'all your father's fortune. They can never accuse me of robbery there'" (640), her refusal to pass along to him manuscripts and knowledge of his father's and grandfather's religion appears as a kind of a theft, legal as well as moral.[75] In contrast with English law, Judaism has traditionally maintained a rule of matrilineal descent: during the nineteenth century, observant practitioners would have considered any child of a Jewish mother to be a Jew. In that sense, neither Mirah's father nor Daniel's mother can alter or actually steal Mirah or Daniel's religious identity. Yet even in making Jewish identity more a function of the maternal tie than of a father's or grandfather's wish, matrilineal descent was passive, a function of blood rather than choice. It would not have granted women the ability to change their children's religious identity. Thus despite its blurring of relational lines and its shift away from material property, *Daniel Deronda*'s Jewish plotline maintains the limitations on women's ownership we have seen in the novel as a whole: it refuses to grant women the inheritance it reserves for men; it privileges patrilineal descent over marital or matrilineal rights; it makes even their earnings "repugnant" when they exceed the domestic bounds of traditionally feminine labor; and it portrays women as the victims and agents of cultural theft rather than as possessors of legal rights to children or heritage. Unlike the troubled diamonds, estates, servants, and painted ceilings at stake in Gwendolen's story, however, the property proposed by Daniel's tale—communal religious identity— is one that, the novel suggests, cannot be taken away. Hence his mother's sense that she has been *compelled* to return Daniel to the Jewish community, "'forced to tell you that you are a Jew, and deliver to you what [my father] commanded me to deliver'" (631). His inheritance has become a form of inalienable possession,[76] not something like his father's diamond ring, which he can pawn in commercial districts, but a form of wealth more easily recognized in familial than financial

---

[74] Shanley 135.

[75] These laws may not apply; Daniel's mother, raised partially in Genoa, was born to an English mother of Portuguese descent and an Italian father who married in England, but Daniel was living (possibly born?) in Naples when his mother chooses to part ways with him and have him raised as an Englishman (663, 634).

[76] For cultures in which "reproduction of kinship is legitimated in each generation through the transmission of inalienable possessions," as well as women's involvement "in their production and guardianship," see Annette B. Weiner, *Inalienable Possessions: The Paradox of Keeping-While-Giving* (Berkeley: University of California Press, 1992): 11.

WOMEN'S PROPERTY LAW AND JEWISH CULTURAL INHERITANCE 149

terms. When he receives his grandfather's papers, Daniel recognizes their symbolic value: "'I shall be more careful of this than of any other property [...]. I never before possessed anything that was a sign to me of so much cherished hope and effort'" (722). Like Daniel, Eliot valued textual legacies. Nancy Henry notes that "[s]he took care to finish Lewes's unfinished work, to intervene in whatever was written about him when she could," and "implicitly authorized [her own chosen] biographer"; her personal life and novel alike emphasized associations of inheritance and transmission with the written word.[77] And in *Daniel Deronda*, papers and the cultural "hope and effort" they represent become more important than "any other property."

Daniel's cautious receipt of this "sign," this spiritual heritage, makes him less mindful of material belongings. Whereas Gwendolen (like Lizzie Eustace) finds it impossible to detach herself from the "stolen" wealth she is compelled to wear,[78] Daniel, secure in his inheritance and his intimacies, learns to see his "'heavy ring'" as a "superfluit[y]" (789): "'I have been wearing my memorable ring ever since I came home [...]. But [...] I constantly put it off as a burthen when I am doing anything'" (789). Heavy, burdensome, and superfluous for his "absorb[ing]" work (789), his diamond ring—having served the purpose of connecting him to Mordecai and his deceased Jewish father—is finally "detached" from his hand because Daniel has already acquired the spiritual inheritance it has come to represent and no longer needs its physical symbol (790).

The final theft of the novel—Lapidoth's acquisition of Daniel's diamond ring—differs significantly from the earlier thefts both because its value is resolutely and immediately financial and because it facilitates, rather than hinders, proper affiliations and transmission. When "[h]is rambling eyes quickly alighted on the ring that sparkled on the bit of dark mahogany," Lapidoth registers this ring as material wealth, a comfortable replacement for the "sum of ready money" he has hoped to obtain from Daniel (789). "[D]etached, and within easy grasp," the ring Lapidoth pockets offers him the present guarantee of a "solid fact" instead of the still greater but "imaginary sums" he desires (790). Unlike Gwendolen's possession of Grandcourt's diamonds, Lapidoth's "theft" of Mirah, or the Alcharisi's "robbery" of Daniel's cultural identity, this incident seems to offer a relatively clear picture of ownership and theft: Lapidoth makes off with a ring that is legally Daniel's. Yet even here, the novel refuses to make legality the predominant factor in assessing property acquisition. Lapidoth, who "appeared to himself to have a claim on any property his children might possess" (774) and "thought that he ought to have had what he wanted of [his daughter's] other earnings as he had of her apple-tart" (788), surmises correctly that he will not be punished for walking away with the ring:

---

[77] Henry, *George Eliot* 266, 265.
[78] See Plotz 33 for Lizzie's inability to detach herself from her diamonds.

150   IMAGINING WOMEN'S PROPERTY IN VICTORIAN FICTION

> For any property of Deronda's (available without his formal consent) was all one with his children's property, since their father would never be prosecuted for taking it. [...] [L]arceny is a form of appropriation for which people are punished by law; and to take this ring from a virtual relation, who would have been willing to make a much heavier gift, would not come under the head of larceny.   (790)

So Lapidoth's theft again signals a problem with property. While the novel is much more obviously sympathetic to children's inheritance of their father's property than to a father's appropriation of his children's property, this passage reminds us of the disparity between legal policy and personal feeling or action. Lapidoth may define terms such as "larceny" as they suit his needs, but the plot essentially accedes to his definitions by refusing to prosecute him for the crime he commits. If he feels less guilt for his actions than Gwendolen and, ultimately, the Alcharisi do, it may be in part because he understands that laws and customs will protect him as a father, despite his marginalized social standing as a Jew.

Lapidoth's theft of his ring is far less distressing to Daniel than the earlier "theft" of "poisoned" diamonds is to both Gwendolen and Lydia, but I do not think, *pace* Gallagher, that this is because the ring once belonged to Daniel's "money-changing" father or that its theft provides the "alienation of all the negative things Jewishness stands for in the book," particularly the troubling commercial exchanges of both usury and art.[79] Even leaving aside the fact that Daniel continues to benefit, without qualms, from his father's money (628, 640), the problems and passions we have seen with property in *Daniel Deronda* are as much family matters as commercial affairs; Daniel's father, hardly the negative stereotype of financial "Jewishness," actually "'wound up his money-changing and banking'" to "'devote himself'" to his wife (633). Usury, as Cleere has shown, signified divergent family relations as well as commerce in nineteenth-century texts.[80] And family by the end of the novel means more than what Gallagher has described as "the pure exchange of souls symbolized in Daniel's marriage to both Mirah and Mordecai."[81] Indeed, the discovery of Lapidoth's theft hastens the formation of new kinship ties between them all by serving as the impetus for Daniel's proposal to Mirah. When he implores his humiliated lover to "'let me think that he is my father as well as yours—that we can have no sorrow, no disgrace, no joy apart'" (792), he not only claims Lapidoth as kin and merges his feelings of fraternity for the siblings with his desire for a wife, but also proposes a form of marriage purged of the property anxieties contained in Gwendolen's union with Grandcourt. Here, in this fullest rendering of coverture, the wife is absolved from any financial liability. Unlike a host of other Victorian characters

[79] Gallagher, "George Eliot" 58; see also Munich 137.
[80] Cleere 112, 113; also 147, 150.
[81] Gallagher, "George Eliot" 58.

WOMEN'S PROPERTY LAW AND JEWISH CULTURAL INHERITANCE 151

including those from Dickens's *Little Dorrit* or, as the next chapter will discuss, Margaret Oliphant's *Hester*, she cannot be held personally accountable for parental or other debts. In exchange for this dubious protection, however, Mirah can no longer make any claims for personal possession. Nothing—not even her "father," her "sorrow," or her "joy"—will be Mirah's "own." Upon this engagement, she ceases to be an economic agent, despite her previous ability to "'make an income'" (486) through her singing. Having earlier acknowledged that she "'owe[s] everything to him'" (561), Mirah poses no threat to Daniel's property rights or to ongoing or future transmission. Significantly, neither does material theft. By this point, Daniel's "fine diamond ring" has ceased to be much more than "heavy" and "superflu[ous]" to his real wealth (789). Lapidoth's theft does not, can not, rob Mordecai and Daniel of their cultural inheritance—something aligned with but not identical to a much more generalized sense of "moral" economy.

This theft of Daniel's ring thus resolves certain problems of ownership revealed in Gwendolen's plotline, elevating inalienable cultural wealth above private material property to demonstrate that other, more valuable property can *not* be stolen, that inheritance may finally be secured through a "blent transmission" that entails multiple kinship ties working together in the interest of this inheritance. It does so by removing a wife's claim to anything of her "own,"[82] offering no resolution for a woman such as Gwendolen, who lacks paternal fortune or cultural inheritance and who even in her final encounter with Daniel finds it difficult to think of "whatever surrounded her [...] as rightfully belonging to others more than to her" (804). Nor can it help Daniel's mother, who, unlike Mirah, insists upon her "'rightful claim'" in the world and tells him that she "'was never willingly subject to any man'" (664, 666). Similarly, while the substitution of immaterial property for tangible belongings seems appropriate for Mordecai, whose death concludes the novel, and for Daniel, who has appreciated his friend's "brilliant eyes" (809) more than diamonds, this substitution appears untenable for the Sir Hugos of the nation, who were being asked to consider new legislation for married women's property. Politically and financially, the resolution cannot work: alongside their symbolic registers, English wealth and property law are also material problems. Fiction, however, offers us different ways to understand and grapple with these problems. Narratively, Daniel's Jewish mission—to travel East and "'restor[e] a political existence to my people, making them a nation again, giving them a national centre, such as the English have'" (803)—supplants these material concerns; the competing claims of son and wife, seen in Gwendolen's "poisoned gems," are a small matter compared with the larger claims of kinship that Daniel acknowledges as he devotes himself to restoring the inheritance he shares with his fellow Jews. By shifting focus to this transmission and this kinship, the

---

[82] For the reinstatement of patriarchal power at the novel's close, see, e.g., Linehan 342.

152 IMAGINING WOMEN'S PROPERTY IN VICTORIAN FICTION

novel expands and perhaps attempts to purify the meaning of the property rights that Victorian women were endeavoring to claim. It is worth remembering, too, that Daniel's proposal— to "'have no sorrow, no disgrace, no joy apart'" from Mirah—cedes his own privileged economic and legal status in favor of something more like the mutuality we have seen in Gaskell's *Wives and Daughters*. If his promise to similarly have nothing of his own seems meaningless in the context of British property law, the fact that Daniel is guided by another tradition as well— one emphasizing religious patriarchy but also driven by matrilineal descent—gives that law a somewhat less powerful hold. And even if Daniel's words to Mirah are, finally, only words, then, like all of the other words and novels examined in this study so far—by Austen, Dickens, Gaskell, Trollope, and Eliot—they remind us of the importance and changing nature of words about women's property during this period. In *Daniel Deronda*, one of those words, "robbery," becomes, finally, not the corollary for marriage or the attempt of wives and mothers to insert them-selves into male lines of inheritance but a way to recognize the inadequacy of contemporary property law, which undermines both marriage and entire nations by pitting family members against one another, apparently leaving women no economic choices except dispossession or theft.

5

"Giv[ing] All She Had"

Hester's Pearls and the Obligations of Women's Property

I. "Awful Clever" Women

Although Victorian fiction often showcases women's financial dispossession—the self-proclaimed "'degradingly poor, offensively poor'" plight of characters such as Bella Wilfer alongside those, like Lizzie Hexam, who "'work [...] and plan and contrive [...] how to get together a shilling now, and a shilling then'" (*Our Mutual Friend* 37, 27)—such images, as this study has shown, coexist with others featuring women of means. And despite some resistance to their riches—Dorothea Casaubon's passionate "'I hate my wealth'" (*Middlemarch* 811), for example—many well-heeled women in novels from this period possess and use their property with confidence. Yet fiction often teaches us to be suspicious of wealthy women. Showing how women's poverty was aligned with virtue throughout the nineteenth century, Elsie B. Michie describes "a tradition that goes back as far as Lady Catherine [...] in which rich women talk too loudly about their wealth and become figures we laugh at and disparage."[1] For Austen, she argues, "wealth-fueled egoism [...] transform[s] concern for others into an occasion to assert one's own superiority."[2] Thus in *Pride and Prejudice*, Lady Catherine is both rich and meddling, an "active magistrate in her own parish" (112) and beyond, proving equally intrusive in Mr. Collins's closets, cottagers' quarrels, and her nephew's marriage (46, 112, 230–4): "nothing escaped her observation" (112). In her desire for Darcy to marry her own daughter—"'Their fortune on both sides is splendid'" (232)—she symbolizes the "engrossment" or amassing of wealth which Michie has shown to be aligned with a dangerous egoism.[3] Property ownership similarly corresponds with distorted forms of egoistic "concern" in Dickens's *Little Dorrit*, where Mrs. Clennam exerts the same "'judgment and watchfulness'" over her son and "dependant" that she uses to manage her late husband's uncle's business (60, 68). "[G]rim," "immoveable," and "austere" (49, 50, 59), she is another "'awful clever'" woman (52) with significant economic agency despite the progressive "'decline'" of a business that has "'not [kept] the

---

[1] Michie xiii.
[2] Michie 38.
[3] Michie 45.

Imagining Women's Property in Victorian Fiction. Jill Rappoport, Oxford University Press. © Jill Rappoport 2023.
DOI: 10.1093/oso/9780192867261.003.0006

154 IMAGINING WOMEN'S PROPERTY IN VICTORIAN FICTION

track of the time'" (60). In both cases, the sense of superiority enabled by family property appears to come at the expense of warmer family feeling. These women are "awful" in the sense of wonder they occasion but also in the more colloquial sense, as almost entirely unlikeable characters.

In Margaret Oliphant's *Hester* (1883), Catherine Vernon, like her titled name-sake in Austen's novel, appears to follow suit as one more clever, controlling, and unpleasant woman of property. Holding "reign" with "great firmness" as "almost the most important person" in town (23), Catherine similarly suffers from "the deteriorating influences of too much prosperity" (32). One character observes that "'Aunt Catherine [is] powerful [...] because she is rich—rich and kind; very kind in her way'" (50), yet the narrator also notes that "It is so much easier to be substantially kind than to show that tender regard for other people's feelings which is the only thing which ever calls forth true gratitude" (32). Though in many regards this portrayal seems to fit the nineteenth-century tradition of denigrating rich women, I'm interested here in how—in the wake of the Married Women's Property Act of 1882—*Hester* also gives us tools to revise that legacy. By juxtaposing Catherine Vernon not only with poor women but with those who claim other, largely disregarded forms of economic agency, *Hester*, I argue, highlights an understanding of these women's property and economic relationships that sees women as more than a "makeshift link" between (generally male) heirs (*Daniel Deronda* 631); replaces the consolidation of wealth with women's ability to main-tain and protect separate property streams; and acknowledges that family feelings, obligations, and traditions, not just legal rights, shaped the ways in which Victorian fiction imagined women's property. With a primary focus on how women's prop-erty reform offers a lens through which to see a wider range of women's economic relationships and choices in *Hester*, these arguments will allow us to briefly revisit *Pride and Prejudice* and *Little Dorrit* as well. I opened this study with tales of Elizabeth Bennet and Amy Dorrit's dispossession. Returning to these novels in the present chapter permits emphasis on different characters and allegiances, allowing us to see how the financial actions of Lady Catherine and Mrs. Clennam derive in large part from relationships that are generally relegated to the margins of these texts. The forms of loyalty, stewardship, and duty that they demonstrate persist in Oliphant's novel and suggest the ongoing importance of these extralegal factors for women of property even after the reform of married women's property law.

II. A Wife's Rights

Two parallel financial crises bookend Oliphant's novel: Catherine Vernon saves the Vernon family bank when her cousin John's negligence threatens it some thirty years before the novel's present action; his daughter Hester joins Catherine years later to come to the bank's rescue when Edward (Hester's suitor, Catherine's

HESTER'S PEARLS AND THE OBLIGATIONS OF WOMEN'S PROPERTY   155

younger cousin and adopted son) speculates wildly and again brings the bank to the brink of failure. In each case, a man's recklessness threatens the bank's stability. In each case, a woman's intelligence, loyalty, ambition, and private wealth resuscitate it. The paired nature of these events and characters makes all the more glaring the only major mismatch, the withholding of Hester's sole item of value—her mother's pearl necklace—from the financial resolution, the cash infusion from Catherine that saves the bank for the second time. Characters and narrator alike fall oddly, utterly silent about the pearls and their value at this second crisis, despite their extreme fascination and heated opinions about them prior to this event.

Anton Chekhov, arguing in 1889 that a play should include only necessary elements, famously wrote, "One must never place a loaded rifle on the stage if it isn't going to go off."[4] Necklaces in Victorian narrative are like Chekhov's rifle, crucial plot objects, loaded things, accessories more to crime than couture: think of the diamond necklace, worth ten thousand pounds, that Trollope's Lizzie Eustace is accused of stealing from her husband's estate, or the wedding present of "poisoned gems" that Eliot's Gwendolen Grandcourt receives from her husband's mistress.[5] When a valuable pearl necklace appears under questionable circumstances and for considerable space in a Victorian novel, then, we expect a narrative reckoning. But we don't get one in *Hester*. This necklace's conspicuous appearance and anticlimactic removal from the narrative highlight women's changing relationship toward money in the late Victorian period. They not only suggest how the reform of marital property law might have affected wives but also offer us ways to think about the personal choices women made regarding property in their other and sometimes competing relational roles—in this case, as mothers and daughters, though also, as we have seen in other chapters, as sisters, cousins, and friends.

Discussions of Oliphant's novel focus chiefly on its two similarly strong-minded and initially feuding single women,[6] the wealthy Catherine and her much younger and impoverished cousin, Hester, who comes of age in the town dominated by Catherine's generosity, ignorant of her father's misdeeds and resentful of Catherine's "reign."[7] Hester's mother, "poor Mrs John" Vernon,[8]

---

[4] Quoted in Leah Goldberg, *Russian Literature in the Nineteenth Century: Essays* (Jerusalem: Magnes Press, The Hebrew University, 1976): 163.

[5] Diamonds in particular have received substantial critical attention. See Chapters 3 and 4 of this study.

[6] From their first introduction they are in conflict. In a scene reminiscent of Elizabeth Bennet's offended dismissal of Lady Catherine from her lawn in *Pride and Prejudice*—"'You can *now* have nothing farther to say [...] I must beg to return to the house'" (*PP* 233)—both women are "hostile" as Hester denies Catherine access to her new home, despite it being a house owned and loaned to Hester and her mother by Catherine (36).

[7] E.g., Aeron Hunt, *Personal Business: Character and Commerce in Victorian Literature and Culture* (Charlottesville: University of Virginia Press, 2014); Nancy Henry, *Women*; Michie, *Vulgar*.

[8] Margaret Oliphant, *Hester* [1883] (Oxford: Oxford University Press, 2003): 62. Subsequent references to this work will be made as parenthetical citations.

156   IMAGINING WOMEN'S PROPERTY IN VICTORIAN FICTION

is a foil to both. A satisfied product of separate-spheres ideology, she is ignorant of her husband's work and even his whereabouts during the bank's moment of crisis. When her husband dies, she is left, like Margaret Oliphant herself, abroad and in debt, with difficult maternal duties to shoulder.[9] Years later, she acknowledges the injury arising from her late husband's financial irresponsibility, both in precipitating the bank crisis and in taking on subsequent debts. "'Your poor papa was incautious about money, Hester, and that has done a great deal of harm to both of us, for we are poor, and we ought to have been rich'" (375). Nevertheless, she wears her ignorance as a point of pride: "'he always had too much respect for me to mix me up with business'" (375). Content to be covered by his choices, whatever they are, she is such a stand-in for coverture that we never even learn her first name; Mrs. John evokes the one-flesh doctrine at every mention, despite her absentee husband and subsequent widowhood. If, at the long-ago moment of crisis, Catherine resembles "a soldier springing instantly to the alert, rallying all his resources at the first word of danger" (18–19), Mrs. John is "bewildered" (12), "helpless" (11). Learning of an expected run on the family bank, Catherine immediately offers up her substantial independent fortune, money inherited from her mother, dismissing the head clerk's promise that the bank would "'make it up to [her] afterwards'" by stressing her economic right to invest, spend, or even throw away these private financial resources as she wishes: "'if not, I don't know who is to stop me from doing what I like with my own'" (21). When, in contrast, the clerk begs Mrs. John to help save the bank, she "[runs] to a pretty ornamental desk" and nervously offers the "twenty pounds" it contains (14), seemingly—as she comes from "a county family [...] with no money to keep up her pretensions"—the only money she can access in her husband's absence (7). Unlike Lady Catherine and Mrs. Clennam, two widows who take on the concerns of their late husbands' estates, Mrs. John could have no future role in the bank even if her husband had not forsaken it. In short, as critics such as Patricia E. Johnson have noted, the novel's introductory scenes pit a strong, single woman with financial knowledge and economic rights against a helpless wife whose marriage deprives her of both information and independent property, two distinct economic positions for women in the nineteenth century.[10]

That's part of the story, at least. The pearls, which belong to Mrs. John but appear on her daughter's neck halfway through the novel and introduce a heated debate about ownership, offer a more complicated meditation on women's property rights and compel us to reconsider those characterizations. Mrs. John treasures her pearls. Not only are they "more beautiful than any other ornament in the

---

[9] Margaret Oliphant, *The Autobiography of Margaret Oliphant*, ed. Elisabeth Jay (Peterborough: Broadview Press, Ltd., 2002): 42, 121.

[10] Patricia E. Johnson, "Unlimited Liability: Women and Capital in Margaret Oliphant's *Hester*," *Nineteenth-Century Gender Studies* 6.1 (2010): para. 10.

HESTER'S PEARLS AND THE OBLIGATIONS OF WOMEN'S PROPERTY   157

room" (220) but they allow her to cling to her sense of status and "pride of descent" despite her otherwise impoverished state: "'you can say you got them from your mother, and your grandmother before her—which is more than they ever had'" (213). (As the story continues, the lineage extends to Mrs. John's grandmother as well [261].) Significantly, though, the pearls are also "'worth a good deal of money'" (244), "'something nobody can turn up their noses at'" (213). Trouble arises when Catherine, learning of the pearls and contemplating their (high though unspecified) monetary value, begins saying that Mrs. John has had no right to keep them. For Catherine, Mrs. John's possession of the pearls is illegitimate because they represent wealth owed to others on two separate occasions: her husband died under debt that the necklace might have paid off and he also caused the bank crisis that provoked Catherine's dramatic financial intervention. Mrs. John made no mention of her valuable necklace at that time, despite the head clerk's frustrated response to her offer of £20—"'If it were twenty thousand it might do something'" (14). When Catherine first learns that Mrs. John has kept these pearls all along, she attributes the ongoing possession to ignorance. "'Poor little thing! I suppose she did not understand what it meant, and that she was cheating her husband's creditors'" (244). Pearls—as signs of purity, innocence—support this sense of Mrs. John's financial ignorance in a way that mitigates her possible wrongdoing. (Lizzie Eustace's diamonds are never read in such a way.) But Catherine grows increasingly angry about Hester wearing the pearls, speaking of them to others with "contempt" (244), a "mingled sense of pity and disdain" (258), and "a sternness of virtue [...] which justified her dislike" (278). "'She should not have them; knowing her father's story, as I suppose you do.—Don't you see,' cried Catherine with sudden energy, 'that she ought not to appear in Redborough in those pearls?'" (259) After seeing the pearls, Catherine becomes fixated on what she perceives to be the injustice of Mrs. John's continued possession: she "could not keep her mind from dwelling upon these ornaments" (258), and for a brief but intense space—forty-five references over sixty-five pages!—the novel is similarly obsessed with them. Catherine even indulges in fantasies about how Hester might react to the pearls upon learning the truth about her father: "[...] what would the girl do? Pocket the shame and continue to wear them [...] or tear them from her neck and trample them under foot?" (258).

What these impassioned scenes stage is, to a certain extent, a debate about married women's property rights. Does a wife, such as Mrs. John, have any right to keep property apart from her husband's estate? Mrs. John, in her quiet way, affirms that she does. Catherine, far less quietly, objects. Astonished by Catherine's disapproval of Hester's adornment, Mrs. John speculates that "'She must mean [...] that they are too good for you to wear because we are poor'" (261); to Catherine's stern insinuation that "'their value is [...] the worst thing about them,'" Mrs. John "stood her ground. / 'I don't think so,' she said simply. 'I like them to be worth a great deal, for they are all she will have'" (278). Mrs. John, consistently represented as "simple," "poor," and "tender," does not seem, even in the privacy of her own home and maternal interactions, to knowingly conceal any wrongdoing. In fact, it does not appear to have ever crossed her mind that the pearls might be thought of as anything other than her own, unlike the £20 of Vernon marital money that she previously offered the bank manager. Relieved to have kept something fine for her daughter throughout difficult circumstances, she merely marvels "'what a good thing that I did not part with my pearls!'" (213), and again, "'Oh, how glad I am I kept my pearls!'" (214) We enter her perspective long enough to learn that "If there was anything in the world that was her individual property, and in which no one else had any share, it was her pearls" (261). Ironically, Mrs. John here becomes the novel's champion for married women's independent property rights. In contrast, Catherine, at once one of Victorian fiction's more radical businesswomen and this novel's strongest proponent of the conservative common law, angrily refutes the idea that the pearls can or should constitute Mrs. John's "individual property." Whereas an unmarried woman such as Catherine could own property, the doctrine of coverture mandated that wives could not; a woman's property belonged to her husband upon marriage. Thirty years before *Hester's* publication, around the time of the fictional bank's first crisis, this doctrine, which Catherine seems eager to enforce, meant that Mrs. John's pearls would likely have belonged to Mr. John.

Oliphant's writing from that earlier period does not seem to have opposed this doctrine. Indeed, in an 1856 essay responding to Barbara Leigh Smith [later Bodichon]'s "A Brief Summary, in Plain Language, of the Most Important Laws Concerning Women," she affirms that a marriage can have only one "public representative, the acknowledged head of the house," and suggests that autonomy within marriage can have dire consequences: "The more independent husband and wife are of each other, the less sure is the basis of society."[11] Even in the 1850s, however, having one "head of the house" did not necessarily mean settling all property by common law, and Oliphant's writing suggests an openness to the benefits of various financial arrangements within marriage. Wealthy families often secured brides' private fortunes for a future generation through special legal settlements, and *Hester* apparently grants Mrs. John such a marriage settlement, though its income is diminished because so much of it went to pay her husband's debts. Catherine blames Mrs. John both for keeping and losing the income: "'She has only a scrap of it. Poor little thing! She neither knew it was wrong to take it, nor that if she did keep it, it ought not to have been allowed to go for his after debts. She got muddled altogether among them. The greater part of it she mortgaged for him, so that there was only a pittance left'" (244). This "muddled" state—property that should and shouldn't be protected as hers—speaks to a

[11] Margaret Oliphant, "The Laws Concerning Women," *Blackwood's Edinburgh Magazine* 486.79 (1856): 379–87, 384, 380.

HESTER'S PEARLS AND THE OBLIGATIONS OF WOMEN'S PROPERTY   159

cultural confusion regarding a wife's property rights under coverture, but seems to leave Mrs. John with some legal latitude, once having kept the pearls, "'not to have allowed [them] to go for his after debts.'"

As Trollope shows us in *The Eustace Diamonds*, a widow could sometimes claim jewelry or other personal property as paraphernalia for her own private use, separate from her husband's estate, while Leonore Davidoff and Catherine Hall note that though a married woman's "liquid property" along with "the whole of the family's resources were open to seizure for debt," there are exceptions in cases where "there had been a trust."[12] But we do not know if Mrs. John has a trust of this kind. We do not know if the pearls are specifically named as part of her marriage settlement. We do not even know whether Mr. John is aware that the pearls remain in Mrs. John's possession. (If he does, he apparently declines to claim them, a point which significantly—and perhaps cunningly—protects them from his creditors.) Oliphant's novel remains silent on these topics, refusing an easy answer about the pearls' legal status or their place in the marriage and its aftermath. In the 1850s, then, Mrs. John's pearls could have been subject to some of the questions that Catherine raises, and hopeful creditors would have needed additional information before seizing them.[13] But this is information the novel refuses to supply. More importantly, it is an anachronistic debate in 1883, when *Hester* was published. By that point, as Oliphant—the author of an 1880 essay on "The Grievances of Women"—must have known and regardless of what may have been the case thirty years before, a wife was newly entitled to keep any property she had inherited or earned, and such property could not be forfeited to a husband's debts.[14]

We could say, then, that the Married Women's Property Act of 1882 wins the argument for Mrs. John, silencing Catherine and protecting Mrs. John's most

---

[12] Davidoff and Hall, *Family Fortunes* 210.

[13] The question of John Vernon's debt depends first, since he died abroad, on whether or not it was acquired in England and subject to English law, and, if so, at what precise point in the 1850s or 1860s he died indebted. Until 1861, different laws existed for bankruptcy (for "traders") and insolvency (for "non-traders"); a bankrupt, unlike an insolvent debtor, "could, under certain circumstances, be discharged from his indebtedness." See V. Markham Lester, *Victorian Insolvency: Bankruptcy, Imprisonment for Debt, and Company Winding-Up in Nineteenth-Century England* (Oxford: Clarendon Press, 1995): 88. In 1842 a bill was introduced to enable debtors to petition the bankruptcy court (Lester 115) and in 1861 bankruptcy status was extended to non-traders (Lester 116). After the Bankruptcy Act of 1869, bankruptcy administration was managed by creditors rather than government, but small debts were rarely worth the time and energy of recovery (Lester 174). Creditors were less likely to receive payment in real life than in fiction, where debt was typically seen as "a moral wrong." See Barbara Weiss, *The Hell of the English: Bankruptcy and the Victorian Novel* (Lewisburg: Bucknell University Press, 1986): 74, 76, 73.

[14] Margaret Oliphant, "The Grievances of Women," *Fraser's Magazine*, New Series 21 (1880): 698–710. As Erika Diane Rappaport discusses, earlier debate about marital debt in the 1850s and '60s largely suggested that a husband should not be liable for the consumer debts his wife had run up on his credit. Limitations on women's liability persisted even after the Married Women's Property Acts of 1870 and 1882 (57, 63), and "married women did not gain full contractual rights and liabilities until 1935" (64).

160   IMAGINING WOMEN'S PROPERTY IN VICTORIAN FICTION

valuable item for her own possession, use, or bequest. Aeron Hunt has argued that the pearls drop out of an otherwise doubled plot to emphasize character;[15] that is, Hester doesn't rush in with the valuable pearls to save the bank at its second crisis as Catherine once did with her own maternal inheritance—there's no mention of pearls at all by that point—because her individual traits matter more to the business than her family legacy. But I think that another reason why the pearls disappear from the narrative is that Mrs. John's perspective prevails. *Hester* supports her standpoint that these pearls are her "individual property." I don't mean to suggest Mrs. John as the novel's unequivocal model for women's financial aptitude. Even if Catherine's financial genius meets with ambivalence, Hester's approach to business—much more engaged and interested than her mother's— indicates a progression of women's accepted roles in the economy and has narrative backing over (deceitful, villainous) Edward's belief that a knowledge of business "'is not what a man wants in a woman'" (370) or even Roland Ashton's somewhat more tactful concession:

> "These women, who step out of their sphere, they may do much to be respected, they may be of great use; but—"
> "You mean that men don't like them," said Hester, with a smile.   (307)

Whether or not Hester's suitors are correct about Victorian men's desires in general, Oliphant's novel suggests that financial knowledge is important for women. In essays for *Blackwood's*, Oliphant further praises women's general economic understanding, noting of working-class wives that "Every one is aware how entirely the expenditure and economy of the house lies in her hands" and of the middle classes that "it is his daughter who keeps the tradesman's books, and makes out his bills, almost universally."[16] Oliphant recalls in her *Autobiography* how her own mother "kept everything going, and comfortably going, on the small income she had to administer," while Oliphant herself took financial responsibility not only for her biological children but for her brothers, nephew, and nieces.[17] Mrs. John's financial ignorance makes her an outlier—a relic of an earlier moment—but the novel ultimately endorses her conviction that her maternal property is or should be something separate from her husband's or his family's, free from the consequences of his poor financial management. Although she doesn't exactly get the last word—the final statements about the pearls come from petty and unreliable gossips—her statement that the pearls are "'all [her daughter] will have'" silences Catherine and finishes the novel's serious

---

[15] Aeron Hunt 166.

[16] Oliphant, "The Laws" 387; Margaret Oliphant, "The Condition of Women," *Blackwood's Edinburgh Magazine* 508.83 (1858): 139–54, 150.

[17] Oliphant, *The Autobiography* 55–6, 52, 123, 179; Henry, *Women* 230–1.

HESTER'S PEARLS AND THE OBLIGATIONS OF WOMEN'S PROPERTY 161

commentary on the topic. It is no small thing that Catherine's indignation about creditors is silenced by a mother's pleasure at being able to pass down something of value to her daughter. Along these lines, Oliphant showcases the significance of changes in economic law and popular sympathy with those changes; Catherine's is the sole voice of protest. Mrs. John's insistence that nobody—neither creditor nor family—has the right to "interfere" with her pearls (261) shows how Married Women's Property Acts permitted different forms of economic action and allowed writers such as Oliphant to imagine different sites of economic agency.

III. Family Obligations

This kind of argument is important for understanding the significance of marital property reforms to wives, and it is one worth making, in recognition of the dramatic shift in their legal rights during the period. But this kind of argument also, ironically, prevents us from seeing the economics of relationships beyond marriage and from assessing the larger implications of debates about women's property. If we think about Mrs. John's necklace only in terms of the relative, legal, individual property rights of husband and wife, married versus unmarried women, we miss how the debate about her pearls illuminates different interpersonal connections and the ways in which they are constituted by or engaged in other economic traditions and obligations.

Oliphant envisions these pearls as property which can at once be both individual and shared, personal and familial, present and future, making them a key example of law's inadequacy to distribute hereditary property outside the legal categories of heirlooms, entailments, primogeniture, and coverture. Unlike Gwendolen Grandcourt or Lizzie Eustace from our previous discussions, Mrs. John gets to enjoy possession of her "own" jewels, taking pleasure in them in her own way as she "hold[s] them up, all warm and shining, to the light, before she deposited them in their carefully padded bed" (261). And unlike *Daniel Deronda*'s Alcharisi, who resents being the "makeshift link" between her father and son, Mrs. John feels confident that "no one else had any share" in her legacy of "individual property" (261). Indeed, the novel pairs the pearls most frequently with her name, possessive pronouns, and maternal designation (e.g., "my mother's pearls").[18] Yet Hester, too, refers to "'my pearls'" (259), and the narrator twice, in describing Hester, mentions "her pearls" (219, 292). Catherine addresses Hester, not Mrs. John, in her stern observation of "'your lovely pearls'" (278), while Mrs. John's fierce claim to the pearls is not for her own personal adornment but for her

---

[18] An online search of Volume 2, for instance, links the pearls to Mrs. John six times as "my pearls," three times as "her pearls," five times as Hester's "mother's pearls," twice as "Mrs. John's pearls," once as "your pearls," and once more as "pearls [that] are my mother's": https://www.gutenberg.org/ebooks/48198.

162 IMAGINING WOMEN'S PROPERTY IN VICTORIAN FICTION

daughter's: "'I wear them, Hester! Oh, no! They have been in their box all these years, and I have never put them on, you know. I kept them for you.'" (277) Looking forward to gifting them to her ("'they are all she will have'") (278) Mrs. John appreciates at once her own "individual property," its future bequest to her daughter, and the maternal line that brought them to her: "'they were her grandmother's, and her great grandmother's, Catherine. It is not only for their value that one is fond of things like these'" (278).

Like *Our Mutual Friend, Daniel Deronda*, the Trollope novels I have discussed, and indeed the Married Women's Property Act of 1870 itself, *Hester* privileges a child's inheritance over a parent's use (or abuse) of property. Yet whereas other so-called "family property"—the Grandcourt diamonds in *Daniel Deronda*, Lizzie's *"Eustace"* diamonds, or the Hamley estate in *Wives and Daughters*— refused simultaneity, unable to be of service to both generations at once, functioning more to incite family rancor than harmony, Mrs. John's pearls, as her mother's family property, work differently. Hester "will have" them but also already benefits from their use. At least rhetorically, then, mother and daughter seem to both share and possess separate personal claims to these pearls, a vision that merges one woman's "individual property" with more inclusive ideas of matrilineal family and is echoed in one catty complaint about "'*their* pearls'" (285, emphasis added). Legally, of course, Hester is a future, not current owner. The Married Women's Property Act of 1882, recognizing the rights of married women to bequeath their property just as an unmarried woman or widow might, did not alter the idea of sequential ownership. But *Hester* repeatedly underscores tensions between the letter of the law and cultural assumptions about the dispersal of property.

To a large extent, after all, a wife's hold on property in this novel is not about her legal *rights*. John Vernon treats the money from Mrs. John's legal marriage settlement as his own: it "secured their income, but he had spent as much as it was possible to spend of that, and forestalled every penny that he could manage to forestall" (28). Oliphant in an 1856 essay about "The Laws Concerning Women" argues on the conservative side of reform that such legal settlements and property rights are irrelevant to the practical terms of marriage.

> Let everything possible be done to protect the property of the wife. Let the law ordain her fortune and her earnings as exclusively her own as if she were unmarried. What then? [...] If the man is a brute, he may *take* his wife's money, rudely, by force of cruelty, physical or mental [...]. If he does it lovingly, all the laws in the world, all the friends in the world, all the panoply of right and personal possession will not save a woman's fortune.[19]

---

[19] Oliphant, "The Laws" 385. We might think also of Anne Brontë's *The Tenant of Wildfell Hall*, with Helen's rueful acknowledgment that "by my own desire, nearly the whole of the income of my fortune is devoted, for years to come, to the paying off of his [her husband's] debts" (208–9).

HESTER'S PEARLS AND THE OBLIGATIONS OF WOMEN'S PROPERTY   163

Brute force and kindness alike make legal protections inconsequential here. No working woman, Oliphant declares, "however induced to give her hard-won shillings to her drunken husband, has the remotest idea that he has any *right* to them. She gives them because he would take them—or she gives them for peace—or with the forlorn hope of redeeming him by kindness."[20] Highlighting the disparity between "words" (or legal decree) and "practice" (marital life), Oliphant reminds us of law's limitations, even as she perhaps undervalues the significance of its protections or its importance for women of all classes.[21] As she reiterates in another essay published two years before the passage of the 1882 Act, the law can be "righted [...] by contracts and compromises, by affection, by the natural force of character, even by family pride."[22] We see those same extralegal forces contribute, albeit less "right[fully]," to the loss of Mrs. John's income and her questionable hold on the pearls. Whether Oliphant is naïvely idealizing relationships by claiming that affection can mitigate women's marital subordination or is simply resigned to a state of affairs in which laws, no matter how necessary, can do no good, married women's property laws are not sacrosanct in *Hester's* understanding of women's property.

Marital property law cannot fully account for characters' economic decisions in part because of the way that affects associated with family obligation—anger, hope, loyalty, passion—shape them. Catherine's fiery reaction to the pearls, for instance, falls somewhere outside of both the "genius for business" (22) she has inherited from her paternal great-grandfather and the economic behavior found in nineteenth-century theories of capitalism as a rational science.[23] *Hester* reminds us of the importance of feelings, beyond desire or pity, to property dispersal and economic choice. But marital property law also fails to account for characters' economic decisions because the novel is interested in women's property as more than a function of marriage—as something other than that negotiated (legally or not) between husband and wife. As we have begun to see, *Hester* also emphasizes daughters.

---

[20] Oliphant, "The Laws," 387. The plight of virtuous working women with drunken husbands was a common theme in discussions about married women's property reform. While it stemmed in part from prejudice against the working classes, it also, as the first chapter of this study has discussed, served the rhetorical purpose of rallying legislators to extend women's rights as a form of protection (rather than empowerment).

[21] Ibid. 385.

[22] Oliphant, "Grievances" 700.

[23] For neoclassical economics' emphasis on rationality as well as its critical refutation, see Hadley, Jaffe, and Winter 10, 12, 14; Dalley and Rappoport, ed., "Introducing Economic Women," *Economic Women: Essays on Desire and Dispossession in Nineteenth-Century British Culture* (Columbus: Ohio State University Press, 2013): 2; John Stuart Mill, "On the Definition of Political Economy; and On the Method of Investigation in That Science," *The London and Westminster Review*, American ed. (New York: Theodore Foster) nos. 7 and 50 (1836): 1–16, 7. For "economic science" as a function of "utility and self-interest," see William Stanley Jevons, "Preface to the Second Edition," in *Theory of Political Economy* (1871), 2nd ed. (1879), online ed.: https://www.econlib.org/library/YPDBooks/Jevons/jvnPE.html?chapter_num=2#book-reader, accessed Nov. 18, 2019.

164   IMAGINING WOMEN'S PROPERTY IN VICTORIAN FICTION

Catherine is a harsh judge of Mrs. John's legal responsibilities, her financial debts to the bank and to her husbands' creditors, but her anger about the pearls reveals a far more personal sense of injury and alerts us to another set of economic obligations and relationships. In a moment of free indirect discourse that takes us into Catherine's bitter thoughts, we see her conviction that the pearls "were Catherine's, they were the creditors' by rights. Mrs John was not wise enough to understand all that; but Hester, if she knew, would understand" (258). With this statement, the debate about the pearls exits the legal realm. They were *Catherine's*? No. Even had the pearls been part of Mr. John's indebted estate and hence up for seizure by his creditors, Catherine would have no legal grounds for claiming them. The blurred distinction between Catherine and the bank, between the bank and Mr. John's later creditors, does more here than provide further evidence of the ongoing confusion regarding Mrs. John's obligations as a wife and widow. It also indicates a collapse of the personal and professional that Catherine's own feelings of obligation to a family sanction but that Mrs. John does not share. And, I think, in this bitterness about their different sense of obligation, we can also see the possibility of Catherine's resentment—and maybe remorse?—that, unlike Mrs. John, she didn't hold anything back.

This view of the characters sharpens if instead of simply viewing the two women's economic choices in terms of their marital status—as a single woman vs. a wife, with different economic *rights*—we think of them also as two daughters, each with a maternal legacy to use or protect, but with different perceptions of their economic *duties*. At the first bank crisis, Catherine offers up her "'mother's money [which] has accumulated till it is quite a little fortune'" (20); at the second, though she "had not now the independent fortune which on the former occasion [...] had remained in the business" (423), she again "place[s] everything she had in the world in the common stock" (446). Though there was legal justification for her action in the first instance, Catherine is governed primarily by the cultural traditions of family business, not by law, when she gives "everything she had" *twice*.

At the bank's first crisis, Catherine's behavior accords with ideas of family partnerships and the legal principles that used to govern them. In throwing her independent fortune into Vernon's to save the bank, she acts according to the principle of unlimited liability that was expected of shareholders at that time, holding herself accountable personally as well as professionally for its failings. This first crisis, presumably in the 1850s, would have occurred around a time when other banks were also failing (1857, in particular, saw a commercial crisis).[24] The Joint Stock Act of 1856 limited the liability of investors in joint stock

---

[24] See James Taylor, "Company Fraud in Victorian Britain: The Royal British Bank Scandal of 1856," *English Historical Review* 122.497 (2007): 700–24, 720.

companies,[25] and even though its principles of limited liability did not then actually apply to banks, "the views underlying the change in the law affected attitudes to the unlimited liability of the British Bank shareholders" at its crisis.[26] Later in the decade, joint-stock banks were "permitted [...] to trade with limited liability."[27] Thus by the second bank crisis, Catherine's commitment to taking full financial responsibility for the bank is out of step with banking trends that had moved away from unlimited liability, because her primary motivation is extralegal. Her actions stem more from "honor" than necessity[28] and align with internalized family pressure to save the family business and name: "Vernon's would continue" (448), though with "'new blood'" and "a great deal of supplementary aid" (447, 450). In the strong pulls of loyalty and obligation that Catherine experiences, Oliphant demonstrates the inadequacy of self-interest as the only model for understanding economic choices and of rights as the primary means of improving women's economic status.

Catherine's longstanding sense of honor and duty to the family bank shapes her initial perception of Mrs. John's first response to the early crisis. She originally shows some respect (coupled with "amusement and sympathy") for Mrs. John's offer of £20: "'That shall always be remembered to her credit,' she said. 'I did not think she had any feeling for the bank. Let us always remember it to her credit. She was ready to give all she had, and who can do any more?'" (22) At that point, thirty years before the pearls appear on Hester's neck, she sees Mrs. John as acting in equal manner if not degree with her—"'giv[ing] all she had'" out of "'feeling for the bank.'" Critically, it is a matter of feeling, not law, of "credit," not compulsion, for good behavior. "Credit" is a key word for Oliphant in distinguishing between "sentiment" and legal status; in an 1880 essay she invokes it to ask not for the reform of economic law but for women to "receive the credit which is our due" for their household contributions.[29] In Hester, she again ties "credit" to personal "feeling" and economic choice in order to emphasize the extralegal pressures contributing to women's financial decisions and duties. The same financial "feeling" that Catherine first praises but later finds lacking in Mrs. John's sense of the Vernon fortune guided her own economic actions as a younger woman. Such feeling also formed the root of the argument that John's mother earlier made to Catherine when it first became clear that the cousins would not wed: "she bade Catherine remember that it would be almost dishonest to enrich another family with money which the Vernons had toiled for" (6). We "smile [...] perhaps a little

---

[25] As Andrew H. Miller has pointed out, the Joint Stock Act of 1856 also altered ethical attitudes about business. See "Subjectivity Ltd: The Discourse of Liability in the Joint Stock Companies Act of 1856 and Gaskell's *Cranford*," *ELH* 61.1 (1994): 139–57, 146. Catherine's behavior at the first crisis is in keeping with the idea of unlimited liability that motivates Miss Matty of *Cranford* in Miller's discussion (149).

[26] Taylor 708.

[27] Ibid. 722.

[28] See also, e.g., Weiss 73.

[29] Oliphant, "Grievances" 700, 701, 704, 706.

166 IMAGINING WOMEN'S PROPERTY IN VICTORIAN FICTION

sadly" with Catherine when she ignores that argument as a reason to marry John (6), in part because we don't like women marrying out of duress, in part because the Vernons' toil has nothing to do with Catherine's maternal fortune—but despite Catherine's smile, her subsequent actions suggest that the advice resonates with her own sense (if not Mrs. John's) of patriarchal familial obligation, whether through a father or a spouse.

The feelings invoked by the pearl necklace thus point to two different models for thinking about women's relationship to property during the nineteenth century. The first, illustrated by Mrs. John's position as a wife, is that of the changing legal rights I have discussed, the shift, over thirty years, from coverture to independent property ownership, as principles of equity were incorporated into the common law. The second, which attention to these legal patterns sometimes obscures, is that of family feeling and tradition. This is the tradition that we perhaps see in Oliphant's own readiness to support so many members of her family, at tremendous financial and personal cost.[30] It is certainly one of the traditions at play in the "fond[ness]" Mrs. John has for her mother's legacy and in the sense of "honour and credit"[31] illustrated by Catherine's readiness to put everything she has at the disposal of a family business. As Davidoff and Hall have shown, women's financial "involvement" in family businesses was expected, important, and "widespread"; not only did wives play a "vital part," but "the direct contribution of women's capital to the family enterprise" included that of "daughters, sisters, nieces, mothers, aunts, cousins, and occasionally unrelated female 'friends.'"[32] A daughter's wealth was a necessary part of its sustainability and growth. Catherine, who takes seriously her legacy as "'old Edward Vernon's granddaughter'" and as "the heir of her great-grandfather's genius for business" (20, 22), sees herself in terms of her filial position to the paternal bank, putting her mother's money at the service of that business without a second thought—until, perhaps, Mrs. John's pearls offer her another vision of what a daughter's wealth might do. The contrast isn't in their financial dedication to "family" as much as it is a difference in what that familial dedication entails; they differ in their relative ability to recognize and maintain ideas of separate property when that property comes from two separate sources, in this case paternal and maternal, the Vernon bank's finances and their mothers' independent fortune, whether in the form of money or pearls.

Rather than finding in Catherine's bitterness only a conservative diatribe against wives' property rights, then, we might see also the disparity between two

---

[30] Oliphant, The Autobiography 9–10, 51, 179.

[31] "Grievances" 701.

[32] Davidoff and Hall 279. See also Patricia E. Johnson paras. 5, 6; Davidoff and Hall 279–80, 289, 311; Stana Nenadic, "The Small Family Firm in Victorian Britain," Business History 35 (1993): 86–114, 101, 103; Mary Rose, "The Family Firm in British Business, 1780–1914," in Business Enterprise in Modern Britain: From the Eighteenth to the Twentieth Century, ed. Maurice W. Kirby and Mary B. Rose (London: Routledge, 1994), 61–87, 67.

HESTER'S PEARLS AND THE OBLIGATIONS OF WOMEN'S PROPERTY 167

daughters' lots. One daughter is urged and ultimately persuaded, early on, to consider her maternal wealth as belonging to her paternal family, to recognize only one side's all-encompassing claims to property. She is guided entirely by this duty to protect her family's credit and livelihood, losing everything she has in the service of relatives who mock, resent, and even betray her. The other daughter is also motivated by family ties, but she appears to recognize that they have generated two separate estates. Her "feeling for the bank" of her conjugal family neither is nor apparently has to be as strong as her consanguineal commitments, and she is therefore able to give her daughter as a maternal legacy an item that has been held by three generations of women.[33]

And this is where—returning briefly to *Little Dorrit*, *Pride and Prejudice*, and the relational dynamics that opened this chapter—I find *Hester*'s two models of family obligation and economic choice useful for understanding other women of property in earlier nineteenth-century literature. We can see in Dickens's Mrs. Clennam some of the paternal pressures, both marital and economic, that *Hester*'s Catherine Vernon also faced. Mrs. Clennam's marriage is arranged by a father and uncle—"'old Mr Gilbert Clennam proposed his orphan nephew to my father for my husband'" (807)—who are either ignorant of her husband's prior romantic relationship or choose to deceive her about it for their family's interest. Underscoring her filial trust in and obedience to a father, who, having "'brought [her] up strictly, and straitly,'" then "'impressed upon [her]'" the similar circumstances of her new husband's upbringing (807), she recalls the series of her father's false assurances ("'He told me [. . .] He told me [. . .]'") with her belated awareness of both the truth and, perhaps, her own overreliance on paternal dictate: "'within a twelvemonth of our marriage I found my husband, *at that time when my father spoke of him*, to have sinned [. . .]'" (807, emphasis added). In the repeated references to her father's speech, we learn not only of the "'wrongs'" that this new husband has committed against her but also of the failures of a father and uncle-in-law to fulfill their own obligations (808). In her determination to raise her husband's child as "'a daily reproach to his father,'" we might see the unspoken reproach of her own father as well (810). "'[H]umbled and deceived,'" she grows "wrathful" and "vindictive," her life "'darkened with [their] sin'" (812, 808, 811).

Despite this "strife and struggle" (808), and acknowledging a lack of the maternal ties[34] that offer *Hester*'s Mrs. John her own purpose as well as her property, Mrs. Clennam nevertheless maintains a strict sense of familial duty to the child himself ("'I devoted myself to reclaim the otherwise predestined and lost

---

[33] For lineage through maternal jewelry, see Marcia Pointon, *Strategies for Showing: Women, Possession, and Representation in English Visual Culture 1665–1800* (Oxford: Oxford University Press, 1997): 43–4.

[34] Forced, with "quiver[ing] lips" to admit that she is "'[n]ot Arthur's mother!'" (806, 807), she later adds that "'[h]e never loved me, as I once half-hoped he might'" (*LD* 807, 824).

168   IMAGINING WOMEN'S PROPERTY IN VICTORIAN FICTION

boy; to give him the reputation of an honest origin [...] I have seen that child grow up [...] to be just and upright'" [810, 824]) and even to his great uncle's unwelcome will. Though she explicitly disregards the law, as she suppresses Gilbert Clennam's "'unmerited'" but legal deathbed bequest, her sense of extra-legal responsibility to this family head's final words is nonetheless strong enough that she cannot entirely ignore their obligations, finding and financially assisting in smaller degree the young woman he belatedly and even "'delusion[ally]'" wished to benefit (811).[35] Mrs. Clennam's sense of familial duty appears even more extensively in her work with the family business, a commercial House which she oversees.[36] She takes care of its domestic concerns during her estranged husband's life, and, following his death, has the "'direction and management of the estate'" (62, 60). When the child she has raised relinquishes his place in the business, he does so with the knowledge that he gives it up "'To my mother, of course,'" who "'will continue it, I see,'" notwithstanding the lack of personal pleasure or even financial profit it offers her (67, 61). Bound by invalidism to her room (49), she persists in her work, "'attend[ing] to my business duties'" there, "'shelter[ed]'" (61) in a home that was once "'a place of business'" but now, as her son reminds her, "'out of date and out of purpose'" (60). The outdated collapse of personal and professional obligations that we have seen in Catherine Vernon's fixation on Hester's pearls appears not only in the Clennam house, as a place of business and domestic shelter, but in the way that the form of account-keeping she must maintain for her work also enters and informs Mrs. Clennam's bitter religiosity ("always balancing her bargain with the Majesty of heaven, posting up the entries to her credit, strictly keeping her set-off, and claiming her due" [64]). *Little Dorrit* literalizes Mrs. Clennam's dangerous collapse of business and domestic concerns when the joined site of the Clennam home and House of commerce actually crumbles: "it heaved, surged outward, opened asunder in fifty places, collapsed, and fell" (827). Mrs. Clennam's immobility following that collapse ("she never from that hour moved so much as a finger again [...]. She lived and died a statue" [827]) dramatically represents, in part, the paralysis of a woman trapped by

[35] Although Mrs. Clennam suppresses his bequests "with the knowledge of Arthur's father" (813), she nevertheless recognizes one convoluted and rather bizarre part of its claim, however unmerited she feels it to be; she locates the youngest niece of her husband's mistress's patron and notes that "'She herself was innocent, and I might not have forgotten to relinquish [the bequest] to her, at my death'" (813). A full discussion of the bequest at the heart of *Little Dorrit*'s plot is beyond the scope of this chapter, but it is significant that, in comparison with the accusations of theft we have seen in previous chapters for women who claim property of their own, and despite the much clearer sense of legal wrong committed in her case, Mrs. Clennam protests fiercely against the idea that she has "stolen money," emphasizing that her actions were "'Not for the money's sake'" (811) but rather in retaliation for a greater "'injustice'" than that recognized by law (812). In her case as in so many of the cases this study has examined, women's economic actions operate outside of the bounds of the law and call attention to its inadequacy.

[36] The Clennam "House" "lend[s] credit to European clients, but its wider dealings are not explained" (*LD* 930: ch. v, n. 2).

HESTER'S PEARLS AND THE OBLIGATIONS OF WOMEN'S PROPERTY   169

devastating adherence to paternal mandates, strict obligation to a family business, and the stultifying duty to protect the credit of her husband's family line.

Whereas Mrs. Clennam's crushing sense of credit, debt, and duty to a father and family business aligns with Catherine Vernon's outdated obligations to her great-grandfather's bank, both women continuing to hold the professional reins, at personal cost, in compensation for the actions of irresponsible men, the fierce allegiance that *Hester*'s Mrs. John feels to a separate legacy, which allows her to retain an independent voice, family line, and property apart from her marital identity finds a surprising counterpoint in Austen's Lady Catherine de Bourgh. We see the resemblance when we focus on Lady Catherine not as *Pride and Prejudice*'s intrusive, arrogant aunt but as another mother who is desperately trying to pass along a legacy to her own daughter. Anne de Bourgh is, as Mrs. Bennet observes, "'better off than many girls'" (46); the "'heiress of Rosings, and of very extensive property'" (46), she is the financial beneficiary of both parents' wealth because they disregarded the principle of primogeniture: "'entailing estates from the female line [...] was not thought necessary in Sir Lewis de Bourgh's family'" (109). Yet any maternal inheritance that makes Anne "better off" appears to be only monetary. Her "'sickly constitution'" and "'indifferent state of health'" (46) are frequent subjects of discussion, as is her appearance, "'so thin and small'" (106), "pale and sickly; her features [...] insignificant" (108). Among Lady Catherine's most narratively mocked moments are those when she attempts to attribute to her daughter talents that Anne does not possess. "'Anne would have been a delightful performer, had her health allowed her to learn'" (117), "'if her health had allowed her to apply'" (115). In these protests to her nephew about what Anne could (but doesn't) have, Lady Catherine seems anxious not only to give her daughter a "'share in the conversation'" that she infamously grabs for herself but also, perhaps, to bequeath something else of non-monetary value to this apparently incapacitated daughter who has gone without the hereditary gifts of her mother's strength, confidence, or ability. Though Anne's maternal wealth has seemingly been subsumed in her father's "extensive property," Lady Catherine's strongest desire is one that might restore to her some of the other advantages of her own separate, consanguineal line. Whatever else nineteenth-century fiction has taught us to think of pre-arranged aristocratic marriages, the engrossing consolidation of family wealth, or the snobbery that makes her dwell upon the dangers of her nephew marrying a "'woman of inferior birth'" (231), the urgency with which Lady Catherine travels "'nearly fifty miles'" (118) not simply to defend Darcy from possible "'disgrace'" (233) but also to protect her daughter's future and the "'favourite wish'" of her late sister (231) suggests an understanding of family more closely aligned to that of Mrs. John than we might expect, despite admittedly important distinctions between these women of different generations, status, and temperament and also despite our earlier linkage of Lady Catherine to her Vernon namesake. This understanding of family is one that continues to value

170   IMAGINING WOMEN'S PROPERTY IN VICTORIAN FICTION

her maternal line and what it can offer to the next generation, apart from a paternal legacy. And it is based at least in part upon her strong feelings for that family, "'the wishes of both sisters'" (231), not just the consolidation of wealth: again we might recall Mrs. John's remark, "'[i]t is not only for their value that one is fond of things like these'" (*Hester* 278).

Returning to *Hester*'s case, it matters, I think, that we never learn the monetary value of Mrs. John's pearls. Trollope's Eustace diamonds have a price tag from the start, their value of £10,000 suggesting their inevitable relationship to the market, to extrafamilial exchange. The eponymous Moonstone of Wilkie Collins's novel, despite the "serious difficulties" of "accurately valuing it," is estimated at "twenty thousand pounds."[37] Pearls at this time were more rare and sometimes more highly valued even than diamonds, cultured pearls not appearing on the market until the 1920s;[38] hence Ellen Merridew's envy of Hester's necklace: "'do you mean to say these are real pearls? Oh go away, or I shall kill you! Why have not I pearls? They are far more *distingués*—oh, far more!—than my paltry bits of diamonds!'" (219) By refusing to appraise Hester's necklace, Oliphant's novel effectively acts with Mrs. John, taking the pearls off the market and emphasizing instead their value as inalienable possessions in a maternal line.[39]

Mrs. John operates without the explicit sanction of property law, and in this way the novel again gestures toward the *de facto* ways that many nineteenth-century women achieved economic agency despite legal restrictions. Yet the history of Married Women's Property reform remains as significant to our understanding of Catherine and Mrs. John as two daughters as it was to our understanding of them a single woman and a wife. Only at a time when a wife is legally permitted to make choices regarding her "individual property" (in Mrs. John's case, the choice to enrich blood kin rather than a spouse's family) can the novel so clearly show and support the way her nonbinding and extralegal but nonetheless firm financial commitments as a daughter and mother supersede those as a wife. The key point for me here is not just that some women had economic agency but that married women's property law reform has potential to shape our understanding of other economic relationships, beyond the spousal. When we see Mrs. John and Catherine as daughters, our sense of whose actions are more financially savvy shifts. Instead of just pitting a naïve, helpless wife against a successful businesswoman, the novel also compares the daughter who manages to protect her mother's legacy for herself and the next generation, against one who couldn't, or doesn't; and it forces us to see how these roles coexist, in tension, changing how we perceive and prioritize characters' relational choices.

---

[37] Collins, *The Moonstone* 50.

[38] Dona M. Dirlam, Elise B. Misiorowski, and Sally A. Thomas, "Pearl Fashion through the Ages," *Gems & Gemology* (1985): 63–78, 76, 77. See also Pointon, *Rocks* 32.

[39] See Weiner 11, *passim* and Maurice Godelier, *The Enigma of the Gift*, trans. Nora Scott (Chicago: University of Chicago Press, 1999): 33.

HESTER'S PEARLS AND THE OBLIGATIONS OF WOMEN'S PROPERTY 171

Along these lines, when Catherine dies, impoverished, we might see her as a daughter who fails, tragically, because family obligations have a stronger pull on women, by 1883, than the common law restrictions on a wife's property. This is an important reminder that despite the significance of legal change for improving economic agency, other cultural pressures, extralegal forces, and relational obligations continued—and continue—to shape women's financial lives.

When Catherine speculates on Hester's reaction—her shame, anger, or sorrow—she attributes to Hester the same crushing sense of familial obligation that made it seemingly impossible for Catherine to do anything but give her mother's wealth to her father's family bank but, by the end of the novel, has compromised her own financial position, leaving her to die in drastically reduced circumstances (452, 455). Mrs. John has kept her mother's pearls separate not only from her husband's estate but also from everyone else, rejecting her marital kin's "'right [...] to interfere'" (261) with them in favor of a different relationship. Her refusal to give them up models a new possibility for women's financial management at a time when more women were to begin keeping their income and inheritance. She passes the pearls along to her daughter as maternal property which Hester will not feel obliged to give to the bank, despite the shame, anger, and sorrow that she eventually feels when she understands her father's role in its failure.

IV. "She Never Looked One Ten-Thousandth Part So Well All Her Life"

Beyond marking separate estates and the significance of maternal property lines, pearls have additional meaning in *Hester* through their ability to enhance the erotic and financial value of a marriageable woman. Though, as I'll go on to argue, Hester herself ultimately rejects this vision of her mother's property and her own prospects, it is one that occupies the novel at length. Looking at the pearls through the lens of heterosexual exchange—a form of transaction that has traditionally positioned women as objects rather than economic agents—counterintuitively allows us to see a different, more empowered female subject: Mrs. John, who takes an active role in her own property management. Rather than serve as a passive vehicle for her necklace's transmission—that "makeshift link" of the Alcharisi and many women whose inheritance was never really intended to be their own—Mrs. John uses the occasion of Hester's adornment to make decisions regarding the use, sale, and purchase of other property as well. By juxtaposing her pearls with another prized possession, the novel not only showcases Mrs. John's role as a property owner making economic choices but also emphasizes the way that property takes different forms, and that those forms, and their unique affordances, matter when we discuss fictional representations of wealth and

172 IMAGINING WOMEN'S PROPERTY IN VICTORIAN FICTION

ownership.[40] Jewels, as tangible, feminized personal property, appear particularly suited for debates about women's economic claims and relationships in Victorian fiction.

The pearl necklace is not the only item of value that Mrs. John retains during her downward plunge into poverty, and is in fact the second one that she mentions, after "'my Indian shawl'" (213). The shawl receives far less commentary than the necklace, but it constitutes a significant portion of the personal property Mrs. John has treasured for all these years. "Mrs John's Indian shawl [...] after Hester and the pearls, was the thing in the world which the poor lady held most dear" (277). Nevertheless, she parts with it apparently without commentary, its "sacrifice" providing her with the money necessary for purchasing the clothing she deems appropriate for her daughter's new social engagements (277). "Indian" or Kashmir shawls, expensive, labor-intensive productions "coveted" because of their "exquisite softness, delicacy, and warmth,"[41] were most popular in Victorian Britain at mid-century, when Mrs. John would likely have acquired hers. The shawl—unlike her pearls—might have made a material difference in Mrs. John's physical comfort, but the novel presents this as irrelevant next to its cultural status and monetary value. It is a luxury item. In Charlotte Brontë's 1853 *Villette*, "that majestic drapery [...] *a real Indian shawl*— 'un véritable Cachmire,'" evokes "mixed reverence and amaze."[42] Suzanne Daly has observed that mid-century novels tend to "remov[e] the shawls from the cash nexus [... portraying them] either as old but stately garments that women seem always to have owned, or explicitly as heirlooms that women inherit rather than purchase."[43] Mrs. John's shawl calls attention to its exoticized origins by its very name,[44] but whatever its origins, and in contrast with Daly's observations, it matters most in *Hester* because of its market price. Worth far more than the twenty pounds Mrs. John offers at the Bank's first crisis, a genuine "Kashmiri

---

[40] See Levine, *Forms*.

[41] Chitralekha Zutshi, "'Designed for Eternity': Kashmiri Shawls, Empire, and Cultures of Production and Consumption in Mid-Victorian Britain," *Journal of British Studies* 48.2 (2009): 420–40, 423, 425: https://www.jstor.org/stable/25483041, accessed Sept. 25, 2019.

[42] Brontë, *Villette* 78.

[43] Suzanne Daly, "Kashmir Shawls in Mid-Victorian Novels," *Victorian Literature and Culture* 30.1 (2002): 237–55, 249: https://www.jstor.org/stable/25058583, accessed Sept. 25, 2019.

[44] The "Indian" shawl thus offers an exotic contrast with pearls that were likely either from the United States or Scotland and that may have seemed more appropriate for Hester, who despite having "never been in England before" the start of the novel's present action, nevertheless "prided herself on being an English girl" (30); see Dirlam, Misiorowski, and Thomas 74. While investments, like the shawl itself, remind us that global trade finances the lives depicted in the novel, *Hester* shows some preference for the local. Vernon's bank is a Redborough fixture, tied to the town and, in the imagination of Emma Ashton who wishes to see "'where all the Vernon money comes from'" (240), a specific physical structure. In contrast with Hester, Edward is not the "home-loving" son Catherine believes him to be (129); after speculating wildly with the bank's money, he eventually flees England (448). To a certain extent, *Hester* attempts to expunge the foreign from the novel, even while showing the impossibility of doing so, in its choice of pearls over shawl, Hester over Edward, Vernon's local bank over risky financial speculation.

HESTER'S PEARLS AND THE OBLIGATIONS OF WOMEN'S PROPERTY   173

shawl could cost upward of £200," according to Chitralekha Zutshi.[45] Mid-century novels such as Elizabeth Gaskell's *North and South* (1854–5) remind us that "Indian shawls" don't fall around the shoulders of every young woman who wants them. As one mother in that novel remarks about her daughter's desire, "'really when I found what an extravagant price was asked, I was obliged to refuse her.'"[46]

Given Catherine's great interest in the topic of Mrs. John's debts, though, it is worth noting that John Vernon's creditors never learn about her "Indian shawl" either. Unlike the pearls, it appears only twice in the novel, both times in a woman's financial deliberations rather than displayed on her. Perhaps because it is so little visible Catherine never knows enough about this shawl to resent its continued possession or subsequent sale. Yet the novel's joint invocation of shawl and pearls, twice within the same sentences, throws into relief the very different treatment that Mrs. John's two most valuable items receive in this novel, one becoming the bitter subject of debates about a woman's property rights and obligations and the other given something of a free pass.

Why are the pearls so much more important than the shawl in this novel's accounting of the widow's property? The necklace—which appears more spectacularly and more often than the shawl—has greater financial value, most likely tallied in the thousands, while the shawl, worth roughly £200, approximates the amount that the first Married Women's Property Act (1870) conceded to wives— not much for a wealthy woman such as Catherine to count, but of extreme importance to the working classes or a relatively impoverished gentlewoman such as Mrs. John. It is odd, though, that the shawl's financial value matters less than Mrs. John's flustered offer of £20 in the novel's (and Catherine's) fierce tallying of the property that should or should not have either helped the bank or paid her husband's debts. It suggests that the pearls raise issues for the novel and Catherine that go beyond their monetary value.

To some extent, this is a function of their status as rare and stylish objects. Extravagant Ellen Merridew envies her cousin's uncommon necklace because it is "'far more *distingués*'" than her own jewelry, not because she cannot afford its price (219). In contrast, the Kashmir shawl no longer has the cultural heft it once had, its British market having taken a downturn by the time of *Hester*. Suzanne Daly, counting it among the "outworn fashions Oliphant carefully evokes," notes "the wisdom of Mrs. John's decision, when forced to part with one of the two prized possessions of her own youth in the 1840s, to sell her Indian shawl [. . . .T]he shawl could no longer do the crucial work of marking Hester as a

---

[45] Even the best imitations manufactured in England, "a much more accessible option for the middle classes [. . .] cost between £20–25" (Zutshi 424). The shawl that allows Mrs. John to purchase and maintain her daughter's dresses is unlikely to have been an imitation, since it dates from her wealthier days.

[46] Gaskell, *North and South* 9.

174   IMAGINING WOMEN'S PROPERTY IN VICTORIAN FICTION

young woman of distinction, work the pearls perform flawlessly."[47] Ordinary shawls are ubiquitous in *Hester*; leaving a party at Catherine's home all of "the ladies [are] shawled" (279), and ten out of the novel's sixteen mentions of "shawls" appear on or in reference to Mrs. John and Catherine, making them as much or more the fashion of widows and unmarried elderly women as of young women. Even an "Indian shawl" more exquisite or costly than others might not grab attention or set Hester apart. But nobody else in the novel wears pearls. As Marcia Pointon notes, jewelry has long functioned as "the most spectacular way of displaying extraordinary wealth while simultaneously disguising capital as artistry,"[48] and the symbolic weight of necklaces in Victorian fiction far exceeds their measurement in carats. In the growing consumer culture of the nineteenth century, such displays were not limited to the extraordinarily rich, and jewels served as markers of both class status and marital or other familial wealth.[49] Though she has fallen from her former rank—previously "there was nothing in the county to equal Mrs John Vernon's dresses and diamonds" (9)—Mrs. John, as we have seen, sustains her own sense of status as well as her daughter's primarily through her pearl necklace.

Status in this case is specifically gendered. Both pearls and shawls are worn close to and associated with a woman's body in ways that other costly household possessions—silver candlesticks, a porcelain vase, a portrait or carriage—are not. Even as the category of "paraphernalia" may make it more legally straightforward for women to cling to a necklace or garment after a household has broken up,[50] these objects' physical touch grants them a still closer connection. The pearls' proximity to bare skin, their encircling of the neck, constitutes an especially intimate embrace, even more than that of the shawl, which would have been worn over other attire. A hopeful suitor might assist with or adjust a woman's shawl, but was unlikely to have the privilege of fastening her necklace. When, in *Daniel Deronda*, Grandcourt compels Gwendolen to wear her diamonds, "fasten[ing] them" while she "stood still" with the awareness that "he had been used to fasten them on someone else" (427), his unwanted, close contact and her response are framed in terms of his sexual[ized] claim to her body, his physical access first to "someone else" and now to his wife. Hester's pearls, like Gwendolen's diamonds, draw attention to and invite interpretations of their relationship to the female body.

Victorian jewelry suggested "the standing of a family and their ability to provide a dowry"[51] and in this way highlighted the potential—of both jewels and the woman they adorn—for heterosexual exchange. The crucial necklace,

[47] Daly 252.
[48] Marcia Pointon, "Intriguing" 493–516, 493.
[49] Arnold, *Victorian Jewelry* 1–7.
[50] Marcia Pointon, *Strategies* 32, 39.
[51] Marcia Pointon, "Women and Their Jewels," in *Women and Material Culture, 1660–1830*, ed. Jennie Batchelor and Cora Kaplan (Houndmills: Palgrave Macmillan, 2007): 11–30, 13.

worn only by Hester and never by Mrs. John within the novel's present action, comes into play when Hester is to make an appearance at her cousin's fashionable parties. Her mother, who "'would rather go without my dinner [...] for a whole year'" than send her daughter in a "'dowdy'" dress, expresses relief that she has not parted with her pearls (213). Mrs. John's maternal pride and sense of matrilineal descent remain important to her understanding of the pearls—"'You shan't go at all if you can't go as my daughter should'" (214)—but once they appear around Hester's neck as adornments they function differently, attracting sexual admiration and marking her as an object of erotic attention. The pearls are repeatedly presented as effecting Hester's transformation from "'a dowdy little girl [...] with no ornaments at all'" (244) to "'much handsomer than I should have expected, [...] very well dressed, with beautiful pearls'" (244). Descriptions of her "with her pearls round her throat" (219) or "with her mother's pearls about her white throat" (242) call attention to an exposed and apparently titillating part of her body, along with the pearls that touch it. This sight provokes a visceral response from her viewers: "[...] even young Mrs Merridew herself held her breath" (219); "The sight of her had intoxicated Edward" (242). When Catherine observes, "'they must have dazzled you, [...] these pearls,'" he acknowledges "'they took away my breath'" (244). Though Hester's rejected suitor Harry maintains faithfully that "'she always looks nice, whatever she puts on'" (220) and that the pearls, pretty as they are, "'are nothing to me at least'" (259), his steady breath, like her ability to "walk [...] without noticing Harry by her side" (300), does not bode well for his suit. The narrator, on the other hand, seconds the fashionable hostess's claim, "'She never looked one ten-thousandth part so well all her life' [...]. No, she had never looked so well in all her nineteen years" (220). The loosely chaperoned parties where Hester wears the pearls are explicitly framed as places for romance. "Flirtation was openly recognised in this youthful house as one of the portions of the evening's entertainment" (225), and the single-minded Emma Ashton, finding that these events are likely to offer her the best matrimonial "'chance'" of her visit to Redborough (230, 231) quickly angles for an invitation. The pearls, then, work to position Hester as a desirable young woman within a likely marriage plot.

Catherine's objection to their presence around her neck thus seems as much about her ongoing competition with other women as it is about any property Mrs. John may have withheld from the bank. Catherine, after all, "'was to have married John Vernon [...] and he preferred—'" (227). Decades later, she recalls her rival's pearls unusually well, with the altered breath both Mrs. Merridew and Edward experience, when she first hears of them appearing on Hester. "'Ah!' said Catherine, with a long breath; 'then her mother kept her pearls!'" (244) The pearls remind her of her earlier rivalry, but by this point her jealousy seems less about the widowed Mrs. John than it is about Hester, who is receiving Edward's attention and affection. This adopted son appears to betrays Catherine as much by secretly

176   IMAGINING WOMEN'S PROPERTY IN VICTORIAN FICTION

desiring Hester as by ruining the bank. Learning "that it was Hester who was the object of his love [...] had caused her perhaps the greatest mental conflict she had ever known in her life" (379); "the idea that Hester had *him* at her feet was bitter to her" (389). In this reading of Catherine's hostility toward Mrs. John's pearls, relationships between women again have as much or more significance than spousal property dynamics. Along these lines, it makes sense that the pearls vanish from the narrative without any further commentary about debts or putting them to use in the service of saving the bank. Once Edward has run away from Hester, Catherine, and the bank he has failed, there is no more rivalry; they have all been abandoned. Hester's pearls no longer mark his choice between (adopted) mother and lover (381). The object of competition having been removed, Catherine's dislike vanishes as well, along with any further mention of the pearls.

V. "What Can a Young Woman Desire More Than to Have Such a Possibility of Choice?"

This reading of eroticized jewelry offers us one useful way to account for the problematic pearls, but—like viewing Mrs. John primarily through the lens of marital coverture—it again makes marriage and heterosexual competition the primary explanations of women's property matters and motivations. Oliphant's novel, I am arguing, also recognizes other relationships of equal importance for women's economic deliberations. Just as our understanding of Mrs. John's financial choices broadens when we view her as a daughter and mother as well as a wife, our understanding of Hester's adornment and even of Catherine's eventual silence about this property can shift if we pursue the thought experiment of taking Hester, like the pearls, off the market.

Hester's ending note reminds us that marriage remains one possibility for its heroine: "And as for Hester, all that can be said for her is that there are two men whom she may choose between, and marry either if she please [...]. *What can a young woman desire more* than to have such a possibility of choice?" (456, emphasis added). Many critics find it difficult to reconcile this conclusion with the novel's "history of a family business" and its strong female protagonist.[52] After Hester has been deserted by the romantically and financially treacherous Edward and left to pick up the pieces of the Vernon bank with Catherine, "the novel returns to the shreds of its marriage plot," submits Johnson.[53] Linda Peterson similarly suggests that Oliphant appears "unable to imagine closure without marriage. Perhaps she felt neither satisfied with the traditional feminine plot of marriage and motherhood, nor comfortable with the masculine pattern of quest

---

[52] E.g., Patricia E. Johnson, "Unlimited Liability" para. 29.
[53] Ibid.

HESTER'S PEARLS AND THE OBLIGATIONS OF WOMEN'S PROPERTY   177

and self-fulfillment, and so ended in the only way possible—with a question."[54] Yet this question resembles, both in form and, I think, in irony, an earlier moment from the novel when the narrator, describing Edward's deceptively pleasing relations to his "Aunt Catherine," notes: "No mother could have had sons more respectful and devoted. Good and virtuous and kind children—*what could a woman have more?*" (26, emphasis added). Much more, as it happens. This Catherine, like her titled and similarly intrusive predecessor in *Pride and Prejudice*, cannot trust her "nephew" to show the devotion she wishes in his financial or marital decisions. Moreover, as the narrative makes clear over the course of four hundred pages, Edward, who manipulates and steals from her, is neither respectful nor good. Catherine learns belatedly just how very little she has really had. Hindsight undercuts this initial interrogative. The similarly phrased query in Hester's case thus invites us to read ironically, imagining what another four hundred pages might do to undercut the question and reminding us of all that this particular young woman might actually want. Along such lines, Aeron Hunt reads the ending query as a "bittersweet" acknowledgment of the other desires Hester has expressed throughout the novel, "pointedly [leaving her] in position to exercise 'choice' and just as pointedly left with the choice unmade and perhaps even refused."[55] Nancy Henry too notes that, despite the "ambivalence" that prevents Oliphant "from turning Hester into a business heroine," Catherine's death and Hester's rejection of marriage "raise the possibility that she might find her way to a business career."[56] As we will see, the pearls specifically, like the plot in general, support a reading in which Hester refuses to conform with a marriage plot that even Oliphant's novel takes pains to undermine. In doing so, they offer one final insight on the terms by which *Hester* can imagine a woman's right to individual property.

Removing Hester from the marriage market is work that she herself initiates and reiterates, despite what for her is the real temptation of eloping with Edward. From her early rejection of Harry—" 'I would rather not marry—any one. I don't see the need for it' " (138–9)—to her realization that Roland Ashton, who "had taken possession of her mind and thoughts for a few weeks with a completeness of influence which probably he never intended" (301), "did not affect her any more" (315), romance or even the idea of a secure establishment is never Hester's aim, as her juxtaposition with Emma (so fixated on getting her " 'chance' ") makes even more evident. Fantasizing not about a husband or household but about "an opportunity, to show the mettle that was in her," Hester longs for "the occasion to do a heroic deed, to save some one, to venture your own life, to escape the bonds

---

[54] Linda Peterson, "The Female *Bildungsroman*: Tradition and Revision in Margaret Oliphant's Fiction," in *Margaret Oliphant: Critical Essays on a Gentle Subversive*, ed. D. J. Trela (Selinsgrove, PA: Susquehanna University Press, 1995): 66–89, 81.

[55] Hunt 168.

[56] Henry, *Women* 244.

178   IMAGINING WOMEN'S PROPERTY IN VICTORIAN FICTION

of every day, and once have a chance of showing what was in you! This was not the 'chance' which Emma Ashton desired, but it appealed to every sentiment in Hester" (300). Nothing about these dreams of her "own life" entails merging it with someone else's.

Her pearls signal, in part, Hester's eventual choice to remain single. These jewels, according to Marcia Pointon, are associated at once with luxury and the consumption of "male vitality"; reproduction ("generative powers" and "maternal authority"); and also virginity (along with the moon and traditions linking the moon to virginity).[57] In accordance with the first two of these meanings, Catherine, in her accusations of what she believes to be Mrs. John's unwarranted wealth, sees them as inappropriately luxurious tokens of marital consumption, while Mrs. John appreciates their maternal lineage and their condition as property that she can pass along to her own daughter. If these two understandings (luxury and reproduction) come into conflict with each other in *Hester*, the novel perhaps resolves them in the third, their (virginal) association with Hester's chosen single status. Despite having invited speculation on Hester's marital value and her rivalry with Catherine, her pearls also "signify purity and sweetness" and were, during much of the nineteenth century, "the only suitable ornament for an unmarried daughter."[58] The association of pearls with virginity aligns with her mother's understanding that Hester may never acquire marital wealth: "'I like them to be worth a great deal, for they are all she will have'" (278). By the end of the novel, that comment seems an astute prediction of Hester's unmarried status, not simply an account of her net worth for a potential suitor.

Given the choice between leaving town with the man she explicitly calls her "'love'" (404) and staying behind to help make things right with the bank, Hester is clear about her priorities, putting the family business before Edward's promises of "'Safety and happiness and everything we can wish'" (402). "'[T]here is everything to detain us,'" she tells him, "'I am not going [....] Oh, how could you think it!'" (402) Or again: "'If it was right I would go,'" she explains, but "'I am a Vernon too [...] when things are going badly—Oh no, no [...]'" (403). These repeated refusals importantly acknowledge her love for him—when she later realizes that he is not coming back "[s]he could have flung herself upon the earth in her misery" (435)—but the very heartbreak they indicate underscores just how much these refusals insist on privileging ties of wider kinship and work. This is family loyalty, not filial guilt. She chooses her family bank over her lover's plans even before she knows the backstory of her father's role in the first crisis. Once Edward reveals that backstory, however, she dismisses him completely: "'There is not another word to be said [...] I will never go with you!'" (405). Hester, "stricken to the heart" by her new knowledge about the bank (404) as much as

---

[57] Pointon, "Intriguing" 507, 508, 504, 503–4; Pointon, *Rocks* 193.
[58] Dirlam, Misiorowski, and Thomas 73, 74.

HESTER'S PEARLS AND THE OBLIGATIONS OF WOMEN'S PROPERTY   179

by Edward's desertion, chooses responsible business practices over unethical profit-seeking, but this is also a choice of extended familial relationships over romance. Hester is more invested in her larger family—"'for God's sake, think of Catherine'" (404)—than in self-interest or personal desire. In the nomenclature Talia Schaffer has given us, Edward initially appears to be a "familiar" suitor for his cousin Hester, but when it becomes clear to her that he cannot actually fulfill that role, that he cannot reinforce and actually threatens her ties to her Vernon kin, family wins out as she rejects the untethered romantic suitor in her decision to stay and support Catherine and the bank rather than flee with her lover. She declares twice in her last narrated conversation, "'I will never marry'" (454). To take seriously the narrator's comment two pages later that she will marry either Roland or Harry or that this possibility is really "all that can be said for her" (456) requires us to discredit her explicit resolve or endorse reading practices which insist that "no" doesn't really mean no. There are critical reasons to be skeptical of such practices, and no textual reasons to tie up a marriage plot that Oliphant deliberately leaves untied.

Of course, Hester rarely waits for other people to speak *for* her, so in this sense, too, the question of "all that can be said for her" is irrelevant. She speaks for herself "with eager eyes" about the prospect of learning and working for the family business (454) and rejects love at the price of dishonor with strength and clarity, "pushing [Edward] from her with all her force" (405). If what others say "for her" may not matter, however, what Oliphant says elsewhere might. Significantly, Oliphant treats single women and the choice to remain single with respect. In "The Condition of Women," for example, single women are a valued and even "remarkable" fact of life, not the problem that other Victorian essays pondering the issue of "surplus" women posed:[59]

Many hundred, nay thousand years ago, there was even a certain characteristic and remarkable person called Miriam, who, willful and womanlike, and unquestionably unmarried, was still so far from being disrespected or unimportant, that a whole nation waited for her, till she was able to join their journey. Our age, which likes so much to declare itself the origin of changes, is not the inventor of feminine celibacy. There were unmarried women before our time, and there will be unmarried women after it.[60]

---

[59] See William Rathbone Greg, "Why Are Women Redundant?" (*National Review*, 1862), in *The Broadview Anthology of British Literature: The Victorian Era*, 2nd ed. (Ontario: Broadview Press, 2012): 106–7; Frances Power Cobbe, "What Shall We Do with Our Old Maids?" (*Fraser's Magazine*, Nov., 1862), in *Prose by Victorian Women: An Anthology*, ed. Andrea Broomfield and Sally Mitchell (New York: Garland, 1996): 244–5.
[60] Oliphant, "Condition" 148.

180   IMAGINING WOMEN'S PROPERTY IN VICTORIAN FICTION

Although Catherine, who urges Hester to forget Edward and marry—"'Your heart will not be empty for ever'" (454)—is single, solitary, and largely unloved, the novel faults her mocking manner, not her unmarried status, for limiting her close connection with other kin.[61] It also, crucially, allows her to eventually develop a more emotionally fulfilling relationship with her younger, female relative. Recognizing that "'you are like me, Hester'" (455), Catherine is finally granted, for the brief remainder of her life, a different kind of familial love and support. Catherine tells her former rival, "'you and I have hated each other because we were meant to love each other, child.' 'I think I have always done both,' said Hester" (442). Oliphant's novel and essay alike reject activists' idea that without marriage a woman must be solitary or "unimportant," refuting the idea that such a woman is even, in the larger sense of the word, single: "not only unmarried and unmarriageable, but without father, mother, brother, or family, sole units standing each upon her own responsibility before the world!"[62] In Oliphant's formulation, marriage is not the only means of affection; nor is it the only means of financial subsistence, since single women need not "stand [...] each upon her own responsibility." A larger network of family ties (parents, siblings, and other kin) offers economic as well as emotional support. We see the significance of these wider relationships to property management in *Hester* as well, in Catherine's efforts to support her poorer relatives and in Hester's decision not to flee with Edward.

Rather than being "unable to imagine closure without marriage," as Peterson suggests, Oliphant finds a different form of closure for an unmarried woman with property. Though, as we have seen, her earlier essays express skepticism about the ability of legal reform to protect women's property, she does make the point that remaining single (or proceeding cautiously into marriage) can be financially advantageous, the best way to avoid married women's property restrictions. A single woman, she argues, "cannot be compelled to marry any but her own choice; nay, she has the alternative of not marrying at all."[63] Along these lines, Hester's decision to remain single is both a matter for respect in itself—like Miriam, she can be "far from being disrespected or unimportant"—and also, possibly, a financial benefit. Here we might think of that other nineteenth-century "Hester" who of course also and famously possessed a "Pearl," this one "her mother's only treasure!"[64] Oliphant was quite familiar with Nathaniel Hawthorne's works and *The Scarlet Letter* (1850) in particular, discussing his writing in detail in her essay "Modern Novelists—Great and Small."[65] In granting her fictional Hester pearls of

---

[61] Nevertheless, Catherine's limited connection with others certainly takes part in a larger literary tradition that treats unmarried women disrespectfully, as spinsters and old maids.

[62] Oliphant, "Condition" 141.

[63] Oliphant, "The Laws" 386.

[64] Nathaniel Hawthorne, *The Scarlet Letter* [1850] (New York: Collier Books, 1962): 94.

[65] Margaret Oliphant, "Modern Novelists—Great and Small." *Blackwood's Edinburgh Magazine* 475.77 (1855): 554–68, 562–5.

HESTER'S PEARLS AND THE OBLIGATIONS OF WOMEN'S PROPERTY   181

her own, she consciously or unconsciously references Hawthorne's earlier tale, acknowledging through the borrowed name her heroine's nonconformity, a possible future outside of traditional marital bounds, and, through her necklace, the possession of "her mother's only treasure."

When Hester stands by the family business—"'Think of Vernon's, which we have all been so proud of, which gives us our place in the country,'" she urges Edward before his flight (404)—she aligns herself, heart, pride, and status alike, with her father's larger family. Her other property, that notable maternal pearl necklace, is absent from discussion about this family business or her personal life. Perhaps the weight of the failing bank overshadows all other economic decisions for Catherine and Hester by the end of the novel, but as the former sells all of her own property and the latter acknowledges her father's wrongdoing—"'I never knew it—I never knew it,' she said, with sobs. 'I am going to Catherine to ask her pardon on my knees'" (405)—it is striking that Catherine does not now demand and Hester does not now offer up those pearls. As Catherine learns to recognize her likeness to Hester in terms of personality and marital status, however, she also learns to understand their likeness in economic terms: they share their fervent "feeling for the bank." When Catherine eavesdrops on Hester's final conversation with Edward, she hears something she never expected from this particular rival and the daughter of Mrs. John: real, reiterated, actionable devotion to Vernon's.

In Catherine's life, "feeling for the bank" could not coexist with holding property back. Her paternal, familial commitments counteract and even make irrelevant the legal rights she has, as a *feme sole*, to her own property, a separate estate, a maternal fortune kept apart from other familial claims. Mrs. John, after the first bank crisis, has little property but even less "feeling for the bank"; through her insistence on keeping her maternal pearls separate from her husband's paternal family business, the novel makes a case for married women's property rights but suggests that they could come at the expense of loyalty to longstanding, patriarchal family traditions. Hester offers a third way of thinking about women's property. Despite what she has learned of the father who owed so much, she keeps her mother's valuable pearls away from the bank, as private property, which, as I've noted, the novel treats as her own and her mother's alike. Nevertheless, she stands by the family business at great personal cost. "'Think of Vernon's,'" she urges Edward before their aborted elopement, "'think of Catherine.'" Choosing the bank and ties of wider kinship over romantic love, she is a reminder of the economic commitments women make outside of marriage and of the steep emotional price that Victorian fiction demands from such women. Alongside this sacrifice, though, the novel makes an important concession. By letting Hester retain her maternal pearls even as she forcefully prioritizes her paternal family's economic well-being, Oliphant suggests that women's independent property ownership might not have to preclude those other family duties that once so ardently drove Catherine. Hester's pearls, we see, do not interfere with her

182   IMAGINING WOMEN'S PROPERTY IN VICTORIAN FICTION

commitment to the Vernon family's economic welfare or its financial institution. Catherine, like other opponents of married women's property rights, has viewed a wife's separate property as a sign of insufficient commitment to her family, a threat to traditional bonds. After seeing how Hester's possession of her mother's pearls does nothing to diminish her feelings of obligation to the family bank, however, Catherine no longer feels a need to contest it.

Unmarried women such as Hester were entitled to their own property well before the laws changed for married women in 1870 and 1882, so in this sense Hester's pearls may not tell us anything new about her rights. But again, Oliphant's novel understands women's property as a function of much more than their rights. If, as we have seen here and in the previous two chapters of this study, a key argument for keeping married women economically dependent upon their husbands was women's presumed financial neglect of or even theft from family, Hester's keen, self-sacrificing dedication to the Vernon bank despite her ability to retain property apart from it counters that argument, regardless of her marital status or legal rights. This idea that the right to private property will not make women abandon other family traditions would have been an important point in favor of the new married women's property laws which, like the pearls, were a fiercely contested legacy for a new generation of women—beautiful and valuable, even if they came with strings of unwritten obligations attached.

Afterword

Women's Property Matters Now

I. Marginal Accounts

In the legal battle for women's property rights, Victorian reformers emphasized the small earnings accrued by working women's labor before setting their sights on the greater wealth of inherited property. Protecting poor women and their children initially proved a more popular rationale for reform than recognizing the property rights of relatively privileged wives, but this shift in attention from women's work to the circulation of women's wealth also reflects the fact that, before widespread higher education and professional opportunities for women, substantial property was less likely to result from their income than from family gifts. Today, of course, income has become a much more important component of middle-class women's economic independence. As I turn, in the next two sections of this Afterword, to the challenges facing contemporary women's property rights, I focus primarily on the twenty-first-century workplace rather than on inheritance. First, however, I want to address why it matters that this transition, from legislating women's income to legislating women's wealth, occurs during the specific time-frame of these property reforms. In the brief remarks that follow, I suggest that the shift in *legal attention* in the 1870s offers us a window into women's invisibility within the *economic theory* that also arose in the 1870s. Looking at these legal and theoretical developments together illuminates not only the difficulties still facing women's economic lives but also some ways to address and perhaps resolve them.

The history of economics, as narrated by many scholars of Victorian literature, follows a trajectory disengaged from questions of women's economic actions, economic subjectivities, or legal reforms. It begins with political economy's focus on labor and the distribution of wealth and then turns to calculations of desire and demand within the emerging discipline of economics. In this disciplinary arc, economics' theoretical grounding moves from production to consumption, from "economic man's" self interest to the market choices of so-called rational agents, from the distribution of wealth to neoclassical equations of marginal utility.[1]

---

[1] For a discussion of the "marginal revolution," see Gagnier 40–3 and Claudia C. Klaver, *A/Moral Economics: Classical Political Economy and Cultural Authority in Nineteenth-Century England* (Columbus: Ohio State University Press, 2003): xi, 173–5, 182–3; Kreisel 59, 62–3. Multiple economic

184   IMAGINING WOMEN'S PROPERTY IN VICTORIAN FICTION

Feminist economists have challenged some of these foundational myths largely by expanding the models available for understanding these market choices.[2] More recently, literary and cultural critics have reminded us that economics is more than a series of mathematical equations and that individualism is only one roadmap for economic behavior.[3] The fiction I've discussed, for instance, demonstrates how collaboration becomes an important strategy for women's economic agency. But as Elaine Hadley, Audrey Jaffe, and Sarah Winter observe, "[feminist economists] have had a modest impact on the embedded gendered suppositions of the field."[4]

There are many reasons for disciplinary fixity, but one of the ongoing difficulties presented by an economic model that posits a shift from labor to consumer choice during the nineteenth century is its failure to engage with the changing legal parameters and cultural traditions that made those choices possible. The reform of married women's property law constituted a fundamental structural change to the economic underpinning of British families and to the history of economics, as Janette Rutterford, David R. Green, Josephine Maltby, and Alastair Owens have shown.[5] Yet accounts of how nineteenth-century economics developed as a discipline ignore the fact that *the focus of theory shifted from production to consumption precisely when women gained the power to keep their money.* Why did this theoretical move correspond with the first major changes to women's property law and amidst heightened debate about further change?[6] Coincidence? Recognition of the many new financial agents populating the economic field? Or, perhaps, a disavowal of women's productivity, inheritance, investments, and other

theorists (William Stanley Jevons and Carl Menger in 1871, Léon Walras in 1874) turned in the early 1870s to examining individuals' "subjective valuation" of commodities and calculating it according to mathematical equations (Klaver 175).

[2] See, e.g., Paula England, "The Separative Self: Androcentric Bias in Neoclassical Assumptions," in *Beyond Economic Man: Feminist Theory and Economics*, ed. Marianne A. Ferber and Julie A. Nelson (Chicago: University of Chicago Press, 1993): 37–53, 37, 40; Susan F. Feiner, "Reading Neoclassical Economics: Toward an Erotic Economy of Sharing," in *Out of the Margins: Feminist Perspectives on Economics*, ed. Edith Kuiper and Jolande Sap (London: Routledge, 1995): 151–66, 155; Nancy Folbre and Heidi Hartman, "The Rhetoric of Self-Interest: Ideology and Gender in Economic Theory," in *The Consequences of Economic Rhetoric*, ed. Arjo Klamer, Deirdre Nansen McCloskey, and Robert M. Solow (Cambridge: Cambridge University Press, 1988): 184–203. See also Elaine Hadley, Audrey Jaffe, and Sarah Winter, eds., *From Political Economy to Economics through Nineteenth-Century Literature: Reclaiming the Social* (Cham: Palgrave Macmillan, 2019): 14.

[3] Klaver *passim*, e.g., xvi, 8, 29, 134, 161–2; see also Kreisel 28–9, 65–7, 69; Dalley and Rappoport, "Introducing Economic Women" 2–4.

[4] Hadley, Jaffe, and Winter 14. Their volume inadvertently repeats some of neoclassical economics' "embedded gendered suppositions" by ignoring the history of women's legal progress in its cultural history of economics.

[5] See, e.g., Janette Rutterford, David R. Green, Josephine Maltby, and Alastair Owens, "Who Comprised the Nation of Shareholders? Gender and Investment in Great Britain, c. 1870–1935," *The Economic History Review* 64.1 (2011): 157–87, 170–2: http://www.jstor.com/stable/27919486.

[6] For the place of slavery in modern capitalism and how the shift from political economy to economics also "roughly coincides with the era of Reconstruction in the United States," see Gordon Bigelow, "Forgetting Cairnes: *The Slave Power* (1862) and the Political Economy of Racism," in *From Political Economy to Economics through Nineteenth-Century Literature: Reclaiming the Social*, ed. Elaine Hadley, Audrey Jaffe, and Sarah Winter (Cham: Palgrave Macmillan, 2019): 85–105, 85.

WOMEN'S PROPERTY MATTERS NOW   185

financial activities not centered in consumption? Did the distribution of wealth seem less important once women's property entered the mix? Either way, ignoring these legal and theoretical intersections distorts our understanding of the period.[7] And, I suspect, it also contributes to the continued marginalization of women's labor today. If, as Catherine Gallagher has observed, production rather than circulation was considered the primary "source of value, the source of real wealth" in nineteenth-century thought,[8] then the fact that economic models did not have to take women into account as legal financial agents until they were already focusing on circulation means that women's productive contributions to the economy were made secondary from the start: economic theory shifted before having to account for theories of labor that included women's work.

II. Invisible Labor

What might it have meant for labor theories to take women into account? "Women's work" is not and never has been only one thing, of course, but if we trace just a few of the models presented by the nineteenth-century fiction this study has addressed, we see how the failures of economic theory to account for various forms of gendered economic agency might contribute to the ways in which women's productive labor is often both overlooked and even punished in today's workplaces, with tangible costs to their financial lives.

In attempting to bridge the many gaps—historical, national, fictional, racial— between Victorian literary characters and twenty-first-century people, between imagined property and contemporary labor forces, these concluding remarks are necessarily speculative. They grow out of connections I have observed between the twenty-first-century, professional middle-class workplace I inhabit in the United States and the Victorian patterns of property-based agency I study. But they are nonetheless suggestive. As *Imagining Women's Property* has demonstrated, Victorian novels written during the period of married women's property reform frequently emphasize the benefit of women's collaborative approaches to property as an alternative to competitive individualism. They sacrifice women's claims for the careers of male kin, vilifying those women whose personal ambitions, business

---

[7] This is not to devalue scholarship on consumerism, to which my own work is indebted. Historians who have turned to "consumption-oriented analysis" of "persons whose working lives were often located outside the formal economy and whose economic activities were as much implicated in the reproduction of families as they were in the production of marketable goods" have rightly celebrated the "new academic legitimacy" given to studying households and "the myriad intersections between class and gender identity." See Margot Finn, "Working-Class Women and the Contest for Consumer Control in Victorian County Courts," *Past and Present* 161 (1998), 116–54, 116: http://www.jstor.com/stable/651074. For men's consumer activities and interests in the early nineteenth century, see Margot Finn, "Men's Things: Masculine Possession in the Consumer Revolution," *Social History* 25.2 (2000): 133–55, 134–5, 142: http://www.jstor.com/stable/4286642.

[8] Gallagher, "George Eliot and *Daniel Deronda*" 42.

186   IMAGINING WOMEN'S PROPERTY IN VICTORIAN FICTION

acumen, or professional talents give them the prospect of self-reliant lifestyles or profitable careers. And they favor future family lines, requiring women to prioritize their (future) husband and children's financial well-being over their own or anyone else's. Whether the literary models that emerge during this period of reform reflect real women's actions or register cultural anxieties toward women's growing economic agency, the discursive patterns we find in these works contributed to and reinforced attitudes toward Victorian women. And in nearing the end of this book, I am struck by how these patterns persist, with longstanding consequences for individuals and families today.

Collaborative approaches continue to appear in twenty-first-century gendered professional norms. Contemporary women in the workplace are "more likely to care for the collective" than their male colleagues.[9] Even when being a "team player" seems to be a shared principle of operation, Pam Heim, Tammy Hughes, and Susan K. Golant have found gendered differences in its definitions and deployment; women are more likely to value interpersonal support and cooperation, while men more frequently interpret being a team player as carrying out their own work in accordance with a leader's agenda.[10] Despite recognition of women's disproportionately collaborative approach, however, economic conventions and employment law do not fully account for collaboration when assessing models of agency, labor, or choice. Many of our workforces similarly lack ways to measure or reward such efforts equitably.

Indeed, the inability to assess or compensate collaboration as an important economic mode has turned what Victorian writers such as Gaskell treated as a tool for women's progress into something of a trap today. Studies of "collaboration overload," for instance, have shown that contemporary women in the workplace "fe[el] the burden disproportionately."[11] Such collaborative efforts—"helping behavior" or "altruistic citizenship behavior," as they are sometimes called—are not only demanded along gender lines ("routinely expected for women") but then

[9] Renee Cullinan, "In Collaborative Cultures, Women Carry More of the Weight," *Harvard Business Review* (July 24, 2018): 2 of 7 pdf pages: https://hbr.org/2018/07/in-collaborative-work-cultures-women-carry-more-of-the-weight.

[10] Pat Heim, Tammy Hughes, and Susan K. Golant, *Hardball for Women: Winning at the Game of Business*, 3rd ed. (New York: Penguin, 2015): 115–16. See also Rose Bryant-Smith, "Talking at Cross Purposes: How Gender Informs Our Communications in the Workplace," *Worklogic* 34: https://www.worklogic.com.au/resources/newsletters/workplace-culture/talking-cross-purposes-gender-informs-communications-workplace/, accessed Dec. 10, 2020. For the gendered significance of evolving collaborative cultures within the discipline of science, see Mary C. Murphy, Amanda F. Mejia, Jorge Mejia, Xiaoran Yan, Sapna Cheryan, Nilanjana Dasgupta, Mesmin Destin, Stephanie A. Fryberg, Julie A. Garcia, Elizabeth L. Haines, Judith M. Harackiewicz, Alison Ledgerwood, Corinne A. Moss-Racusin, Lora E. Park, Sylvia P. Perry, Kate A. Ratliff, Aneeta Rattan, Diana T. Sanchez, Krishna Savani, Denise Sekaquaptewa, Jessi L. Smith, Valerie Jones Taylor, Dustin B. Thoman, Daryl A. Wout, Patricia L. Mabry, Susanne Ressl, Amanda B. Diekman, and Franco Pestilli, "Open Science, Communal Culture, and Women's Participation in the Movement to Improve Science," *Proceedings of the National Academy of Sciences* 117.39 (2020): 24154–64; https://doi.org/10.1073/pnas.1921320117.

[11] Cullinan 2.

WOMEN'S PROPERTY MATTERS NOW   187

"likely to be disregarded or ignored" when performed. Women are "penalized more than men for their failure to act altruistically," and also less likely than their male colleagues to be noticed or rewarded for their efforts along these lines.[12] Since existing theories and metrics for workplace evaluations fail to account for models of the collective, many of women's contributions—helping a co-worker, engaging in service commitments, resolving conflict, or taking care of time-consuming but not quantitatively productive "office housework" for the good of the group—amount to invisible (and unrewarded) labor.[13] Women of color face particularly excessive burdens in these forms of unrecognized work.[14] Within current frameworks, an emphasis on mutual help, cost-sharing, or teamwork has both direct and indirect costs to women's career advancement, financial achievement, and related property ownership. The work of supporting others is important for many reasons, but it is also difficult to leverage for advancement when performance reviews tally individual contributions. Meanwhile, effort spent on behalf of the team, department, or collective rather than on individual tasks can directly detract from the time necessary for women to achieve their own professional goals.[15]

III. "The Reasons Women Should Get the Same Things as Men"[16]

Disproportionate service mandates, invisible labor, and a legacy of Victorian economic theories that fail to see or reward collaborative efforts account for

[12] Madeline E. Heilman and Julie J. Chen, "Same Behavior, Different Consequences: Reactions to Men's and Women's Altruistic Citizenship Behavior," *Journal of Applied Psychology* 90.3 (2005): 431–41, 431, 432, 437, 439. See also Deborah L. Kidder, "The Influence of Gender on the Performance of Organizational Citizenship Behaviors," *Journal of Management* 28.5 (2002): 629–48, 632.

[13] See, e.g., Joan C. Williams and Rachel Dempsey, *What Works for Women at Work: Four Patterns Working Women Need to Know* (New York: New York University Press, 2014, updated ed. 2018): 68–70, 110–16. Also relevant is Talia Schaffer's discussion of "[i]nvisibilized work [a]s a big part of care" (*Communities of Care* 6).

[14] See many of the essays in *Presumed Incompetent: The Intersections of Race and Class for Women in Academia*, ed. Gabriella Gutiérrez y Muhs, Yolanda Flores Niemann, Carmen G. González, and Angela P. Harris (Boulder: University Press of Colorado, 2012): Sherrée Wilson, "They Forgot Mammy Had a Brain," 65–77, 71; Angela Onwuachi-Willig, "Silence of the Lambs," 142–51, 145; Michelle M. Jacob, "Native Women Maintaining Their Culture in the White Academy," 242–9, 244; Yolanda Flores Niemann, "The Making of a Token: A Case Study of Stereotype Threat, Stigma, Racism, and Tokenism in Academe," 336–55, 433–5; Adrien Katherine Wing, "Lessons from a Portrait: Keep Calm and Carry On," 356–71, 357, 364; Jessica Lavariega Monforti, "La Lucha: Latinas Surviving Political Science," 393–407, 395; Sherri L. Wallace, Sharon E. Moore, Linda L. Wilson, and Brenda G. Hart, "African American Women in the Academy: Quelling the Myth of Presumed Incompetence," 421–38, 423; Yolanda Flores Niemann, "Lessons from the Experiences of Women of Color Working in Academia," 446–99, 460, 481, 483, 484.

[15] E.g., Joyce K. Fletcher, "Relational Practice: A Feminist Reconstruction of Work," *Journal of Management Inquiry* 7.2 (1998): 163–86, 167, 175–80; Paolo Gaudiano, "Are Women Penalized for Being Team Players?" *Forbes* (July 30, 2018): 4 of 5: https://www.forbes.com/sites/paologaudiano/2018/07/30/are-women-penalized-for-being-team-players/?sh=61cd4746453d, accessed Dec. 9, 2020.

[16] See first and penultimate paragraphs of my earlier Acknowledgments.

188 IMAGINING WOMEN'S PROPERTY IN VICTORIAN FICTION

some of the pay disparities between men and women in the workforce. Another way in which we see the afterlife of Victorian attitudes about women's property is in ongoing expectations of "altruistic" behavior more generally, which contribute to gendered differences in salary negotiations today. Like Lizzie Eustace, that "blood-sucking harpy" of Trollope's novel, many women today are penalized for showing what is perceived as greed or even basic self-interest. Women negotiate job offers and salaries less frequently than men, largely because of the greater "social cost" of self-promotion.[17] Accordingly, women tend to be more active in negotiating on behalf of another person than for themselves.[18] But even small salary increases can have huge impact on property accrued over the course of a career.[19]

The often unspoken stipulation that women put others' needs before their own resembles nineteenth-century expectations that "good" women will sideline their own ambitions and agency for the well-being of their family, making "acts of self-sacrifice habitual."[20] The Alcharisi's choice to put her personal career and earning power ahead of her maternal role remains uniquely unforgiveable in Eliot's *Daniel Deronda*. In the U.S. workforce today, women still perform the greater percentage of parenting, household, and other caregiving responsibilities.[21]

[17] Deborah A. Small, Michele Gelfand, Linda Babcock, and Hilary Gettman, "Who Goes to the Bargaining Table? The Influence of Gender and Framing on the Initiation of Negotiation," *Journal of Personality and Social Psychology* 93.4 (2007): 600–13, 601, 604: https://doi.org/10.1037/0022-3514.93. 4.600; Hannah Riley Bowles, Linda Babcock, and Lei Lai, "Social Incentives for Gender Differences in the Propensity to Initiate Negotiations: Sometimes It Does Hurt to Ask," *Organizational Behavior and Human Decision Processes* 103 (2007): 84–103, 85, 91; Hannah Riley Bowles, Linda Babcock, and Kathleen L. McGinn, "Constraints and Triggers: Situational Mechanics of Gender in Negotiation," *Journal of Personality and Social Psychology* 89.6 (2005): 951–65, 953: https://doi.org/10.1037/0022-3514.89.6.951.

[18] Bowles, Babcock, and McGinn, "Constraints and Triggers" 959.

[19] In this calculation, for instance, a $3,500 difference in starting salary or initial raises can make a difference of over *a quarter million dollars* of property ownership over thirty years, before taxes and adjusting for inflation, cost-of-living increases, and modest interest on investments. Even a $1,500 difference amounts to over $120,000. See (and play around with the numbers at): https://www.calcula tor.net/savings-calculator.html?cstartingprinciple=0&cannualaddition=3500&cannualadditionyears=30& cannualadditionincrease=2&cmonthlyaddition=0&cmonthlyadditionmonths=0&cmonthlyaddition increase=0&cadditionat1=beginning&cinterestrate=3&ccompound=annually&cyears=30&ctaxtrate=0& cinflationrate=3&printit=0&x=53&y=16#savingresult.

[20] Ellis 123.

[21] Pew Research Center, "Raising Kids and Running a Household: How Working Parents Share the Load" (Nov. 2015): 1–23, 3, 7, 9–10: https://www.pewsocialtrends.org/2015/11/04/raising-kids-and-running-a-household-how-working-parents-share-the-load/, accessed Dec. 13, 2020. See also Modern Language Association, "Standing Still: The Associate Professor Survey: Report of the Committee on the Status of Women in the Profession" (Apr. 27, 2009): 1–35, 12; Kim A. Weedon, Youngjoo Cha, and Mauricio Bucca, "Long Work Hours, Part Time Work, and Trends in the Gender Gap in Pay, the Motherhood Wage Penalty, and the Fatherhood Wage Premium," *RSF: The Russell Sage Foundation Journal of the Social Sciences* 2.4 (2016): 71–102: https://doi.org/10.7758/RSF.2016.2.4.03. For a discussion of domestic labor as both "essential" and "unwaged" in relation to Silvia Federici and the 1970s Wages for Housework movement which has reentered cultural discourses since the pandemic, see Jordan Kisner, "The Lockdown Showed How the Economy Exploits Women. She Already Knew," *New York Times* (Feb. 17, 2021; updated Feb. 22, 2021): https://www.nytimes.com/2021/02/17/magazine/waged-housework.html.

WOMEN'S PROPERTY MATTERS NOW   189

Family responsibilities slow women's career advancement and have compounding consequences on their lifelong earnings, benefits, and savings. These disparities are evident in my own field, where studies suggest the "unequal treatment of women and men" and show "unambiguously" that "women spend significantly more time at the rank of associate professor than do men" before attaining the rank and financial benefits of full professorship.[22]

These dynamics have material consequences for women's economic lives. The gendered earnings gap at the start of individuals' work lives and its widening over time, "particularly for [...] those who were ever-married" and especially "when families are being formed," has been well documented.[23] In 2019, "women were paid 82 cents for every dollar paid to men."[24] This ratio, substantial in itself, fails to reflect racial, occupational, and educational differences among women; the disparity increases when we compare the earnings of Black women (62 cents on the dollar) and Latinas (54 cents on the dollar) to those of white, non-Hispanic men,[25] or when we consider the "disproportionate economic toll on women, most notably women of color" taken by the COVID-19 coronavirus pandemic, which is likely to "have economic ramifications for years."[26] Such income disparities have direct consequences for women's ability to save, invest, and exercise other choices with regard to their property.

Women of color not only receive significantly less income than white men but also benefit less from the accrued family property that, as both nineteenth-century literature and contemporary studies of socioeconomic status demonstrate, has material impact on life opportunities. Not until 1882 did the power to inherit money for their own use and to direct the ways in which that money would be left to future generations become a common-law right for married Englishwomen. As I noted earlier, such inheritance, more than income, was historically "the most important component of wealth."[27] Persisting class disparities coincide with, and in part stem from, racial wealth inequalities; in the United States, white families are more likely than Black families both to receive inheritances and to receive larger sums.[28] Wealth inequality, according to economists, contributes to a

[22] "Standing Still" 20, 19.
[23] Claudia Goldin, Sari Pekkala Kerr, Claudia Olivetti, and Erling Barth, "The Expanding Gender Earnings Gap: Evidence from the LEHD-2000 Census," *American Economic Review: Papers & Proceedings* 107.5 (2017): 110–14, 113, 114: https://doi.org/10.1257/aer.p20171065, accessed Dec. 10, 2020. See also American Association of University Women (AAUW), "The Simple Truth about the Gender Pay Gap" (Fall 2018 ed.): 1–32: www.aauw.org, accessed Nov. 16, 2020.
[24] American Association of University Women, "The Simple Truth about the Gender Pay Gap" (2020 Update): 1–6, 2: https://www.aauw.org/app/uploads/2020/10/SimpleTruth_1.8.pdf, accessed Nov. 16, 2020.
[25] Ibid.
[26] AAUW, "2020 Update" 1. See also Kisner, "The Lockdown Showed How the Economy Exploits Women."
[27] Erickson, *Women and Property* 3. For depictions of heiresses in Victorian fiction, see Michie, *Vulgar.*
[28] Clymer 10.

190   IMAGINING WOMEN'S PROPERTY IN VICTORIAN FICTION

significant educational gap. Youth from families with money are more likely to complete at least two years of college, attend more selective institutions, take on less debt, and pursue graduate degrees.[29] As Lynn Arner demonstrates, such inequalities also shape the experiences and success rates of job candidates pursuing careers in academia, particularly in English and the humanities.[30]

From a legal standpoint, many women today have significantly more economic protections than they did during the period discussed in this book, both within their domestic lives and in their careers. As a working woman in the United States, for example, I am protected by the 1963 Equal Pay Act and Title VII of the Civil Rights Act of 1964, both of which prohibit sex-based pay discrimination, while the Lilly Ledbetter Fair Pay Act of 2009 clarifies and safeguards these rights.[31] As a working mother of three, I have also benefited from the 1993 Family and Medical Leave Act (FMLA), along with university and department policies regarding parental leave.[32] But not all women or work situations have these protections. As writers from Austen to Oliphant show us, law and institutional directives are only part of this story. The novels I have discussed remind us powerfully of the extralegal forces—including tradition and social pressure and fiction itself—that shape women's financial realities and relationships. We need to recognize and address the myriad ways in which cultures of work and life create ongoing gender disparities as well as other inequities today.

One starting point may be to remember that women's economic rights are never "just" about women, individually or even collectively. *Imagining Women's Property* has shown not only the cultural expectations for women's property and the tremendous backlash that can arise when women make independent

---

[29] For completion of postsecondary education, see Breno Braga, Signe-Mary McKernan, Caroline Ratcliffe, and Sandy Baum, "Wealth Inequality Is a Barrier to Education and Social Mobility" (Apr. 2017): 1–12. Urban Institute: https://www.urban.org/sites/default/files/publication/89976/wealth_and_education_4.pdf, accessed Dec. 28, 2020; "Postsecondary Attainment: Differences by Socioeconomic Status," Annual Report, NCES: National Center for Education Statistics, *The Condition of Education* (May 2015): 1–7: https://nces.ed.gov/programs/coe/pdf/Indicator_TVA/coe_tva_2015_05.pdf, accessed Dec. 28, 2020; Sandy Baum and Patricia Steele, "Who Goes to Graduate School and Who Succeeds?" (Jan. 2017): 1–16: https://www.urban.org/research/publication/who-goes-graduate-school-and-who-succeeds, accessed Dec. 28, 2020; Sharon O'Dair, "Class Work: Site of Egalitarian Activism or Site of Embourgeoisement?" *College English* 65.6 (2003): 593–606, 600: https://www.jstor.org/stable/3594272; for attendance at elite universities and the longlasting advantages of such attendance, see Anthony P. Carnevale and Stephen J. Rose, "Socioeconomic Status, Race/Ethnicity, and Selective College Admissions," *America's Untapped Resources: Low-Income Students in Higher Education*, ed. Richard D. Kahlenberg (New York: Century Foundation Press, 2004): 101–56, 106–9; Ann L. Mullen, *Degrees of Inequality: Culture, Class, and Gender in American Higher Education* (Baltimore: Johns Hopkins University Press, 2010), 5–11.
[30] For the significance of family wealth within academia, particularly English and the humanities, see Lynn Arner, "Working-Class Women at the MLA Interview," *Rhizomes: Cultural Studies in Emerging Knowledge* 27 (2014): http://www.rhizomes.net/issue27/arner.html#_edn24, ISSN 1555–9998, accessed Dec. 28, 2020.
[31] See AAUW, "The Simple Truth about the Gender Pay Gap" (Fall 2018 ed.): 23–4.
[32] Policies regarding parental leave still vary greatly among universities and even among colleges within a single university.

professional or financial choices, but also the ways in which their economic lives matter within local and global communities and depend upon intersecting conditions including those of family, class, ethnicity, sexuality, religion, and race. This is worth emphasis, because women's finances are still imagined as somehow operating outside of larger economic relationships. The fact that financial inequalities are often seen as primarily women's problems appears in some of the solutions—support groups, professional mentorship and training, suggestions that women simply learn to ask for what they need or to just say no to unfair requests—that have been proposed to address them. But financial inequality is a social injustice requiring attention to institutional structures, national protections, access to wealth, and a shifting of cultural norms, not simply a matter of one woman's ability to request a raise or refuse a committee assignment.

Similarly, just as in Victorian literature we saw how women's changing economic agency had the potential to transform family, communities, and even financial industries, we would do well to remember that women's financial equality can affect not just their own lives and those of their immediate families but also the larger networks, corporations, and non-profits into which they invest their resources. As we rethink cultures of work and life in relation to women's financial claims, we need to remember those capacious forms of kinship and community that shape and are shaped by women's (and indeed all) economic choices. Just as Victorian fiction emphasizes a wide range of connections— through single women's ties, elective and non-nuclear families, friendships, mutual dependence—we might think seriously about the significance of multiple forms of community, the priorities indicated by women's investments and bequests, the structures of connection and reciprocity forged by women's disproportionate gift-giving,[33] the consequences of mentorship and collaboration. We might find new ways to account for the "relational self"[34] within the workplace, including systems of evaluation that more effectively represent and reward diverse work strategies, teamwork, and service. And, by better recognizing and addressing the ways in which parental leave or spousal benefits do not currently cover the requirements of all domestic arrangements, we might also take seriously some people's expansive caregiving needs and commitments (to close friends, unmarried partners, young or elderly relatives, and other communities) that may not fall under the legal protections or privileges of family or medical leave.

As we do so, we might finally begin to place greater value, material and otherwise, on professional and personal contributions that do not operate solely according to theories of economic individualism. Rather than penalize people for the collaboration or service that supports so much necessary and valuable work,

---

[33] Aafke E. Komter, *Social Solidarity and the Gift* (Cambridge: Cambridge University Press, 2005): 79, 81–5. See also Rappoport, *Giving Women*.

[34] E.g., Bowles, Babcock, and Lai 86, 101; Small, Gelfand, Babcock, and Gettman 602.

192 IMAGINING WOMEN'S PROPERTY IN VICTORIAN FICTION

we might more fully recognize, celebrate, and even incentivize these commitments and the communities they strengthen. The solution to ignoring, devaluing, and unfairly demanding certain forms of economic agency is not for us to eliminate collaboration or service, but rather to create more even distribution, more equitable evaluation, and more balanced understanding of these and other forms of economic actions.

One of the core insights that I take from my years with this project is the extent to which even this "single-authored monograph," the primary point of professional labor for my individual promotion, can only in the narrowest way be considered an individual endeavor. And though my words constitute a poor substitute for the wealth I have discussed, it seems appropriate to recognize again here in some small way the many, many people—family, friends, writing groups, University staff and students, but also my children's elementary school teachers and our religious community, as well as others (yoga instructors, physicians, housekeeping services, grocery delivery drivers, and so many more)—who have enabled me to complete this book at this time. In countless ways, some long-term, others occasional, I have benefited tremendously from their time, energy, diligence, and care. Without this substantial and varied support, this book, as well as the stage of my life and the career that it represents, would have been greatly impoverished.

Works Cited

Ablow, Rachel. *The Marriage of Minds: Reading Sympathy in the Victorian Marriage Plot.* Stanford: Stanford University Press, 2007.

Ablow, Rachel. "'One Flesh,' One Person, and the 1870 Married Women's Property Act." In *BRANCH: Britain, Representation and Nineteenth-Century History.* Ed. Dino Franco Felluga. Extension of *Romanticism and Victorianism on the Net.* https://branchcollective.org/?ps_articles=rachel-ablow-one-flesh-one-person-and-the-1870-married-womens-property-act.

Adler, Judith. "Hidden Allusion in the Finale of *Middlemarch*: George Eliot and the Jewish Myth of the *Lamed Vov.*" *George Eliot—George Henry Lewes Studies* 70.2 (2018): 143–71. https://doi.org/10.5325/georelioghlstud.70.2.0143.

Alborn, Timothy. *All that Glittered: Britain's Most Precious Metal from Adam Smith to the Gold Rush.* Oxford: Oxford University Press, 2019.

Allen, Michelle. *Cleansing the City: Sanitary Geographies in Victorian London.* Athens: Ohio University Press, 2008.

Altick, Richard D. "Education, Print, and Paper in *Our Mutual Friend.*" In *Nineteenth-Century Literary Perspectives: Essays in Honor of Lionel Stevenson.* Ed. Clyde de L. Ryals. Durham: Duke University Press, 1974, 237–54.

American Association of University Women (AAUW). "The Simple Truth about the Gender Pay Gap." Fall 2018 ed. 1–32. www.aauw.org. Accessed Nov. 16, 2020.

American Association of University Women (AAUW). "The Simple Truth about the Gender Pay Gap" (2020 Update): 1–6. https://www.aauw.org/app/uploads/2020/10/SimpleTruth_1.8.pdf. Accessed Nov. 16, 2020.

Anderson, Amanda. *The Powers of Distance: Cosmopolitanism and the Cultivation of Detachment.* Princeton: Princeton University Press, 2001.

Anderson, Amanda. "Trollope's Modernity." *ELH* 74.3 (2007): 509–34.

Andrews, Malcolm. *Charles Dickens and His Performing Selves: Dickens and the Public Readings.* Oxford: Oxford University Press, 2006.

Appel, Peter A. "A Funhouse Mirror of Law: The Entailment in Jane Austen's *Pride and Prejudice.*" *Georgia Journal of International & Comparative Law* 41 (2013): 609–36.

Armstrong, Nancy. *Desire and Domestic Fiction: A Political History of the Novel.* New York and Oxford: Oxford University Press, 1987.

Arner, Lynn. "Working-Class Women at the MLA Interview." *Rhizomes: Cultural Studies in Emerging Knowledge* 27 (2014). http://www.rhizomes.net/issue27/arner.html#_edn24. ISSN 1555-9998. Accessed Dec. 28, 2020.

Arnold, Jean. *Victorian Jewelry, Identity, and the Novel: Prisms of Culture.* Burlington: Ashgate, 2011.

Ashton, Rosemary. *G. H. Lewes: A Life.* Oxford: Clarendon Press, 1991.

Ashton, Rosemary. *George Eliot: A Life.* London: Hamish Hamilton, 1996.

Austen, Jane. *Mansfield Park* [1814]: *Authoritative Text, Contexts, Criticism.* Ed. Claudia L. Johnson. New York: W. W. Norton & Company, 1998.

Austen, Jane. *Persuasion* [1818]: *A Norton Critical Edition,* 2nd ed. Ed. Patricia Meyer Spacks. New York: W. W. Norton & Company, 2013.

194 WORKS CITED

Austen, Jane. *Pride and Prejudice* [1813]: *An Authoritative Text, Backgrounds and Sources, Criticism*, 3rd ed. Ed. Donald Gray. New York: W. W. Norton & Company, 2001.

Austen, Jane. *Sense and Sensibility* [1811]: *Authoritative Text, Contexts, Criticism*. Ed. Claudia L. Johnson. New York: W. W. Norton & Company, 2002.

Babcock, David. "Professional Subjectivity and the Attenuation of Character in J. M. Coetzee's 'Life & Times of Michael K.'" *PMLA* 127.4 (2012): 890–904. https://www.jstor.org/stable/23489094.

Bailey, Joanne. "Favoured or Oppressed? Married Women, Property, and 'Coverture' in England, 1660–1800." *Continuity and Change* 17.3 (2002): 351–72.

Baum, Sandy and Patricia Steele, "Who Goes to Graduate School and Who Succeeds?" (2017): 1–16. Urban Institute: https://www.urban.org/research/publication/who-goes-graduate-school-and-who-succeeds. Accessed Dec. 28, 2020.

Beer, Gillian. *Darwin's Plots: Evolutionary Narrative in Darwin, George Eliot, and Nineteenth-Century Fiction*, 2nd ed. Cambridge: Cambridge University Press, 1983, 2000.

Ben-Yishai, Ayelet. *Common Precedents: The Presentness of the Past in Victorian Law and Fiction*. Oxford: Oxford University Press, 2013.

Bennet, Judith M. and Amy M. Froide. "Introduction." In *Singlewomen in the European Past, 1250–1800*. Ed. Judith M. Bennett and Amy M. Froide. Philadelphia: University of Pennsylvania Press, 1999, 1–37.

Best, Stephen M. *The Fugitive's Properties: Law and the Poetics of Possession*. Chicago and London: University of Chicago Press, 2004.

Bigelow, Gordon. "The Cost of Everything in *Middlemarch*." In *Economic Women: Essays on Desire and Dispossession in Nineteenth-Century British Culture*. Ed. Lana L. Dalley and Jill Rappoport. Columbus: Ohio State University Press, 2013, 97–109.

Bigelow, Gordon. "Forgetting Cairnes: *The Slave Power* (1862) and the Political Economy of Racism." In *From Political Economy to Economics through Nineteenth-Century Literature: Reclaiming the Social*. Ed. Elaine Hadley, Audrey Jaffe, and Sarah Winter. Cham: Palgrave Macmillan, 2019. 85–105.

Blanton, C. D., Colleen Lye, and Kent Puckett. *Representations* 126.1 (2014, special issue: Financialization and the Culture Industry): 1–8. https://www.jstor.org/stable/10.1525/rep.2014.126.1.1.

Blumberg, Ilana M. "Collins's *Moonstone*: The Victorian Novel as Sacrifice, Theft, Gift and Debt." *Studies in the Novel* 37.2 (2005): 162–86.

Blumberg, Ilana M. "'Love Yourself as Your Neighbor': The Limits of Altruism and the Ethics of Personal Benefit in *Adam Bede*." *VLC* 37 (2009): 543–60.

Blumberg, Ilana M. "'Unnatural Self-Sacrifice': Trollope's Ethic of Mutual Benefit." *Nineteenth-Century Literature* 58.4 (2004): 506–46.

Blumberg, Ilana M. *Victorian Sacrifice: Ethics and Economics in Mid-Century Novels*. Columbus: Ohio State University Press, 2013.

Bodichon, Barbara Leigh Smith. "A Brief Summary, in Plain Language, of the Most Important Laws Concerning Women: Together with a Few Observations Thereon" [1854]. Excerpt. ed.

Boiko, Karen. "Reading and (Re)Writing Class: Elizabeth Gaskell's *Wives and Daughters*." *Victorian Literature and Culture* 33.1 (2005): 85–106.

Bowen, John. *Other Dickens: Pickwick to Chuzzlewit*. Oxford: Oxford University Press, 2000.

Bowles, Hannah Riley, Linda Babcock, and Lei Lai. "Social Incentives for Gender Differences in the Propensity to Initiate Negotiations: Sometimes It Does Hurt to Ask." *Organizational Behavior and Human Decision Processes* 103 (2007): 84–103.

WORKS CITED   195

Bowles, Hannah Riley, Linda Babcock, and Kathleen L. McGinn, "Constraints and Triggers: Situational Mechanics of Gender in Negotiation." *Journal of Personality and Social Psychology* 89.6 (2005): 951–65, 953, 959. http://doi.org/10.1037/0022-3514.89.6.951.

Braga, Breno, Signe-Mary McKernan, Caroline Ratcliffe, and Sandy Baum. "Wealth Inequality Is a Barrier to Education and Social Mobility" (April 2017): 1–12. Urban Institute: https://www.urban.org/sites/default/files/publication/89976/wealth_and_education_4.pdf. Accessed Dec. 28, 2020.

Brantlinger, Patrick. *The Reading Lesson: The Threat of Mass Literacy in Nineteenth-Century British Fiction.* Bloomington: Indiana University Press, 1988.

Bresden, Dagni. "'What's a Woman to Do?': Managing Money and Manipulating Fictions in Trollope's *Can You Forgive Her?* and *The Eustace Diamonds.*" *Victorian Review* 31.2 (2005): 99–122.

Briefel, Aviva. *The Deceivers: Art Forgery and Identity in the Nineteenth Century.* Ithaca: Cornell University Press, 2006.

Brontë, Anne. *The Tenant of Wildfell Hall* [1848]. Ed. Herbert Rosengarten. Oxford: Oxford University Press, 1992, 2008.

Brontë, Charlotte. *Jane Eyre* [1847]. Ed. Richard J. Dunn, 3rd ed. New York and London: W. W. Norton & Company, 2001.

Brontë, Charlotte. *Villette* [1853]. Ed. Helen M. Cooper. London: Penguin Random House, 2004.

Brooks, Peter. *Realist Vision.* New Haven: Yale University Press, 2005.

Bryant-Smith, Rose. "Talking at Cross Purposes: How Gender Informs Our Communications in the Workplace." *Worklogic* 34, Web. https://www.worklogic.com.au/resources/newsletters/workplace-culture/talking-cross-purposes-gender-informs-communications-workplace/. Accessed Dec. 10, 2020.

Carnevale, Anthony P. and Stephen J. Rose. "Socioeconomic Status, Race/Ethnicity, and Selective College Admissions." In *America's Untapped Resources: Low-Income Students in Higher Education.* Ed. Richard D. Kahlenberg. New York: Century Foundation Press, 2004, 101–56.

Carpenter, Mary Wilson. "The Apocalypse of the Old Testament: Daniel Deronda and the Interpretation of Interpretation." *PMLA* 99.1 (1984): 56–71.

Castillo, Larisa T. "Natural Authority in Charles Dickens's *Martin Chuzzlewit* and the Copyright Act of 1842." *Nineteenth-Century Literature* 62.4 (2008): 435–64.

Cave, Terence. "Introduction." In George Eliot, *Daniel Deronda* [1876]. Ed. Terence Cave. London: Penguin Books, 1995, ix–xxxv.

"Central Criminal Court, Jan. 14." *The Times* Jan. 15, 1869: 9. *The Times Digital Archive.* Sept. 21, 2015.

Černý, Lothar. "'Life in Death': Art in Dickens's *Our Mutual Friend.*" *Dickens Quarterly* 17.1 (2000): 22–36.

Chase, Karen. *The Victorians and Old Age.* Oxford and New York: Oxford University Press, 2009.

Chase, Karen and Michael Levenson. *The Spectacle of Intimacy: A Public Life for the Victorian Family.* Princeton: Princeton University Press, 2000.

Cheyette, Bryan. *Constructions of "the Jew" in English Literature and Society: Racial Representation, 1875–1945.* New York: Cambridge University Press, 1995.

Clark, Cumberland. *Dickens and Talfourd. With an Address & Three Unpublished Letters to Talfourd, the Father of the First Copyright Act Which Put an End to the Piracy of Dickens' Writings.* London: Chiswick Press, 1919.

196   WORKS CITED

Cleere, Eileen. *Avuncularism: Capitalism, Patriarchy, and Nineteenth-Century English Culture*. Stanford: Stanford University Press, 2004.

Clymer, Jeff. *Family Money: Property, Race, and Literature in the Nineteenth Century*. Oxford: Oxford University Press, 2013.

Cobbe, Frances Power. "What Shall We Do with Our Old Maids?" [*Fraser's Magazine*, Nov. 1862]. Reprinted in *Prose by Victorian Women: An Anthology*. Ed. Andrea Broomfield and Sally Mitchell. New York: Garland, 1996, 236–61.

Cobbe, Frances Power. "Wife-Torture in England" [*Contemporary Review*, April 1878]. Reprinted in *Prose by Victorian Women: An Anthology*. Ed. Andrea Broomfield and Sally Mitchell. New York and London: Garland Publishing, Inc., 1996, 291–333.

Cohen, Deborah. *Family Secrets: Shame and Privacy in Modern Britain*. Oxford: Oxford University Press, 2013.

Cohen, Monica. "From Home to Homeland: The Bohemian in *Daniel Deronda*." *Studies in the Novel* 30.3 (1998): 324–54.

Cohen, Monica F. *Pirating Fictions: Ownership and Creativity in Nineteenth-Century Popular Culture*. Charlottesville: University of Virginia Press, 2017.

Cohen, Monica F. *Professional Domesticity in the Victorian Novel: Women, Work and Home*. Cambridge: Cambridge University Press, 1998.

Cohen, William A. "The Palliser Novels." In *The Cambridge Companion to Anthony Trollope*. Ed. Carolyn Dever and Lisa Niles. Cambridge: Cambridge University Press, 2011, 44–57.

Cohen, William A. *Sex Scandal: The Private Parts of Victorian Fiction*. Durham: Duke University Press, 1996.

Collins, Wilkie. *The Moonstone* [1868]. Ed. Sandra Kemp. London: Penguin Books Ltd., 1998.

Collins, Wilkie. *The Woman in White* [1860]. Ed. John Sutherland. Oxford: Oxford University Press, 1998.

Colón, Susan. "'One Function in Particular': Professionalism and Specialization in *Daniel Deronda*." *Studies in the Novel* 37.3 (2005): 292–307.

Combs, Mary Beth. "'A Measure of Legal Independence': The 1870 Married Women's Property Act and the Portfolio Allocations of British Wives." *Journal of Economic History* 65.4 (2005): 1028–57. http://www.jstor.com/stable/3874913.

Corbett, Mary Jean. "Afterword: Real Figures." In *Replotting Marriage in Nineteenth-Century British Literature*. Ed. Jill Galvan and Elsie Michie. Columbus: Ohio State University Press, 2018, 229–37.

Corbett, Mary Jean. *Family Likeness: Sex, Marriage, and Incest from Jane Austen to Virginia Woolf*. Ithaca: Cornell University Press, 2008.

Cullinan, Renee. "In Collaborative Cultures, Women Carry More of the Weight." *Harvard Business Review* (July 24, 2018): 7 pdf pages. https://hbr.org/2018/07/in-collaborative-work-cultures-women-carry-more-of-the-weight.

"Curious Wills." *The Saturday Review of Politics, Literature, Science and Art* 36.942 (1873): 630–1.

Dalley, Lana L. and Jill Rappoport. "Introducing Economic Women." In *Economic Women: Essays on Desire and Dispossession in Nineteenth-Century British Culture*. Ed. Lana L. Dalley and Jill Rappoport. Columbus: Ohio State University Press, 2013, 1–21.

Daly, Nicholas. *Modernism, Romance, and the Fin De Siècle: Popular Fiction and British Culture, 1880–1914*. Cambridge: Cambridge University Press, 1999.

Daly, Suzanne. "Indiscreet Jewels: The Eustace Diamonds." *Nineteenth-Century Studies* 19 (2005): 69–81.

WORKS CITED 197

Daly, Suzanne. "Kashmir Shawls in Mid-Victorian Novels." *Victorian Literature and Culture* 30.1 (2002): 237–55, 249. https://www.jstor.org/stable/25058583. Accessed Sept. 25, 2019.

Dames, Nicholas. "Trollope and the Career: Vocational Trajectories and the Management of Ambition." *Victorian Studies* 45.2 (2003): 247–78.

Darwin, Charles. *The Descent of Man, and Selection in Relation to Sex* [1871]. Ed. James Moore and Adrian Desmond. London: Penguin Books Ltd., 2004.

Darwin, Charles. *On the Origin of Species by Means of Natural Selection, or the Preservation of Favoured Races in the Struggle for Life.* London: John Murray, 1850. *A Facsimile of the First Edition with an Introduction by Ernst Mayr.* Cambridge, MA: Harvard University Press, 1964.

Darwin, Charles. *On the Origin of Species by Means of Natural Selection, Or, The Preservation of Favoured Races In the Struggle for Life,* 4th ed., with additions and corrections. London: John Murray, 1866. https://catalog.hathitrust.org/Record/011619025/Home.

David, Deirdre. *Fictions of Resolution in Three Victorian Novels: North and South, Our Mutual Friend, Daniel Deronda.* New York: Columbia University Press, 1981.

David, Deirdre. *Rule Britannia: Women, Empire, and Victorian Writing.* Ithaca: Cornell University Press, 1995.

Davidoff, Leonore. *Thicker Than Water: Siblings and Their Relations, 1780–1920.* Oxford: Oxford University Press, 2012.

Davidoff, Leonore and Catherine Hall. *Family Fortunes: Men and Women of the English Middle Class, 1780–1850,* rev. ed. London: Routledge, 1987, 2002.

Debrabant, Mary. "Birds, Bees and Darwinian Survival Strategies in *Wives and Daughters.*" *Gaskell Society Journal* 16 (2002): 14–29.

Dekel, Mikhal. "'Who Taught This Foreign Woman about the Ways and Lives of the Jews?': George Eliot and the Hebrew Renaissance." *ELH* 74.4 (2007): 783–98.

DeMaria, Joanne Long. "The Wondrous Marriages of *Daniel Deronda*: Gender, Work, and Love." *Studies in the Novel* 22.4 (1990): 402–17.

Dever, Carolyn. *Death and the Mother from Dickens to Freud: Victorian Fiction and the Anxiety of Origins.* Cambridge: Cambridge University Press, 1998.

DeWitt, Anne. "Moral Uses, Narrative Effects: Natural History in Victorian Periodicals and Elizabeth Gaskell's *Wives and Daughters.*" *Victorian Periodicals Review* 43.1 (2010): 1–18.

Dickens, Charles. *A Christmas Carol* [1843] *and Other Christmas Writings.* Ed. Michael Slater. London: Penguin Books Ltd., 2003.

Dickens, Charles. *Little Dorrit* [1855–7]. Ed. Stephen Wall and Helen Small. London: Penguin Books Ltd., 2003.

Dickens, Charles. *Oliver Twist* [1838]. Ed. Kathleen Tillotson and Stephen Gill. Oxford: Oxford University Press, 1999.

Dickens, Charles. *Our Mutual Friend* [1864–5]. Ed. Michael Cotsell. Oxford: Oxford University Press, 2008.

Dickens, Charles. *The Pickwick Papers* [1836–7]. Ed. James Kinsley. Oxford: Oxford University Press, 1988.

Dirlam, Dona M., Elise B. Misiorowski, and Sally A. Thomas. "Pearl Fashion through the Ages." *Gems & Gemology* 21.2 (1985): 63–78.

"Divorce." *John Bull and Britannia* (Feb. 21, 1857): 121.

Doe, Helen. "Waiting for Her Ship to Come In? The Female Investor in Nineteenth-Century Sailing Vessels." *The Economic History Review* 63.1 (2010): 85–106. http://www.jstor.com/stable/27771571.

198 WORKS CITED

Dolin, Tim. *Mistress of the House: Women of Property in the Victorian Novel.* New York: Routledge, 2016. First published 1997 by Ashgate.

Draper, Nicholas. *The Price of Emancipation: Slave-Ownership, Compensation and British Society at the End of Slavery.* Cambridge: Cambridge University Press, 2010.

"Duties of Executors and Administrators." *The Leisure Hour: A Family Journal of Instruction and Recreation* 998 (1871): 91–4.

Eliot, George. *Daniel Deronda* [1876]. Ed. Terence Cave. London: Penguin Books Ltd., 1995.

Eliot, George. *Middlemarch* [1871]. Ed. Rosemary Ashton. London: Penguin Books Ltd., 1994.

Eliot, George. *The Mill on the* Floss [1860]. Ed. A. S. Byatt. London: Penguin Books Ltd., 1979, 2003.

Elliott, Dorice Williams. *The Angel Out of the House: Philanthropy and Gender in Nineteenth-Century England.* Charlottesville: University of Virginia Press, 2002.

Ellis, Sarah Stickney. *The Women of England, Their Social Duties, and Domestic Habits.* New York: Appleton, 1843.

Endersby, Jim. "Sympathetic Science: Charles Darwin, Joseph Hooker, and the Passions of Victorian Naturalists." *Victorian Studies: An Interdisciplinary Journal of Social, Political, and Cultural Studies* 51.2 (2009): 299–320.

England, Paula. "The Separative Self: Androcentric Bias in Neoclassical Assumptions." In *Beyond Economic Man: Feminist Theory and Economics.* Ed. Marianne A. Ferber and Julie A. Nelson. Chicago: University of Chicago Press, 1993, 37–53.

"English Laws of Divorce with Regard to Women." *Englishwoman's Domestic Magazine.* n.d. 82–6.

Erickson, Amy Louise. *Women and Property in Early Modern England.* London: Routledge, 1993.

Faber, Adele and Elaine Mazlish. *Siblings without Rivalry: How to Help Your Children Live Together So You Can Live Too.* New York: W. W. Norton & Company, Inc., 2012.

Feiner, Susan F. "Reading Neoclassical Economics: Toward an Erotic Economy of Sharing." In *Out of the Margins: Feminist Perspectives on Economics.* Ed. Edith Kuiper and Jolande Sap. London: Routledge, 1995, 151–66.

Finch, Janet, Lynn Hayes, Jennifer Mason, Judith Masson, and Lorraine Wallis. *Wills, Inheritance, and Families.* Oxford: Clarendon Press, 1996.

Finn, Margot. "Men's Things: Masculine Possession in the Consumer Revolution." *Social History* 25.2 (2000): 133–55. http://www.jstor.com/stable/4286642.

Finn, Margot. "Women, Consumption and Coverture in England, c. 1760–1860." *The Historical Journal* 39.3 (1996), 703–22. http://www.jstor.com/stable/2639966.

Finn, Margot. "Working-Class Women and the Contest for Consumer Control in Victorian County Courts." *Past and Present* 161 (1998), 116–54.

Fletcher, Joyce K. "Relational Practice: A Feminist Reconstruction of Work." *Journal of Management Inquiry* 7.2 (1998): 163–86.

Folbre, Nancy and Heidi Hartman. "The Rhetoric of Self-Interest: Ideology and Gender in Economic Theory." In *The Consequences of Economic Rhetoric.* Ed. Arjo Klamer, Deirdre Nansen McCloskey, and Robert M. Solow. Cambridge: Cambridge University Press, 1988, 184–203.

Frank, Cathrine O. *Law, Literature, and the Transmission of Culture in England, 1837–1925.* London and New York: Routledge, 2016 (first published by Ashgate, 2010).

Freedgood, Elaine. *The Ideas in Things: Fugitive Meaning in the Victorian Novel.* Chicago: University of Chicago Press, 2006.

WORKS CITED 199

Froide, Amy M. *Never Married: Singlewomen in Early Modern England*. Oxford: Oxford University Press, 2005.

Frost, Ginger S. *Living in Sin: Cohabiting as Husband and Wife in Nineteenth-Century England*. Manchester and New York: Manchester University Press, 2008.

Furneaux, Holly. "Sexuality." In *Charles Dickens in Context*. Ed. Sally Ledger and Holly Furneaux. Cambridge: Cambridge University Press, 2011, 358–64.

Gagnier, Regenia. "Conclusion: Gender, Liberalism, and Resentment." In *The Politics of Gender in Anthony Trollope's Novels: New Readings for the Twenty-First Century*. Ed. Margaret Markwick, Deborah Denenholz Morse, and Regenia Gagnier. Burlington: Ashgate, 2009, 235–48.

Gagnier, Regenia. *The Insatiability of Human Wants: Economics and Aesthetics in Market Society*. Chicago: University of Chicago Press, 2000.

Gallagher, Catherine. *The Body Economic: Life, Death, and Sensation in Political Economy and the Victorian Novel*. Princeton: Princeton University Press, 2006.

Gallagher, Catherine. "George Eliot and *Daniel Deronda*: The Prostitute and the Jewish Question." In *Sex, Politics, and Science in the Nineteenth-Century Novel: Selected Papers from the English Institute, 1983–84, New Series, No. 10*. Ed. Ruth Bernard Yeazell. Baltimore: Johns Hopkins University Press, 1986, 39–62.

Galvan, Jill and Elsie Michie. "Introduction." In *Replotting Marriage in Nineteenth-Century British Literature*. Ed. Jill Galvan and Elsie Michie. Columbus: Ohio State University Press, 2018, 1–11.

Gaskell, Elizabeth. *Cranford* [1851–3]. Oxford: Oxford University Press, 1998.

Gaskell, Elizabeth. *North and South* [1854]. Ed. Patricia Ingham. London: Penguin Books Ltd., 1995.

Gaskell, Elizabeth. *Ruth* [1853]. Ed. Angus Easson. London: Penguin Books Ltd., 1997.

Gaskell, Elizabeth. *Wives and Daughters* [1864–66, 1866]. Ed. Pam Morris. London: Penguin Books Ltd., 1996.

Gates, Sarah. "'A Difference of Native Language': Gender, Genre, and Realism in *Daniel Deronda*." *ELH* 68.3 (2001): 699–724.

Gaudiano, Paolo. "Are Women Penalized for Being Team Players?" *Forbes* (July 30, 2018): 5 pages. https://www.forbes.com/sites/paologaudiano/2018/07/30/are-women-penalized-for-being-team-players/?sh=61cd4746453d. Accessed Dec. 9, 2020.

Gissing, George. *The Odd Women* [1893]. Ed. Elaine Showalter. London: Penguin Books Ltd., 1983.

Godelier, Maurice. *The Enigma of the Gift*. Trans. Nora Scott. Chicago: University of Chicago Press, 1999.

Godfrey, Esther. "'Absolutely Miss Fairlie's own': Emasculating Economics in *The Woman in White*." In *Economic Women: Essays on Desire and Dispossession in Nineteenth-Century British Culture*. Ed. Lana L. Dalley and Jill Rappoport. Columbus: Ohio State University Press, 2013, 162–75.

Goldberg, Leah. *Russian Literature in the Nineteenth Century: Essays*. Jerusalem: Magnes Press, The Hebrew University, 1976.

Goldin, Claudia, Sari Pekkala Kerr, Claudia Olivetti, and Erling Barth. "The Expanding Gender Earnings Gap: Evidence from the LEHD-2000 Census." *American Economic Review: Papers & Proceedings* 107.5 (2017): 110–14. https://doi.org/10.1257/aer.p20171065. Accessed Dec. 10, 2020.

Goodlad, Lauren M. E. "'Trollopian Foreign Policy': Rootedness and Cosmopolitanism in the Mid-Victorian Global Imaginary." *PMLA* 124.2 (2009): 437–54.

200 WORKS CITED

Grass, Sean. *Charles Dickens's* Our Mutual Friend: *A Publishing History*. Burlington: Ashgate, 2014.

Grass, Sean. "Commodity and Identity in *Great Expectations*." *Victorian Literature and Culture* 40.2 (2012): 617–41.

Gray, Donald. "A Note on Money." In Jane Austen, *Pride and Prejudice* [1813]: *An Authoritative Text, Backgrounds and Sources, Criticism*, 3rd ed. Ed. Donald Gray. New York: W. W. Norton & Company, 2001, 403–5.

Green, David R. "To Do the Right Thing: Gender, Wealth, Inheritance and the London Middle Class." In *Women and Their Money 1700–1950: Essays on Women and Finance*. Ed. Anne Laurence, Josephine Maltby, and Janette Rutterford. London and New York: Routledge, 2009, 133–50.

Green, David R. and Alastair Owens. "Gentlewomanly Capitalism? Spinsters, Widows, and Wealth Holding in England and Wales, c. 1800–1860." *The Economic History Review* 56.3 (2003): 510–36. http://www.jstor.com/stable/3698573.

Greg, William Rathbone. "Why Are Women Redundant?" [*National Review*, 1862]. Reprinted in *The Broadview Anthology of British Literature: The Victorian Era*, 2nd ed. Ontario: Broadview Press, 2012, 106–7.

Habakkuk, John. *Marriage, Debt, and the Estates System: English Landownership 1650–1950*. Oxford: Clarendon Press. 1994.

Hack, Daniel. "Literary Paupers and Professional Authors: The Guild of Literature and Art." *Studies in English Literature, 1500–1900* 39.4 (1999): 691–713.

Hadley, Elaine. "Human Capital: Becker the Obscure: Human-Capital Theory, Liberalisms, and the Future of Higher Education." In *From Political Economy to Economics through Nineteenth-Century Literature: Reclaiming the Social*. Ed. Elaine Hadley, Audrey Jaffe, Sarah Winter. Cham: Palgrave Macmillan, 2019, 29–57.

Hadley, Elaine. "The Past Is a Foreign Country: The Neo-Conservative Romance with Victorian Liberalism." *The Yale Journal of Criticism* 10.1 (1997): 7–38. https://doi.org/10.1353/yale.1997.0003.

Hadley, Elaine, Audrey Jaffe, and Sarah Winter, eds. *From Political Economy to Economics Through Nineteenth-Century Literature: Reclaiming the Social*. Cham: Palgrave Macmillan, 2019.

Hager, Kelly and Talia Schaffer. "Introduction: Extending Families." *Victorian Review* 39.2 (2013): 7–21, 10. https://doi.org/10.1353/vcr.2013.0055.

Hager, Lisa. "A Case for a Trans Studies Turn in Victorian Studies: 'Female Husbands' of the Nineteenth Century." *Victorian Review* 44.1 (2018): 37–54.

Haight, Gordon S., ed. *The George Eliot Letters*, Vol. VII. New Haven: Yale University Press, 1954.

Hall, John N. *Trollope: A Biography*. Oxford: Clarendon, 1991.

Hancher, Michael. "Grafting *A Christmas Carol*." *SEL* 48.4 (2008): 813–27.

Harris, Margaret. "Afterlife." In *George Eliot in Context*. Ed. Margaret Harris. Cambridge: Cambridge University Press, 2013, 52–62.

Harris, Margaret. "Charles Lewes's Career." *George Eliot-George Henry Lewes Studies* 72.1 (2020): 1–19.

Harris, Margaret. "George Eliot's Reputation." In *The Cambridge Companion to George Eliot*. Ed. George Levine and Nancy Henry. Cambridge: Cambridge University Press, 2019, 236–58

Hawthorne, Nathaniel. *The Scarlet Letter* [1850]. New York: Collier Books, 1962.

Heath, Kay. *Aging by the Book: The Emergence of Midlife in Victorian Britain*. Albany: State University of New York Press, 2009.

WORKS CITED 201

Heilman, Madeline E. and Julie J. Chen. "Same Behavior, Different Consequences: Reactions to Men's and Women's Altruistic Citizenship Behavior." *Journal of Applied Psychology* 90.3 (2005): 431–41.

Heim, Pat, Tammy Hughes, and Susan K. Golant. *Hardball for Women: Winning at the Game of Business*, 3rd ed. New York: Penguin, 2015.

Henry, Nancy. *The Life of George Eliot: A Critical Biography*. Chichester: John Wiley & Sons, Ltd., 2012.

Henry, Nancy. *Women, Literature and Finance in Victorian Britain: Cultures of Investment*. Cham: Palgrave Macmillan, 2018.

Henry, Nancy and Cannon Schmitt. "Introduction: Finance, Capital, Culture." In *Victorian Investments: New Perspectives on Finance and Culture*. Ed. Nancy Henry and Cannon Schmitt. Bloomington: Indiana University Press, 2009, 1–12.

Hepburn, Allan, ed. "Introduction: Inheritance and Disinheritance in the Novel." In *Troubled Legacies: Narrative and Inheritance*. Toronto: University of Toronto Press, 2007, 3–25.

Hoeckley, Cheri Larsen. "Anomalous Ownership: Copyright, Coverture, and *Aurora Leigh.*" *Victorian Poetry* 35.2 (1998): 135–61.

Holcombe, Lee. *Wives and Property: Reform of the Married Women's Property Law in Nineteenth-Century England*. Toronto and Buffalo: University of Toronto Press, 1983.

Hollingsworth, Keith. *The Newgate Novel 1830–1847: Bulwer, Ainsworth, Dickens, and Thackeray*. Detroit: Wayne State University Press, 1963.

Huelman, Lisieux. "The (Feminist) Epistemology of the Nineteenth-Century Periodical Press: Professional Men in Elizabeth Gaskell's *Wives and Daughters.*" *Nineteenth-Century Gender Studies* 5.2 (2009), 35 paragraphs. Electronic publication.

Hughes, Linda K. "*Cousin Phillis, Wives and Daughters*, and Modernity." In *The Cambridge Companion to Elizabeth Gaskell*. Ed. Jill L. Matus. Cambridge: Cambridge University Press, 2007, 90–107.

Hunt, Aeron Hunt. *Personal Business: Character and Commerce in Victorian Literature and Culture*. Charlottesville: University of Virginia Press, 2014.

Hunt, Margaret R. "The Sapphic Strain: English Lesbians in the Long Eighteenth Century." In *Singlewomen in the European Past, 1250–1800*. Ed. Judith M. Bennett and Amy M. Froide. Philadelphia: University of Pennsylvania Press, 1999, 270–96.

"Imperial Parliament: The Property of Married Women." *Bell's Life in London and Sporting Chronicle* Mar. 16, 1856: 8.

Irigaray, Luce. "Women on the Market." In *The Logic of the Gift: Toward an Ethic of Generosity*. Ed. Alan D. Schrift. New York: Routledge, 1997, 174–89.

Jacob, Michelle M. "Native Women Maintaining Their Culture in the White Academy." In *Presumed Incompetent: The Intersections of Race and Class for Women in Academia*. Ed. Gabriella Gutiérrez y Muhs, Yolanda Flores Niemann, Carmen G. González, and Angela P. Harris. Boulder: University Press of Colorado, 2012, 242–9, 244.

Jaffe, Audrey. "Trollope in the Stock Market: Irrational Exuberance and *The Prime Minister.*" *Victorian Studies* 45.1 (2002): 43–64.

Jevons, William Stanley. "Preface to the Second Edition." In *Theory of Political Economy* (1871), 2nd ed. (1879), online ed. https://www.econlib.org/library/YPDBooks/Jevons/jvnPE.html?chapter_num=2#book-reader. Accessed Nov. 18, 2019.

Johnson, Patricia E. "Unlimited Liability: Women and Capital in Margaret Oliphant's *Hester.*" *Nineteenth-Century Gender Studies* 6.1 (2010). Online issue.

Jones-Rogers, Stephanie E. *They Were Her Property: White Women as Slave Owners in the American South*. New Haven: Yale University Press, 2019.

202 WORKS CITED

Jones, Wendy S. *Consensual Fictions: Women, Liberalism, and the English Novel.* Toronto: University of Toronto Press, 2005.

Kaufman, Heidi. "*King Solomon's Mines*?: African Jewry, British Imperialism, and H. Rider Haggard's Diamonds." *Victorian Literature and Culture* 33 (2005): 517–39.

Keatley, Paula. "'It's about a Will': Liberal Protestant Theology in Dickens' *Bleak House.*" *Nineteenth-Century Contexts* 39.2 (2017): 77–86.

Kendrick, Walter M. "The Eustace Diamonds: The Truth of Trollope's Fiction." *ELH* 46.1 (1979): 136–57.

Kendrick, Walter M. *The Novel-Machine: The Theory and Fiction of Anthony Trollope.* Baltimore: Johns Hopkins University Press, 1980.

Kidder, Deborah L. "The Influence of Gender on the Performance of Organizational Citizenship Behaviors." *Journal of Management* 28.5 (2002): 629–48.

King, Margaret F. "'Certain Learned Ladies': Trollope's *Can You Forgive Her?* and the Langham Place Circle." *Victorian Literature and Culture* 21 (1993): 307–26.

Kinsey, Danielle C. "Koh-i-Noor: Empire, Diamonds, and the Performance of British Material Culture." *Journal of British Studies* 48.2 (2009): 391–419.

Kisner, Jordan. "The Lockdown Showed How the Economy Exploits Women. She Already Knew." *New York Times.* Feb. 17, 2021 (updated Feb. 22, 2021). https://www.nytimes.com/2021/02/17/magazine/waged-housework.html.

Klaver, Claudia C. *A/Moral Economics: Classical Political Economy and Cultural Authority in Nineteenth-Century England.* Columbus: Ohio State University Press, 2003.

Komter, Aafke E. *Social Solidarity and the Gift.* Cambridge: Cambridge University Press, 2005.

Kornbluh, Anna. *Realizing Capital: Financial and Psychic Economies in Victorian Form.* New York: Fordham University Press, 2014.

Kreisel, Deanna K. *Economic Woman: Demand, Gender, and Narrative Closure in Eliot and Hardy.* Toronto: University of Toronto Press, 2012.

Kuper, Adam. *Incest and Influence: The Private Life of Bourgeois England.* Cambridge, MA: Harvard University Press, 2009.

"The Lady and Her Marriage Settlement." *Englishwoman's Domestic Magazine* (Mar. 1, 1864): 207–11.

Langland, Elizabeth. *Nobody's Angels: Middle-Class Women and Domestic Ideology in Victorian Culture.* Ithaca: Cornell University Press, 1995.

Laurence, Anne, Josephine Maltby, and Janette Rutterford, eds. *Women and Their Money, 1700–1950: Essays on Women and Finance.* New York: Routledge, 2009.

Leighton, Mary Elizabeth and Lisa Surridge. "Evolutionary Discourse and the Credit Economy in Elizabeth Gaskell's *Wives and Daughters.*" *Victorian Literature and Culture* 41.3 (2013): 487–501.

Lester, V. Markham. *Victorian Insolvency: Bankruptcy, Imprisonment for Debt, and Company Winding-Up in Nineteenth-Century England.* Oxford: Clarendon Press, 1995.

Levenson, Alan T. "Writing the Philosemitic Novel: *Daniel Deronda* Revisited." *Prooftexts* 28.2 (2008): 129–56.

Levine, Caroline. *Forms: Whole, Rhythm, Hierarchy, Network.* Princeton: Princeton University Press, 2015.

Levine, George. *Darwin and the Novelists: Patterns of Science in Victorian Fiction.* Cambridge, MA: Harvard University Press, 1988.

Levine, George. *Darwin Loves You: Natural Selection and the Re-Enchantment of the World.* Princeton: Princeton University Press, 2006.

WORKS CITED 203

Levine, George. *Dying to Know: Scientific Epistemology and Narrative in Victorian England.* Chicago: University of Chicago Press, 2002.

Lewis, Michael D. "The Challenge of Female Homoeroticism in *Our Mutual Friend.*" *Dickens Studies Annual: Essays on Victorian Fiction* 48 (2017): 207–29.

Lewis, Michael D. "Pictures of Revolutionary Reform in Carlyle, Arnold, and *Punch.*" *Nineteenth-Century Contexts: An Interdisciplinary Journal* 34.5 (2012): 533–52.

Lightman, Bernard. *Victorian Popularizers of Science: Designing Nature for New Audiences.* Chicago and London: University of Chicago Press, 2007.

Linehan, Katherine Bailey. "Mixed Politics: The Critique of Imperialism in *Daniel Deronda.*" *Texas Studies in Literature and Language* 34.3 (1992): 323–46.

Lysack, Krista. *Come Buy, Come Buy: Shopping and the Culture of Consumption in Victorian Women's Writing.* Athens: Ohio University Press, 2008.

M. S. R. "The Property of Married Women." *Englishwoman's Domestic Magazine*, n.d. 234–8.

Macpherson, Sandra. "Rent to Own: or, What's Entailed in *Pride and Prejudice.*" *Representations* 82.1 (2003): 1–23.

Malton, Sara. *Forgery in Nineteenth-Century Literature and Culture: Fictions of Finance from Dickens to Wilde.* New York: Palgrave Macmillan, 2009.

Marcus, Sharon. *Between Women: Friendship, Desire, and Marriage in Victorian England.* Princeton: Princeton University Press, 2007.

Markovits, Stefanie. "Form Things: Looking at Genre through Victorian Diamonds." *Victorian Studies* 52.4 (2010): 591–619.

Markwick, Margaret. *New Men in Trollope's Novels: Rewriting the Victorian Male.* Burlington: Ashgate, 2007.

"Married Women's Property." *Women's Union Journal: The Organ of the Women's Protective and Provident League* (Sept. 1, 1882): 72.

Martin, Claudia J. "Place and Displacement: The Unsettling Connection of Women, Property, and the Law in British Novels of the Long Nineteenth Century." Diss. Binghamton University—SUNY (2018). *Graduate Dissertations and Theses* 70. https://orb.binghamton.edu/dissertation_and_theses/70. Accessed July 8, 2020.

Matthews, J. B., ed. *Hayes & Jarman's Concise Forms of Wills, With Practical Notes*, 12th ed. London: Sweet and Maxwell, Limited, 1905.

Matus, Jill L. *Shock, Memory, and the Unconscious in Victorian Fiction.* Cambridge: Cambridge University Press, 2009.

Maurer, Sara L. *The Dispossessed State: Narratives of Ownership in 19th-Century Britain and Ireland.* Baltimore: Johns Hopkins University Press, 2012.

McCormack, Kathleen. "Yachting with Grandcourt: Gwendolen's Mutiny in *Daniel Deronda.*" *Victorian Literature and Culture* 43 (2015): 83–95.

McMaster, R. D. *Trollope and the Law.* Houndmills: Macmillan, 1986.

Mermin, Dorothy and Herbert F. Tucker. *Victorian Literature 1830–1900.* Fort Worth and Philadelphia: Harcourt College Publishers, 2002, 87–90.

Meyer, Susan. *Imperialism at Home: Race and Victorian Women's Fiction.* Ithaca: Cornell University Press, 1996.

Meyer, Susan. "'Safely to Their Own Borders': Proto-Zionism, Feminism, and Nationalism in *Daniel Deronda.*" *ELH* 60.3 (1993): 733–58.

Michie, Elsie B. *The Vulgar Question of Money: Heiresses, Materialism, and the Novel of Manners from Jane Austen to Henry James.* Baltimore: Johns Hopkins University Press, 2011.

204 WORKS CITED

Michie, Helena. *Sororophobia: Differences among Women in Literature and Culture.* New York: Oxford University Press, 1992.

Mill, John Stuart. "On the Definition of Political Economy; and on the Method of Investigation in that Science." In *The London and Westminster Review*, American ed. New York: Theodore Foster, nos. 7 and 50 (Oct. 1836): 1–16.

Miller, Andrew H. *Novels behind Glass: Commodity Culture and Victorian Narrative.* Cambridge: Cambridge University Press, 1995.

Miller, Andrew H. "Subjectivity Ltd: The Discourse of Liability in the Joint Stock Companies Act of 1856 and Gaskell's *Cranford.*" *ELH* 61.1 (1994): 139–57.

Miller, D. A. *The Novel and the Police.* Berkeley: University of California Press, 1988.

Miller, J. Hillis. *"Our Mutual Friend." Dickens: A Collection of Critical Essays.* Ed. Martin Price. Englewood Cliffs, NJ: Prentice-Hall, Inc., 1967, 169–77.

Milton, Heather. "'Bland, Adoring, and Gently Tearful Women': Debunking the Maternal Ideal in George Eliot's *Felix Holt.*" In *Other Mothers: Beyond the Maternal Ideal.* Ed. Ellen Bayuk Rosenman and Claudia C. Klaver. Columbus: Ohio State University Press, 2008, 55–74.

Modern Language Association (MLA). "Standing Still: The Associate Professor Survey: Report of the Committee on the Status of Women in the Profession." Web Publication (April 27, 2009): 1–35.

Monforti, Jessica Lavariega. "La Lucha: Latinas Surviving Political Science." In *Presumed Incompetent: The Intersections of Race and Class for Women in Academia.* Ed. Gabriella Gutiérrez y Muhs, Yolanda Flores Niemann, Carmen G. González, and Angela P. Harris. Boulder: University Press of Colorado, 2012, 393–407, 395.

Morgentaler, Goldie. "Dickens and the Scattered Identity of Silas Wegg." *Dickens Quarterly* 22.2 (2005): 92–100.

Morris, Pam. "Introduction." In Elizabeth Gaskell, *Wives and Daughters* [1864–66, 1866]. Ed. Pam Morris. London: Penguin Books Ltd., 1996, xi–xxxv.

Morris, R. J. *Men, Women and Property in England, 1780–1870.* Cambridge: Cambridge University Press, 2005.

Morse, Deborah Denenholz. *Reforming Trollope: Race, Gender, and Englishness in the Novels of Anthony Trollope.* Burlington: Ashgate, 2013.

Morse, Deborah Denenholz. *Women in Trollope's Palliser Novels.* Ann Arbor: University of Michigan Press, 1987.

Mullen, Ann L. *Degrees of Inequality: Culture, Class, and Gender in American Higher Education.* Baltimore: Johns Hopkins University Press, 2010.

Munich, Adrienne. *Empire of Diamonds: Victorian Gems in Imperial Settings.* Charlottesville: University of Virginia Press, 2020.

Murphy, Mary C., Amanda F. Mejia, Jorge Mejia, Xiaoran Yan, Sapna Cheryan, Nilanjana Dasgupta, Mesmin Destin, Stephanie A. Fryberg, Julie A. Garcia, Elizabeth L. Haines, Judith M. Harackiewicz, Alison Ledgerwood, Corinne A. Moss-Racusin, Lora E. Park, Sylvia P. Perry, Kate A. Ratliff, Aneeta Rattan, Diana T. Sanchez, Krishna Savani, Denise Sekaquaptewa, Jessi L. Smith, Valerie Jones Taylor, Dustin B. Thoman, Daryl A. Wout, Patricia L. Mabry, Susanne Ressl, Amanda B. Diekman, and Franco Pestilli. "Open Science, Communal Culture, and Women's Participation in the Movement to Improve Science." *Proceedings of the National Academy of Sciences* 117.39 (2020): 24154–64. https://doi.org/10.1073/pnas.1921320117.

Najarian, James. "'Mr. Osbourne's Secret': Elizabeth Gaskell, *Wives and Daughters*, and the Gender of Romanticism." In *Romantic Echoes in the Victorian Era.* Ed. Andrew Radford and Mark Sandy. Aldershot: Ashgate, 2008, 85–101.

WORKS CITED 205

Nardin, Jane. *He Knew She Was Right: The Independent Woman in the Novels of Anthony Trollope.* Carbondale: Southern Illinois University Press, 1989.

Nayder, Lillian. "'The Omission of His Only Sister's Name': Letitia Austin and the Legacies of Charles Dickens." *Dickens Quarterly* 28.4 (2011): 251–60.

Nenadic, Stana. "The Small Family Firm in Victorian Britain." *Business History* 35 (1993): 86–114.

Newton, Lucy A., Philip L. Cottrell, Josephine Maltby, and Janette Rutterford. "Women and Wealth: The Nineteenth Century in Great Britain." In *Women and Their Money, 1700–1950: Essays on Women and Finance.* Ed. Anne Laurence, Josephine Maltby, and Janette Rutterford. London: Routledge, 2009, 86–94.

Niemann, Yolanda Flores. "Lessons from the Experiences of Women of Color Working in Academia." In *Presumed Incompetent: The Intersections of Race and Class for Women in Academia.* Ed. Gabriella Gutiérrez y Muhs, Yolanda Flores Niemann, Carmen G. González, and Angela P. Harris. Boulder: University Press of Colorado, 2012, 446–99, 460, 481, 483, 484.

Niemann, Yolanda Flores. "The Making of a Token: A Case Study of Stereotype Threat, Stigma, Racism, and Tokenism in Academe." In *Presumed Incompetent: The Intersections of Race and Class for Women in Academia.* Ed. Gabriella Gutiérrez y Muhs, Yolanda Flores Niemann, Carmen G. González, and Angela P. Harris. Boulder: University Press of Colorado, 2012, 336–55, 433–5.

Noble, Christopher S. "Otherwise Occupied: Masculine Widows in Trollope's Novels." In *The Politics of Gender in Anthony Trollope's Novels: New Readings for the Twenty-First Century.* Ed. Margaret Markwick, Deborah Denenholz Morse, and Regenia Gagnier. Burlington: Ashgate, 2009, 177–90.

Nunokawa, Jeff. *The Afterlife of Property: Domestic Security and the Victorian Novel.* Princeton: Princeton University Press, 1994.

O'Brien, Monica. "The Politics of Blood and Soil: Hannah Arendt, George Eliot, and the Jewish Question in Modern Europe." *Comparative Literature Studies* 44.1/2 (2007): 97–117. https://www.jstor.org/stable/25659563.

O'Connor, Frank. *The Mirror in the Roadway: A Study of the Modern Novel.* London: Hamish Hamilton, 1957.

O'Dair, Sharon. "Class Work: Site of Egalitarian Activism or Site of Embourgeoisement?" *College English* 65.6 (2003): 593–606, 600. https://www.jstor.org/stable/3594272.

Oliphant, Margaret. *The Autobiography of Margaret Oliphant.* Ed. Elisabeth Jay. Peterborough: Broadview Press, Ltd., 2002.

Oliphant, Margaret."The Condition of Women." *Blackwood's Edinburgh Magazine* 508.83 (1858): 139–54.

Oliphant, Margaret. "The Grievances of Women." *Fraser's Magazine,* New Series 21 (1880): 698–710.

Oliphant, Margaret. *Hester* [1883]. Oxford: Oxford University Press, 2003.

Oliphant, Margaret. "The Laws Concerning Women." *Blackwood's Edinburgh Magazine* 486.79 (1856): 379–87.

Oliphant, Margaret. "Modern Novelists—Great and Small." *Blackwood's Edinburgh Magazine* 475.77 (1855): 554–68.

Onwuachi-Willig, Angela. "Silence of the Lambs." In *Presumed Incompetent: The Intersections of Race and Class for Women in Academia.* Ed. Gabriella Gutiérrez y Muhs, Yolanda Flores Niemann, Carmen G. González, and Angela P. Harris. Boulder: University Press of Colorado, 2012, 142–51, 145.

206 WORKS CITED

Osborne, Katherine Dunagan. "Inherited Emotions: George Eliot and the Politics of Heirlooms." *Nineteenth-Century Literature* 64.4 (2010): 465–93.

Outhwaite, R. B. *The Rise and Fall of the English Ecclesiastical Courts, 1500–1860.* Cambridge: Cambridge University Press, 2006.

Owens, Alastair. "Property, Gender and the Life Course: Inheritance and Family Welfare Provision in Early Nineteenth-Century England." *Social History* 26.3 (2001): 299–317.

Panek, Jennifer. "Constructions of Masculinity in *Adam Bede* and *Wives and Daughters.*" *Victorian Review: The Journal of the Victorian Studies Association of Western Canada and the Victorian Studies Association of Ontario* 22.2 (1996): 127–51.

Patten, Robert L. *Charles Dickens and His Publishers.* University of California, Santa Cruz: The Dickens Project, 1978.

Patten, Robert L. "Copyright." In *Oxford Reader's Companion to Dickens.* Ed. Paul Schlicke. Oxford: Oxford University Press, 1999, 119–22.

Pecora, Vincent P. "Inheritances, Gifts, and Expectations." *Law and Literature* 20.2 (2008): 177–96.

Perkin, Harold. *The Rise of Professional Society: England since 1880.* London and New York: Routledge, 1989, 2002.

Perry, Ruth. *Novel Relations: The Transformation of Kinship in English Literature and Culture, 1748–1818.* Cambridge: Cambridge University Press, 2004.

Peterson, Linda. "The Female *Bildungsroman*: Tradition and Revision in Margaret Oliphant's Fiction." In *Margaret Oliphant: Critical Essays on a Gentle Subversive.*" Ed. D. J. Trela. Selinsgrove, PA: Susquehanna University Press, 1995, 66–89.

Pettitt, Clare. *Patent Inventions: Intellectual Property and the Victorian Novel.* Oxford: Oxford University Press, 2004.

Pew Research Center. "Raising Kids and Running a Household: How Working Parents Share the Load" (Nov. 2015): 1–23. https://www.pewsocialtrends.org/2015/11/04/raising-kids-and-running-a-household-how-working-parents-share-the-load/. Accessed Dec. 13, 2020.

Plotz, John. *Portable Property: Victorian Culture on the Move.* Princeton: Princeton University Press, 2008.

Pointon, Marcia. "Intriguing Jewellery: Royal Bodies and Luxurious Consumption." *Textual Practice* 11.3 (1997): 493–516.

Pointon, Marcia. *Rocks, Ice and Dirty Stones: Diamond Histories.* London: Reaktion Books, 2017.

Pointon, Marcia. *Strategies for Showing: Women, Possession, and Representation in English Visual Culture 1665–1800.* Oxford: Oxford University Press, 1997.

Pointon, Marcia. "Women and Their Jewels." In *Women and Material Culture, 1660–1830.* Ed. Jennie Batchelor and Cora Kaplan. Houndmills: Palgrave Macmillan, 2007, 11–30.

Poon, Phoebe. "Popular Evolutionism: Scientific, Legal and Literary Discourse in Gaskell's *Wives and Daughters.*" In *Elizabeth Gaskell: Victorian Culture and the Art of Fiction: Original Essays for the Bicentenary.* Ed. Sandro Jung. Lebanon, NH: Academia, 2010, 195–213.

Poon, Phoebe. "Trust and Conscience in *Bleak House* and *Our Mutual Friend.*" *Dickens Quarterly* 28.1 (2011): 3–21.

Poovey, Mary. *Genres of the Credit Economy: Mediating Value in Eighteenth- and Nineteenth-Century Britain.* Chicago: University of Chicago Press, 2008.

Poovey, Mary. *Making a Social Body: British Cultural Formation, 1830–1864.* Chicago: University of Chicago Press, 1995.

Poovey, Mary. *Uneven Developments: The Ideological Work of Gender in Mid-Victorian England.* Chicago: University of Chicago Press, 1988.

WORKS CITED   207

"Postsecondary Attainment: Differences by Socioeconomic Status." Annual Report, NCES: National Center for Education Statistics. *The Condition of Education* (May 2015): 1–7. https://nces.ed.gov/programs/coe/pdf/Indicator_TVA/coe_tva_2015_05.pdf. Accessed Dec. 28, 2020.

"I.—The Property Earnings and Maintenance of Married Women." *Englishwoman's Review* 1 (1867): 263–75.

"The Property of Married Women." *Lady's Newspaper and Pictorial Times* (June 7, 1856): 355.

Psomiades, Kathy Alexis. *"He Knew He Was Right*: The Sensational Tyranny of the Sexual Contract and the Problem of Liberal Progress." In *The Politics of Gender in Anthony Trollope's Novels: New Readings for the Twenty-First Century.* Ed. Margaret Markwick, Deborah Denenholz Morse, and Regenia Gagnier (Burlington: Ashgate, 2009): 31–44.

Psomiades, Kathy Alexis. "Heterosexual Exchange and Other Victorian Fictions: *The Eustace Diamonds* and Victorian Anthropology." *NOVEL: A Forum on Fiction* 33.1 (1999): 93–118.

Ragussis, Michael. *Figures of Conversion: "The Jewish Question" and English National Identity.* Durham: Duke University Press, 1995.

Rainof, Rebecca. *The Victorian Novel of Adulthood: Plot and Purgatory in Fictions of Maturity.* Athens: Ohio University Press, 2015.

Raitt, Suzanne. "Marital Law in *He Knew He Was Right.*" In *The Ashgate Research Companion to Anthony Trollope.* Ed. Margaret Markwick, Deborah Denenholz Morse, and Mark W. Turner. Farnham: Ashgate, 2016.

Rappaport, Erika Diane. *Shopping for Pleasure: Women in the Making of London's West End.* Princeton: Princeton University Press, 2000.

Rappoport, Jill. "'Clutch[ing] Gold': Wives, Mothers, and Property Law in *The Ring and the Book.*" *Victorian Poetry* 60.1 (2022): 1–26.

Rappoport, Jill. *Giving Women: Alliance and Exchange in Victorian Culture.* Oxford: Oxford University Press, 2012.

Rappoport, Jill. "Wives and Sons: Coverture, Primogeniture, and Married Women's Property." In *BRANCH: Britain, Representation and Nineteenth-Century History.* Ed. Dino Franco Felluga. Extension of *Romanticism and Victorianism on the Net* (Nov. 30, 2015). https://branchcollective.org/?ps_articles=jill-rappoport-wives-and-sons-coverture-primogeniture-and-married-womens-property

Reed, John R. "The Riches of Redundancy: *Our Mutual Friend.*" *Studies in the Novel* 38.1 (2006): 15–35.

Regaignon, Dara Rossman. *Writing Maternity: Medicine, Anxiety, Rhetoric, and Genre.* Columbus: Ohio State University Press, 2021.

Reich, Noa. *Relational Speculation: Rereading Inheritance in Victorian Fiction.* Diss. University of Toronto. 2018. Digital File shared by Author. Accessed Sept. 2020.

Richardson, Ruth. *Death, Dissection, and the Destitute,* 2nd ed. Chicago: University of Chicago Press, 1987, 2000.

Robb, George. "Ladies of the Ticker; Women, Investment, and Fraud in England and America, 1850–1930." In *Victorian Investments: New Perspectives on Finance and Culture.* Ed. Nancy Henry and Cannon Schmitt. Bloomington: Indiana University Press, 2009, 120–40.

Robb, George. *Ladies of the Ticker: Women and Wall Street from the Gilded Age to the Great Depression.* Urbana: University of Illinois Press, 2017.

Robb, George. *White-Collar Crime in Modern England: Financial Fraud and Business Morality, 1845–1929.* Cambridge: Cambridge University Press, 1992.

208 WORKS CITED

Robbins, Bruce. "How to Be a Benefactor without Any Money: The Chill of Welfare in *Great Expectations.*" In *Knowing the Past: Victorian Literature and Culture.* Ed. Suzy Anger. Ithaca: Cornell University Press, 2001, 172–91. https://www.jstor.org/stable/10.7591/j.ctv3s8qqv.12.

Robbins, Bruce. "The Village of the Liberal Managerial Class." In *Cosmopolitan Geographies: New Locations in Literature and Culture.* Ed. Vinay Dharwadker. New York: Routledge, 2001, 15–32.

Rose, Mary. "The Family Firm in British Business, 1780–1914." In *Business Enterprise in Modern Britain: From the Eighteenth to the Twentieth Century.* Ed. Maurice W. Kirby and Mary B. Rose. London: Routledge, 1994, 61–87.

Rosenman, Ellen Bayuk and Claudia C. Klaver. "Introduction." In *Other Mothers: Beyond the Maternal Ideal.* Ed. Ellen Bayuk Rosenman and Claudia C. Klaver. Columbus: Ohio State University Press, 2008, 1–22.

Ross, Ellen. *Love and Toil: Motherhood in Outcast London, 1870–1918.* New York and Oxford: Oxford University Press, 1993.

Roth, Alan. "He Thought He Was Right (But Wasn't): Property Law in Anthony Trollope's *The Eustace Diamonds.*" *Stanford Law Review* 44.4 (1992): 879–97.

Rotunno, Laura. "The Long History of 'In Short': Mr. Micawber, Letter-Writers, and Literary Men." *Victorian Literature and Culture* 33 (2005): 415–33.

Rowlinson, Matthew. *Real Money and Romanticism.* Cambridge: Cambridge University Press, 2010.

Rubin, Gayle. "The Traffic in Women: Notes on the 'Political Economy' of Sex." In *Toward an Anthropology of Women.* Ed. Rayna R. Reiter. New York: Monthly Review Press, 1975, 157–210

Ruoff, Gene. "Wills." In *Sense and Sensibility* [1811]: *Authoritative Text, Contexts, Criticism.* Ed. Claudia L. Johnson. New York: W. W. Norton & Company, 2002, 348–59.

Rutterford, Janette. "'A *Pauper* Every Wife Is': Lady Westmeath, Money, Marriage, and Divorce in Early Nineteenth-Century England." In *Economic Women: Essays on Desire and Dispossession in Nineteenth-Century British Culture.* Ed. Lana L. Dalley and Jill Rappoport. Columbus: Ohio State University Press, 2013, 127–42.

Rutterford, Janette, David R. Green, Josephine Maltby, and Alastair Owens. "Who Comprised the Nation of Shareholders? Gender and Investment in Great Britain, c. 1870–1935." *Economic History Review* 64.1 (2011): 157–87. http://www.jstor.com/stable/27919486.

Rutterford, Janette and Josephine Maltby. "Frank Must Marry Money: Men, Women, and Property in Trollope's Novels." *Accounting Historians Journal* 33.2 (2006): 169–99. http://www.jstor.com/stable/40698346.

Sadrin, Anny. *Parentage and Inheritance in the Novels of Charles Dickens.* Cambridge: Cambridge University Press, 1994.

Sahlins, Marshall. *Stone Age Economics.* Chicago: Aldine & Atherton, Inc., 1972.

Sanders, Valerie. *The Brother-Sister Culture in Nineteenth-Century Literature: From Austen to Woolf.* Houndmills: Palgrave, 2002.

Schaffer, Talia. *Communities of Care: The Social Ethics of Victorian Fiction.* Princeton: Princeton University Press, 2021.

Schaffer, Talia. *Novel Craft: Victorian Domestic Handicraft and Nineteenth-Century Fiction.* Oxford: Oxford University Press, 2011.

Schaffer, Talia. *Romance's Rival: Familiar Marriage in Victorian Fiction.* New York and Oxford: Oxford University Press, 2016.

Schaffer, Talia. "Why You Can't Forgive Her: Vocational Women and the Suppressive Hypothesis." *Victorians: A Journal of Culture and Literature* 128 (2015): 15–35.

WORKS CITED 209

Schaul-Yoder, Richard. "British Inheritance Legislation: Discretionary Distribution at Death." *Boston College International and Comparative Law Review* 205 (1985), vol. 8.1 article 8.204–36. http://lawdigitalcommons.bc.edu/iclr/vol8/iss1/8.

Schor, Hilary M. *Dickens and the Daughter of the House.* Cambridge: Cambridge University Press, 1999.

Sedgwick, Eve. *Between Men: English Literature and Male Homosocial Desire.* New York: Columbia University Press, 1985.

Sen, Sambudha. "From Dispossession to Dissection: The Bare Life of the English Pauper in the Age of the Anatomy Act and the New Poor Law." *Victorian Studies* 59.2 (2017): 235–9.

Shanley, Mary Lyndon. *Feminism, Marriage, and the Law in Victorian England.* Princeton: Princeton University Press, 1989.

Shelley, Mary. "Introduction to *Frankenstein*, Third Edition (1831)." In *Frankenstein* [1818]. Ed. J. Paul Hunter. New York: W. W. Norton & Company, Inc., 1996, 169–73.

Shuman, Cathy. "Invigilating *Our Mutual Friend*: Gender and the Legitimation of Professional Authority." *Novel* 28.2 (1995): 154–72.

Small, Deborah A., Michele Gelfand, Linda Babcock, and Hilary Gettman. "Who Goes to the Bargaining Table? The Influence of Gender and Framing on the Initiation of Negotiation." *Journal of Personality and Social Psychology* 93.4 (2007): 600–13. https://doi.org/10.1037/0022-3514.93.4.600.

Smith, Jonathan. "Introduction: Darwin and the Evolution of Victorian Studies." *Victorian Studies* 51.2 (2009): 215–21.

Spring, Eileen. "Landowners, Lawyers, and Land Law Reform in Nineteenth-Century England." *American Journal of Legal History* 21.1 (1977): 40–59. https://www.jstor.org/stable/844924. Accessed Sept. 25, 2020.

Spring, Eileen. "Law and the Theory of the Affective Family." *Albion: A Quarterly Journal Concerned with British Studies* 16.1 (1984): 1–20. https://www.jstor.org/stable/4048903. Accessed Sept. 25, 2020.

Spring, Eileen. "The Settlement of Land in Nineteenth-Century England." *American Journal of Legal History* 8.3 (1964): 209–23. Accessed Sept. 25, 2020. https://www.jstor.org/stable/844170.

Spring, Eileen. "The Strict Settlement: Its Role in Family History." *Economic History Review* 41.3 (1988): 454–60. https://www.jstor.org/stable/2597370. Accessed Sept. 25, 2020.

Staves, Susan. *Married Women's Separate Property in England, 1660–1833.* Cambridge, MA: Harvard University Press, 1990.

Sugarman, David. "Chancery." In *Oxford Reader's Companion to Dickens.* Ed. Paul Schlicke. Oxford: Oxford University Press, 1999, 70.

Surridge, Lisa. *Bleak Houses: Marital Violence in Victorian Fiction.* Athens: Ohio University Press, 2005.

Sutherland, John. "Introduction." In *He Knew He Was Right.* By Anthony Trollope. Ed. John Sutherland. Oxford: Oxford University Press, 2008, vii–xxiii.

Taylor, James. "Company Fraud in Victorian Britain: The Royal British Bank Scandal of 1856." *The English Historical Review* 122.497 (2007): 700–24.

Tennyson, Lord Alfred. *In Memoriam A. H. H.* 56: 15. *Tennyson's Poetry: A Norton Critical Edition.* Ed. Robert W. Hill, Jr. New York: W. W. Norton & Company, 1971, 1991.

Thierauf, Doreen. "*Daniel Deronda*, Marital Rape, and the End of Reproduction." *Victorian Review* 43.2 (2017): 247–69.

Thierauf, Doreen. "Guns and Blood: Reading *The Tenant of Wildfell Hall* in the Age of #MeToo." Special Issue: Victorian Literature in the Age of #MeToo. Ed. Lana L. Dalley and Kellie Holzer. *Nineteenth Century Gender Studies* 16.2 (2020), Online Journal: <23>.

210 WORKS CITED

"The Thwaytes Will Case." *The Saturday Review of Politics, Literature, Science and Art* 24.615 (1867): 181–2.

Toise, David W. "'As Good as Nowhere': Dickens's *Dombey and Son*, the Contingency of Value, and Theories of Domesticity." *Criticism* 41.3 (1999): 323–48.

Toise, David W. "Sexuality's Uncertain History: Or, 'Narrative Disjunction' in 'Daniel Deronda.'" *Victorian Literature and Culture* 38.1 (2010): 127–50.

Tracy, Robert. "Trollope Redux: The Later Novels." In *The Cambridge Companion to Anthony Trollope.* Ed. Carolyn Dever and Lisa Niles. Cambridge: Cambridge University Press, 2011, 58–70.

Trollope, Anthony. *An Autobiography.* Vol. 1. London: Blackwood, 1883.

Trollope, Anthony. *Barchester Towers* [1857]. Ed. John Sutherland. Oxford: Oxford University Press, 1998.

Trollope, Anthony. *Can You Forgive Her?* [1865]. Ed. Andrew Swarbrick. Oxford: Oxford University Press, 2008.

Trollope, Anthony. *Doctor Thorne* [1858]. Ed. Simon Dentith. Oxford: Oxford University Press, 2014.

Trollope, Anthony. *Framley Parsonage* [1861]. Ed. Katherine Mullin and Francis O'Gorman. Oxford: Oxford University Press, 2014.

Trollope, Anthony. *He Knew He Was Right* [1869]. Ed. John Sutherland. Oxford: Oxford University Press, 2008.

Trollope, Anthony. *Orley Farm* [1862]. Ed. David Skilton. Oxford and New York: Oxford University Press, 2008.

Trollope, Anthony. *Phineas Finn* [1869]. Ed. Simon Dentith. Oxford: Oxford University Press, 2011.

Trollope, Anthony. *Phineas Redux* [1874]. Ed. John Bowen. Oxford: Oxford University Press, 2011.

Trollope, Anthony. *Ralph The Heir* [1871]. Ed. John Sutherland. Oxford: Oxford University Press, 1990.

Trollope, Anthony. *The Duke's Children* [1880]. Ed. Katherine Mullin and Francis O'Gorman. Oxford: Oxford University Press, 2011.

Trollope, Anthony. *The Eustace Diamonds* [1873]. Ed. W. J. McCormack. Oxford: Oxford University Press, 2008.

Trollope, Anthony. *The Prime Minister* [1876]. Ed. Nicholas Shrimpton. Oxford: Oxford University Press, 2011.

Tromp, Marlene. "Gwendolen's Madness." *Victorian Literature and Culture* 28.2 (2000): 451–67.

Tromp, Marlene. *The Private Rod: Marital Violence, Sensation, and the Law in Victorian Britain.* Charlottesville: University Press of Virginia, 2000.

Tromp, Marlene."'Til Death Do Us Part: Marriage, Murder, and Confession." In *Replotting Marriage in Nineteenth-Century British Literature.* Ed. Jill Galvan and Elsie Michie. Columbus: Ohio State University Press, 2018, 127–44.

Tross, Ruth. "Dickens and the Crime of Literacy." *Dickens Quarterly* 21.4 (2004): 235–45.

Turner, Mark W. *Trollope and the Magazines: Gendered Issues in Mid-Victorian Britain.* New York: St. Martin's, 2000.

Unsworth, Anna. "Some Social Themes in *Wives and Daughters,* I: Education, Science, and Heredity." *Gaskell Society Journal* 4 (1990): 40–51.

Vanden Bossche, Chris R. "The Value of Literature: Representations of Print Culture in the Copyright Debate of 1837–1842." *Victorian Studies* 38.1 (1994): 41–68.

Vicinus, Martha. *Independent Women: Work and Community for Single Women, 1850–1920.* Chicago: University of Chicago Press, 1985.

WORKS CITED 211

Vicinus, Martha. *Intimate Friends: Women Who Loved Women, 1778–1928.* Chicago: University of Chicago Press, 2004.

Vickery, Amanda. "Golden Age to Separate Spheres? A Review of the Categories and Chronology of English Women's History." *The Historical Journal* 36.2 (1993): 383–414.

Vickery, Amanda."Women and the World of Goods: A Lancashire Consumer and Her Possessions, 1751–81." In *Consumption and the World of Goods.* Ed. John Brewer and Roy Porter. London: Routledge, 1993, 274–301.

Vlasopolos, Anca. "The Weight of Religion and History: Women Dying of Virtue in Trollope's Later Short Fiction." In *The Politics of Gender in Anthony Trollope's Novels: New Readings for the Twenty-First Century.* Ed. Margaret Markwick, Deborah Denenholz Morse, and Regenia Gagnier. Burlington: Ashgate, 2009, 221–33.

Wagner, Tamara S. *The Victorian Baby in Print: Infancy, Infant Care, and Nineteenth-Century Popular Culture.* Oxford: Oxford University Press, 2020.

Walkowitz, Judith R. *Prostitution and Victorian Society: Women, Class, and the State.* Cambridge: Cambridge University Press, 1980.

Wallace, Sherri L. Sharon E. Moore, Linda L. Wilson, and Brenda G. Hart. "African American Women in the Academy: Quelling the Myth of Presumed Incompetence." In *Presumed Incompetent: The Intersections of Race and Class for Women in Academia.* Ed. Gabriella Gutiérrez y Muhs, Yolanda Flores Niemann, Carmen G. González, and Angela P. Harris. Boulder: University Press of Colorado, 2012, 421–38, 423.

Weedon, Kim A., Youngjoo Cha, and Mauricio Bucca, "Long Work Hours, Part Time Work, and Trends in the Gender Gap in Pay, the Motherhood Wage Penalty, and the Fatherhood Wage Premium." *RSF: The Russell Sage Foundation Journal of the Social Sciences* 2.4 (2016): 71–102. https://doi.org/10.7758/RSF.2016.2.4.03.

Weiner, Annette B. *Inalienable Possessions: The Paradox of Keeping-While-Giving.* Berkeley: University of California Press, 1992.

Weiss, Barbara. *The Hell of the English: Bankruptcy and the Victorian Novel.* Lewisburg: Bucknell University Press, 1986.

Welsh, Alexander. *From Copyright to Copperfield: The Identity of Dickens.* Cambridge, MA: Harvard University Press, 1987.

Williams, Joan C. and Rachel Dempsey. *What Works for Women at Work: Four Patterns Working Women Need to Know.* New York: New York University Press, 2014. Updated ed. 2018.

Wilson, Sherrée. "They Forgot Mammy Had a Brain." In *Presumed Incompetent: The Intersections of Race and Class for Women in Academia.* Ed. Gabriella Gutiérrez y Muhs, Yolanda Flores Niemann, Carmen G. González, and Angela P. Harris. Boulder: University Press of Colorado, 2012, 65–77, 71.

Wing, Adrien Katherine. "Lessons from a Portrait: Keep Calm and Carry On." In *Presumed Incompetent: The Intersections of Race and Class for Women in Academia.* Ed. Gabriella Gutiérrez y Muhs, Yolanda Flores Niemann, Carmen G. González, and Angela P. Harris. Boulder: University Press of Colorado, 2012, 356–71, 357, 364.

Wynne, Deborah. *Women and Personal Property in the Victorian Novel.* New York: Routledge, 2016. First published 2010 by Ashgate.

Ziegler, Garrett. "The City of London, Real and Unreal." *Victorian Studies* 49.3 (2007): 431–55. https://www.jstor.org/stable/4626329.

Zutshi, Chitralekha. "'Designed for Eternity': Kashmiri Shawls, Empire, and Cultures of Production and Consumption in Mid-Victorian Britain." *Journal of British Studies* 48.2 (2009): 420–40. https://www.jstor.org/stable/25483041. Accessed Sept. 25, 2019.

Index

For the benefit of digital users, indexed terms that span two pages (e.g., 52–53) may, on occasion, appear on only one of those pages.

agency. *See* economic agency, women's
altruism 68–9, 85–6, 186–8
Arner, Lynn 189–90
Austen, Jane
  earnings and financial dependence of 6–8
  Mansfield Park 66–7, 111–12
  Pride and Prejudice 6–8, 11–12, 20–1,
    27–8, 66–7, 93–4, 98, 153–4, 167,
    169–70, 176–7
  Sense and Sensibility 6–8, 13–14

Bank Act (1844) 45n.37
Bankruptcy Act (1869) 159n.13
Beer, Gillian 130
Blumberg, Ilana M. 127–8
Brontë, Anne: *Tenant of Wildfell Hall* 14–15,
  90–2
Brontë, Charlotte
  Jane Eyre 14–15, 36–7
  Villette 3–4, 172–3
Browning, Elizabeth Barrett 66–7

Castillo, Larisa 47–8
Chekhov, Anton 155
Cheyette, Bryan 141–2
children 4–5, 14–16, 28
  bequests of 55–9
  competition between spouses and 18–20, 101,
    104–8
  illegitimate children 24–6, 124–5, 130–2, 136,
    143–4
  orphans 46–7, 54–5, 64–5, 167
  religious identity of 147–9
  textual legacy of 53–4
Civil Rights Act (1864) 190
Cleere, Eileen 18–20, 73n.21, 74n.24, 141–2,
  150–1
Collins, Wilkie 16–17, 66–7, 127–8, 140, 170
  The Woman in White 16–17, 66–7
common law 1–3, 98–9, 104–5, 107–8, 113–14,
  136–7, 158–9, 166, 170–1, 189–90. *See also*
  coverture; primogeniture
conduct books 71

consanguineal kinship
  conjugal ties competing with 18, 101, 110–12,
    116–17
  debt and 118–19
  "familiar" marriage and 20–1
  legitimacy and 130
copyright 45–50, 60, 63
Corbett, Mary Jean 9, 96–7, 111–12, 117, 143
cost-sharing practices 32, 66–7, 69–70, 186–7
coverture 2–3
  Daniel Deronda and 125–7, 135–7, 150–1
  definition of 5–6
  disadvantages of for women 6, 9, 21
  feme covert 5–6
  Hester and 155–9, 161–2, 166, 176
  Jane Eyre and 14–15
  lateral transmission of property 6, 18, 76–7,
    104–5, 116, 132–3, 142–3
  marriage property reform and 15–18
  Middlemarch and 16–17
  one-flesh doctrine 5–6, 15–16, 50–2, 72, 80–1,
    90–2, 125–7, 155–6
  Our Mutual Friend and 38–9, 50–2
  overcoming limitations of 10–12
  Pride and Prejudice and 6–9, 20–1
  quasi-marital arrangements and 11–12
  relationship to primogeniture 6–18, 85
  Sense and Sensibility and 13–14
  Tenant of Wildfell Hall and 14–15
  Trollope's novels and 99–100, 103–7, 110,
    118–19
  Wives and Daughters and 67–8, 72–3, 75–6,
    79–81, 85, 89–92
  The Woman in White and 16–17
  See also settlements, financial

Daniel Deronda (Eliot) 123–5
  childless marriage in 130
  Christianity in 138–9, 143
  coverture and 125–7, 135–7, 150–1
  eroticized jewelry in 174
  family property in 124–5, 132–3, 135–7, 142
  greed and 138–40, 142–3

214 INDEX

Daniel Deronda (Eliot) (*cont.*)
  heterosexual exchange in 125–7, 143
  illegitimacy in 124–5, 130–2, 136, 143–4
  Jewish cultural inheritance in 33–4, 124,
    136–52
  Judaism in 33–4, 143–52
  legal property rights and 34, 125–7, 135–7
  marriage property reform and 130–2, 135–6
  primogeniture and 132–3, 136, 144–6
  problematic feelings and competing priorities
    in 125–36
  textual legacy in 148–9
  wealth as theft in 123–5, 127, 133–6
Darwinism 68–70, 76–8, 85–9, 93–4
Davidoff, Leonore 18–20, 23, 112, 117, 159, 166
Debrabant, Mary 68–9
debt and credit 10–11, 24–6, 28, 189–90
  in *Hester* 155–9, 156n.9, 164, 173
  in Hester 155–9, 156n.9, 164, 173
  in Trollope's fiction 98–102, 108–9, 111–12,
    115–22
  in *Wives and Daughters* 67, 74–5, 82–4,
    89–90, 93–4, 98
DeWitt, Anne 85–6
diamonds. *See under* jewelry
Dickens, Charles
  Bleak House 37, 44
  A Christmas Carol 37
  literary piracy of works of 46–7
  Little Dorrit 1–2, 5, 11–12, 21, 36–7, 150–1,
    153–4, 167–9
  Nicholas Nickleby 46–7
  Oliver Twist 37, 46–7
  The Pickwick Papers 46–7
  Sketches by Boz 46–7
  wills and distribution of property in works
    of 37
  See also *Our Mutual Friend* (Dickens)
Divorce or Matrimonial Causes Act (1857) 6,
  15–17, 80–1
Dolin, Tim 2n.6, 9, 72
Dower Act (1833) 9, 9n.26, 43, 43n.27, 135–6

economic agency, women's 2–6, 10, 18,
  21–3, 29–30, 36–7, 185–6,
  188–9, 191–2
  in *Daniel Deronda* 125–7, 146–7, 150–1
  in *Hester* 10–11, 31, 154, 160–1, 170–2
  in *Little Dorrit* 21, 153–4
  Married Women's Property Act (1882)
    and 18, 22–3
  mercenary marriage and 134
  in *Middlemarch* 16–17
  in *Our Mutual Friend* 10–11, 54, 60–3
  in *Pride and Prejudice* 20–1

  in *Sense and Sensibility* 14
  through contribution of wealth and
    labor 10–11, 23
  in Trollope's novels 29–30, 108–10, 119–21
  in *Wives and Daughters* 67–8, 89–92
  working-class women and 62–3
economic theory and history 183–7
  disciplinary fixity 183–5
  feminist economists 183–4
  shift from production to consumption 183–5
Eliot, George
  Middlemarch 3–4, 16–17, 27–8, 36–7, 109,
    127–8, 132–3, 142–3
  Mill on the Floss (Eliot) 28, 36
  romantic relationships 130–2
  See also *Daniel Deronda* (Eliot)
Ellis, Sarah Stickney 71, 76–7
endogamous alliances and marriage 11–12, 110,
  112–13, 117, 143
entailment 6–9, 7n.19, 8n.21, 9n.23, 16–17, 21,
  75–6, 161–2, 169–70
exogamous alliances and marriage 9, 110–12,
  143–4

Family and Medical Leave Act (1993) 190
feme sole 5–6, 24–6, 63–4, 108–11, 181–2
feminized men 68–9, 90–2, 144–5
Finn, Margot 10–11
forgiveness 117–22
friendship 18–23, 191
  in *Hester* 166
  in *Our Mutual Friend* 60–2, 64–5
  in Trollope's fiction 66–7, 103–4, 106
  in *Wives and Daughters* 32, 69–70, 78–97
Froide, Amy M. 23–4
Frost, Ginger S. 11–12

Gallagher, Catherine 41, 62, 125–7, 141–2,
  146–7, 150–1, 184–5
Gaskell, Elizabeth
  Darwin, Charles, and 68–9
  economic agency of 67–8
  North and South 67, 172–3
  Ruth 67
  support for marriage property reform
    67–8, 98
  See also *Wives and Daughters* (Gaskell)
Gissing, George 134
Golant, Susan K. 186
greed 187–8
  Daniel Deronda and 138–40, 142–3
  Sense and Sensibility and 14
  in Trollope's fiction 100–4, 106, 108,
    116–17, 121
Green, David R. 44, 184–5

INDEX 215

Hadley, Elaine 183–4
Hager, Kelly 18–20
Hall, Catherine 23, 112, 117, 159, 166
Heim, Pam 186
heirlooms 102, 161–2, 172–3
Henry, Nancy 10–11, 18–20, 24–6, 31, 75n.25, 141–2, 148–9, 176–7
Hester (Oliphant) 154
  debt and credit in 155–61, 156n.9, 164–6, 169–70, 173
  economic and family duty in 161–71, 176–82
  eroticized jewelry in 171–6
  financial crises in 154–5
  gendered status in 173–4
  heterosexual exchange in 171–2, 174–5
  "Indian shawl" in 172–4
  investment and speculation in 30
  legal property rights and 154, 159–60, 162
  primogeniture and 161–2, 169–70
  women's economic agency in 154, 160–1, 170–2
heterosexual exchange 33, 98–103, 116, 125–7, 143, 171–2, 174–5
Hughes, Tammy 186
Hunt, Aeron 159–60, 176–7

illegitimacy. *See under* children
Infant Custody Act (1839) 144–5
Infant Custody Act (1873) 144–5
Infant Custody Act (1886) 104–5, 144–5, 145n.68
Inheritance (Family Provision) Act (1938) 43

Jaffe, Audrey 183–4
jewelry
  diamonds, in *Daniel Deronda* 29–30, 123–9, 132–4, 137–43, 148–52, 162, 174
  diamonds, in *The Eustace Diamonds* 24–6, 29–30, 33–4, 100–6, 120–1, 155–7, 159, 162, 170
  eroticized jewelry 171–6
  as paraphernalia 102–6, 159
  pearls, in *Hester* 29–30, 34, 44, 144–5, 154–64, 166, 170–8, 180–2
Johnson, Patricia E. 155–6, 176–7
Joint Stock Act (1856) 164–5
Judicature Act (1873) 11–12

Kendrick, Walter M. 120
Kirkpatrick, Hyacinth 32, 68–9, 72, 81–2
Kuper, Adam 117

labor, contemporary 185–92
  COVID-19 pandemic and 189
  gendered caregiving norms 187–9
  gendered earnings gap 189

  gendered norms of collaboration 186
  gendered professional norms 186
  legal protections 190
  racial and class disparities 189–90
  relationship self and 190–2
  wealth inequality 189–90
Leavis, F. R. 124
Leighton, Mary Elizabeth 68–9, 83–4, 93–4
Lilly Ledbetter Fair Pay Act (2009) 190
literacy piracy 46–7

Maltby, Josephine 113–14, 184–5
Marcus, Sharon 18–21, 23–4
marriage
  childless marriages 129–30
  cousin marriages 109–12, 143
  "familiar" marriage 20–1, 92–3
  marriage-plot economics 18–21
  mercenary marriage 15–18, 21–2, 33–4, 53–4, 124–7, 135–6
  pre-arranged marriages 169–70
  second marriages 13–17, 99–100, 120–1
  unsuccessful and unhappy marriages 15–16, 31, 51, 121, 129–30, 136
  See also coverture
Married Women's Property Act (1870) 11–12, 12n.41, 17–18, 22–8, 33, 40–1, 55, 63–4, 66–7, 80–1, 90–2, 101–2, 104–5, 107–8, 115–16, 135–6, 162
Married Women's Property Act (1882) 11–12, 12n.41, 17–18, 22–3, 27–8, 80–1, 90–2, 107–8, 154, 159–60, 162
Michie, Elsie B. 8n.20, 14, 98, 129–30, 140–2, 153–4
Miller, Andrew H. 102–3, 120
Miller, D. A. 102–3, 121
Moonstone, The (Collins) 127–8, 140, 170
Morse, Deborah Denenholz 109, 119

Nunokawa, Jeff 39–40, 42, 42n.23, 116

Odd Women, The (Gissing) 134
Oliphant, Margaret
  Autobiography 160–1
  Blackwood's essays 160–1
  "The Grievances of Women," 159
  "The Laws Concerning Women," 158–9, 162–3
  See also *Hester* (Oliphant)
one-flesh doctrine. *See under* coverture
Our Mutual Friend (Dickens) 10–11, 15–16
  ambivalence toward literacy in 48–9
  collaborative marital partnership in 51–4
  coverture and 38–9, 50–2
  gendered authorship in 49–50
  marriage property reform and 40–1, 55, 63–4

216 INDEX

Our Mutual Friend (Dickens) (*cont.*)
  primogeniture and 54
  publication of 40–1
  speculation in 21–2, 40–1, 64–5
  testamentary agency in 36–7
  textual legacy in 50, 53–4
  value of speech over writing in 55–9
  wills, oral bequests, and burial wishes 31–2,
    38–48, 53–62
  working-class women's economic agency
    in 62–5
  written texts in 46–50
Owens, Alistair 8, 184–5

paraphernalia, property as 28, 102–6, 159, 174
pearls. *See under* jewelry
Perry, Ruth 6–8, 110–11
Peterson, Linda 176–7, 180–1
Petition for Reform of the Married Women's
  Property Law (1856) 11–12, 15–16, 21–2,
  31, 40–1, 67–8, 80–1, 106–8, 130–2, 135–6
Plotz, John 29–30, 132–3
Pointon, Marcia 139, 173–4, 178
Poovey, Mary 42, 42n.23
primogeniture
  "customary primogeniture," 6, 6n.12
  Daniel Deronda and 132–3, 136, 144–6
  definition of 5–6
  disadvantages of 6
  entailment and 6–9, 6n.12, 7n.19, 8n.21,
    16–17
  Hester and 161–2, 169–70
  marriage property reform and 6, 15–16
  Our Mutual Friend and 54
  patrilineal transmission of property 14–15,
    17, 31–2, 38–9, 54, 75–6, 104–5, 148–9
  Pride and Prejudice and 6–8
  relationship to coverture 6–18, 85
  Wives and Daughters and 67–8, 75–7,
    82–5, 87
property, historical conceptions of 26–31
  in *Daniel Deronda* 29–30
  diamonds and jewelry 29–30
  in *The Eustace Diamonds* 29–30
  financial investments and speculation 30–1
  in *Hester* 30
  liquid property 159
  in *Middlemarch* 27–8
  in *The on the Floss* 28
  in *Our Mutual Friend* 30–1
  in *Pride and Prejudice* 27–8
  Reform Acts and 26–8
  tangible goods 28–30

property, transmission of
  consanguineal transmission 18, 101, 110–12,
    116–17, 130, 142–3, 167, 169–70
  lateral transmission 6, 18, 76–7, 104–5, 116,
    132–3, 142–3
  patrilineal transmission 14–15, 17, 31–2,
    38–9, 54, 75–6, 104–5, 148–9
  vertical, generational transmission 6, 104–5,
    113–14, 116, 132–3, 142–4
Psomiades, Kathy 102–3, 125–7

Reform Act (1832) 26–7
Reform Act (1867) 26–7, 29n.90
Rossetti, Christina 66–7
Rutterford, Janette 113–14, 184–5

Sahlins, Marshall 89–90
Schaffer, Talia 9, 11–12, 18–21, 23–4, 89–90,
  90n.52, 92–3, 143–4, 144n.67, 178–9
separate spheres ideology 10–11, 14, 51, 90–2,
  155–6
settlements, financial 1–2, 6–8, 11–14, 51–2
  marriage settlements 11–12, 17–18, 20–1,
    103–4, 113–15, 158–9, 162
  prenuptial settlements 11–12, 113, 120–1
  separate estates 11–14, 72, 99–100, 166–7,
    171–2, 181–2
  strict settlements 7n.19, 8n.21
  trusts 11–14, 115, 159
Shelley, Mary 48
Smith, Adam 9n.23
Smith, Barbara Leigh 158–9
speculation
  in *Hester* 30–1
  in *North and South* 67
  in *Our Mutual Friend* 21–2, 40–1, 64–5
Spring, Eileen 6
step-siblings 68–9, 76–82, 89, 92–3
Surridge, Lisa 68–9, 83–4, 93–4

Talfourd, Thomas 46–7
textual legacy 50, 53–4, 148–9
Trollope, Anthony
  The Belton Estate 106
  blame and punishment in fiction of 102–3,
    108–12, 117–18, 120–2
  Can You Forgive Her? 108–20
  Castle Richmond 106
  children's rights in fiction of 104–8
  debt and credit in fiction of 98–102, 108–9,
    111–12, 115–22
  Doctor Thorne 106
  The Eustace Diamonds 100–8, 117, 120, 159

INDEX 217

forgiveness in fiction of 117–22
generosity in fiction of 33, 100–1, 108–17, 121
He Knew He Was Right 66–7, 99–100
marital property reform in fiction of 101–2, 104–8, 115, 117–18
Orley Farm 15–16, 36–7, 45–6, 106
Phineas Finn 33, 99–101, 108–9, 115–18
Phineas Redux 36–7, 56–7, 108–9, 117–18, 120–1, 140–1
The Prime Minister 120
property as paraphernalia in fiction of 102–6, 159
Ralph the Heir 106, 116

Unsworth, Anna 81–2
usury 141–2, 146–7, 150–1

vertical (generational) wealth transmission 6, 17–18, 104–5, 113–14, 116, 132–3, 142–4

wills
copyright compared to 45–8
fictional representations of 42–4
multiple versions and revisions of 44–5
nineteenth-century laws and statistics 43–4
secrecy of 45–6

Wills Act (1837) 44, 56, 60n.67
Winter, Sarah 183–4
Wives and Daughters (Gaskell) 15–16, 32, 66–70, 106, 123, 132–3, 151–2, 162
common interest in 81–97
common law and 67–8, 72–3, 75–6, 79–85, 87, 89–92, 95
coverture and 67–8, 72–3, 75–6, 79–81, 85, 89–92
debt and credit in 67, 74–5, 82–4, 89–90, 93–4, 98
gift-giving in 67, 84, 88–9, 93–5
"hive-building" Darwinsim and 87–9, 93–4
individualistic Darwinism and 67–70, 76–8, 85–6
intimacy in 67–70, 72–5, 77–80, 95–7
marriage property reform and 72, 80–1, 85, 90–2
primogeniture and 67–8, 75–7, 82–5, 87, 89–90
"purse in common" in 83–4, 88–90, 93–6
self-interest in 70–81
sibling relationships in 67–9, 74–7, 80–4, 89–92, 94–7
step-siblings in 68–9, 76–82, 89, 92–3
sympathy in 68–76, 78–84, 86–7, 89–92